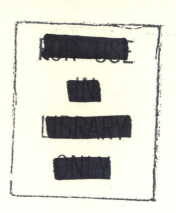

THE BOOK OF REVELATION

BOOKS OF THE BIBLE
VOLUME 2
GARLAND REFERENCE LIBRARY OF THE HUMANITIES
VOLUME 1387

BOOKS OF THE BIBLE
HENRY O. THOMPSON, *Series Editor*

THE BOOK OF PSALMS
An Annotated Bibliography
Thorne Wittstruck

THE BOOK OF REVELATION
An Annotated Bibliography
Robert L. Muse

THE BOOK OF DANIEL
An Annotated Bibliography
Henry O. Thompson

THE BOOK OF RUTH
An Annotated Bibliography
Mishael Maswari Caspi

THE BOOK OF EPHESIANS
An Annotated Bibliography
William W. Klein

THE BOOK OF REVELATION
AN ANNOTATED BIBLIOGRAPHY

ROBERT L. MUSE

GARLAND PUBLISHING, INC.
NEW YORK AND LONDON
1996

Library of Congress Cataloging-in-Publication Data

Muse, Robert L.
    The book of Revelation : an annotated bibliography / Robert L. Muse.
        p.   cm. — (Books of the Bible ; vol. 2)   (Garland reference
library of the humanities ; vol. 1387)
    Includes bibliographical references and indexes.
    ISBN 0-8240-7394-0 (alk. paper)
    1. Bible. N.T. Revelation—Criticism, interpretation, etc.—
Bibliography.   I. Title.   II. Series.   III. Series: Garland reference library of
the humanities ; vol. 1387.
    Z7772.R1M87   1996
    [BS2825.2]
    016.228—dc20   95-39196
                                                                         CIP

Printed on acid-free, 250-year-life paper
Manufactured in the United States of America

Presented

to the glory of God

and dedicated

with love and appreciation to my parents

Mildred Louise Scales Muse (died 7/8/77)

and

Robert Shields Muse

Advisory Board

CONTENTS

Editor's Foreword ix
Preface xi
Sources xv
Introduction xvii
List of Abbreviations xxix

1. Introduction to the Study of the Revelation
   A. General Research of Literature and Bibliography 1
   B. General Introduction/Survey 10
   C. Interpretation/Hermeneutics 19

2. Historical-Critical Research on the Revelation
   A. General Works 49
   B. Essay Collections 50
   C. Manuscript/Textual Research 51
   D. Archaeology 60
   E. Authorship and Date 68
   F. Canonical Questions 73
   G. Cultural, Religious, Socio-Political Life-Setting Studies 73
   H. Form-, Tradition-History, History-of-Religions Studies 87
   I. Source and Revision Hypotheses 95

3. Compositional Studies
   A. General Works 99
   B. Genre Study 101
   C. Language, Grammar, Style 113
   D. Literary and Motif Relationships (Extrabiblical,
      Biblical Traditions) 125
   E. Structure/Plan of the Book 149
   F. Symbolism (and Semiotics) 161
   G. Rhetoric 172

4. Exegetical/Expositional Studies
   A. Commentaries on the Revelation 177
   B. Studies of Specific Sections 211

5. Theological/Thematic Studies
   A. General Works   233
   B. God   236
   C. Jesus Christ   237
   D. Holy Spirit   245
   E. The Trinity   247
   F. The Church   247
   G. Eschatology   250
   H. Other Themes (Angels - Worship)   264

6. The Revelation in the Life of the Church
   A. General Works   303
   B. Art/Music   305
   C. Secular and Devotional Literature   305
   D. Homiletics   308
   E. Liturgy   328
   F. Pedagogy   329

Index of Authors   333
Index of Scripture and Ancient Texts   345

EDITOR'S FOREWORD

It is a personal and professional pleasure to recommend this annotated bibliography to the public. The Book of Revelation has had a varied and widespread impact. The "Preface" points out studies of the book as a whole, but also themes related to it, and studies peripheral to the main text but which touch on it in a variety of ways. Revelation has meant so many things to so many people. Some see it as a rich source of history for the early church. Others look to its theological insights. It is often seen as the only full length example of the apocalyptic genre in the New Testament and thus a primary source for this type of literature. Revelation has frequently been seen as prediction with its fulfillment hailed here and there. The fulfillment is now anticipated by some for the millennial year 2,000, though others claim Jesus was born in 6 BCE so the millennial year was 1994. And one must not forget those who in the past have thrown up their hands and given up trying to understand what they see as a weird book.

Robert Muse's thorough search will certainly facilitate the study, understanding, and appreciation of all concerned with what some have called the great mystery of the Bible. The arrangement of the entries will guide users to the several approaches for special study or casual interest. His introduction gives a useful overview of Revelation itself.

This volume is one of a series. These Bible bibliographies should be of value to everyone interested in the biblical text--teachers, students, professional clergy, the laity, students at the undergraduate and graduate levels--and several fields or disciplines of study--Bible, Church History, Literature, History of Religions. The annotated bibliographies will serve as reference works in libraries for colleges, theological schools, the public, religious groups, individuals.

The projected series was planned to have an annotated bibliography on the books of the Judeo-Christian Scriptures (canon, rule of faith). Jews call the Hebrew Scriptures the Tenak or Tanakh, from the first letters: Torah (Instruction or Law), Nabiim (Prophets), and Kethubim (Writings; Hebrew for "cut" as in preparing a reed or quill pen). Christians call these Scriptures the Old Testament (OT). The Christian Bible includes the New Testament (NT). Jews and Protestant Christians have the same books in the Tenak or OT, but they arrange some of the books in different orders. Roman Catholic and Eastern Orthodox Christians have fifteen (more or less) additional Writings called deuterocanonical, "second canon," or Apocrypha ("Hidden").

The writers are drawn from across doctrinal perspectives and across the Judeo-Christian perspective. Each person has had the academic freedom of selecting what to include with the understanding the result would reflect the field of study for the book presented, and the items would be comprehensive for the post-World War II era with greater selectivity prior to that. This does not mean everything ever published, probably an impossible goal. It does mean available, though not necessarily in the compiler's own hands, e.g., doctoral dissertations. The annotation is selective.

Users can be helpful to the series. Please share new materials, items missed in the general search, or appearing later than the volume's coverage. Please correct factual errors. Perfection is an ideal but it remains a goal.

As in giving birth, editing involves labor and sometimes labor pains. The end of the process, however, is joy and joy remains. It is a special privilege to thank Rev. Robert Muse for his work on this volume. Without his commitment and effort, it would not exist. The thank you spreads out to other authors and the editorial board and all who have helped make the series viable. This of course includes Garland Publishing for producing these volumes. A very special thank you to Editor Phyllis Korper, for commissioning the series, for editorial advice and direction, for a listening ear, a friendly voice. Final thank you's go out to Assistant Editor Jennifer Sorenson and all who brought the final manuscript into print, publication, distribution, and into the hands of you the reader.

Henry O. Thompson
Series Editor

PREFACE

This is a book about books and articles on the New Testament Book of Revelation. It covers roughly the period 1940-1990. Several things need to be stated about the method of this volume before the reader can benefit from its contents. First, the reader must remember that this is an annotated bibliography, i.e., it is a listing of sources of information on various aspects and facets of a given subject (in this case, the Book of Revelation) with accompanying descriptive and/or explanatory (occasionally critical) remarks attached to each of the sources. No attempt is made respecting commentary, comprehensive analysis, or historical-theological discussion. All or some of these elements may appear in the bibliography entries, but they are not presented as a part of the author's annotation. The Introduction that follows this Preface attempts to present a brief overview and outline of the biblical material and some of the major issues involved in the study of the Revelation. This is as far as the author goes toward offering any commentary on the Revelation per se.

Similarly, the present volume does not attempt to incorporate any material that deals with the Revelation only in indirect terms. For example, there are many ideas and phrases found in the book that are contained in other biblical and extrabiblical literature, viz., "Apocalypse," "prophecy," "Son of Man," "judgment," "salvation," and so forth. Much of that scholarship has concentrated on other sources, e.g., Daniel, Ezekiel, and Jeremiah, or other topics, such as history of doctrine, biblical theology, or eschatology. Generally these non-Revelation sources make only occasional references to the Revelation and are not cited in the bibliography. Some works however may be cited because of their relative importance to the field of eschatology and/or apocalyptic literature and their consideration of the Revelation as an important element in the discussion. Thus while the reader may discover numerous references to ideas such as "Apocalypse," "prophecy," or "Son of Man" in this volume, he/she will soon learn that this is not a bibliography on those ideas.

The bibliography reflects the author's original intention to be somewhat comprehensive in his task, i.e., to treat the most important English, German, and French scholarship on the Book of Revelation. But time restraints and limited resources have made it impossible to include all the foreign language works in time to meet the publication date. Still, the reader will find a large representation of literature from German and

French scholars. The inclusion of foreign language works is highly selective. Also, there are some Italian, Spanish, Dutch, and Greek entries included. These were added without annotation and according to the nature of each title.

As stated in the introductory sentence, this volume was originally planned to concentrate roughly on the last fifty years of scholarship on the Book of Revelation. However, I have decided to include selective works beyond those limits (but not beyond the turn of the century) because of the very important contribution to Revelation studies by some earlier scholars. (The exclusion of such names as Lohmeyer, Schmidt, Ramsay, Charles, Bousset, Allo, Loisey, Beckwith, and Swete would be indefensible in any bibliography.) Furthermore, the reader will find the titles of a select number of unpublished doctoral dissertations taken from **American Doctoral Dissertations** (Ann Arbor, MI: University Microfilms) listed under the appropriate chapters in the main body of the bibliography. Many other dissertations have been consulted via **Dissertation Abstracts International** (computer, Speer Library, Princeton Theological Seminary) and are included in the main body of the bibliography as a separate listing (through 1994) at the end of each chapter.

The main part of this bibliography is structured to provide scholars, graduate students, and interested nonprofessionals with an idea of the general development of scholarly literature on the Book of Revelation. Each section begins with the most recent research. This is shown under six general headings: 1. Introduction, 2. Historical-Critical Research, 3. Compositional Studies, 4. Exegetical / Expositional Studies, 5. Theological / Thematic Studies, and 6. The Revelation in the Life of the Church. A major problem of researching and compiling a bibliography such as this (stated also by other bibliography authors--see Chapter 1, A.) has to do with thematic overlap and the methodological inclusiveness of academic scholarship in general. It is hard to find any biblical research that tries to make one main point or uses one strict methodology. The nature of modern biblical scholarship is increasingly eclectic and interdisciplinary and therefore very difficult to categorize.

Where the nature of a work is obvious from its title, e.g., Introduction, Commentary, Theology, it is easy to classify. Other works, however, are more difficult to place, e.g. an essay's title may purport to investigate a specific motif in the Book of Revelation. But by the time the essay concludes, the author has utilized a variety of methods and treated several themes in the process. When this is the case, the present bibliography tries to select the section of the chapter that most readily touches the major emphasis of the essay. When it is impossible to classify a work, the present author (at times) has had to flip the proverbial coin in order to make a decision. These entries are usually followed by cross-referencing to one or more other sections of the text. No doubt, some scholars will disagree with many of the decisions made to categorize a work in the course of preparing this volume. Those who would be critics after the fact are cordially invited to send their constructive criticisms to the author for future revised editions.

Annotation has been selective and conservative with respect to the length of annotation entries. Because of their impact on the field of biblical research, some items may run long (nine or ten lines of description and/or explanation). Other items may run only one or two lines due to their minimal impact on scholarship or lack of unique contribution to the field. This is, of course, a subjective decision made by the author and he takes sole responsibility for each decision.

Book titles and journals are included in bold print in the text. References to foreign words (German, French, Greek, etc.) are set in *italics*, and Hebrew terms are also transliterated. For easy reference to authors and/or Scripture passages in the bibliography, indexes are included at the end of the volume.

Finally, I must say words of appreciation to many people who contributed to the completion of this book. First, sincere appreciation is extended to my academic colleagues, who offered advice, and to students, especially Doozie Emaus, who occasionally helped with the research. Appreciation also goes to Dr. Henry O. Thompson, Series Editor, who has been especially patient and helpful in terms of suggestions and encouragement to keep the project going, and to Garland Publishing, for producing this important project. A very special thank you goes to Phyllis Korper, Editor, and to Jennifer Sorenson, Assistant Editor, who gave valuable advice, correction, and direction to the manuscript's final form and content.

I am deeply indebted to the librarians and staff at Eastern Baptist Theological Seminary, Eastern College, Speer Library (Princeton Theological Seminary), and Villanova and Rutgers universities who offered generous assistance when I visited their campuses. Sincere thanks is extended to Alan Lisk and Sharyn Silverman at Eastern College (DCP) for the use of college offices and printer, and to Kamalesh Stephen for helping to put the manuscript into final copy form. Also, I must thank my congregation, The King's Community Baptist Church, Cherry Hill, New Jersey, who graciously provided me with the time and the computer to complete this writing assignment. And to Mike Swartz, computerphile and skilled MS-Word expert, many thanks for ideas and suggestions that kept my hours in front of the tiny screen bearable. Lastly, to my family, Carol, Andy, Janet, and Joe, I want to say thank you for your patience and for caring for me during the years, and the times when, because of the book, I was absent from our home both in body and in spirit. You are all deeply appreciated.

SOURCES

American Doctoral Dissertations. Ann Arbor: University Microfilm International, 1946-present.

The Anchor Bible. W.F. Albright and D.N. Freedman, eds. Garden City, NY: Doubleday, 1964 ff.

A Basic Bibliography for Ministers, 2nd Ed. D. McPhail, ed. NY: Union Theological Seminary, 1960.

The Bible as Literature: A Selective Bibliography. J.H. Gottcent. Boston, MA: Hall, 1979.

The Bible Book: Resources for Reading the New Testament. E. Hort. NY: Crossroads, 1983.

Bibliographie Biblique, Biblical Bibliography, 3 vols. P.-E. Langevin, ed. Quebec: Les Presses de L'Université Laval, 1930-1985.

A Bibliography of New Testament Bibliographies. J.C. Hurd, Jr. NY: Seabury Press, 1966.

The Cambridge Bible Commentary on the New English Bible. P.R. Ackroyd, A.R.C. Leaney, and J.W. Packer, eds. Cambridge, UK: Cambridge University Press, 1963 ff.

The Catholic Periodical and Literature Index. Haverford, PA: Catholic Library Association, 1940 ff.

Christian Periodical Index. Buffalo, NY: Christian Librarians' Fellowship, 1956 ff.

A Decade of Bible Bibliography: The Book Lists of the Society for Old Testament Study 1957-1966. G. W. Anderson, ed. Oxford: Basil Blackwell, 1967.

Elenchus of Biblica, 1985 - present (preceded by **Elenchus**

Bibliographicus   Biblicus,   1968-85;   Elenchus Bibliographicus   Biblicus, 1950-67; "Elenchus Bibliographicus Biblicus" of **Biblica,   1924-49).** Rome: Biblical Institute Press.

Hermenia. F.M. Cross, Jr., *et al.,* eds. Philadelphia, PA: Fortress Press, 1971 ff.

Internationale   Zeitschriftenschau   für   Bibelwissenschaft und Grenzgebiete. Stuttgart: Katholisches Bibelwerk, 1951 ff.; Düsseldorf: Patmos, 1986 ff.

Multipurpose   Tools   for   Bible   Study, 3rd ed. F.W. Danker. St. Louis, MO: Concordia, 1970.

New   Testament   Abstracts. Cambridge, MA: Weston School of Theology, 1956 ff.

New   Testament   Literature: An   Annotated Bibliography.   Vol 1. Lyons, N.L. and Parvis, M.M.   Chicago, IL: The University of Chicago Press, 1948.

"Recent Trends in Johannine Studies." A.M. Hunter. **ET** 71 (1959-60): 164-167; 219-222.

Theological   and   Religious   Reference   Materials: General Resources   and   Biblical   Studies,   Vol.   1. G.E. Gorman and L. Gorman, eds. Westport, CT: Greenwood Press, 1984.

Tools   for   Bible   Study. B.H. Kelly and D.G. Miller.   Richmond, VA: John Knox, 1956.

Religion   Index   One--Periodicals. Chicago, IL: Association of Theological Librarians of America, 1949 ff.

Religion   Index   Two--Multi-Author   Works. Chicago,   IL: Association of Theological Librarians of America, 1950 ff.

Religious and   Theological   Abstracts. Myerstown, PA: RTA, 1958 ff.

INTRODUCTION

The Revelation of John, called the Apocalypse, is the last book of the canonical Christian writings. It has been considered by many to be one of the most fascinating and yet most frustrating pieces of literature in the Judeo-Christian Bible. The history of research and exposition on the book, which the present text undertakes to categorize and identify chronologically, supports the notion that the search continues for answers to many fascinating and frustrating questions.

Textual criticism of the Book of Revelation is discussed only infrequently today. Some early twentieth-century commentators on the text (cf. Swete,1911 and Charles, 1920) have been supplanted by and large to this date by the work of Lagrange, Weiss, Hoskier, and Schmid. Metzger (1971) confirms that only three papyri and four letter uncials contain all or a part of the Greek text of the Revelation of John, viz., p^{18}, p^{24}, p^{47}, and Aleph, A, C, and P (025). The numbered uncials include 046, 051, 052, 0207, and 0229. Of the multitude of Greek minuscules, there are approximately nineteen somewhat relevant between the eleventh and fourteenth centuries. The United Bible Societies' latest **Greek New Testament Text** (1993) is generally accepted today by most scholars.

The content of the Book of Revelation itself has been analyzed first, structurally, according to obvious surface literary units (see earliest genre and form studies and commentaries in Chaps. 2, H; 3, E; and 4 of this volume). Most recent analyses have discussed the deeper literary and rhetorical structures (see Chap. 3, E, and G). Although heading titles for the literary units of the Revelation vary from author to author, the separate major units of the book usually fall along these lines of division: I. Prologue (1:1-8); II. Initial/Inaugural Vision (1:9-20); III. Seven Messages to Seven Churches in Asia (2:1-3:22); IV. Future Judgments, including Heavenly Scenes, Seven Action Events, and the Fall of the Great City (4:1-18:24); V. Final Victory, including the Parousia, the Final Battle, the Millennium, and the New Jerusalem (19:1-22:5); VI. Epilogue (22:6-21).

I. *The Prologue (1:1-8).* The author calls his work a "revelation" and a "prophecy," which the Church should read aloud for effect and edification. The superscription (1:1-3) is followed by a salutation greeting (1:4-8) to seven Asiatic churches and a doxology to Christ, who is praised for his present love, saving work, and anticipated future return "on the clouds."

This unit has been an object of interest for many scholars, especially as it has been understood in terms of John's use of the terms *Apocalypse* (vs. 1) and *prophecy* (vs. 3), which has generated lengthy debate. Chapter 3 of this volume reveals some of the ongoing (often heated) debate concerning literary genre. Critical scholars have tended to allow the apocalyptic nature of the work (presupposing Jewish antecedents) to be the defining rubric. Most conservative scholars, on the other hand, have usually argued for the classical OT prophetic influence. A bone of continual contention is the question, just how much extrabiblical Jewish material (e.g., Enoch, Esdras, Sibylline Oracles, etc.) should we admit into the discussion in order to determine the influence on genre? Conservatives are much happier to stay exclusively within the context of the canon. Most critical research, on the other hand, has been very inclusive in terms of the debate. There have also been some mediators (See, e.g., Ladd, "Why Not Prophetic-Apocalyptic," 1957) who have tried to reconcile the two positions. The history of research on the Revelation of John, probably not unlike most biblical research in general, has tended to follow the Hegelian method, with critical scholars arguing strongly for their new (and often radical) theses, and the conservative (and often fundamental) scholars countering with their antitheses. Only after an agreeable synthesis has developed do we finally discover that the (battle?) field of research is allowed a period of relative peace and quiet.

Another relatively important area of interest and debate is the thematic and grammatical connection between the Prologue and the Epilogue (22:6-21). As connections are established between the two units, scholars interpret the link to suggest single authorship and a unified literary structure. Others suggest that the grammatical and linguistic similarities simply highlight the work of one or more redactors.

The salutation and doxology (1:4-8) have drawn interest in terms of their historical connection with the area of Asia Minor and the character of the local church and community as background to interpretation. Chapter 2 of this volume records a multitude of discussions surrounding the evidence drawn from basic historical-critical research. Major lines for the general hermeneutical and interpretative approaches to the Revelation are usually drawn from these opening units of the book. There are at least four basic approaches recognized today: Preterist (*zeitgeschichtlich*), historicist (historical), futurist (eschatological), and idealist (timeless).

Also, the lofty Christological statement in vss. 5-8 has prompted numerous books and articles on the Christocentric character of theology in the primitive church. Such titles attributed to Jesus as "faithful witness," "first born of the dead," "ruler of kings," "He who cometh with the clouds," "Alpha and Omega," lend support to many scholars who suggest that John's book may reflect the highest Christology of all the NT writings. Certainly the Jewish background to such sublime attributes and their specific connection to the OT references to Yahweh have been of no little interest to the ongoing discussion of NT theology. Also the issue of eschatology and the Parousia of Christ are inextricably linked to discussions of the divine attributes of Jesus Christ in the second half of the Prologue.

II. *The Initial/Inaugural Vision (1:9-20).* In this section John identifies the *Sitz im Leben* of and the reason for his writing. Christ is shown to be in the midst of the churches through a variety of images that connect to traditional Jewish themes and symbols. The vision finally commands John to write to the seven churches about what he has seen and the vision explains the "mystery" of the seven stars and the seven lampstands.

The literary section under consideration has held special scholarly interest for those who are drawn to the history of the Roman world, the Emperor cult, or the persecution of the Church in the first Christian century. John's further reference to being "in the Spirit on the Lord's Day" has prompted a number of debates on the rationale for shifting Sabbath celebrations from Saturday to Sunday based on 1:10. The rest of the material in the initial vision has drawn interest, in the main, because of its clear tie into the OT imagery, which seems to suggest that John was identifying the character of Jesus with some divine, heavenly figure, who was personally active among the churches in the present tense. The form of this literary (visionary) unit here adds weight to the contention that the basic genre structure is more apocalyptic than prophetic. This has led a number of scholars to conclude that the best way to view the book for interpretative purposes is to recognize that it is basically prophetic in content but apocalyptic in form and structure.

Noteworthy in this section is vs. 19. This text apparently has provided for mostly conservative and fundamental scholars a clear indication of the two-part outline of the contents of the book, viz., "the things which are" (= the present) and "the things which shall come to pass hereafter" (= future). Critical scholars, on the other hand, suggest that this conclusion is too simplistic and not in keeping with the complex nature of John's formal structure.

III. *Seven Messages to Seven Churches in Asia (2:1-3:22).* The author pronounces what appears to be seven prophetic messages to seven specific church communities in Asia Minor in order to meet some specific internal conditions of each church. Each message concludes with a conditional promise of victory to those churches who remain faithful to the eschatological "End." Ephesus is praised for an excellent past; but is warned about a loveless present condition (2:1-7). Smyrna receives no condemnation. The Church has been under attack from Satan, but if the Christians there remain faithful they will receive their reward (2:8-11). Pergamum is also threatened by a satanic climate and some have been deceived by false teachers. The Church is called to repent before it is too late (2:12-17). Thyatira has been infected by immorality; but there are many who have not fallen prey to the sickness. Christ pleads for them to hold on to what they currently possess (2:18-29). Sardis is described as a dead Church and not many of its members have not been effected by its godless environment. The Church is urged to wake up (3:1-6). Philadelphia, like Symrna, receives no condemnation from the Lord. The Church has been loyal in the past and will receive special protection from the Lord during the imminent trial that is coming on the whole world (3:7-13). Lastly, Laodicea is roundly condemned for compromise and "lukewarm" indifference; but the Church has the opportunity to repent before the Lord comes in final parousia judgment (3:14-22).

Due to the form and structure of these messages, scholars have found interest in debating the relative literary connections between Rev. 1, 2-3, and 4-22. Some research concludes that Rev. 2-3 were later redactions to a proto-apocalyptic document. Others point out the strong thematic and grammatical connections between the Rev. 2-3 and 1:9-20, which suggests the author's intended structural purpose and identifies the work, at least partly, as an epistle intended originally for distribution among the seven churches. The most recent form studies have concluded that the designation "letters" does not fit the literary form of Rev. 2-3. These two chapters are highly structured and stylized prophetic message forms with numerous prophetic formula in the tradition of Amos and other literary prophets.

Archaeological research has added significant background information to these chapters, which has been helpful in translating and clarifying some of the local city references and identifying some of John's cryptic statements. These chapters have been rich soil for investigating the psychological, sociological, political, and religious milieu in relationship to each church community. Scholarship has been quite successful in identifying points of tension and conflict between the primitive church and its environment. Themes relevant to each community touch on such notions as persecution/tribulation, church division, good works, repentance, endurance, love and the spirit, and conquering/victory through martyrdom.

IV. *Future Judgments, including Heavenly Throne Scenes, Seven Action Events, and the Fall of the Great City (4:1-18:24).* The major scene after the seven messages focuses on a two-part vision (4:1-5:14): 1) God's throne and the worship offered to Him. 2) Christ, the Lamb, who is the only one worthy to open the scroll with seven seals. The scene depicts worship in which both the Lamb and God are equally praised. This section has stimulated scholarly interest in liturgical and Christological issues. Literary and theological antecedents relevant to extrabiblical writings that depict heavenly trips (Enoch, *et al.*) have also been analyzed at great length and compared to John's work. Form studies have identified certain hymnic units that connect with OT cultic practices. The throne scene, describing the relative status of God and Jesus Christ respecting worship and praise, has been a focus for much debate surrounding the divinity of Jesus and his role in the divine scheme of history. Also, the form and function of the seven-sealed book have been debated in relationship to its OT traditions. Many bizarre symbols and literary images abound in this unit as well, and numerous investigations have offered many suggestions regarding their meaning and application for both ancient and modern audiences.

There are seven action events that follow the throne scene (6:1-16:21): 1) The first six seals of the seven-sealed book are opened (6:1-8:1). After each of numbers one through four is broken, a rider on a horse appears representing conquest, war, famine, and death. As the fifth seal is opened the martyrs cry out, but are told to be still for just a little while longer. After this, as the sixth seal is opened, the Lamb reveals his wrath by sending terrible calamities to earth. The people of God (12,000 from each tribe) are sealed against the wrath to come. Shortly thereafter a dialogue takes place between one of the elders and John the author, who learns of the meaning of the great multitude of worshippers. Finally, the seventh seal is opened and there is absolute silence in heaven for one hour.

2) Following that period of time seven trumpets are then revealed (8:2-13:18). First, we learn about the identity of the seven trumpeters. Then we watch as an eighth trumpeter comes on the scene and throws to earth a censer that causes great disturbances in nature. There is a suggestion in this action that we are getting a foretaste of things to come when all the trumpets are finally blown. Next, the first four trumpets are blown and there follows hail and fire, volcanic eruptions, a star named Wormwood (Bitterness) falls from the sky, and the sun, moon, and stars

are all darkened. An eagle flies in the heavens expressing woe, which introduces a dramatic expectation for the next three trumpets. The fifth and sixth trumpets are then blown revealing a bottomless pit and four angels on a mission of destruction. Still, we are told, the people on earth refuse to repent.

The author is then commanded to eat a little scroll, to prophesy, and measure the temple. Before the final trumpet blasts, two witnesses must prophesy for three and a half years. They meet opposition from the Beast from the pit, and are eventually killed; but they are soon resurrected and return to heaven. Before the final woe is announced we are again offered a vision of worship in heaven. This time the emphasis is on God's wrath. As thunder and earthquakes develop there now appears on the scene a pregnant woman who is bothered by a dragon. A child is then born but is immediately taken up to heaven. This is the apparent signal for a battle to begin between Michael and his angelic army against the great dragon. Victory is then announced in heaven. However the dragon is persistent and attacks the woman and her children.

At this point in the vision the opponents of God's forces are described. One terrible-looking Beast emerges from the sea and is immediately worshipped. It appears to be a tyrant who speaks all kinds of blasphemous things. A second powerful Beast appears from the earth and deceives the people while compelling all to receive his cryptic mark, "666."

3) Visions of those who worship the Lamb then appear (14:1-20), followed by 4) an introduction to and description of the seven bowls of wrath (15:1-16:21), which are poured out at the command of a voice from within the temple. In succession there are produced ulcers, pollution of the sea, pollution (blood-like) of rivers and springs, scorching heat, darkness and anguish, drying up of the Euphrates, and the appearance of frog-like creatures, and finally, the dramatic proclamation of the End. 5) The fall of the great city "Babylon" concludes the section (17:1-18:24). The city is described in terms of her great sins. Babylon is called a harlot and is closely identified with Rome. In spite of that city's power, the Lamb of God will be victorious over it. From this there follows a symbolic description of the fall of Babylon, with the ultimate symbolic act being the casting of a great stone into the sea.

As a major unit in the Book of Revelation, this one has drawn a great amount of interest. Certain attempts to deal with the violent (sometimes sub-Christian) language and imagery have sparked numerous debates concerning the relevance of apocalyptic and/or prophetic language to Christian thought and practice. Suggestions of possible Near Eastern combat myth sources have raised further questions concerning John's role in the writing, i.e., as both creative author and/or redactor. Again, the best critical scholarship of the period under consideration seems to turn away from traditionally prescribed doctrinal issues and toward the question of John's basic theology and purpose. How do these things help to inform our understanding of the literary units? Or, do the literary units help to inform us regarding the author's theology and purpose? And what is the relationship between the medium and the message?

The section also provides rich soil for raising scholarly discussion over the relative form/structure of the main part of the book. Chapter 2 (H and I) of this volume provides a number of interesting and insightful works related to structural commentary. The most obvious categories covered deal with the number patterns--in particular, three and seven--that appear between Rev. 6 and 16. Many elaborate charts and diagrams have been produced from the three series of sevens: seals (6:1-8:1); trumpets (8:6-11:19); bowls (15:5-16:21). The various interludes and digressions have also drawn scholarly attention, especially in terms of John's artistic and dramatic creativity. Even the best scholarship of each period has come away from this literary unit in the Revelation saying that final conclusions about meaning and practical application are at best a puzzling maze of divergent symbols and themes. Thus, scholars have eventually tried to argue for a reasonable structure that is most consistent to the notions of strict chronology, repetition and combinations of the two resulting in the final structuring of this so-called eschatological drama.

No little interest has also been directed to the little "surrealistic drama" in Rev. 12:1-14:20 (Boring, 1989), as John attempts to spotlight the action sequences related to the evil powers of the universe. Again, the debate frequently gets bogged down in the question, Do we or do we not interpret the text literally? The conclusions drawn often suggest nothing more than a scholar's commitment to her/his own parochial hermeneutic principle rather than to discussion. Rev. 12:1-14:20 seems to have been explained best by serious investigations into the literary context and structure, the cultural milieu, the mythological imagery, and by discussions that provide dialogue with the dramatic characters and their actions (Boring).

Within this section one of the most controversial texts has occupied scholarly attention from the earliest times, viz., Rev. 13:18. This verse identifies the beast from the earth as "666." The history of interpretation demonstrates no clear consensus among the scholars. Even rigorous applications of gematria have been at best inconclusive. Probably the most popular Roman character that research has identified as this "evil" personage is Nero Caesar (which is also possible through the variant reading "616"). But in order to accept this theory readers are asked to accept a Hebrew transliteration of a Latinized Greek proper name. Another, perhaps more interesting and popular view among the more moderate critical scholars (Minear, Hendriksen, Torrance, Mounce, Boring, *et al.*) states that the number 666, whether identified with a particular person or not, continues to evoke mysterious power in every age, even where the original intention of John has been lost or forgotten. Thus each generation is called upon to discern and identify its own source of "evil" that threatens to make idols of political (state) power.

The fall of the great city Babylon has been discussed and debated from a number of perspectives and across numerous disciplines. Agreement over the clear structure (major sections and subsections) of the unit is lacking among most scholars. Where one section ends and another begins has frequently been a toss-up, depending on which scholarly presupposition is voiced most vociferously. Traditional research has identified the start of the unit at Rev. 17:1. The question raised most frequently is, where did John intend to end this unit of thought? Many (including older, traditional) scholars argue for 19:5 or 19:10, which includes the final hymn of vindication of the saints as the best termination point. Others suggest that the final lament of 18:21-24 affixes an appropriate conclusion to a very disturbing and lamentable unit of thought.

Discussion about the identity of the great city (Babylon=Rome) traces the roots of the material to a prophetic Jewish tradition that has frequently pictured evil, secular cities/civilizations in relationship to the form of an alluring woman/harlot/prostitute. The city of Rome emerges clearly from the author's perspective at several levels, which include the notions of the goddess, the city of Rome, the Roman Empire, and the Emperors with their cult and mythology. Furthermore, other debates have tried to focus on the specific seven-headed beast upon which the woman is seated and the naming of the particular Emperor associated with the most contemporary time for the author. These discussions have been crucial in terms of trying to date the writing/editing of John's Revelation within a definite time span and to describe the specific *Sitz im Leben*, subsequently, to identify the particular kind of persecution that seems to be background to the whole story.

Finally, John (coincidentally and paradoxically) seems to celebrate and lament the fall of the great city Babylon (18:1-24). Attempts to locate the essential sources behind this chapter have proven to be less than convincing. Research has concluded that the creative genius of the author must be allowed full force in order to understand how John used his own mind to blend a variety of biblical laments, dirges, and taunt-songs that seem to be taken freely from the prophetic traditions of Isaiah, Jeremiah, and Zephaniah. Thematic and theological discussions have then taken the debate a step further by underlining some of the "sins" of Babylon, viz., idolatry, the emperor cult, state violence, self-glory, blasphemy of pride, wealth, etc. Ecclesiastical studies, including extensive homiletic presentations, have then attempted to suggest the proper posture and attitude of the church in the middle of all this eschatological activity. Times and seasons in relationship to scholarly trends and interests have produced volume upon volume of advice (and command!) for Christian communities of every age. Occasionally the reader/researcher does find agreement over the basic principles that should motivate the Church in the End-Time period.

V. *Final Victory, including the Parousia, the Final Battle, the Millennium, and the New Jerusalem (19:1-22:5).* This last major unit in the Revelation begins with visions of worship and praise in heaven (Rev. 19:1-11). Hymns are offered to God for 1) judging the great harlot and vindicating the martyrs and 2) the marriage of the Lamb to the Church, which is attired as the bride clothed "in fine linen, bright and pure . . ." i.e., "the righteous acts of the saints" (Rev. 19:8). John is then commanded to worship God.

Rev. 19:12-20:15 describes seven visions of the End or the Last Absolute Judgment. The Warrior King, who is also the Victor before the fact, moves toward his eschatological Parousia (19:11-16). The imagery draws from a variety of sources to identify the figure as "word of God," Jesus Christ, the Messiah, who now comes in wrath. There follows 1) the destruction of the Beast, the false prophet, and all their followers (19:17-21); 2) the binding of Satan for a millennium (20:1-3); 3) the millennial reign of Christ (20:4-6); 4) the final destruction of Satan in the defeat of Gog and Magog (20:7-10); and 5) the last absolute judgment (20:11-15). In this final action sequence the contemporary natural order ceases to exist and the second resurrection begins as death and Hades are thrown in the lake of eternal fire.

Visions of the new world order especially understood in terms of the new Jerusalem complete the last major section of the book (21:1-22:5). Included here are 1) A description of the new creation (21:1-8). The old order passes away as the New Jerusalem descends. It is a place that seems to include the highest hopes and aspirations of the perfect future state of existence. There is no sea there, no tears, death, sorrow, crying, and no pain. There is no place there for people who are cowardly, faithless, etc., (i.e., sinners). 2) A description of the glorious splendor of the new Jerusalem (21:9-22:5). In the new Jerusalem there is no need for a temple, or sun, moon, night, and closed gates. Accordingly, there is found there no curse, as was necessary in the old order due to the Genesis Fall tradition. The time has come to acknowledge the redeemed order through the transforming grace of a Holy God. The new city contrasts old Babylon. It is a special city that is expansive, inclusive, and renewed. It is a "holy" city that communicates not only moral purity but also separate *"otherness"* (Boring). Finally, John concludes the section by stating that there will be eternal light in the new order because God Himself will give light forever.

Critical scholarship has tended to focus attention mainly on the structure of the last major unit in terms of its comparison to the previous section, with special emphasis on the seven events. Form and symbolic elements have also been studied in order to discuss the interconnections between authorship, redaction, and sources. Similarities have been noted between the unit and the other two major units (1:9-20; 4:1-5:14) as to their worship introductions. Thematic and source studies have traced the author's preferences for literary traditions in order to determine the meaning of the rich imagery and symbolism.

No little interest on behalf of fundamental scholarship (opposed to the views of critical, nonconservative scholars) has been directed to Rev. 20:4-6 respecting the Millennium. Fundamental (and some conservative) literalists suggest that the passage is the interpretative key to the book. Critical (including, also, many conservative) scholars argue that John's own interest in the Millennium is precisely three (3!) verses and therefore Rev. 20:4-6 should be viewed in that light, i.e., seen as simply one small scene among many components of John's final eschatological act. Interpretations of the thousand years seem to vary according to each scholar's hermeneutical preferences. Most nonfundamentalists tend to view the unit as a symbolic/figurative description of a long period of time during the final stages of the eschatological End.

The final scenes of judgment and the new creation, including the new Jerusalem, have also drawn much theological argument and speculation concerning the author's use of sources to explain his own theology. Is the final battle, with Jesus Christ, the Lamb of God at center stage as warrior and judge, consistent with NT theology in general? Or, has John's apocalyptic tendencies emerging in the midst of his own hardships, caused him to express a sub-Christian position? Scholars have also debated the question of the place of the Revelation in the whole context of NT theology. And, lastly, the crucial question, Is the final judgment of God to be understood as thoroughly inclusive (universal) or exclusive (limited) according to John's theology?

VI. *Epilogue (22:6-21)*. The work concludes with a series of exhortations: 1) Divine endorsement is given through an angel saying that the words in the book are true and that the promise of an imminent Parousia is genuine. 2) John offers exhortation and then attempts to worship the angel. 3) Christ speaks against angel worship and promises that he is "coming soon." 4) The invitation is given by the Spirit and the Church to Christ to come. 5) The concluding warning is directed against adding anything to the words of the Book of Revelation. 6) The final benediction is then offered up.

Scholars seem to have been puzzled by the apparently haphazard collection of sayings appended to this last section of the book. However, more careful analysis convinces the reader that the answer is to be found in the overall structure of the work, which is in part, epistolary. Thus the Prologue and Epilogue (with epistolary benediction) function to remind us that the Revelation of John was written to seven church communities. The vision finally ends with victorious exhortations and imperatives to the church communities: 1) To offer up worship to God alone; 2) To remember that God will be coming soon in Jesus Christ; and 3) To watch faithfully and to pray for the Lord to come.

After nearly two millennia the Book of Revelation continues to be hotly debated but also joyfully received by millions of scholars and general readers around the world. The following pages of this bibliography represent but a small fraction of the scholarly and general interest that has developed through the last fifty-plus years. It is hoped that these brief, annotated entries might serve the interests of all who continue to delight in the study of the Bible as the Word of God.

LIST OF ABBREVIATIONS

ABR	Australian Biblical Review (Melbourne)
AC	L'Ami du Clergé (Langres)
AER	American Ecclesiastical Review
AJA	American Journal of Archaeology
AJT	American Journal of Theology (Continued as JR)
Ang	Angelicum (Rome)
AnJBI	Annual of the Japanese Biblical Institute (Tokyo)
ANQ	Andover Newton Quarterly
Ant	Antonianum (Rome)
AQ	Augustana Quarterly
AS	Assemblées du Seigneur (Paris)
ATR	Anglican Theological Review
Aug	Augustiniana (Louvain)
AUSS	Andrews University Seminary Studies
AW	Auf der Warte
B	Biblica (Rome)
BA	Biblical Archaeologist
BASOR	Bulletin of the American Schools of Oriental Research
BCPE	Bulletin du Centre Protestant d'Etudes (Geneva)
BETS	Bulletin of the Evangelical Theological Society (Continued as JETS)
BF	Blackfriars (London)
BibSac	Bibliotheca Sacra
BJRL	Bulletin of the John Rylands Library (Manchester)
BK	Bibel und Kirche (Stuttgart)
BL	Bibel und Leben (Düsseldorf)
BLE	Bulletin de Littérature Ecclésiastique (Toulouse)
BM	Benediktinische Monatschrift (Beuron, Ger.)

BN	Biblical Notes
BO	Biblica et Orientalia (Rome)
BRep	Biblical Repository
BRes	Biblical Research
BRev	Biblia Revuo = Biblia kaj Oriento (Esperanto)
BrL	Brethern Life
BT	The Bible Today
BTB	Biblical Theology Bulletin
BTh	Biblical Theology (Belfast)
BTr	Bible Translator (London)
BTS	Bible et Terre Sainte (Paris)
BuH	Buried History (Melbourne)
BVCh	Bible et Vie Chrétienne (Denee, Bel.)
BW	Biblical World (Previously **ONTS**)
BZ	Biblische Zeitschrift (Paderborn, Ger.)
CBQ	Catholic Biblical Quarterly
CBTJ	Calvary Baptist Theological Journal
CC	Cross and Crown
CCER	Cahiers du Cercle Ernest Renan (Paris)
CH	Church History
Chr	Christus (Paris)
ChSR	Christian Scholar's Review (Previously **GR**)
ChT	Christianity Today
CJTh	Canadian Journal of Theology (Continued as **SR/SR**) (Toronto)
Col	Colloquium (Auckland)
ColM	Collectanea Mechliniensia (Mechelen)
ComV	Communio Viatorum (Prague)
Con	Concilium (London)
ConN	Coniectanea Neotestamentica (Uppsala)
CQ	Crozer Quarterly
CQR	Church Quarterly Review (London)
CS	Cristianesimo nella Storia (Bologna)
CTJ	Calvin Theological Journal
CTQ	Concordia Theological Quarterly (Continued as **CTM**)
CTM	Concordia Theological Monthly (Previously **CTQ**)
CuTM	Currents in Theology and Mission
DAI	Dissertation Abstracts International
DBM	Deltion Biblikon Meleton (Athens)

DV	Dieu Vivant (Paris)
É	Études (Paris)
EA	Erbe und Auftrag (Beuron, Ger.)
EcO	Ecclesia Orans (Rome)
ElB	Elenchus of Biblica (Rome)
Em	Emmanuel
EpM	Ephemerides Mariologicae (Madrid)
EpR	Epworth Review (London)
EQ	The Evangelical Quarterly (Exeter, Eng.)
EQR	Evangelical Quarterly Review (Previously **ER**; continued as **LQ**)
ERT	Evangelical Review of Theology
EsB	Estudios Biblicos (Madrid)
EsV	Esprit et Vie (Langres)
ET	The Expository Times (Edinburgh)
ETL	Ephemerides Theologicae Lovanienses (Lorvain)
EuD	Euntes Docete (Rome)
EvT	Evangelische Theologie (München)
Exp	Expositor (London)
Expl	Explor [sic]: A Journal of Theology
F	Furrow (Maynooth, Ireland)
FV	Foi et Vie (Paris)
GL	Geist und Leben (Würzburg)
GR	Gordon Review (Continued as **ChSR**)
Gre	Gregorianum (Rome)
GTJ	Grace Theological Journal
HBT	Horizons in Biblical Theology
HibJ	Hibbert Journal (London)
HJ	The Heythrop Journal (London)
HMC	Homiletic Monthly and Catechist (Continued as **HMPR**)
HMPR	Homiletic Monthly and Pastoral Review (Previously **HMC**; continued as **HPR**)
HPR	Homiletic and Pastoral Review (Previously **HMPR**)
HS	Hebrew Student (Continued as **OTS**)
HTR	Harvard Theological Review

HUCA	Hebrew Union College Annual
IBRR	Index to Book Reviews in Religion
IBS	Irish Biblical Studies (Belfast)
IEJ	Israel Exploration Journal (Jerusalem)
IKZC	Internationale Katholisches Zeitschrift Communio (Rodenkirchen, Ger.)
Int	Interpretation (Previously **USR**)
Interp	The Interpreter (London)
IR	The Iliff Review
ITQ	Irish Theological Quarterly (Maynooth)
JAAR	Journal of the American Academy of Religion (Previously **JBR**)
JBL	Journal of Biblical Literature
JBR	Journal of Bible and Religion (Previously **JNABI**; continued as **JAAR**)
JCS	Journal of Church and State
JES	Journal of Ecumenical Studies
JETS	Journal of the Evangelical Theological Society (Previously **BEThS**)
JHS	Journal of Hellenic Studies (London)
JNABI	Journal of the National Association of Biblical Instructors (Continued as **JBR**)
JNES	Journal of Near Eastern Studies
JQR	Jewish Quarterly Review
JR	Journal of Religion (Previously **AJTh**)
JRS	Journal of Roman Studies (London)
JSJ	Journal for the Study of Judaism (Leiden, Neth.)
JSNT	Journal for the Study of the New Testament (Sheffield)
JSP	Journal for Study of the Pseudepigrapha (Sheffield)
JSS	Journal of Semitic Studies (Manchester)
JTS	Journal of Theololgical Studies (Oxford/London)
JTSA	Journal of Theology for South Africa (Braamfontein, Transavaal, S.A.)
Kar	Kardia

Kat/B	Katallagete/Be Reconciled
KRS	Kirchenblatt für die Reformierte Schweiz (Basel)
LChQ	Lutheran Church Quarterly (Previously **LChR**; continued as **LQ[LThS]**)
LChR	Lutheran Church Review (Previously **LQ**; continued as **LChQ**)
LingBib	Linguistica Biblica (Bonn)
LQ	Lutheran Quarterly (Previously **EQR**; continued as **LChR**)
LQ (LThS)	Lutheran Quarterly -- Lutheran Theological Seminaries (Previously **LChQ & AQ**)
LuVS	Lumiere et Vie, Supplement (Lyon)
LV	Lumen Vitae (Brussels)
LW	Lutheran World (Geneva)
M	Le Muséon (Louvain)
Mar	Marianum (Rome)
MC	The Modern Churchman (Ludlow, Eng.)
McQ	McCormick Quarterly
MS	Marian Studies
NBF	New Blackfriars (Previously **BF**) (London)
Neo	Neotestamentica (Pretoria, S.A.)
NGTT	Nederduits-GereformeerdeTeologiese Tydskvif (Kaapstad)
NovT	Novum Testamentum (Leiden)
NRT	Nouvelle Revue Théologique (Tournai)
NTA	New Testament Abstracts
NTS	New Testament Studies (London)
NTT	Nederlands Theologisch Tijdschrift (Wageningen)
OF	Orate Fratres (Continued as **Wor**)
ONTS	The Old and New Testament Student (Previously **OTS**; continued as **BW**)
OTS	Old Testament Student (Previously **HS**; continued as **ONTS**)
PIBA	Proceedings of the Irish Biblical Association (Belfast)

Pne	Pneuma
PP	Priests & People (London)
PR	Presbyterian Review (Continued as **PRR**)
Pres	Presbyterion
PRR	Presbyterian and Reformed Review (Previously **PR**; continued as **PThR**)
PThR	Princeton Theological Review (Previously **PRR**)
QR	Quarterly Review: A Journal of Theological Resources for Ministry
RB	Review Biblique (Jerusalem/Paris)
RE	Religious Education
Rel	Religion (London)
Ren	Renovatio (Köln/Genova)
ReScR	Recherches de Science Religieuse (Paris)
RevB	Revista Biblica (Buenos Aires)
RevCT	Revista Catalana de Teologia (Barcelona)
RevET	Revista Española de Teologia (Madrid)
RevSR	Revue des Sciences Religieuses (Strassbourg)
RevThom	Review Thomiste (Toulouse/Brussels)
REx	Review and Expositor
RHPR	Revue d'Histoire et de Philosophie Religieuses (Strasbourg)
RHR	Revue de l'Histoire des Religions (Paris)
RivB	Rivista Biblica Italiana (Bologna)
RL	Religion in Life
RQ	Restoration Quarterly
RQum	Revue de Qumran (Paris)
RR	Reformed Review
RRé	Revue Réformée (Saint-Germain-en-Lage)
RS	Religious Studies (Cambridge, Eng.)
RSR	Religious Studies Review
RTP	Revue de Théologie et de Philosophie (Epalinges)
RTR	Reformed Theological Review
RuBL	Ruch Biblijny i Liturgiczny (Krakow)
Sal	Salmanticensis (Salamanca, Spain)
SBFLA	Studii Biblici Franciscani Liber Annuus (Jerusalem)

ScC	La Scuola Cattolica (Venegono Inferiore, Varese)
ScEsp	Science et Esprit (Montreal)
Scrip	Scripture (Continued as **ScripB**)
ScripB	Scripture Bulletin (Previously **Scrip**)
SD	Sacra Doctrina (Milano)
SE	Studia Evangelica
SEAJT	South East Asia Journal of Theology
Sem	Semeia
SémB	Sémiotique et Bible (Lyons)
SJT	Scottish Journal of Theology (Edinburgh)
SKZ	Schweizerische Kirchenzeitung (Luzern)
SMR	St. Mark's Review (Canberra, Australia)
SNTU	Studien zum NT und seiner Umwelt (Linz)
SO	Soundings
Sp	Spiritus (Paris)
SPa	Studia Papyrologica (Barcelonia)
SR/SR	Studies in Religion/Sciences Religieuses (Previously CJTh)
STh	Studia Theologica (Oslo)
STV	Studia Theoloica Varsaviensia (Warsaw)
SvEA	Svensk Exegetisk Arsbok (Uppsala)
SWJT	Southwestern Journal of Theology
Sym	Symbolisme
TBei	Theologische Beiträge (Wuppertal)
TD	Theology Digest
TE	Theologia Evangelica (Pretoria, South Africa)
TG	Theologie und Glaube (Paderborn)
Th	Theology (London)
TLz	Theologische Literaturzeitung (Berlin)
TM	Theological Monthly (Previously **TQ**; continued as **CTM**)
TPQ	Theologisch Praktische Quartalschrift (Linz)
TQ	Theological Quarterly (Continued as **TM**)
TRu	Theologische Rundschau (Tübingen)
TS	Theological Studies
TT	Theology Today
TTS	Trierer Theologische Studien (Continued as **TTZ**)
TTZ	Trierer Theologische Zeitschrift (Trier, Ger.)
TVia	Theologia Viatorum (Berlin)

TyB	Tyndale Bulletin (Previously **TyHB**)
TyHB	Tyndale House Bulletin
TZ	Theologische Zeitschrift (Basel)
UMI	University Microfilms, Inc.
UR	Union Review (Continued as **USQR**)
US	Una Sancta (Augsburg-Meitingen/Brooklyn)
USM	Union Seminary Magazine (Continued as **USR**)
USQR	Union Seminary Quarterly Review (Previously **UR**)
USR	Union Seminary Review (Previously **USM**; continued as **Int**)
VC	Vigiliae Christianae (Leiden)
VE	Vox Evangelica (London)
VerC	Verbum (Communio) Caro (Neuchâtel)
VerD	Verbum (Communio) Domini (Roma)
VS	La Vie Spirituelle (Paris)
VT	Vetus Testamentum (Leiden)
Way	The Way
Wor	Worship (Previously **OF**)
WTJ	Westminster Theological Journal
WW	Word and World
ZNW	Zeitschrift für die Neutestamentliche Wissenschaft (Berlin)
ZTK	Zeitschrift für Theologie und Kirche (Tübingen)

Chapter 1

Introduction to the Study
of the Revelation

A. GENERAL RESEARCH OF LITERATURE AND BIBLIOGRAPHY

[1989]
1. Fiorenza, E.S. "Revelation" in **The New Testament and Its Modern Interpreters**. Eldon Jay Epp and George W. MacRae, S.J., eds. Atlanta, GA: Scholars Press, 1989. Pp. 407-427.

Surveying and evaluating the scholarly work on the Revelation for the period 1945-1980, F. concludes that since the work of Allo (1933), with the possible exception of the commentary of Kraft (1974), there have been no scientific commentaries with "research breadth." The essay outlines the following areas: I. Research on Revelation; II. Historical-Critical Analyses; III. Literary-Functional Interpretation. Section I surveys the trends in research in bibliographical studies and concludes that conservatives have dominated the scene and most scholarship tends to be popular and "fundamental." Section II concludes that redaction-critical studies have tended to view the Revelation as the theological work of one author and as an "authentic Christian prophetic work" addressed to real congregations in Asia Minor. Section III focuses on the "evocative power" and "theological intention" of the author in calling Christians to counter economic, political, and religious opposition in the world.

2. Shepherd, W.H. "Revelation and the Hermeneutics of Dispensationalism." **ATR** 71 (1989): 281-299.

Investigates the history and main ideas of dispensationalism, the hermeneutical and exegetical principles used in the Revelation, and concludes that dispensationalism embraces figurative interpretation and biblical diversity in order to hold to the primacy of literal interpretation and the unity of the biblical message. Dispensationalism is an awkward and artificial system of thought that sets up a rigid presuppositional commitment to inerrancy. Where the Bible does not fit the accepted (dispensational) model, it is reshaped to fit that mode.

3. Tabbernee, W. "Revelation 21 and the Montanist 'New Jerusalem.'" **ABR** 37 (1989): 52-60.

Argues that Quintilla (late third or early fourth century) and not Montanus was responsible for identifying Pepouza with the biblical New Jerusalem. Montanus referred to Pepouza-Tymion, Phrygia as "Jerusalem" and Quintilla may have extended the idea by means of a word association prompted by a literal interpretation of Rev. 21:10.

[1988]
4. Jeske, R.L. and Barr, D.L. "The Study of the Apocalypse Today." **RSR** 14 (1988): 337-344.

Reviews six recent works on the Revelation (three are collections of articles edited by Hellholm, A.Y. Collins, and Lambrecht and three are scholarly efforts by A.Y. Collins, Fiorenza, and Hemer) under the broad rubrics of literary analyses, historical analyses, and theological analyses. Although there is little attempt to maintain dialogue between modern scholars, overlapping between each category is acknowledged. The writer concludes that clarity will be coming rapidly to a most misunderstood biblical book. B. does an analytic survey concentrating on the work of Collins and Fiorenza and notes that this scholarship moves beyond the "old historical-critical paradigm" into the newer "historical," "aesthetic literary," and "social analysis" methods. B. concludes that these scholars are setting trends for future research in the areas of oral discourse, literary narrative, and the social history of the period. The focus of these brief essays is on conclusions relevant to new methods and trends in research on the Revelation.

5. Paulien, J. "Recent Developments in the Study of the Book of Revelation." **AUSS** 26 (1988): 159-170.

Reviews and critiques recent publications: E.S. Fiorenza, **The Book of Revelation: Justice and Judgment** (1985) and A.Y. Collins, **Crisis and Catharsis: The Power of the Apocalypse** (1984). Both suggest that correct interpretation is based upon the recognition of the author's intent within the social life-situation. The former stresses the eschatological perspective and the latter emphasizes the sociopsychological. S. Thompson's work, **The Apocalypse and Semitic Syntax** (1985), identifies the language and style of the Revelation with OT ideas and images. G. Goldsworthy's **The Lion and the Lamb: The Gospel in Revelation** (1984) proposes the thesis that the good news of the Gospel, seen in the images of the the lion and the lamb, is the major motif of the Revelation.

[1986]
6. Collins, A.Y. "Reading the Book of Revelation in the Twentieth Century." **Int** XL (July, 1986): 229-242.

Reviews the ways the Revelation has been read (interpreted) within the history of the Church, beginning with the early Father's debate over the literal versus the spiritual (allegorical) interpretation. The ancient debate is carried on in the present by the "premillennialists" and the "amillennialists." Premillennial faith maintains an imminent expectation of the End based on a certain reading of historical events. Suggests that an historical-critical study of the Revelation highlights the failure of the premillennial position because, in its attempt to predict the future, it fails to appreciate the historical character of the Bible. Serious interpretation of a text from another time and place demands that the text be interpreted in terms of its original historical situation. After treating the history-of-religions approach, the genre "apocalypse," and the literary and social functions of apocalypses, C. concludes that at its deepest level, the Book of Revelation offers a story in and through which the people of God discover who they are and what they should do.

[1985]
7. Michaud, J.-P. "Sur l'Apocalypse de Jean, un ouvrage important." **ScEsp** 37 (1985): 231-246.

Reviews the work of E. Corsini (**L'Apocalypse maintenant,** French trans. by R. Arright) and commends the author for his coherent and comprehensive reading of the text as one unit. Suggests that the Revelation is really a Christological statement about the past and the present and not about the future.

[1983]
8. Brady, D. **The Contribution of British Writers between 1560 and 1830 to the Interpretation of Revelation 13.16-18 (The Number of the**

Beast). A Study in the History of Exegesis. Beitrage zur Geschichte der biblischen Exegese 27. Tübingen: Mohr-Siebeck, 1983.

Surveys British interpretations of Rev. 13:16-18 (especially 666) from a chronological and thematic perspective, from the periods of the Geneva Bible to the death of Elizabeth I (1560-1603), James I (1603-1625), Charles I (1626-1649), the interregnum (1649-1660), the late seventh century (1660-1699), new ideas (1700-1830), and the older interpretations from 1560 to 1830. Appendixes discuss Greek and Hebrew characters and their numerical values and decrees against heretical interpretations of Rev. 13:17. Concludes that the Beast of Rev. 13 probably had both specific and general meaning for the early church in terms of opposition to Christ and his people.

[1980]
9. Vanni, U. "L'Apocalypse johannique: État de la question" in **L'Apocalyopse johannique et l'Apocalyptique dans le Nouveau Testament.** J. Lambrecht, ed. BETL 53. Paris and Gembloux: Duculot; Louvain: Leuven University Press, 1980.

Introduces the work by first discussing briefly the scholarship and publications on the Revelation to date. After addressing the problems of hermeneutics, literary analysis, and the historical-religious background of the book, V. suggests that there may be five areas ripe for future research (including the above), viz., the relationship between the book and OT and NT studies, as well as the connection with Jewish and Christian apocalypticism. Finally, V. proposes the need for a new type to commentary that would interact more intensely with and incorporate modern research.

[1979]
10. Lambrecht, J. "The Book of Revelation and Apocalyptic in the New Testament: Colloquium Biblicum Lovaniense XXX (August 28-30, 1979)." **ETL** 55 (1979): 391-397.

Describes the papers and topics presented at the Louvain Biblical Conference: Introductory questions, specific passages, themes, and Johannine relationships.Concludes with a discussion of apocalyptic texts in Paul, John, 2 Peter, and the Synoptics.

[1978]
11. Megivern, J.J. "Wrestling With Revelation." **BTB** 8 (1978): 147-154.

Reviews a wide range of literature on the Revelation from the "apocalyptic pornography" of Lindsey and Ryrie to the dialectical philosophy of Jacques Ellul. Current scholars agree that the "calendarizing approach" to Revelation is not acceptable. M. suggests that interpretations that follow strict denominational lines (e.g., Literalism, dispensationalism, as well as the historical-critical method of the more liberal denominations (ignoring the "ecumenical dimension") are ultimately inferior. Modern studies have been reluctant to adopt "classical" approaches like preterist, futurist, etc., and to offer any new hermeneutic. The radical literary method of Ford (1975) is too problematic, and general disagreement and confusion among the best scholars have opened the door, again, to the "crassest literalism" of fundamentalism. Preferring the dialectical approach of Ellul, M. concludes that this method of study of the Revelation is superior to the "so-called scientific method" because it is best suited to the genre and it restores relevance to the text.

12. Pilch, J.J. What Are They Saying about the Book of Revelation? New York: Paulist Press, 1978.

Offers an introductory survey of the status of recent scholarship regarding the Revelation in four short chapters, beginning with the apocalyptic work of D. Russell, K. Koch, and P. Hanson. Chaps. 2-3 treat the specific works of A. Y. Collins and E. S. Fiorenza in connection with the CBA Task Force's publication on apocalyptic (1977), which identified the Revelation as "a prophetic-apocalyptic treatise" in letter form to serve as a public, pastoral letter to the faithful Christians in Asia. The last chapter identifies some problems related to the failure of scholars to communicate their findings to the general public, and suggests appropriate "popular" interpretations of the book as well as liturgical usage for the Church today.

[1976]
13. Vanni, U. "Rassegna bibliografica sull'Apocalisse (1970-1975)." **RivB** 24 (1976): 277-301.

Not seen. See summary in **NTA** 21 (2, '77): #527.

[1975]
14. Böcher, O. Die Johannesapokalypse. Erträge der forschung, 41. Darmstadt: Wissenschaftliche Buchgesellschaft, 1975.

Examines the results of scholarly research on the Revelation of John from the eighteenth century until 1974 in two parts: Part 1 discusses the history-of-religions method of the twentieth century and then evaluates several critical schools, e.g., British exegetes (Charles, Ramsay), and the diversity of Roman Catholic scholars (Allo, Schmid, Oliver). Part 2 treats some of the critical problems (e.g., authorship, date, setting, Christology, the 144,000, etc.) while engaging in a dialogue with a number of European commentators, e.g., Bousset, Lohmeyer, Hadorn). Omits any discussion of modern specialists' work on the Revelation, but suggests the need for further research in such areas as theology of the Revelation; the relationship between Revelation and the other Johannine writings; and the social, political, and pastoral aspects of the language of the Revelation. See also 1, B.

15. Clymer, D., and Lowery, R. **Index to Periodical Literature on the Book of Revelation.** S. Hamilton, MS: (s.n.), 1975.

Categorizes a list of 1,225 articles on the Book of Revelation based on the authors' examination of one hundred English-language journals from the first date of publication through 1973. Chapter titles include "Introduction" (I), "Texts and Versions" (II), "Literary and Historical Criticism" (III), "Exegesis" (IV), "Theology" (V), "History of Interpretation" (VI), "Revelation in Various Aspects of the Church's Life" (VII). The last chapter treats, among other things, thirteen pages of "Sermons" on the Book of Revelation.

[1973]
16. Hemer, C.J. "Unpublished Letters of Sir W. M. Ramsay in the Cambridge University Library." **EQ** 45 (1973): 166-171.

Examines the correspondence between Ramsay and W.R. Smith, M.R. James, E.H. Blakeney, and F.C. Burkitt in order to understand more fully Ramsay's research and scholarship on Asia Minor and, more particularly, the background to Rev. 2-3.

17. Kraft, H. "Zur Offenbarung des Johannes." **TRu** 38 (1973): 81-98.

Reviews the scholarly trends and literature on the Revelation from 1962 to 1973 (cf. Feuillet, Holtz, Comblin, Müller) and comments more briefly on the studies of Prigent, Jörns, Fiorenza, Rissi, Vanni, Lancellotti and Mussies. Regarding the more useful commentaries, K. singles out the work of Lohse (1960) because it combines scientific precision and intelligibility. He concludes that one of the keys to the interpretation of the Revelation is the connection between the author's time and the end of time. The essay is very selective and does not treat comprehensively the trends and directions of research up to 1973.

18. Strand, K.A. "The Book of Revelation: A Review Article on Some Recent Literature." **AUSS** 11 (1973): 181-193.

Reviews and critiques the books of Minear (1968), Morris (1969), and Ladd (1972). Regarding Minear's **I Saw a New Earth**, S. supports most of the author's findings, with the exception of the theory that John is dealing with an internal problem within the Church and not external opponents. Regarding Morris' Tyndale commentary, **The Revelation of St. John**, S. takes issue with the eight points that (according to Morris) mark off the Revelation from Jewish apocalyptic. Lastly, regarding Ladd's independent **A Commentary on the Revelation of John**, S. suggests that the work does well to break off from traditional dispensational futurism (e.g., Rev. 4:1-16:21), but Ladd does not go far enough in failing to identify numerous "historical" references.

[1967]
19. Langgärtner, G. "Der Apokalypse-Kommentar des Caesarius von Arles." **TG** 57 (1967): 210-225.

Builds on the work of G. Morin and the scholars who identified this Revelation commentary of Caesarius of Arles as either a pseudo-Augustinian work or a writing of Gennadius of Marseille. Suggests that the 19 sermons (*sequentiae*) that compose the commentary are really an abstract of a fifth-century commentary by Ticonius (dated prior to 400), which included material from a commentary of Victorinus of Pettau (ca. 304). Ticonius used a nontraditional "spiritualistic" method to interpret the Revelation. Caesarius copied the method of Ticonius. This commentator's use of the Old Latin text of the Bible is of great importance for modern scholars. Caesarius, one-time bishop of the church (502-542), interpreted the Revelation to be a statement of God's help for the persecuted church and not a prophetic report of the imminent end of the world. See also 6, A and E.

[1965]
20. Feuillet, A. **The Apocalypse.** T. E. Crane, trans. Staten Island, NY: Alba House, 1965.

Reports briefly on the scholarly research on the Revelation for the period 1920-1960 in seven chapters. Chap. 1 covers the general tendencies and methods of interpretation; Chap. 2, composition and literary structure; Chap. 3, interpretation of Rev. 2-3 and 4-21; Chap. 4, the doctrine(s) of the book; Chap. 5, date and place of composition; Chap. 6, authorship; Chap. 7, particular problems, e.g., the "woman" of Rev. 12, the millennium, etc. Draws short conclusions at the end of each chapter, e.g., regarding Rev. 2-3, he says that the "letters" never existed independently, but they are "prophetic" in that they address the whole church of every age. A general conclusion urges further "scientific research and investigation" and indicates the kind of creative writing and art that the Revelation of John has inspired during the history of the Church.

21. Molnar, A. "Apocalypse XII dans l'interprétation hussite." **RHPR** 45 (1965): 212-231.

Surveys three hundred years of Hussite scholarship on Rev. 12 and concludes that Hussite interpretation of the chapter identified the conflict there with their conflict with the papacy. Furthermore they interpreted the theme of the book to be a call to action in the last days that began with the coming of Christ. See also 1, A.

22. Roberts, J.W. "The Interpretation of the Apocalypse: The State of the Question." **RQ** 8 (1965): 154-162.

Uses the work of A. Feuillet, **L'Apocalypse. État de la question** (1963) as springboard for his discussion of scholarship on the Revelation since 1923. Reviews and evaluates (pro and con) the studies of Kuyper (1963), Greer (1963), and Pack (1965). The article concludes with several suggestions for future studies.

[1963]
23. Beasley-Murray, G.R. "Commentaries on the Book of Revelation." **Th** 66 (1963): 52-56.

Surveys the latest commentaries for general readers and recommends the works of Preston and Hanson, D.T. Niles, and Kiddle. Of the older, more popular works, he commends Milligan, Scott, and Peake, but disapproves of Newbott and Kepler. The most outstanding commentaries are identified as those of Swete, Charles, Moffatt, and Ramsay. Among the German works, the author mentions Bousset, Zahn, Lohmeyer, and Gunkel, especially for his **Schöpfung und Chaos** (1895). Among the French commentaries, the author praises the work of Allo.

24. Danner, D. "A History of Interpretation of Revelation 20:1-10 in the Restoration Movement." **RQ** 7 (1963): 217- 235.

Traces the history of the Movement's interpretation of the millennium from 1825 to 1865 and concludes that the postmillennial view of Campbell and Milligan had a big impact on subsequent Restoration leaders. This particular emphasis is best explained by the spirit of the times and the Restoration hope that Christendom would be converted into the millennium. Concludes that this may not be the most sound apocalyptic hermeneutic. See also 4, B.

25. James, E. "Commentaries on Revelation." **Th** 66 (1963): 158.

Writes to the editor of *Theology* regarding the omission of Lilje's commentary in Beasley-Murray's article (66, 1963).

26. Montagnini, F. "Problemi dell'Apocalisse in alcuni studi degli ultimi anni." **RivB** 11 (1963): 400-424.

See summary in **NTA** 9 (1, '64) #280.

[1956]
27. Stanley, D.M. "Bulletin of the New Testament: The Johannine Literature." **TS** 17 (1956): 516-531.

Reviews contemporary scholarship on the Johannine corpus and offers advice on the interpretation of the Revelation while not addressing the authorship problem. Says that the interpreter should not separate the book's ideas from the literary imagery and/or overstress the tradition of Jewish mythology in connection to the writing. Dangers of interpretation are, 1) Insufficient attention given to the "suppleness of the symbolism." 2) The "historicisation" of images, taking them simply as concrete, historical events.

[1954]
28. Barrett, C.K. "New Testament Commentaries, Pt. 3. Epistles and Revelation." **ET** 65 (1953-54): 177-180.

Reviews and evaluates briefly the commentaries of Swete, Charles, Beckwith, Moffatt, Scott, Kiddle, Weiss, Heitmüller, Behm, Bouset, and Lohmeyer. Offers special praise for the work of Charles in terms of its critical superiority.

[1947]
29. Theissen, A. "Catholic Bibliography of Acts, Catholic Epistles and the Apocalypse." **Scrip** 2 (1947): 53-57.

Lists some of the most recent Catholic publications on the Apocalypse.

[1942]
30. Wikenhauser, A. **Das neueste Schrifttum über die Apokalypse.** Oberrhein: Pastoralbl., 1942.

Reviews and critiques the latest scholarship on the book.

[1935]
31. Lohmeyer, E. "Die Offenbarung des Johannes 1920-1934." **TRu** 6 (1934):269-314; 7 (1935):28-62.

Vol. 6 (1934) reviews a wide range of scholarly research on the Revelation under two headings: 1) Method and 2) Commentary and Cognate studies. Under the latter, L. considers the scholarship of England, France, Holland, and Germany. His opinion of the various methods (e.g., "*kirchengeschichtlichen*," "*formgeschichtliche*," "*zeitgeschichtlich*,") varies in terms of their relative value. He urges caution while concluding that the many answers proposed to the critical questions may only suggest the inadequacies and problems of the book itself. The work of Charles, Oman, Loisy, Köhler, Zahn, Hadorn, and Allo are singled out for special analysis and commendation. Vol. 7 (1935) treats seven problem areas of research: 1. Text and Canon; 2. Literary Problems; 3. Stylistic and Religio-Psychological Problems, etc. Number 7, "Einzel fragen," deals with eschatology, not from the perspective of a distant goal, but from the "last things," which are always present where God acts.

B. GENERAL INTRODUCTION/SURVEY

[1987]
32. Moore, H. "The Book of Revelation." **IBS** 9 (1987): 158-174.

Offers general information regarding the form and content of the book: 1) In terms of literary characteristics, it is to be understood as an apocalyptic and prophetic epistle; 2) In terms of its historical setting and basic ideas, it is Christian; 3) In terms of its apocalypticism, it is changed by the author in light of the Christ-event, but it maintains the apocalyptic hope.

[1982]
33. Palmer, E.F. **1, 2, 3 John, Revelation.** "The Communicator's Commentary, 12." Waco, TX: Word, 1982.

Popular treatment for church pastors and teachers combines contemporary biblical scholarship with modern applications. Includes a brief introduction, book outline, text of the **New King James Version,** and exposition of each literary unit. Stresses the dramatic structure and choral-symphonic character of the Revelation. Problematic questions are avoided in order to offer more positive suggestions for preaching.

34. Wallis, W.B. "The Coming Kingdom. A Survey of the Book of Revelation." **Pres** 8 (1982): 13-70.

Offers an expositional study and an outline of the book following four main visions: 1:9-3:22; 4:1-16:21; 17:1-21:8; 21:9-22:5. The visions are introduced by a prologue (1:1-8) and concluded by an epilogue (22:6-21). The theme of the book is stated in Rev. 1:7, "Behold, he is coming!" Concludes his work with an extended discussion of Rev. 20 in terms of the coming Millennium.

[1978]
35. Garoffalo, S. **"L'Apocalisse è per oggi, Miti, mistero e storia."** Florence: Salani, 1978.

See summary in **NTA** 23 (3, '79): 356.

[1977]
36. Schick, E.A. **Revelation -- The Last Book of the Bible.** Philadelphia, PA: Fortress, 1977.

Uses the analogy of a nine-room picture gallery in order to set the scene and prepare for the interpretation of the text, which he outlines as follows: 1:1-8; 22:6-21 (Entrance and Exit); 1:9-3:22 (The Seven Churches and the One Church); 4:1-5:14 (Thrones and Worship); 6:1-8:1 (Seven Seals); 8:2-11:19 (Seven Trumpets): 12:1-14:20 (Beasts and Church); 15:1-16:21 (New Exodus); 17:1-19:10 (The Great City Babylon); 19:11-22:5 (The New Creation). Underlines five major truths in the book: 1) Disclosure through symbols; 2) Historical realism; 3) Political realism; 4) The oneness of the universe; 5) The finality of God's rule.

37. Sproxton, V. **Good News in Revelation.** "The Revelation to John in **Today's English Version.**" Cleveland, OH: Collins & World/Fount Books, 1977.

Offers an exposition of **Today's English Version** of the Revelation according to each literary section. Suggests that this basic message controls the book's interpretation: "The victory of God's purpose for the world, which evil has no power ultimately to frustrate."

[1976]
38. Fiorenza, E.S. **The Apocalypse.** "Herald Biblical Booklets." Chicago, IL: Franciscan Herald Press, 1976.

Introduces this popular treatment of the Revelation by identifying the work as an apocalyptic-prophetic book written in an epistolary frame. Discusses the various interpretations of the book and the relative value of history and eschatology for interpretation, the literary model, techniques of composition, content, plan, and, finally, John's theological perspective. See also 3, A.

[1975]
39. Feuillet, A. "Jalons pour une meilleure intelligence de l'Apocalypse. Introduction à la partie prophétique." EsV 85 (1975): 209-223; 433-443.

Pages 209-223 discuss literary and historical problems, including the connection between Chaps. 2-3 and 4-21, the condition of the churches, and the link with the prayers of John 17 and III John. Part two examines the theology of the book, especially the Second Coming of Christ, imminent events in the midst of persecution and the doctrine of the Eucharist underlying Rev. 2-3. The Book of Revelation is John's reinterpretation of the OT in light of the new Christian era. Christ is shown to be continually present in His Church and the church depends on Him for her life. Pages 433-443 focus on Chaps. 4-5 as the "prophetic" part of the book where John reveals his plan. F. demonstrates that the Revelation is a book of Christian hope for a suffering people. This theme is suggested by Chaps. 4-5, which interpret a Jewish liturgy into a heavenly liturgy glorifying the Lamb, Jesus Christ. See also 3, A and 4, B.

40. ———. "Jalons pour une meilleure intelligence de l'Apocalypse. Les lettres aux Églises, Chaps. 2 et 3." EsV 85 (1975): 209-223.

Discusses, first, the literary and historical problems of Rev. 2-3, viz., their connection with Rev. 4-22, the spiritual problems in the churches, and their relationship to the prayer of John 17. In the second section of the work, F. discusses doctrinal matters: the Parousia of Christ in history, the meaning of the promises made to Christians (crown of life, white garments, etc.), the activity of the Holy Spirit, persecution, martyrdom, and the Eucharistic doctrine underlying the two chapters. Concludes that John's work is an inspired rereading of the OT in light of the Christian era. It offers the message that Christ is always present to the Church and each Christian, and the Church is always dependent upon Him for life and support. See also 4, B.

41. ———. "Jalons pour une meilleure intelligence de l'Apocalypse. Le prologue et la vision inaugurale (chap. 1)." **EsV** 85 (1975): 65-72.

Identifies the Revelation as a "prophecy" based on the author's immediate past. The crucified and risen Christ is the key to history. Chap. 1 draws on a number of OT traditions in order to introduce the book's message (e.g., 1:5 draws from Ps. 89; 1:7 uses Dan. 7:13; the phrase "Day of the Lord" corresponds to the same expression used by the OT prophets, etc.) Concludes that Rev. 1 exalts Christ as the royal King and Priest who controls the churches. See also 4, B.

[1974]
42. Eller, V. **The Most Revealing Book of the Bible: Making Sense out of Revelation.** Grand Rapids, MI: Eerdmans, 1974.

Offers a popular introduction and survey of the Revelation based on the thesis that Jesus Christ is both the revealer and the content of the book. There follows a discussion of the literary sections based on a traditional outline: 1) Introduction (1:1-20); 2) The revealer's letters to seven actual churches of the End Time (2:1-3:22); 3) The control of history in the End Time (4:1-5:14), etc. Argues for a Christological interpretation of the Revelation.

43. Feuillet, A. "Jalons pour une meilleure intelligence de l'Apocalypse. Vue d'ensemble sur la révélation johannique." **EsV** 84 (1974): 481-490.

Continues a previous study: 1) Approves certain "useful" interpretative approaches, e.g., millennialism, recapitulation, universal history, eschatology, contemporary history, literary analysis, comparative religions. 2) Compares the Book of Revelation with Jewish apocalyptic literature and with the Gospel of John (noting the promises, apocalyptic pseudonymity, esoterism and symbolism, etc. 3) Suggests the relative importance and meaning of the book, the present interest in the message, and the way the Revelation uses OT traditions. Concludes that the Book of Revelation is a magnificent Christian poem composed of references to ancient Christian liturgy and Christian symbolism. See also 1, C.

[1972]
44. Beasley-Murray, G.R. **Highlights of the Book of Revelation**. Nashville, TN: Broadman Press, 1972.

This is an expanded revision of the popular lectures given for the Nationwide Bible Conference in Dallas in 1971. B-M. offers the reader some light concerning their general understanding of the Revelation by suggesting it be read/studied under the theme of Christian hope. A balanced, conservative exposition follows the traditional literary units.

[1970]
45. Anonymous. **L'Apocalypse**. "Traduction oecuménique de la Bible." Paris: Les Bergers & les Mages and Cerf, 1970.

Offers a new, interdenominational French translation, preceded by 21 pages of introductory discussion of questions related to the book's form, structure, and major motifs. Footnotes aimed at a popular audience make up the book's appendix.

46. Pesch, R. "Offenbarung Jesu Christi. Eine Auslegung von Apk 1,1-3." **BL** 11 (1970): 15-29.

Studies the introductory section of the Revelation (1:1-3) in terms of its strophic structure, its literary style, and its theological (apocalyptic, prophetic, Christological) content in connection with the rest of the work. See also 4, B, (1).

[1966]
47. Claudel, P. **Au Milieu des Vitraux de l'Apocalypse**. Paris: Galleruard, 1966.

Presents a view and the milieu of the Apocalypse by setting out a study in two parts: I. Dialogue and letters between a father and a child on the contents of the book (300+ pages) and II. Critical notes and glosses to the text (100+ pages).

[1963]
48. Caird, G.B. "On Deciphering the Book of Revelation: I. Heaven and Earth." **ET** 74 (1962-63): 13-15.

Argues for a Jewish apocalyptic background to the "heaven and earth" themes in the Revelation, suggesting that the two ideas are interconnected symbols and realities about to be accomplished "in their entirety" (14). Says that John's purpose is comparable to John Bunyan's notion of seeing the backside of a burning wall, i.e., John wants to show Christians on trial in the first century the reality of God (in control) behind the wall of fire in order to warn them of the impending crisis with Rome. See also 3, F and 5, H, (12).

49. ————. "On Deciphering the Book of Revelation: II. Past and Future." **ET** 74 (1962-63): 51-53.

Suggests that the literary outline is not to be discovered from Rev. 1:19 (re: past, present, future), but that the line between past and future is to be drawn immediately before each reference to coming martyrdom. The divine qualities of "mercy" and "holiness" define God's reasons for allowing persecution of the Church. Concludes that the blood of the martyrs is "the seed of the church." See also 3, F and 5, H, (24).

50. ————."On Deciphering the Book of Revelation: III. The First and the Last." **ET** 74 (1962-63): 82-84.

Considers five views of eschatology (Dodd, J. A. T. Robinson, Schweitzer, Cadbury, Mowinckel) and argues that biblical eschatology is semitic and only Gentiles ("or pedants") take it literally. The "first and last" terms are used by John to show that his primary concern is with the present and not the future. The Revelation interprets history figuratively in order to point to the impending historical crisis (Rome) and not the end of the world. See also 3, F and 5, G, (1).

51. ————. "On Deciphering the Book of Revelation: IV. Myth and Legend." **ET** 74 (1962-63): 103-105.

After defining "myth" as a story about remote past events that embody ultimate truth and imagery relevant to the present (103), C. traces the images of the sea, the dragon, and the harlot to mythological origins and, further, suggests that John used those myths to offer theological commentary on the political situation of the first century.

[1962]
52. Fannon, P. "The Apocalypse." **Scrip** xiv (1962): 33-43.

Concludes that either John the Evangelist or a disciple wrote the book in order to establish persecuted Christians during a time of trial and crisis. The literary characteristics of symbolism and prophetism are described and several methods of interpretation are mentioned. Views the work as John's philosophy of history as giving hope of victory to a persecuted church and describing God's control of history.

[1959]
53. Collins, J.J. "The Apocalypse." **Wor** 33 (1959): 230-231.

Reviews P. Féret's **The Apocalypse of St. John** (1958), noting with approval the work as well as the influence of E.B. Allo on Féret. The theme appears to be the Lamb of God, who controls all history, and Christ, who is the master of the world and its events. The author rejects the verse-by-verse and outline method of study, and prefers to focus on and develop the key ideas in the Apocalypse. F. disagrees with Allo regarding the interpretation of the 144,000 and the meaning of the Millennium. Allo sees the thousand-year period as the life of the Church, from the Ascension to the Last Judgment; but F. views the Millennium occurring at the end of time. Both interpret the woman of Rev. 12 to be the Church.

[1958]
54. Giblet, J. "Introductio in Apocalypsim S. Joannis. **ColM** 43 (1958): 367-369.

See summary in **NTA** 3 (1, '58): # 177.

[1957]
55. Fransen, I. "Cahier de Bible: Jésus, le Témoin fidèle (Apocalypse)." **BVCh** 16 (1956-57): 66-79.

Offers a two-part study of the Revelation. Part I considers the OT background from prophetic and apocalyptic genre. The book seems to be based on Hebraic concepts and imagery, although F. does suggest that much of the imagery in the book reflects ancient mythology, astrology, and astronomy. These elements are combined by the author to present an epic of triumph from torture and a story of heavenly worship. Part II outlines a comprehensive plan of the whole Revelation, while considering some of the themes, images, and scriptural allusions. See also 1, C and 2, G.

56. Richardson, D.W. **Revelation of Jesus Christ: An Introduction.** Richmond, VA: John Knox Press, 1957.

Addresses the matter of interpretation and exposition in the book. Insists that John is giving a philosophy of history in which faith in God's righteous government is supreme. The study follows traditional chapter-by-chapter method of exposition. Considers the millennium as symbolic literary device.

[1953]
57. Häring, P. **Die Botschaft der Offenbarung des hl. Johannes.** München: Pfeiffer, 1953.

Examines point by point the basic message of the Revelation after a brief discussion of some of the critical problems.

[1952]
58. Newbolt, M.R. **The Book of Unveiling.** London: SPCK, 1952.

Presents an "elementary commentary" for the general reader. After a brief introduction, N. offers an exposition of the main literary units. Frequent references to OT and classical literature punctuate the work. The millennium is interpreted as no fixed period of time.

[1950]
59. Little, C.H. **Explanation of the Book of Revelation.** St. Louis, MO: Concordia Publishing House, 1950.

Offers a popular exposition in accordance with its literary style and context. Uses a hermeneutical method, which considers the prophecies of the Revelation as being progressively fulfilled during the history of the current dispensation. See also 1, C.

[1948]
60. Boyd, R. "The Book of Revelation." **Int** 2 (1948): 467-482.

Considers the character and purpose of the Revelation by examining the style (apocalyptic, nonliteral, symbolic), structure (recapitulation), history (dated ca. A. D. 96), text, and the analogy of the Scriptural principle of interpretation.

[1947]
61. Claudel, P. **Introduction à l'Apocalypse**. Paris: Egloff, 1947.

Offers a brief essay (65 pp.) as an introduction to the general apocalyptic and prophetic character of the Revelation to l'Institut Catholique de Paris.

[1945]
62. Rist, M. "Revelation: A Handbook for Martyrs." **IR** 2 (1945): 269-280.

Studies the Book of Revelation in light of Riddle's **The Martyrs: A Study in Social Control**. Concludes that the Revelation is apocalyptic in form, but martyrological in its intended function. See also 1, C.

[1942]
63. Bellamy, H.S. **The Book of Revelation is History**. London: Faber and Faber, 1942.

Offers a rather bizarre interpretation of the Revelation while arguing that the book is really John's publication of a secret, eyewitness record of a time past when the earth went through cataclysmic events. See also 5, H. (14).

64. Stamm, R.T. "The Revelation of St. John and the Present Crisis." **LChQ** 15 (1942): 285-303.

Studies the Revelation in three sections: I. Original Purpose. John's word is a cry for justice and vindication of suffering Christians. II. Sources, Structure, Symbolism. Sees the influence of OT writings and thoughts, traditional structure. Theme: "No compromise! Stand firm! The Victory is Ours!" III. The Message for 1942-- especially for Lutherans. Suggests that John was not promoting an apocalyptic view of history, which, when rightly understood, is unforgiving and fatalistic in dealing with God's punishment for the wicked in relationship to the balance of divine justice. The Revelation is about standing firm in a time of present crisis.

[1941]
65. Ebor, W. "The Sealed Book." **Th** 42 (1941): 65-71.

Reviews the Revelation with an eye to recovering the author's experience after Chap. 3. Interprets the symbols according to contemporary situations and concludes that the book provides a clue to the interpretation of history and a criterion of progress. The ultimate conflict in history is between the

Lamb and the Wild Beast (i.e., Love and Pride) and true progress comes only in the triumph of the Lamb.

66. Shute, A.L. "The Book of the Revelation: The Church of Jesus Christ on the Field of History." **REx** 38 (1941): 158-183.

Offers a brief introduction that includes principles of interpretation and a view of the Revelation relevant to the Church in history. Contends that John is concerned primarily with sweeping observations and nonparticulars, i.e. symbolism. Five major sections review the movement of the Church in history toward victory. Chap. 20 does not describe a millennium, but, rather, the overthrow of the enemies of the Church. The book ends in hope.

[1940]
67. Lawton, A. **Die Zeit ist Kurz, der herr ist nahe. Eine Einführung in die Offenbarung Johannes.** 2. Aufl. Bad Salzuflen: MBK Verlag, 1940.

Writes an introduction to the Rev., discussing briefly some of the critical issues while offerering an explanation of the text with interpretation.

68. Scott, E.F. **The Book of Revelation.** New York City, NY: Scribner's Sons, 1940.

Presents a four-part introduction to the Revelation: I. Origin and Purpose; II. The Drama; III. Doctrine in the Revelation; and IV. Permanent Message. Concludes with a brief study of the book's apocalyptic genre.

C. INTERPRETATION/HERMENEUTICS

(1) General

[1987]
69. Koser, R.E. "Hermeneutics of the Book of Revelation for Preaching." D. Min. Dissertation. School of Theology at Claremont. Claremont, CA, 1987.

Says that the enigmatic features of the Revelation have discouraged most preachers from using the book in the pulpit. Offers guidelines and hermeneutical axioms for NT exegetes based on linguistic, historical, and theological perspectives so that preachers might use the book's nurturing message to convey hope to the Church. See also 6, D.

[1986]
70. Burkhardt, H. "Ausharren bei Jesus. Überlegungen zum theologischen Verständnis der Johannesoffenbarung." **TBei** 17 (1986): 234-247.

Offers a brief history of the interpretation of the Revelation and four theses concerning a hermeneutic of the book. First, it should be approached as a genuine "revelation" to the prophet and not as the result of human fancy. Second, the book should be taken seriously as a genuine prediction of the future, even though it is situated in the first century. Third, the biggest hindrance to understanding the message of the Revelation is not its strange imagery, but rather, human sin and the inability to comprehend the nature of God's holiness. Fourth, what is most helpful in developing a proper hermeneutic is recognizing that John's purpose in writing was not simply to offer eschatological knowledge but to prepare the Christian community for the coming cosmic catastrophes and general persecution. In thus warning the community, John hopes to cut off the temptation to waver and lose faith.

[1985]
71. Boyer, J.L. "Are the Seven Letters of Revelation 2-3 Prophetic?" **GTJ** 6 (1985): 267-273.

Discusses several hermeneutical approaches to the Revelation and concludes that it is not impossible to interpret Rev. 2-3 prophetically, i.e., in specific terms of periods of progressive history for the Church.

72. Kretschmar, G. **Die Offenbarung des Johannes: Die Geschichte ihrer Auslegung im 1. Jahrtausend.** "Calwer Theologische Monographien B9." Stuttgart: Calwer, 1985.

Identifies traditional Jewish apocalypticism as the background to the Revelation and depicts the book in terms of "promises in pictures." Suggests that Christian apocalypticism is like its Jewish counterpart in terms of form, but the Revelation is special in terms of its origin, intention, and structure. Concludes by tracing the history of interpretation of the Revelation from the early Christian era through the Middle Ages.

[1984]
73. Satre, L.J. "Interpreting the Book of Revelation." **WW** 4 (1984): 57-69.

Describes the Revelation in terms that combine apocalyptic, prophetic, and epistolary elements and discusses critical issues (authorship, recipients, date, and situation). Outlines the work according to literary units, provides practical suggestions for interpretative sessions, and concludes with twelve study goals for interested students.

[1983]
74. Tickle, J. **The Book of Revelation. A Catholic Interpretation of the Apocalypse.** Liguon, MO: Liguri Publications, 1983.

Introduces the Roman Catholic church's traditional interpretation of the theme, message, and symbolism of the Revelation. After treating several critical issues (background, authorship, style, etc.), T. offers an exposition of the book in three sections: 1) The Church incarnate (Rev. 1-3), respecting seven local churches and relevant problems; 2) The church committed (Rev. 4-20), respecting heaven, scrolls, seals, trumpets, plagues and judgment; 3) The church transfigured (Rev. 21-22), respecting the new Jerusalem.

[1979]
75. Strand, K.A. **Interpreting the Book of Revelation: Hermeneutical Guidelines, with Brief Introduction to Literary Analysis.** 2nd rev. ed. Naples, FL: Ann Arbor Publishers, 1979.

Revises the author's 1976 work with the following changes: Pp. 46, 78-79 (text) and p. 52 diagram. Pp. 78-79, rearranged material. See also 1, B.

[1978]
76. Gryglewicz, F. "La interpretado de Apokalipso de Sankta Johano." **BRev** 14 (1978): 35-47.

See summary in **NTA** 23 (2, '79): #603.

77. Megivern, J.J. "Wrestling with Revelation." **BTB** 8 (1978): 147-154.

Criticizes the traditional approaches to the Revelation, e.g., preterist, futurist, historicist, and symbolic, while arguing for the dialectical method used by J. Ellul in his **Apocalypse** (1977).

[1977]
78. Beasley-Murray, G.R., Hobbs, H.H., and Robbins, R.F. **Revelation: Three Viewpoints.** Nashville, TN: Broadman, 1977.

Three biblical scholars interpret the Revelation according to premillennial (Beasley-Murray), amillennial (Hobbs), and apocalyptic (Robbins) perspectives. The editor summarizes the discussion in terms of the Ridgecrest Baptist Conference Center, North Carolina context, noting the agreements and differences of the lecturers.

[1976]
79. Marconcini, B. "Differenti metodi dell'interpretazione dell'Apocalisse." **BO** 18 (1976): 121-131.

See summary in **NTA** 21 (2, '77): #526.

80. Prete, B. "La speranza e sue motivazioni nel libro dell'Apocalisse." **SD** 21 (1976): 277-304.

See summary in **NTA** 21 (3, '77): #864.

81. Strand, K.A. **Interpreting the Book of Revelation. Hermeneutical Guidelines, with Brief Introduction to Literary Analysis.** Worthington, OH: Ann Arbor Publishers, 1976.

A reprint and revision of selective material taken from the author's **The Open Gates of Heaven** (1970; revised 1972). Offers a popular study and discussion of the factors involved in developing an appropriate hermeneutic for interpreting the Revelation of John. Chapters consider the following themes: General approaches to interpretation (e.g., preterist, futurist, etc.), literary milieu, symbols, literary analysis, structure, and several illustrations of interpretation (the dragon and beasts, and the sealed book. The work concludes with a discussion of the contributions of Morris, Ladd, and Minear to the study of Revelation, along with an example of the chiasmatic structure of the OT book of Zechariah. See also 1, B.

82. Vanni, U. "La riflessione sapienziale come atteggiamento ermeneutico costante nell'Apocalisse." **RivB** 24 (1976): 185-197.

See summary in **NTA** 23 (2, '79): #609.

83. Veloso, M. "Simbolos en el Apocalipsis de San Juan." **RevB** 38 (1976): 321-338.

See summary in **NTA** 21 (3, '77): #865.

[1975]
84. Stagg, F. "Interpreting the Book of Revelation." **REx** 72 (1975): 331-343.

Discusses the primary movement of thought in the Revelation and argues for the following points of interpretation: 1) Christ and His cross are fully exalted; 2) The fate of the world is determined; 3) The book was written during the reign of Domitian; 4) The author was concerned with persecution and oppression outside the church, along with moral failure within.

[1972]
85. Roberts, J.W. "The Meaning of Eschatology in the Book of Revelation." **RQ** 15 (1972): 95-110.

Leaning heavily on the work of Caird, R. suggests that the idea of identifying the end of the world with the destruction of Rome is flawed at two major points: 1) There is no basis for making John's apocalyptic eschatology into a unified focus that controls the whole writing. 2) It is erroneous methodology to assume that all references to final (ultimate) eschatology in the Revelation must refer to the end of the world.

[1970]
86. Bandstra, A.J. "History and Eschatology in the Apocalypse." **CTJ** 5 (1970): 180-183.

Examines Fioranza's study (**CBQ** 30 ['68]: 537-569), which argues for eschatology and not history as the organizing theme of the Revelation. Concludes that Fiorenza is essentially correct; however she does not do full justice to the author's history-of-redemption statement. See also 5, H, (14).

[1967]
87. Richards, H.J. **What the Spirit Says to the Churches. A Key to the Apocalypse of John.** New York: P. J. Kennedy & Sons, 1967.

Interprets the book by recapitulation (via diagram) and explains the contents accordingly. Concludes with a three-fold summary under the categories, 1) the death and resurrection of Christ, 2) the death and resurrection of the Church, and 3) the book of hope. See also 3, E.

88. Thomas, R.L. "The Chronological Interpretation of Revelation 2-3." **BibSac** 124 (1967): 321-331.

Summarizes the three prevalent interpretations of Rev. 2-3 ("Prophetical," "Historico-prophetical," and "Historical"), while arguing for the historical approach on the basis of literary genre and context. See also 4, B and 5, H, (14).

[1966]
89. MacL. Gilmour, S. "The Use and Abuse of the Book of Revelation." **ANQ** 7 (1966): 15-28.

Places the origin of the Revelation during the time of Domitian and argues that John's purpose was to encourage Christians to resist emperor worship. John expected the immediate return of Christ and the start of the millennium within weeks (or months) of his writing. Because of the delay of Christ's return, the audience was forced to identify the predictions of the Revelation to contemporary history. This process has continued throughout history to the latest millennial sects.

[1963]
90. Newman, B. "The Fallacy of the Domitian Hypothesis: Critique of the Irenaeus Source as a Witness for the Contemporary-Historical Approach to the Interpretation of the Apocalypse." **NTS** 10 (1963): 133-139.

Challenges the traditional view that the Revelation should be interpreted in light of the first-century Roman persecutions of Domitian. Two objections are raised: 1) Apocalyptic literature need not be connected exclusively and essentially to political-religious persecutions since eschatological gnostic thought is much more essential to the literature. 2) The Irenaeus authority for dating the Revelation connects it to Domitian reign generally, but not for reasons of persecution. Irenaeus considered the Revelation as a polemic against first-century gnosticism. This latter point may in fact be the real background to the writing. See also 2, G.

[1961]
91. Feuillet, A. "Les diverses méthodes d'interprétation de l'Apocalypse et les commentaires récents." **AC** 71 (1961):257-270.

Identifies, analyzes, and critiques several interpretative methods regarding the Revelation. They are millenarism, recapitulation, universal history, eschatology, contemporary history, comparative religion, and literary analysis. F. dismisses millenarianism immediately but finds a modified eschatological and historical method most satisfying. Argues that the Revelation presents a Christian philosophy of history and record of contemporary events but pagan influence has been overstated. Finally, F.

suggests that the book is a rereading of the OT in light of the Christ-event and is extremely difficult to interpret due to its strange genre and synthesis of OT allusions. See also 1, A.

[1959]
92. Michl, J. "Die Deutung der apokalyptischen Frau in der Gegenwart." **BZ** 3 (1959): 301-310.

Reviews the scholarly publications on Rev. 12 since 1950 and concludes that the most popular interpretation of the figure views the woman as the people of God, the church prefigured by Israel but realized in the Christian era. See also 4, B.

[1957]
93. Trabucco, A. "La 'Donna ravvolta di sole' (Apoc. 12). Maria e la Chiesa secondo gli esegeti cattolici dal 1563 alla prima metà del secolo XIX." **Mar** 19 (1957): 289-334.

See summary in **NTA** 2 (3, '58): #616. See also 5, B, (11).

[1951]
94. LeFrois, B.J. "Eschatological Interpretation of the Apocalypse." **CBQ** 13 (1951): 17-20.

Argues against the spiritual and ideal interpretation in favor of the traditional eschatological method. After summarizing the Revelation's description of the great finale of God's Kingdom on Earth, the author suggests that the three parts of the book (1:9-3:22; 4:1-20:15; 21-22) point to the destruction of the godless, the conversion of Israel, the security of "the Marian Church," and the new earth of eternal happiness.

[1944]
95. Hall, G.F. "Luther's Eschatology." **AQ** 23 (1944): 13-19.

Examines Luther's views on eschatology and his rejection of the Revelation as inspired because Christ was not known or taught in it. Contends that Luther used the book as a polemic against his enemies.

96. Mathers, J. "The Book of Revelation in the Twentieth Century." **EQ** 16 (1944): 9-27.

Studies modern treatments of the book according to the historical situation of Christian apocalyptic writings. Dialogues with Charles, *et al.*

Offers impressions of John's "Picture Gallery." Concludes that the central message of the Revelation is "The Lord Reigns."

[1940]
97. Clayton, R.H. **Future History in "The Revelation."** London: Marshall, Morgan, and Scott, 1940.

Offers an original study using a futurist interpretation of the text. Suggests that the "key" to the book is to be found in its apocalyptic structure. See also 5, H, (14).

98. Heitmüller, F. "Die Apocalypse. Ein Versuch zur Deutung des letzten Buches der Bibel." **AW** 37 (1940): 271-273.

Offers an introduction to the various ways the reader can understand the meaning of the book.

[1939]
99. Allo, E.-B. "La Leçon de l'Apocalypse." **VS** 61 (1939): 199-204.

Not seen.

[1919]
100. Case, S.J. **The Revelation of John: A Historical Interpretation.** Chicago, IL: University of Chicago Press, 1919.

Explains to the general reader the meaning of the Revelation as John intended it to be understood by the first recipients. While rendering his own personal English translation (paraphrased at times), comments and interprets each paragraph of the text. Three chapters survey I) the historical situation, II) typical revelations preceding John's Revelation, III) the making of a revelation (including John's ideas, equipment, and composition). C. concludes with a brief survey of "typical" interpretations of the Revelation and then argues for the "historical" method as the best.

(2) Millennialist

General

[1988]
101. Wessel, H."Le livre de l'Apocalypse et la fin des temps." **RR** 39 (1988): 1-8.

Describes and discusses four schools of interpretation regarding the Revelation and the book's life setting. Next, W. underlines the three main ideas connected to the Millennium, concluding that one school of interpretation should not exclude the others but each should help define and complement the other.

102. Zegwaart, H. "Apocalyptic Eschatology and Pentecostalism: The Relevance of John's Millennium for Today." **Pne** 10 (1988): 3-25.

From the perspective of Pentecostalism, Z. argues that John reshaped and Christianized the traditional apocalyptic idea of a messianic interregnum in order to show it as a red thread of doctrine thoughout the work. Christ's lordship in the present and the future is best expressed in terms of hope through the reign of the Messiah and the new Jerusalem.

[1978]
103. Mazzucco, C., and Pietrella, E. "Il rapporto tra la concezione del millennio dei primi autori cristiani e *l'Apocalisse di Giovanni*." **Aug** 18 (1978): 29-45.

See summary in **NTA** 23 (1, '79): #231. See also 5, G, (4).

[1977]
104. Montgomery, J.W. "The Millennium" in **Dreams, Visions and Oracles: The Layman's Guide to Biblical Prophecy**. Carl Armerding and Ward Gasque, eds. Grand Rapids, MI: Baker Book House, 1977: pp. 175-185.

This brief history of Christian thought concerning the millennium concludes that the three positions, "pre," "post," and "a," seem to hold equal value, depending upon one's own theological presuppositions. It is the fact of the Parousia of Christ that is most important and common to all positions.

[1973]
105. Smith, D.C. "The Millennial Reign of Jesus Christ. Some Observations on Rev. 20: 1-10." **RQ** 16 (1973): 219-230.

Argues that the earthly, millennial reign of Christ before the consummation was recognized as early as the second century and was supported by the Revelation of John and other writings (2 Baruch and 4 Ezra). Probably the OT tradition behind the notion was Ez. 37-48. In the Revelation the millennium is the second act in the drama of Christ's kingdom, which is inaugurated by His Parousia, which is preceded by the messianic woes. All Christians, dead and alive, will reign with Christ during the thousand years. S. concludes that the idea of a millennial reign of Christ in the End Time is an important structural element in John's Revelation. See Also 4, B and 5, G, (4).

[1972]
106. Fiorenza, E.S."Die tausendjährige Herrschaft der Auferstandenen (Apk 20,4-6)." **BL** 13 (1972):107-124.

Examines the editorial work of John in Rev. 20:4-6 and demonstrates that the author revises various traditions from Ezekiel and Jewish apocalyptic in order to create a new and more relevant idea for his church community. The thousand years apply, not to some interim messianic kingdom, but to one aspect of eschatological salvation. There is no logical or temporal sequence to the events leading up to the coming Kingdom of God.

[1965]
107. Vaucher, A.-F. "Les 1260 jours prophetiques dans les cercles Joachimites." **AUSS** 3 (1965): 42-48.

Suggests that it was A. Joachim of Floris who first interpreted the 1,260 days as 1,260 years in Rev. 11. Apparently Joachim anticipated some kind of spiritual resurrection in A.D. 1200, but some of his disciples chose the year A.D.1260. Other dates of important expectation emerged after those two passed, e.g., 1290, 1335 (Dan. 12) and, finally, 2300 (Dan. 8).

[1958]
108. Cairns, E.E. "Eschatology and Church History." **BibSac** 115 (1958): 136-142, 229-236.

Contends that Christians have always been interested in eschatology because of the historical process that intersects with the Church. Chiliasm was a preference for the ante-Nicean Fathers but was abandoned in favor of postmillennialism from ca. 325 through the Middle Ages as the Church influenced all of life. The Reformation leaders were generally amillennialists (with the exception of the Anabaptists). From 1648 to the present all of the major approaches have been revived and developed. Concludes with caution, noting that 1) eschatology is more prominent with churches in crisis, 2) date setting should not be encouraged, 3) history and eschatology should not be separated since both have a practical function for Christians.

[1955]
109. Bietenhard, H. **Das tausendjährige Reich: Eine biblisch-theologische Studie.** 2d ed. Zurich: Zwingli, 1955.

Studies the key biblical texts relevant to the notion of the millennial reign recorded in Rev. 19:11-20:10 and especially 20:4. Describes the importance of connecting Jewish thought and early Christian eschatology. See also 5, G, (4).

[1953]
110. ———. "The Millennial Hope in the Early Church." **SJT** 6 (1953): 12-30.

Discusses the interpretation history of the millennial hope as expressed in the early church fathers, beginning with Papias in relationship to Rev. 20. Includes an interesting examination of antichiliasm by Clement and Origen. Concludes that only an eschatological interpretation is consistent with the text; but whether or not the hope is maintained today will be decided by other than exegetical considerations.

[1949]
111. Walvoord, J.F. "The Millennial Issue in Modern Theology." **BibSac** 106 (1949): 34-47.

Reviews current trends in millennial literature, suggesting that amillennialism is the majority view of the Church today. Liberal theology has undercut the doctrine of premillennialism to the detriment of theology. But millennialism continues to be important to the Church since it effects a number of Christian ideas. The main issue is whether there will be a literal reign of Christ on earth following His Second Coming. Concludes that further, objective studies are needed.

[1948]
112. Daniélou, J. "La typologie millenariste de la semaine dans le christianisme primitif." **VC** 2 (1948): 1-16.

Traces historically and theologically the millennial typology of "weeks" in primitive Christianity. Special attention is given to references in the Revelation of John.

Amillennial

[1973]
113. Hughes, J.A. "Revelation 20:4-6 and the Question of the
Millennium." **WTJ** 35 (1973): 281-302.

Argues that Rev. 20:4-6 is to be interpreted according to the "amillennial"
position. The text suggests that the thousand year reign (when Satan is
bound) takes place in heaven and is currently operating, and the saints
reigning with Christ are in a disembodied state. The verb in Rev. 20:4,
εζησαν, should be rendered as the historical aorist, "they lived." This
supports the notion that those involved in the first resurrection are
disembodied, while the first death, of the just and unjust, is physical.
Finally, the second resurrection is, arguably, a physical resurrection of
both just and unjust. See also 4, B.

[1972]
114. Bube, R.H. "Optimism and Pessimism: Science and Eschatology."
JETS 15 (1972): 215-229.

Outlines and discusses a pattern of categorization by which ideas of
present and future, optimism and pessimism may be connected to
traditional and modern forms of eschatology. Critiques a variety of
scholarly views and concludes that an amillennial position (with Escobar
and Ellul) best serves the optimism of God's final consummation.

[1960]
115. Summers, R. "Revelation 20: An Interpretation." **REx** 57 (1960):
176-183.

Interprets Rev. 12:1-20:10 as a symbolic battle between good (the radiant
woman = Israel personified in Mary; the child = Christ; the rest =
Christians; and the rider on the white horse = Christ victorious) and evil
(dragon = Satan; sea beast = Domitian); etc. The thousand-year period
signifies Christ's total victory over emperor worship (one view), and the
time between Christ's death and his Second Coming (Augustine's view).
S. is eclectic at this point. The martyrs will reign with Christ for the
thousand years in the first resurrection (20:4-6) and the ultimate defeat of
Satan is foreshadowed in the defeat of Rome's attempted destruction of
Christianity. See also 1, C, (2) and 4, B.

[1951]
116. Walvoord, J.F."Amillennial Eschatology." **BibSac** 108 (1951): 7-14.

Continues his critical evaluation of amillennialism (especially under the headings of liberalism, Roman Catholicism, and Reformed eschatology). Offers premillennialism as the better doctrine to follow.

[1950]
117. Payne, H.L. "Contemporary Amillennial Literature." **BibSac** 106 (1949): 200-210, 342-351, 486-492; 107 (1950): 103-108.

After suggesting that the key to the amillennial position is the "spiritualizing method of interpretation," P. analyzes a selection of literature by subject in order to offer a body of material for reference and further study. Trends and tendencies are given. Descriptive comments are addressed to Pieters, Allis, Berkhof, Burrows, Case, Hamilton, and Kuyper regarding "Principles." Other categories included are "Covenant Theology," "Israel and the Church," "Dispensational Distinctions." Concludes that amillennialism is in a state of flux and must begin to deal with its inconsistencies and errors before it can make an impact on theology today.

118. Walvoord, J. F. "Amillennial Ecclesiology." **BibSac** 107 (1950): 420-429.

Investigates the unique features of the amillennial doctrine of the Church, with special emphasis on its teaching of the Kingdom of God. Concludes that the amillennial view of the Kingdom, contrary to Scripture, denies any millennial period after the church age and any special promises to Israel.

119. ———. "Amillennial Soteriology." **BibSac** 107 (1950): 281-290.

Considers the historical development of amillennial soteriology and the relatives themes of Covenant Theology and Spiritualizing as primary methods of amillennial interpretation.

120. ———. "Amillennialism as a Method of Interpretation." **BibSac** 107 (1950): 42-50.

Examines and criticizes the amillennial method of Bible interpretation for being inconsistent with its literal and spiritualizing tendencies. Offers seven judgments against the method, concluding that amillennialism has not developed historically from a careful study of prophetic Scripture, but rather through the neglect of it.

121. ———. "Amillennialism as a System of Theology." **BibSac** 107 (1950): 154-167.

Analyzes amillennial theology in terms of its bibliology, angelology, anthropology, soteriology, ecclesiology, and eschatology. Concludes that the last three are the most influential in determining the theology of amillennialism.

[1949]
122. ———. "Amillennialism in the Ancient Church." **BibSac** 106 (1949): 291-302.

Offers the first in a series of historical and theological studies on amillennialism as a distinct theological position. Concludes that Rev. 20 and its six references to Christ's one-thousand year reign on earth is the biggest opponent to amillennialism. Argues strongly against the nonliteralist church fathers who, says W., deviated from the traditional, three-hundred year doctrine of premillennialism.

123. ———. "Amillennialism from Augustine to Modern Times." **BibSac** 106 (1949): 420-431.

Continues his study through an analysis and criticism of Augustine's amillennial position and the failure of modern amillennial thinkers. Rev. 20 is studied in light of Augustine's theological shortcomings.

[1946]
124. Arndt, W.F. "Chiliasm in the **Watchman-Examiner**." CTM 17 (1946): 155.

Examines this Baptist publication and criticizes its blatant chiliasm as erroneous. See also 1, C (2).

125. Mayer, F.E. "Dispensationalism Examined and Found Wanting." **CTM** 17 (1946): 89-94.

Investigates dispensationalism critically as a radical type of premillennialism as, following O. T. Allis (Princeton) offers a four-point critique. See also I, C, (2).

[1944]
126. Arndt, W.F. "Concerning Dispensationalism." **CTM** 15 (1944): 703-704.

Condemns the view of Scofield's dispensationalism as a serious threat to Presbyterianism and a "perversion" of what the Bible teaches. See also I, C (2).

[1943]
127. Mueller, J.T. "Amillennialism." **CTM** 14 (1943): 65-66.

Argues for amillennialism and against dispensationalism as unbiblical. Says that the Bible does not support a physical, literal earthly thousand-year reign of Christ in Palestine. See also 5, G, (4).

128. ———. "Dispensationalism and Premillennialism." **CTM** 14 (1943): 868-870.

Comments on the debate between dispensationalism and premillennialism. Argues that neither are accurately interpreting God's word. See also 1, C, (2) and 5, G, (4).

[1942]
129. Arndt, W.F. "The Exegesis of Premillennialists." **CTM** 13 (1942): 947.

Criticizes the literal exegetical method of the premillennialists as faulty and defective. See also 1, C, (2).

130. ———. "A Premillennialist Warns His Brethern." **CTM** 13 (1942): 948-949.

Describes Stearns' warning of his dispensational brethren against "sensational, unbalanced" interpretations of Scripture related to the last things. See also 1, C, (2).

131. Mennicke, V. "Notes on the History of Chiliasm." **CTM** 13 (1942): 192-207.

Traces the historical development of Chiliasm as a natural inclination of man from the time of Adam and Eve, through the church Fathers, and to the present. Attributing chiliasm to excessive and neurotic enthusiasts, M.

concludes that chiliasm is really a "secular religion" based on material, earthly hopes. See also 1, C, (2).

Postmillennial

[1983]
132. Townsend, J.L. "Is the Present Age the Millennium?" **BibSac** 140 (1983): 206-224.

Argues that, according to the text of Rev. 20, the millennium is to be identified with the present age, and that the eternity described in Rev. 21-22 is the messianic kingdom. Most premillennialists agree that the thousand-year period of Rev. 20:1-10 is an imperfect state, but many arrive at different conclusions respecting the fact of the imperfect kingdom and the connection between Rev. 20:1-10 and the present historical period.

[1953]
133. Leahy, D.J. "Is the 'Millennium,' or 'Thousand Years' of the Apocalypse the Peaceful Expansion of the Church from the Sixth to the Sixteenth Centuries?" **Scrip** 5 (1952-53): 43-47.

Responds to the question, "Is the 'Millennium' the peaceful expansion of the church from the sixth to the sixteenth centuries?" Answers in the negative while using Fr. R. Garcia's study (1940) regarding the eschatological interpretation of Rev. 20.

[1949]
134. Walvoord, J.F. "Postmillennialism." **BibSac** 106 (1949): 149-168.

Sketches the nature, historical development, and theological system of postmillennialism as the youngest of the millennial systems. Concludes that postmillennialism is declining because of the sinful world situation, but amillennialism is on the rise due mainly to its failure of the spiritualizing principle of Bible interpretation.

Premillennialism and/or Dispensationalism

[1988]
135. Crutchfield, L.V. "The Apostle John and Asia Minor as a Source of Premillennialism in the Early Church Fathers." **JETS** 31 (1988): 411-427.

Argues that John's view of Christ's reign (Rev. 20) influenced the spread of millennarianism in Asia Minor, especially in the writings of his disciples Polycarp and Papias, who ultimately influenced the eschatological views of other church leaders up to the time of the Nicean Council.

[1978]
136. Deere, J.S. "Premillennialism in Revelation 20:4-6." **BibSac** 135 (1978): 58-73.

Exegetes the text of Rev. 20:4-6 and, considering the context, concludes that the author predicted an earthly Kingdom would be set up and continued for one-thousand literal years at the second advent of the Messiah.

[1977]
137. Ross, J.R. "Evangelical Alternatives" in **Dreams, Visions and Oracles: The Layman's Guide to Biblical Prophecy.**

Compares the three main schools of interpretation of Rev. 20, while arguing for the premillennial position based on a strict chronological hermeneutic. See also 1, C, (2).

[1972]
138. McCall, T.S. "Problems in Rebuilding the Tribulation Temple." **BibSac** 129 (1972): 75-80.

Admits to a number of "obstacles" to rebuilding the Jerusalem Temple (e.g., Muslim opposition, an extinct priesthood, problems with the whole system of sacrifices), but suggests that the Temple could be rebuilt before the Rapture and that the Jews themselves might take on the work.

[1971]
139. ———. "How Soon the Tribulation Temple?" **BibSac** 128 (1971): 341-351.

Raises the question in light of the events of the Arab-Israeli War in 1967 and suggests that the Bible says that two temples are to be rebuilt, viz., the Tribulation Temple and the Millennial Temple. The latter will be built by Jesus, the Messiah, at His return (Cf. Dan. 9; Mat. 24; II Thes. 2; Rev. 11). A number of benefits may be gained by rebuilding the Tribulation Temple, e.g., more Jews could be reached with the Gospel, and Israel's unity might be maintained.

[1969]
140. Brunk, M.J. "The Seven Churches of Revelation Two and Three."
BibSac 126 (1969): 240-246.

Argues for the interpretation of the seven churches as representations of
seven periods of church history. See also 3, E.

141. Walvoord, J.F. "Revival of Rome." **BibSac** 126 (1969): 317-328.

Argues for a literal interpretation of Daniel's "Fourth Empire" and the
Revelation regarding the revival of Rome politically and religiously at the
end of the age. The ten-nation confederation and world (Roman Catholic)
church are then identified as biblical signs of the End Time.

[1968]
142. Lewis, G.R. "Biblical Evidence for Pretribulationism." **BibSac** 125
(1968): 216-226.

Contends that a serious, literal reading of the NT (especially I & II Thes.
and Mat. 24) points to a pretribulation rapture of the Church. The NT
stress on the two resurrections and the immediacy of Christ's return
underscores the validity of dispensational premillennialism and a
pretribulation rapture.

143. ———. "Theological Antecedents of Pretribulationism." **BibSac**
125 (1968): 129-138.

Considers, briefly, the theological contexts and major ideas of Covenant
Theology, Dispensationalism, Premillennialism, and Dispensational
Premillennialism, and affirms the similarities of each, but excludes
Covenant thinkers because of their confusion concerning Israel and the
Church. Dispensationalists use a method of interpretation that draws
distinctions between Israel and the Church.

144. Morris, H.M. "Biblical Eschatology and Modern Science." **BibSac**
125 (1968): 291-299.

Suggests the reality of Christ's return and some ways of viewing the earth
during the millennial tribulation period. Concludes that restoration of
Edenic conditions will be found on the New Earth, but somewhere in the
universe, when the new earth is complete, the lake of fire will continue to
burn for the wicked.

[1967]
145. Walvoord, J.F. "Prophecy of the Ten-Nation Confederacy." **BibSac** 124 (1967): 99-105.

Proposes a "literal and normative" interpretation of prophecy (Dan. 2, 7; Rev. 13, 17) that forsees a ten-nation confederacy within the future Roman empire and that understands end-time prophecy immediately fulfilled.

[1966]
146. ———. "The Millennial Kingdom and the Eternal State." **BibSac** 123 (1966): 291-300.

Posits the theory that the millennial kingdom will be on earth and Christ will be its supreme ruler over all realms (political and spiritual). Rev. 20-22, when read "normally and literally" point to the chronological developments that move history toward and into eternity. See also 4, B and 5, G, (4).

[1964]
147. Bellshaw, W.G. "Premillennialism: Primary or Peripheral." **BibSac** 121 (1964): 159-169.

Considers "important" questions regarding 1) the Millennium, 2) the Tribulation, and 3) the relative importance between the two. Concludes that these issues are not unimportant (as some liberals suggest), but are crucial to Christian doctrine concerning an understanding of Scripture, salvation, and the Church. How one answers these questions will definitely effect future fellowship among Christians.

[1963]
148. Aldrich, R.L. "A New Look at Dispensationalism." **BibSac** 120 (1963): 42-49.

Attempts to clarify the issues and define terms relevant to the debate over dispensationalism. After identifying the main "dispensational assumptions," of Hodge, Kuiper, Hamilton, and Scofield, A. concludes that dispensationalists have much in common, e.g., definition of the term, Bible time divisions, and views of salvation.

[1961]
149. ———. "An Outline Study on Dispensationalism." **BibSac** 118 (1961): 133-141.

Investigates two important Dispensational movements, viz., its critics ("nondispensationalism") and its supporters ("ultradispensationalists") and tries to refute both. Urges the latter group to return to "direct unsupervised" Bible study as the best antidote to its excesses, and to the former he suggests a more objective approach to dispensationalism as a valid biblical method.

[1960]
150. Ladd, G.E. "Revelation 20 and the Millenium." **REx** 57 (1960): 167-175.

Argues for a contextual approach to the problem of the millenium in Rev. 20, which includes both "preterist" and "futurist" methods of interpretation. The word of the Messiah (19:15) ushers in the "millenial reign" of Rev. 20 and a two-stage resurrection: one at the Parousia and one at the end of the reign. Argues from Pauline theology suggesting that there are three stages in God's victory over death: 1) Christ's resurrection; 2) the Parousia; and 3) the *telos*, or the final death. Thus the millenium is shown to be the interval between the last two stages. But the redeemed already experience this Kingdom "between the times" because they are justified and share eternal life. The final triumph has already begun. See also 4, B.

151. Pentecost, J.D. "The Godly Remnant of the Tribulation Period." **BibSac** 117 (1960): 123-133.

Examines the biblical passages regarding the existence of a remnant of Israel during the tribulation period. Revelation gives special emphasis to such a group, their status, salvation and ministry during that end-time tribulation. The 144,000 (Rev. 7 &14) represent a special part of the remnant nation, Israel, who will lead the nation to Christ. Complete deliverance will occur at the Second Coming.

152. ———. "The Relation Between Living and Resurrected Saints in the Millennium." **BibSac** 117 (1960): 331-341.

Suggests that the millennial age is where the inhabitants are identified as redeemed Jews living in their natural bodies and the resurrected saints of all ages are later united with them in the heavenly city Jerusalem.

[1959]
153. Harrison, W.K. "As Ye See the Day Approaching." **BibSac** 116 (1959): 67-76.

Alludes to the Revelation in identifying four "signs" of the coming of Christ: 1) NATO, 2) Israel, 3) Russia, and 4) Modern Warfare. Concludes that a literal fulfillment of prophecy is imminent.

[1958]
154. Pentecost, J.D. "Salvation in the Tribulation." **BibSac** 115 (1958): 50-61.

Explains the doctrine of salvation during the tribulation period and concludes that Jews and Gentiles will indeed come into the Kingdom by faith, by the blood of Jesus, and by the Holy Spirit. This will culminate in national salvation for Israel and full millennial blessing.

155. Walvoord, J.F. "The Doctrine of the Millennium." **BibSac** 115 (1958): 1-8, 97-108, 193-200, 291-301.

Argues for the millennium as a biblical doctrine in terms of its righteous government, spiritual life, and social and economic justice, with focus on the heavenly Jerusalem and its relevance to the literal new heaven and new earth.

[1957]
156. Mason, C.E., Jr. "A Review of 'Dispensationalism' by John Wick Bowman." **BibSac** 114 (1957): 10-22, 102-122.

Criticizes Bowman's critique of dispensationalism as incomplete, wrong, and too filled with presuppositions to be taken seriously.

157. Ryrie, C.C. "The Necessity of Dispensationalism." **BibSac** 114 (1957): 243-254.

Contends for the validity of dispensationalism based on the validity of its distinctions, the satisfying element of its philosophy of history, along with importance of a consistent biblical literalism as the only valid system of Bible interpretation.

158. Walvoord, J.F. "The Prophetic Context of the Millennium." **BibSac** 114 (1957): 1-9, 97-101, 193-200, 289-307.

Tries to demonstrate that the Kingdom of God on earth (the Millennium) is the one main theme of OT prophecy by treating the tribulation as a key biblical doctrine in addition to the doctrine of the Second Coming and the resurrection from a premillennial perspective.

159. Tenney, M.C. **Interpreting Revelation.** Grand Rapids, MI: Wm. B.
Eerdmans Publishing Company, 1957.

Introduces the undergraduate student to the various methods of
interpreting the Revelation. After explaining the background, theme, and
seven-fold structure of the work, T. gives a brief exposition of each
literary section and concludes with discussions of the O.T. background,
the Christology, the chronological and eschatological methods of
interpretation (T. favors the premillennial one), the terminology, the
symbolism, and the present-age applications.

[1956]
160. Bowman, J.W. "The Bible and Modern Religions, II.
Dispensationalism." **Int** 10 (1956): 170-187.

Critiques the dispensational hypothesis of Scofield, labeling it as
"dangerous heresy" in terms of its insistence on a rigid framework, viz.,
seven (dubious) dispensations and eight (ambiguous) covenants. Also, B.
attacks Scofield's misunderstanding of the connection between prophecy
and the Kingdom of Heaven, as well as his doctrine of an apostate church
(which he finds unbiblical). The latter idea springs from Scofield's
misreading of Rev. 2-3.

161. McClain, A.J. "A Premillennial Philosophy of History." **BibSac** 113
(1956): 111-116.

Discusses Christianity as a philosophy of history based on premillennial
doctrines that lead to optimistic assurances regarding the future.

162. ———. "The Spirituality of the Millennial Kingdom." **BibSac** 113
(1956): 16-23.

Explains what he calls the erroneous (Platonic) use of the term"spiritual"
by some modern theologians. Concludes with his interpretation of the
term by drawing parallels with Paul's usage in I Cor. 10:3. See also 5, G,
(4).

163. Walvoord, J.F. "Premillennialism and the Tribulation." **BibSac** 111
(1954): 193-203, 289-301; 112 (1955): 1-10, 97-106, 193-208, 289-303;
113 (1956): 1-15, 97-110, 193-199.

Addresses the problem of the tribulation for premillennial Christians and
the opposing views of postmillennialism and amillennialism. Suggests

that the doctrine of the tribulation is of exegetical, theological, and practical importance to the Church. Concludes this wordy study with "Fifty Arguments for Pretribulationism" based on a literal translation of the Bible.

[1955]
164. Aldrich, R.L. "An Apologetic for Dispensationalism." **BibSac** 112 (1955): 46-54.

Argues against a growing number of "negative, disillusioned" premillennialists who no longer support dispensationalism. Concludes that the "normal" method of biblical interpretation results in a certain premillennial dispensationalism.

165. McClain, A.J. "The Greatness of the Kingdom: The Mediatorial Kingdom from the Acts Period to the Eternal State." **BibSac** 112 (1955): 304-310.

Investigates the greatness of the Kingdom of God in terms of it being the mediatorial Kingdom from the period of Acts to eternity.

[1954]
166. Walvoord, J.F. "Premillennialism and the Church as a Mystery." **BibSac** 111 (1954): 1-10, 97-104.

Examines the positive revelation in the NT of the Church as a mystery of "One body," "organism," and "Bride" in terms of its distinction from Israel contra amillennialism.

[1953]
167. Mitchell, J.L. "The Question of Millennial Sacrifices." **BibSac** 110 (1953): 248-267, 342-361.

Studies the question of animal sacrifices during the millennium, and reviews several theological positions (cf. Gabelein, Kelly, Wale, et al). Concludes that literal exegesis reveals that the Jews will indeed observe animal sacrifices when they return to their earthly, millennial land.

168. Walvoord, J.F. "The Kingdom Promises to David." **BibSac** 110 (1953): 97-110.

Considers the OT promise to David and his line, and the covenant being fulfilled partially in Jesus Christ's first advent and finally in the Second

Coming. The ultimate reign of David's kingdom will be fulfilled literally during Christ's millennial reign.

169. ———. "The New Covenant with Israel." **BibSac** 110 (1953): 193-205.

Insists that it is premillennialism that best establishes the new covenant of Jer. 31 with Israel and the fulfillment in the millennial kingdom after Christ's return. Key texts such as Heb. 8 do not support amillennialism. Rom. 11:27 points to fulfillment as the outcome of the Second Advent. Concludes that a literal interpretation of the texts is the proper hermeneutic.

170. _____. "Premillennialism and the Church." **BibSac** 110 (1953): 289-298.

Discusses the relationship between premillennial theology and the Church, and opts for dispensational ecclesiology, which views the present age as a "parenthesis" before the final phase of God's final program for both Jews and Gentiles.

[1952]
171. King, W.L. "Millennialism as a Social Ferment." **RL** 21 (1952): 33-44.

Surveys the historical development of millennialism as a political and social force. Offers only occasional references to the text of the Revelation.

172. Kopecky, D.W. "Salvation in the Tribulation." **BibSac** 109 (1952): 266-270, 358-363.

Reviews the Bible teaching on salvation in the tribulation period, based on Jer. 30:7; Dan. 12:1; Mat. 24:21; Rev. 3:10; 7:14; etc., and concludes that the nature of the tribulation reflects God's activity in saving Jews first. Gentiles will be saved only because of the Jews in the tribulation period. They ultimately will have no part in the Church.

173. Scofield, C.I. "The Return of Christ in Relation to the Church." **BibSac** 109 (1952): 77-89.

Tells about the battle of Armageddon as an event preceeding the return of

Christ, and then discusses the specifics of the return as it relates to the rapture of the Church before the great tribulation period.

174. Walvoord, J.F. "The Abrahamic Covenant and Premillennialism. Is the Abrahamic Covenant Unconditional?" **BibSac** 109 (1952): 37-46.

Argues that the Abrahamic Covenant is unconditional (contra amillennial opinions) based on an exegetical treatment of relevant OT texts and confirmation of the NT. This provides a basis for a premillennial and literal interpretation of relevant prophetic predictions, some of which are yet unfulfilled.

175. ————. "The Abrahamic Covenant and Premillennialism. Will Israel Be Restored as a Nation?" **BibSac** 109 (1952): 293-303.

Affirms that Israel (i.e., the Jewish people) will indeed be restored in the End Time as a nation according to a literal reading of the Abrahamic Covenant. This appears to be a natural outcome of the OT promises.

176. ————. "The Abrahamic Covenant and Premillennialism. Will Israel Continue as a Nation?" **BibSac** 109 (1952): 136-150.

Holds that a study of biblical ideas and terms strongly suggests that Israel (i.e., the godly remnant of every age, e.g., Christians, Jews, and the future nations) will continue as a political nation after the return of Christ (contra amillennialism).

177. ————. "The Abrahamic Covenant and Premillennialism. Will Israel Possess the Promised Land?" **BibSac** 109 (1952): 217-225.

Suggests that Israel will be regathered in the End Time and will possess all the land promised to Abraham's seed as long as the present earth continues.

[1951]
178. Scofield, C.I. "The Course and End of the Age." **BibSac** 108 (1951): 105-116.

Continues his discussion of "The Times of the Gentiles" in relation to Daniel and the symbol of the Beast in Rev. 12. Concludes that there will be a literal Armageddon battle before the conclusion of history.

179. ———. "The Last World Empire and Armageddon." **BibSac** 108 (1951): 355-362.

Continues study of the End Time.

180. ———. "The Return of Christ in Relation to the Jew and the Earth." **BibSac** 108 (1951): 477-487.

Argues for two lines of biblical promise at the End Time: 1) Recovery of the Jews and 2) Salvation for the faithful. Jesus' return will accomplish both promises when he finally sits upon the throne of David.

181. Walvoord, J.F. "The Abrahamic Covenant and Premillennialism." **BibSac** 108 (1951): 414-422.

Argues that a literal interpretation of the Abrahamic Covenant (see Gen. 13; 15; etc.) upholds premillennialism and a literal fulfillment of God's promises.

182. ———. "The Historical Context of Premillennialism." **BibSac** 108 (1951): 153-166.

Contends for the historical (OT, NT, second to third century) context of the doctrine of premillennialism. From this the author makes several points: *Infallibility of Scripture, Literal Interpretation of Scripture, Evangelicalism, Opposition to Ecclesiasticism, Emphasis on Prophetic Studies*, etc.

183. ———. "The Theological Context of Premillennialism." **BibSac** 108 (1951): 270-281.

Argues for the theological context of premillennialism as a distinct system of scriptural theology.

[1946]
184. Ehlert, A.D. "A Bibliography of Dispensationalism." **BibSac** 101 (1944): 95-101, 199-209, 319-328, 447-460; 102 (1945): 184-92, 207-219, 322-334, 455-467; 103 (1946): 57-67.

Offers a brief introduction to and comprehensive treatment of the bibliography available on dispensationalism (including books, pamphlets, magazine articles, and charts). Concludes that the doctrine of dispensationalism reaches back into antiquity and the literature available today offers tools for further discussion and debate.

185. Walden, J.W. "The Kingdom of God -- Its Millennial Dispensation." **BibSac** 102 (1945): 433-441; 103 (1946): 39-49.

Argues for a positive premillennial view of the Kingdom based on grace and a negative view of man's efforts to establish the Kingdom before Christ's return.

[1944]
186. Chafer, L.S. "Dispensational Distinctions Denounced." **BibSac** 101 (1944): 257-260.

Disputes the 1944 report of the Assembly of the Presbyterian Church, U.S.A., which itself condemned the doctrine of dispensationalism as "libelous, false and damaging to the church."

[1943]
187. Bear, J.E. "Historic Premillennialism." **USR** 55 (1943): 193-222.

Contrasts modern premillennialism (as modified by dispensationalism) to "historic premillennialism" while reviewing the theological background to the debate through the writings of Tertullian, Mede, Bengel, nineteenth century dispensationalism, etc. Suggests that Tertullian's "Against Marcion" might be read today as "Against Dispensationalism."

188. Chafer, L.S. "Dispensational Distinctions Challenged." **BibSac** 100 (1943): 337-345.

Responds strongly to the criticism of the Presbyterian Assembly's condemnation of dispensationalism. C. says the report is "restrictive and uninformed."

189. Ehlert, A.D. "Dispensational Bibliography." **BibSac** 100 (1943): 345-346.

Informs the reader of the plan of the periodical to publish a comprehensive bibliography of dispensationalism in order to help in the current debate.

[1940]
190. Bear, J.E. "The People of God." **USR** 52 (1940): 33-63.

Debates "dispensationalism" regarding the notion of two "peoples of God" contrary to the (traditional) church's eschatological view of "one people." Reviews the dispensational basis for theological doctrine: the unconditional covenant with Abraham, the Seed of Abraham, the Land of Canaan, and concludes that the traditional eschatological view of the Church regarding *one* people is to be preferred.

191. ————. "The People of God According to the Fathers of the Early Church." **USR** 52 (1940): 351-374.

Investigates the writings of the early Fathers to discover whether or not they held to a belief regarding the Jews as a "peculiar people" to whom God was bound by an unconditional promise that was only fulfilled after Christ's return and the Jewish nation was restored to world power in Palestine. From the Apostolic Fathers through Origen, B. says that of eighteen Fathers only eight had any interest in the general topic and only six (Papias, Barnabas, Justin, Irenaeus, *et al*.) believed in some kind of Millennium and none saw any special interest in the Jews as such. Concludes that dispensationalism seems to run completely counter to Reformed theology.

192. ————. "The People of God in the Light of the Teaching of the New Testament." **USR** 52 (1940): 128-158.

Discusses the NT teaching on the "People of God" and concludes that believing Israelites and Christians alike will benefit as God's people. Only "unbelieving" Israelites will receive eschatological judgment.

-Select Dissertations-

[1987]
193. Koser, R.E. "Hermeneutics of the Book of Revelation for Preaching." Unpublished D.Min. Dissertation. Claremont, CA: School of Theology at Claremont, 1987.

[1977]
194. Rusten, E.M. "A Critical Evaluation of Dispensational Interpretations of the Book of Revelation." Unpublished Doctoral Dissertation. New York, NY: New York University, 1977.

[1959]
195. Mulholland, J.H. "Principles of the Eschatological Interpretation of the Apocalypse." Unpublished Doctoral Dissertation. Dallas, TX: Dallas Theological Seminary, 1959.

Chapter 2

Historical-Critical Research
on the Revelation

INTRODUCTION

Most scholars acknowledge that if the Revelation of John is to be understood at all, it must be studied in its historical, cultural, and religious contexts. Thus, historical-critical investigations that have been useful in other areas of New Testament research have also proven, more or less, to be helpful for the study of the Revelation. But the best results of historical-critical scholarship have been discovered when the method has been used with flexibility and discretion.

A. GENERAL WORKS

[1987]
196. Kealy, S.P. "'At a Loss When Faced with Apocalyptic.'" **ITQ** 53 (1987): 285-302.

Argues that the Revelation has been neglected for years because of its apparent subgospel message, esoteric themes, and inadequate pastoral concerns. But if scholars are able to appreciate the positive accomplishments of the book, as well as the history of Revelation's interpretation (including its limitations), then this NT work will speak to the modern world.

[1983]
197. Léon-Dufour, X. "Bulletin d'exégèse du Nouveau Testament. Autour de l'Apocalypse de Jean." **ReScR** 71 (1983): 309-336.

Offers a two-part study on the authorship of the Revelation. Part I discusses the recent work of five scholars and Part II evaluates particular critical themes, e.g., literary structure, genre, liturgy, and the wisdom tradition.

[1976]
198. Fiorenza, E.S. **The Apocalypse.** "Herald Biblical Booklets."
Chicago: Franciscan Herald Press, 1976.

After treating, briefly, a few critical issues (e.g., literary form and
theological perspective), F. grounds her study on the basis of
understanding the Revelation as a genuine Christian prophetic-
apocalyptic writing set within a letter framework and addressed to life
situations and struggles of the Christian church in western Asia Minor.
She insists that the Revelation basically depicts eternal life and salvation
as a reward for all the earth and all humankind.

[1970]
199. Guthrie, D. "The Book of Revelation" in **New Testament
Introduction.** Downers Grove, IL: Inter-Varsity Press, 1970.

Treats the standard introductory problems, but gives special attention to
the date, symbolism, sources and outline structure. Accepts the unity of
the book and describes the message of Revelation in terms of
encouragement, exhortation and endurance.

[1963]
200. Feuillet, A. **L'Apocalypse. État de la question.** "Studia
Neotestamentica, Sub. III." Paris--Bruges: Desclée de Brouwer, 1963.

Discusses at length many of the critical problems related to the study of
Revelation while arguing for the unity of the book. After identifying the
different types of interpretation of the book (without describing them in
detail), F. seems to support Boismard's view that the book is the result of
a series of redactions starting with the time of Nero. Concludes that Rev.
4:1-11:9, contrary to popular opinion, is a chronological sequence of
events with limited eschatological appeal to the modern reader. See the
review by Giet, NTA 8 (3, '64): #1211r. See also 1, C, (1) and 3, A.

B. ESSAY COLLECTIONS

[1988]
201. Bloom, H., ed. **The Revelation of St. John the Divine.** "Modern
Critical Interpretations." Philadelphia, PA: Chelsea House, 1988.

Includes seven literary-critical interpretations of the Revelation based on
thematic analyses. The studies range from 1931 (D.H. Lawrence) to 1984

(M.H. Abrams on romantic theme variations; A.Y. Collins on the power of apocalyptic rhetoric--catharsis). Other authors included are J.R. May, A. Farrer, N. Frye, E.S. Shaffer, and an introduction by editor Bloom.

[1980]
202. Lambrecht, J., ed. **L'Apocalypse johannique et l'apocalyptique dans le Nouveau Testament.** "Bibliotheca Ephemeridum Theologicarum Lovaniensium, 53." Gembloux: Duculot, 1980.

A summary article and collection of twenty-eight papers given at the 30th Colloquium Biblicum Lovaniense in 1979. Section I deals with "The Book of Revelation" and Section II treats the general theme, "Apocalyptic in the New Testament." The most notable essays are by U. Vanni (in French, pp. 21-46), "The State of the Question," in which he surveys various questions (e.g., hermeneutics, connection with the OT) related to the scholarly study of the Revelation since 1963; P.-M. Bogaert (pp. 47-68) examines various apocalypses contemporary with the Revelation, e.g., 2 Baruch, 4 Esdras; Lambrecht (pp. 77-104) investigates the book's structure; G. Mussies (pp. 167-177) analyzes the Greek language of the Revelation; and M. de Jonge (267-281) does an exegetical comparison of the two phrases, $I\eta\sigma o\upsilon\varsigma \: X\rho\iota\sigma\tau o\varsigma$ and $o \: \chi\rho\iota\sigma\tau o\varsigma$, concluding that in the Revelation both allude to a future eschatological period when God, Jesus, and believers will reign together.

C. MANUSCRIPT / TEXTUAL RESEARCH

[1989]
203. Elliott, J.K. "Manuscripts of the Book of Revelation Collated by H.C. Hoskier." **JTS** 40 (1989): 100-111.

Referring to the apparatus for Hoskier's **Concerning the Text of the Apocalypse** (1929), E. offers conversion tables for the numbering system and then provides the conversions for the cursives where Hoskier's number differs from the Tischendorf (8th) edition.

[1982]
204. King, S.E. **The Revelation of the Apostle John. Arranged as in the Earliest Face of the New Testament.** Ashhurst, New Zealand: Private Publication, 1982.

Makes a new attempt at publishing the original text of the Revelation based on the page displacement theory from the author's earlier work

(1977). The study suggests that, originally, there was a prologue, an epilogue, and seven acts of seven scenes each, including a prelude. Offers his own English translation as well as commentary on the Revelation as Gospel, authorship, and arrangement of the text. Criticism of the text of the Revelation in **Novum Testamentum graece** (26th Edition, 1979) is included.

[1981]
205. Browne, G.M. "An Old Nubian Fragment of Revelation." **SPa** 20 (1981): 73-82.

Presents a copy of a small fragment (P, 13998) from the Berlin Museum published in 1913 by F. Griffith in **The Nubian Texts of the Christian Period**. The fragment contains an Old Nubian translation of Rev. 6:8-9 and 6:15-7:1. B. offers a line-by-line commentary, a discussion of problems related to interpretation and reconstruction, and an English translation.

206. Gwynn, J. ed. **The Apocalypse of John in a Syriac Version Hitherto Unknown [1897]**. Amsterdam: APA-Philo Press, 1981.

This reprint of an 1897 publication presents the Syriac text of the Revelation as it is found in the library of the Earl of Crawford. The publication includes sixty-four pages of notes, a reconstruction of the Greek (with notes) from which the Syriac translator worked, and an introductory essay that discusses the Syriac versions of the NT and the Revelation of John. Suggests that the Crawford manuscript was a part of the Philoxenian NT corpus that was translated in A. D. 508.

[1980]
207. Royse, J.R. "'Their Fifteen Enemies': The Text of Rev. xi. 12 in p[47] and 1611." **JTS** 31 (1980): 78-80.

Argues that 1611 and p[47] have the same reading of Rev. 11:12, i.e., "their fifteen enemies." The variant was probably due to scribal error which read $o\iota$ once and then $\iota\varepsilon$ together as a number, and then ε again as the beginning letter of $\varepsilon\chi\theta\rho o\iota$.

[1978]
208. Birdsall, J.N. "The Georgian Version of the Book of Revelation." **M** 91 (1978): 355-366.

Argues against Molitor's thesis that the Georgian version of the Revelation is a free rendering of the text influenced by the Armenian and Philoxenian Syriac versions. Evidence (positive and negative) regarding any collation with the Greek tradition and the alleged relationship with the Syriac and Armenian sources is not convincing. The Georgian version is a translation of the Greek text.

[1971]
209. Metzger, B.M. **A Textual Commentary on the Greek New Testament**. London; New York: United Bible Societies, 1971.

Offers comprehensive notation and discussion of the Greek New Testament text as a companion volume to the United Bible Societies' third edition. The study includes introduction (adding the criteria used for judging textual superiority), discussion of the most important variant readings among each of the NT writings, and concludes with the Revelation of John (39 pp.). Some textual variants include 1:5-6, 8, 15; 2:2, 10, 13, etc.

[1968]
210. Schmid, J. "Neue griechische Apocalypsehandschriften." **ZNTW** 59 (1968): 250-258.

Catalogues an additional nineteen previously unknown and/or unaccessible manuscripts of the Revelation (see **ZNTW** 52, 1961) and summarizes the text types, e.g., early uncials, the sixth century Andreas text, the so-called Koine text, and four other mixed texts that combine Andreas and the Koine. Concludes that it is impossible to speak of an "official" Byzantine text of the Revelation of John.

[1967]
211. Brieger, P.H., ed. **The Trinity College Apocalypse**. Facsimile. An introduction and description by Peter H. Breiger. Eugrammia Press, 1967.

Praises this thirteenth-century manuscript as the most magnificent work of art of all the Revelation manuscripts. Cf. also **Times Literary Supplement** 66 (May 25, 1967).

212. Rao, K.P. "Studies on the Text of Revelation." Masters Thesis. Philadelphia, PA: Eastern Baptist Theological Seminary, 1967.

Offers a very brief study of Greek texts and some textual problems relevant to the Book of Revelation.

[1966]
213. Trudinger, L.P. "Some Observations Concerning the Text of the Old Testament in the Book of Revelation." **JTS** 17 (1966): 82-88.

Studies the OT texts quoted or alluded to in the Revelation and reaches a two-fold conclusion: 1) The OT texts and versions were fluid during the writing of the Revelation. 2) The author John was steeped in a Palestinian synagogue tradition, which included knowledge of Aramaic Targums, various midrashim, non-Masoretic, and Qumran textual traditions.

[1965]
214. Mussies, G."Antipas [Rev. 2:13]." **NT** 7 (1964-65): 242-244.

Examines the grammar of Rev. 2:13, comparing the language of Palestinian inscriptions, and concludes that the name "Antipas" in the verse could be an indeclinable noun or a first declension name with feminine endings. The verse is to be read as it is shown in the text. See also 4, B.

[1963]
215. Birdsall, J.N. "Rev. XIII. 6." **JTS** 14 (1963): 399-400.

Suggests that the 13:6 reading, "$\tau\eta\nu$ $\sigma\kappa\eta\nu\eta\nu$ $\alpha\upsilon\tau\upsilon$ $\epsilon\nu$ $\tau\omega$ $\upsilon\rho\alpha\nu\omega$," of p^{47} is an attempted simplification of the more difficult text and thus secondary. The Ethiopic and Armenian versions however support p^{47}.

[1962]
216. Hodges, Z.C. "The Critical Text and the Alexandrian Family of Revelation." **BibSac** 119 (1962): 129-138.

Evaluates the text-critical work of J. Schmid on the text of Revelation and argues that manuscripts A and C on the one hand, and Aleph and p^{47} do not constitute two major stems of the textual tradition but rather two branches of a single "*hauptstämme*." Concludes that the Greek of Revelation goes back to an "archetype" that preceded the Alexandrian text. Therefore a new critical text on the Revelation based on a broader representation of Greek manuscript evidence is needed.

[1961]
217. Birdsall, J.N. "The Text of the Revelation of Saint John: A Review of Its Materials and Problems with Especial Reference to the Work of Josef Schmid." **EQ** 33 (1961): 228-237.

Considers the Revelation from a text-critic's prespective. Critiques the work of Hoskier and Schmid. Although generally commending Schmid, B. does point out two deficiencies: 1) The absence of discussion concerning the question, Is a western text to be found in the Revelation? and 2) The question about the relation of the versions to the Greek tradition.

218. Hodges, Z.C. "The Ecclesiastical Text of Revelation -- Does It Exist?" **BibSac** 118 (1961): 113-122.

Argues with Hoskier (see **Concerning the Text of the Apocalypse,** 1929) and contrary to the scholarly opinion of Wescott, Hort, *et al.*, that there may never have been a generally accepted "ecclesiastical" (church) text of the Revelation identified with the so-called Syrian/Byzantine type.

219. Lohse, E. "Die alttestamentliche Sprache des Sehers Johannes. Textkritische Bemerkungen zur Apokalypse." **ZNW** 52 (1961): 122-126.

Argues that modern text criticism of the Revelation must not forget to take into consideration the fact that the author was often using OT phrases and expressions in his writing. Demonstrates the textual problems caused by John's use of Ez. 1:18 in Rev. 4:8; Ez. 2:10 in Rev. 5:1; etc. See also 3, D.

220. Schmid, J. "Unbeachtete und unbekannte griechische Apokalypsehandschriften." **ZNW** 52 (1961): 82-88.

Offers a careful description of thirteen unknown manuscripts of the Revelation. This is a follow-up to his earlier study, **Studien zur Geschichte des griechischen Apokalypsetextes** (1955).

221. Warne, N. "The Book of Revelation [As Translated in The New English Bible]." **ABR** 9 (1961): 32-36.

Discusses the general nature of the New English translation of the book in terms of its presentation and form. Evaluates the strengths and weaknesses of the NEB in relationship to the Hebrew and Greek texts. Finds the NEB to be an able and accurate translation.

[1959]
222. Kilpatrick, G.D. "Professor J. Schmid on the Greek Text of the Apocalypse." **VCh** 13 (1959): 1-13.

Reviews J. Schmid's "monumental work" (**Studien zur Geschichte,** 1955-56) and concludes that Schmid has succeeded in offering the scholarly world a great achievement that reflects sound judgment and excellent scholarship. His treatment of Hoskier's material on the Revelation is useful for future scholarly research. Thus we now have a definitive work on both the language of the Revelation (building from Bousset and Charles) and the text.

223. Schmid, J. "Der Apokalypse-Text des Oikumenios." **B** 40 (1959): 935-942.

Studies the sixth century text of Ecumenius, noting some of the later emendations while trying to restore the original text.

[1957]
224. Kümmel, W.G. "Der Text der Offenbarung des Johannes." **TLZ** 82 (1957): 249-254.

Discusses, first, the work of Lagrange, Weiss, and Hoskier, and then reviews J. Schmid's **Studien zur Geschichte des griechischen Apokalyhpse-Textes** (Part II, Munich, 1955-56). Offers two practical conclusions to the matter: First, because Schmid's excellent work is definitive, all future text-critical questions regarding the Apocalypse must interact with Schmid's findings. Second, the Nestle NT text apparatus for the Apocalypse must be revised accordingly.

225. Mussner, F. "Neue Studien zur Geschichte des griechischen Apokalypse-Textes." **TTZ** 66 (1957): 50-53.

Reviews Schmid's commentary on the Greek text of the Revelation and analysis of the sixth century manuscript commentary by Andrew of Caesarea in Cappadocia. Suggests that the work of S. is excellent, especially his presentation of the textual history of the Revelation and concluding index. Concludes that the older scholarly opinions seem to be verified in holding to the four-textual-family hypothesis for the Revelation, viz., AC, p[47], S, Andrew-Text, and Koine-Text.

226. Oliver, H.H. "A Textual Transposition in Codex C (Ephraemi Syri rescriptus)." **JBL** 76 (1957): 233-236.

Suggests that sometime between the early third and fifth centuries some irresponsible scribe transposed a section of the Greek text of the Revelation in Codex C. Due to the process of folding the large quire of the book, Rev. 7:17-8:3; 8:3-4; 10:10b-11:1; 11:1-3 became Rev. 10:10b-11:1; 11:1-3; 7:17-8:3; 8:3-4.

[1955]
227. Lo Bue, F."Old Latin Readings of the Apocalypse in the 'Wordsworth-White' Edition of the Vulgate." VC 21-24.

Offers a critical study of the Old Latin texts in the "Wordsworth-White" Edition of the Revelation.

228. Schmid, J. **Studien zur Geschichte des griechischen Apokalypse-Textes.** Münchener Theologische Studien. Historische Abteilung 1. 2 Vols. in 3: Munich: Karl Zink, 1955-56.

This massive work investigates the manuscript tradition of the Apocalypse and concludes that our present text has emerged from four major manuscript branches ("*Hauptstämme*"), viz., 1) "Av" and 2) "K" (mainly cursive manuscripts); and 3) "A" and "C" (plus cursive 2053); and, finally, 4) Aleph and p^{47}.

[1954]
229. Sparks, H.F.D. "A Celtic Text of the Latin Apocalypse Preserved in Two Durham Manuscripts of Bede's Commentary on the Apocalypse." **JTS** 5NS (1954): 227-231.

Reviews the two Durham manuscripts (A.iv.28 and B.iv.16) of Bede's commentary on the Revelation. Concludes that these documents represent a deliberate replacement of Bede's original work by a later reviser.

[1950]
230. Schmid, J. "Zur Textkritik [und Exegese] der Apok. [13,10; 18,2]." ZNW 43 (1950): 112-128.

Discusses text-critical and relevant exegetical problems related to Rev. 13:10 and 18:2, and suggests newly corrected renderings.

[1949]
231. Tasker, R.V.G. "The Chester Beatty Papyrus of the Apocalypse of John." **JTS** 50 (1949): 60-68.

Considers the degree to which the Chester Beatty Papyrus (p^{47}) of the Revelation follows or diverges from the author's grammatical "rules"

(Charles). Further, R. asks if the differences in the *Textus Receptus* are really corrections or just exceptions to John's stylistic rules. Concludes that p^{47} is an early revision of the original text of the Revelation.

[1940]
232. Willoughby, H.R. and Colwell, E.C. **The Elizabeth Day McCormick Apocalypse. 2 Vols.** Chicago: University of Chicago Press, 1940.

Vol. 1 by Willoughby offers **A Greek Corpus of Revelation Iconography,** and Colwell presents **History and Text**. Both volumes are a masterful thesaurus of information on iconography and manuscripts relevant to this seventeenth- century vernacular codex on the Revelation of John. Cf., reviews in **JR** 20 (1940): 297-300; **JBL** 60 (1940):71-74.

[1937]
233. Harris J.R. "A New Reading in the Text of the Apocalypse." **ET** 48 (1936-37): 429.

Examines Rev. 18:17 in light of current Egyptian research and notes that the verse should read "all those who sail to Punt (Pont) and all those who work the sea." This probably refers to the OT city of Ophir or Tarshish.

[1936]
234. Schmid, J. "Untersuchungen zur Geschichte des griechischen Apokalypse textes. Der K-Text." **B** 17 (1936): 11-44, 167-201, 273-293, 429-460.

Studies the manuscript texts of the Revelation based on the work of Hoskier and concludes that Hoskier's collation of the available manuscript material is tentative and unimpressive ("*einem Phantom*").

235. ———. "Der Apokalypsetext des Kodex 0207, (Papiri della Societa Italiana 1166)." **BZ** 23 (1935/36): 187-189.

Examines Kodex 0207 and a variety of variant readings (e.g., 9:2, 15). Distinct corrections are seen only from 9:4-12 and the brevity of the fragment does not argue against the text-form or its importance. P^{47} and Aleph are still superior.

[1935]
236. Heikel, I. "Konjecturen zu einigen Stellen des neutestamentlichen Textes." **TStKr** 106 (1935): 314-317.

Investigates a number of NT text readings, including Rev. 1:9 (where he changes the word order); and Rev. 18:17. Regarding the latter, H. emends the text by adding τον between επι and τοπον for what he considers a proper reading.

237. Schmid, J. "Der Apokalypsetext des Chester Beatty Papyrus p47." **Byzantinisch-neugriechische Jahrbucher** 11 (1934-35): 81-108.

Presents candid and critical observations (positive and negative) of p47.

[1934]
238. Lagrange, M.-J. "Les papyrus Chester Beatty pour les epitres de S. Paul et l'Appocalypse." **RB** 43 (1934): 481-493.

Studies and comments on the text of the Pauline letters and the Revelation as found in p47. Sets Rev. 9:10-17:2 aside for special text-critical examination and discussion.

239. Sanders, H.A. "The Beatty Papyrus of Revelation and Hoskier's Edition." **JBL** 53 (1934): 371-380.

Considering that the text of the Beatty Papyrus of Revelation (p47) found in Kenyon's edition treats only its relationship to the better-known uncials (Aleph, A, C, P, and 046) and to the *Textus Receptus*, S. compares p47 to a wider range of cursive manuscripts found in Hoskier's **Concerning the Text of the Apocalypse** (1929). The Beatty Papyrus is supported by 332 readings from various other manuscripts and groups. Three manuscripts/groups in particular stand closer to p47 than the best and oldest of the uncials, viz., Group 95, Cursive 200, and Group 178.

[1929]
240. Hoskier, H.C. **Concerning the Text of the Apocalypse. 2 Vols..** London: Bernard Quaritch, 1929.

Investigates and evaluates the kinds and varieties of texts of the Revelation of John available today.

[1928]
241. Oman, J. **The Text of Revelation: A Revised Theology.** Cambridge, U.K.: University Press, 1928. Revision of 1924 text.

This two-point study attempts to rearrange and restructure the Gebhardt

NT text of the Revelation into twenty-seven sections of thirty-three lines each.

D. ARCHAEOLOGY

NB: Most of the archaelogical interest in the Revelation in the twentieth century took place within the first two decades. The following entries reflect mostly an indirect interest in the study of the Revelation of John.

General Studies

[1974]
242. Meinardus, O.F.A. "The Christian Remains of the Seven Churches of the Apocalypse." **BA** 37 (1974): 69-82.

Reports on the remains and fragments discovered on Patmos and at the sites of the churches mentioned in Rev. 2-3. Several discoveries verify the historicity of the text and inform the traveler concerning the various traditions represented at the sites. Concludes that the traditions about the author of the Revelation and the author of John's Gospel have become mixed since the first century. Photos included.

243. ————. **St. John of Patmos and the Seven Churches of the Apocalypse**. Athens: Lycabettus, 1974.

Describes the present-day sites mentioned in Rev. 1-3 and comments on the connection between the author of the Revelation, John, the island of Patmos on the Aegean Sea, and the sites of Ephesus, Laodicea, etc. Photographs included.

[1971]
244. Mellink, M.J. "Archaeology in Asia Minor." **AJA**, Second Series, 75 (1971): 161-181.

Surveys the "gradual and diversified" excavation work in Anatolia to this date, identifying the sites and the major people connected to the work. Especially noteworthy is the work being done at Old Smyrna, and Sardis (by Hanfmann), Pergamon, and Laodicea.

[1964]
245. Cosmades, T. "Ruins of the Seven Churches." **ChT** 9 (1964): 232-235.

Attempts to connect archaeology and history in reference to the cities mentioned in Rev. 2-3.

[1958]
246. Johnson, S.E. "Early Christianity in Asia Minor." **JBL** 77 (1958): 1-17.

Surveys the state of exploration and excavation in Asia Minor and states that Colossae, Lystra, and Derbe have yet to be seriously investigated. Anatolia presents a problem because of the various forms of Christianity practiced there through the years. Two periods of research are reviewed specifically: 1) 1743-1918; 2) 1918 to the present. Concludes with a brief summary of the secular literature discovered in Anatolia during the first centuries before and after Christ.

[1956]
247. North, R. "Philadelphia and Other Apocalypse-Churches." **CBQ** 18 (1956): 35.

Surveys recent archaeological news on the seven cities of Rev. 2-3. Notes that of the seven cities only two are totally deserted and uninhabited, viz., Sardis and Laodicea. These are the two cities (churches) in Asia Minor condemned without hope in the Book of Revelation.

[1948]
248. Wallace, H. "Leviathan and the Beast in Revelation." **BA** 11 (1948): 61-68.

Discusses the possible sources for the figure and symbol of the Beast in Rev. 12. Suggests that 1) the dragon theme was universally understood and 2) the OT figure of Leviathan is John's particular source.

Specific Studies

(The following entries with a few exceptions are presented without complete annotation insofar as the articles represent very technical research and the authors have made little or no attempt to make connections with the biblical record.)

Ephesus

[1958-70]
249. Mellink, M.J. "Archaeology in Asia Minor: Ephesus." **AJA,**

Second Series, 62 (1958): 99-100; 63 (1959): 84-85; 64 (1960): 66-67; 65 (1961): 48; 66 (1962): 82-83; 67 (1963): 186; 68 (1964): 157-158; 69 (1965): 146-147; 70 (1966): 156-157; 71 (1967): 169; 72 (1968): 140-141; 73 (1969): 221; 74 (1970): 172.

Reviews the ongoing work in this area of Asia Minor, reporting the events and implications of the discoveries of each campaign, from Profs. Miltner to Eichler.

[1951]
250. Jacobsthal, P. "The Date of the Ephesian Foundation-Deposit." **JHS** 71 (1951): 85-95.

Offers a tentative date for this discovery.

251. Robinson, E.S.G. "The Coins from the Ephesian Artemision Reconsidered." **JHS** 71 (1951): 156-167.

Discusses the nature and interpretation of this coin find.

[1946]
252. Luce, S.B. "Archaeological News and Discussions: Early Christian and Byzantine -- Ephesus, Pagan and Christian." **AJA**, Second Series, 50 (1946): 183.

Reviews the 1945 survey of Ephesus by Parvis and Filson (see **BA** viii) and the history of the city, from the first Anatolian settlement to the latest excavation work on the so-called Tomb of St. Luke.

[1945]
253. Filson, F.V. "Ephesus and the New Testament." **BA** 8 (1945): 73-80.

Describes the city in terms of its strategic location, wealth, worship, silver shrines of Artemis, emperor worship, the Jews and, finally, Paul's ministry. Concludes with a discussion of the terms and language of Acts 19 in light of the inscriptions and papyri discovered at Ephesus.

254. Parvis, M.M. "Archaeology and St. Paul's Journeys in Greek Lands. Part IV -- Ephesus." **BA** 8 (1945): 62-73.

Reviews the history of Ephesus from its birth to its decline, ca. A.D. 1365. Archaeological investigation of the city, especially in and around the Temple of Artemis, the Great Theater and later, the Church of St.

Mary (ca. 350-last third of the fifth century). Concludes that archaeological evidence suggests that early Christianity influenced the city a great deal; but the city also influenced Christianity.

Laodicea

[1963-65]
255. Mellink, M.J. "Archaeology in Asia Minor: Laodicea." *AJA*, Second Series 67 (1963): 184; 68 (1964): 160; 69 (1965): 145.

Discusses the major work done here for the period 1963-1965 and offers some insights as to the implications for scholarship.

[1950]
256. Johnson, S.E. "Laodicea and Its Neighbors." **BA** 13 (1950): 1-18.

Traces the history and archaeological work related to the cities of Colossae, Laodicea, and Hierapolis. Discusses the relationship between the biblical data and the facts surrounding the scientific research in these cities.

Pergamum

[1959-70]
257. Mellink, M.J. "Archaeology in Asia Minor: Pergamon." *AJA*, Second Series, 63 (1959): 85; 64 (1960): 68; 65 (1961): 51; 66 (1962): 85; 67 (1963): 189; 68 (1964): 164; 69 (1965): 148; 70 (1966): 158; 71 (1967): 169-170; 72 (1968): 142; 73 (1969): 223; 74 (1970): 173-174.

Reports on the work of the German Archaeological Institute (from Profs. Boehringer to Ziegenaue) at Pergamon for the period 1959 to 1970.

Philadelphia

[1971]
258. Betancourt, P.P. "An Aeolic Shrine in Philadelphia." *AJA*, Second Series, 75 (1971): 427-428.

Identifies the miniature terra-cotta shrine discovered at Philadelphia as belonging to the Aroltic religious order modelled after Mesopotamian cults.

Sardis

[1973]
259. Greenwalt, C.H., Jr. "The Fifteenth Campaign at Sardis (1972)."
BASOR 211 (1973): 14-36.

Reports on the work done in Sardis for 1972.

[1972]
260. Ramage, A. "The Fourteenth Campaign at Sardis (1971)." **BASOR**
206 (1972): 9-39.

Presents the findings of the 1971 work team at Sardis.

[1971]
261. Hanfmann, G.M.A. "Excavations and Restorations at Sardis, 1970."
AJA, Second Series, 75 (1971): 203-204.

Describes the highlights of the digging and restoration during 1970
campaign at Sardis.

262. ———, and Thomas, R.S. "The Thirteenth Campaign at Sardis
(1970)." **BASOR** 203 (1971): 5-22.

Describes the highlights of the 1970 work.

263. Métraux, G.P.R. "A New Head of Zeus from Sardis." **AJA** Second
Series, 75 (1971): 155-159.

Discusses the new head of Zeus find of 1970 along with the possible Zeus
cult connections in Sardis.

[1970]
264. Hanfmann, G.M.A. "Excavations at Sardis, 1969." **AJA**, Second
Series, 74 (1970): 196.

Discusses the new excavations of the pyramid tomb at Sardis in 1969.

265. ———, and Waldbaum, J.C. "The Eleventh and Twelfth Campaigns
at Sardis (1968, 1969)." **BASOR** 199 (1970): 7-58.

Discusses the work done at Sardis between 1968 and 1969.

[1960-70]
266. Mellink, M.J. "Archaeology in Asia Minor: Sardis." **AJA**, Second Series, 64 (1960): 67-68; 65 (1961): 49-51; 66 (1962): 83-84; 67 (1963): 187-189; 68 (1964): 163-164; 69 (1965): 147-148; 70 (1966): 158; 71 (1967): 170-171; 72 (1968): 141-142; 73 (1969): 222-223; 74 (1970): 172-173.

Presents a series of articles on the digs and discoveries at ancient Sardis between 1959 and 1969.

267. ———. "Archaeology in Asia Minor: Sardis-Eski Balikhane." **AJA**, Second Series, 74 (1970): 163.

Reviews the work done in Sardis in 1969 regarding Eski Balikhane.

[1969]
268. Hanfmann, G.M.A. and Mitten, D.C. "Sardis Campaign of 1968: A Summary." **JNES** 28 (1969): 271-272.

Summarizes the latest work at Sardis in 1968.

269. Mellink, M.J. "Archaeology in Asia Minor: Sardis-Ahlatli Tepecik." **AJA**, Second Series, 73 (1969): 209.

Details the 1968 findings at Sardis regarding Ahlatli Tepecik.

[1968]
270. Hanfmann, G.M.A. "The Tenth Campaign at Sardis (1967)." **BASOR** 191 (1968): 2-41.

Summarizes his team's findings for 1967 at Sardis.

[1967]
271. ———. "The Ninth Campaign at Sardis (1966)." **BASOR** 186 (1967): 17-52; 187 (1967): 9-62.

Discusses the 1966 work at Sardis.

[1966]
272. ———. "The Eighth Campaign at Sardis (1965)." **BASOR** 182 (1966): 2-54.

Discusses the 1965 work at Sardis.

273. ———. "Excavations at Sardis, 1965." **AJA**, Second Series, 70 (1966): 190-191.

Presents the results of the 1965 excavations at Sardis.

274. Mitten, D.G. "A New Look at Ancient Sardis." **BA** 29 (1966): 38-68.

Explains and summarizes the major discoveries of the Harvard-Cornell excavation work on urban Sardis.

[1965]
275. Hanfmann, G.M.A. "The Seventh Campaign at Sardis (1964)." **BASOR** 177 (1965): 2-37.

Offers the findings of the 1964 Sardis team of archaeologists.

[1964]
276. ———. "The Sixth Campaign at Sardis (1963)." **BASOR** 174 (1964): 3-58.

Discusses the work of the 1963 team.

[1963]
277. ———. "The Fifth Campaign at Sardis (1962)." **BASOR** 170 (1963): 1-65.

Discusses the 1962 digging at Sardis.

[1962]
278. ———. "The Fourth Campaign at Sardis (1961)." **BASOR** 166 (1962): 1-57.

Presents the findings of the 1961 digging at Sardis.

279. Hansen, D.P. "An Archaic Bronze Boar from Sardis." **BASOR** 168 (1962): 27-36.

Discusses the bronze boar find in 1961 at Sardis.

[1961]
280. Hanfmann, G.M.A. "The Third Campaign at Sardis (1960)."
BASOR 162 (1961): 8-49.

Reports on the work of the 1960 digging at Sardis.

[1960]
281. ———. "Excavations at Sardis, 1959." **BASOR** 157 (1960): 8-43.

Presents the results of the 1959 excavation at Sardis.

282. ——— and Polatkan, K.Z. "A Sepulchral Stele from Sardis." **AJA**,
Second Series, 64 (1960): 49-52.

Describes and comments on the discovery of the classic art stele at Sardis
by the 1959 team.

283. North, R. "Sardis Campaign Published and Continuing." **CBQ** 22
(1960): 82-83.

Summarizes the ongoing work at Sardis by the Hanfmann team.

284. Robert, L. "The Inscription of the Sepulchral Stele from Sardis."
AJA, Second Series, 64 (1960): 53-56.

Discusses the inscription on the sepulchral stele discovered at Sardis.

[1959]
285. Hanfmann, G.M.A. "Excavations at Sardis, 1958." **BASOR** 154
(1959): 5-35.

Reports on the findings of the 1958 archaeological campaign at Sardis.

286. North, R. "First-Season Finds at Sardis." **CBQ** 21 (1959): 55.

Details briefly some results of the latest expedition to Sardis led by G.
Hanfmann.

[1945]
287. Hanfmann, G.M.A. "Horseman from Sardis." **AJA**, Second Series,
49 (1945): 570-581.

Discusses the art and background of the "horseman" pottery fragment discovered at Sardis in 1944.

Smyrna

[1967-70]
288. Mellink, M.J. "Archaeology in Asia Minor: Bayrakli-Old Smyrna." **AJA**, Second Series, 71 (1967): 169; 72 (1968): 141; 74 (1970): 172.

Discusses the development and character of the archaeological work continuing at Bayrakli (Old Smyrna).

E. AUTHORSHIP AND DATE

[1989]
289. Gentry, K.L. **Before Jerusalem Fell. Dating the Book of Revelation.** Tyler, TX: Institute for Christian Economics, 1989.

Argues exegetically and historically for a pre-A.D. 70 date for the composition of the Revelation. Discussion considers internal and external evidence, as well as "Alleged Domitianic Evidences" and concludes for a Neronic dating, ca. A.D. 65-66.

[1987]
290. Trudinger, P. "The 'Nero Redivivus' Rumour and the Date of the Apocalypse of John." **SMR** 131 (1987): 43-44.

Argues (cf. Rev. 17:10) that the Revelation was written ca. mid-A.D. 68--early-69 during the rule of Galba. John evidently believed the Nero *redivivus* rumor concerning the emperor, i.e., he had survived the "death wound," escaped to Parthia, and was preparing to return with a vengeance at some near future date.

[1985]
291. Poythress, V.S. "Johannine Authorship and the Use of Intersentence Conjunctions in the Book of Revelation." **WTJ** 47 (1985): 329-336.

Studies the intersentence Greek conjunctions in Rev. 1-3, concluding that there is authorship unity with the Gospel of John and the Johannine epistles. The pattern of usage in the visionary narratives (4:1-22:17; 1:9-17a) seems to follow the same pattern in which the Greek conjunction και predominates.

292. Ulrichsen, J.H. "Die sieben Häupter und die zehn Hörner. Zur Datierung der Offenbarung des Johannes." **STh** 39 (1985): 1-20.

Investigates Rev. 13:1; 17:9, 12 and argues that the seven heads represent the seven Roman emperors from Caligula and on. The ten horns represent the same emperors, but include the three interregnums Galba, Otho, and Vitellius. Concludes that the Book of Revelation was written during the reign of Domitian (ca. A.D. 90-95). See also 4, B.

[1981]
293. Collins, A.Y. "Dating the Apocalypse of John." **BRes** 26 (1981): 333-45.

Studies the Revelation and questions the popular view that all apocalyptic literature is the product of crisis. Agreeing with Irenaeus' date for the book (ca. A.D. 90-95), C. argues that the internal evidence does support this contention (e.g., calling Rome Babylon, the seven kings in Rev. 17, the Jerusalem Temple in Rev. 11); however, there is no absolute evidence to support the notion that Domitian organized a massive persecution of Christians. References to violence and persecution in the book appear to be just the normal occurrences of opposition and repression that the early church encountered.

294. Gunther, J.J. "The Elder John, Author of Revelation." **JSNT** 11 (1981): 3-20.

Suggests, after critical discussion, that the book of Revelation and other traditions seem to identify John as an ascetic, eschatological Palestinian prophet-teacher-apostle. He was a high priest and chief elder (bishop) in Ephesus after being exiled to Patmos. In terms of personality and apocalyptic perspective, he was probably next in line after the son of Zebedee (Rev. 11:3, 7, 10).

[1978]
295. Bell, A.A. "The Date of John's Apocalypse: The Evidence of Some Roman Historians Reconsidered." **NTS** 25 (1978): 93-102.

Proposes a date in the sixties when the Temple and Jerusalem had not yet been destroyed, although Irenaeus' dating of the Revelation is ca. 95-96. The external evidence of the Roman historians Tacitus, Suetonius and Plutarch, along with the internal evidence suggest a date immediately after Nero's death, ca. A.D. 68. The general political and social circumstances caused John to see an imminent end to the Empire and the beginning of God's rule.

[1976]
296. Robinson, J.A.T. **Redating the New Testament.** Philadelphia: Westminster Press, 1976.

Argues from internal evidence that the Revelation should be dated between A.D. 64 and 70 based on his interpretation of Rev. 11, 17, and 18 in connection with the events in Jerusalem and Rome during this period. Suggests that the psychology of the book seems to indicate Neronic persecution (since there is no evidence for persecution during the reign of Domitian). Also the cryptic number 666 points to the *Nero redivivus* legend.

[1969]
297. Lipinski, E. "L'Apocalypse et Le Martyre de Jean à Jérusalem." **NT** 11 (1969): 225-232.

Maintains that the Revelation was written near the end of A. D. 69 or early 70, that the sixth emperor (mentioned in Rev. 17:9-11) is Nero, and that John knows about the siege of Jerusalem (cf. 11:2). The author of the Revelation knew of John the Apostle's recent martyrdom and thus chose to identify with him and convey his message through the name of John the Apostle. The phrase, "In the spirit on the Lord's Day" (1:10) suggests the Seer's journey to Patmos and also gives apostolic authority to the fourth gospel.

[1966]
298. Isbell, A.C. "The Dating of Revelation." **RQ** 9 (1966): 107-117.

Criticizes the commentaries of F. Wallace ('66) and U. Beeson ('64) regarding their preference for dating the book during the reign of Nero (ca. A.D. 64) without sufficient basis. Opts for a later date (Domitian, ca. A.D. 95/96) because of external and internal evidence relevant to local church situations, use of the phrase "the Lord's Day," and the heresy noted.

[1965]
299. Bruns, J.E. "The Confusion Between John and John Mark in Antiquity." **Script** 17 (1965): 23-26.

Reviews early Patriarchal literature concerning the identities of John the son of Zebedee and John Mark; and after considering an early Christian anecdote by Clement (ca. A.D. 96), suggests that there was some confusion over their identities. Concludes that the author of III John was probably John Mark.

[1964]
300. Strobel, A. "Abfassung und Geschichtstheologie der Apokalypse nach Kap. xvii. 9-12." **NTS** 10 (1964): 433-445.

Investigates the historical context of the Revelation in light of the composition of Rev. 17:9-12. Drawing on the work of Allo, but criticizing him for his insufficient basis for argument, S. suggests that John was interested only in counting Emperors beginning with the new era after the crucifixion and exaltation of Christ during the time of Tiberius. The five "fallen" rulers would then be Caligula, Claudius, Nero, Vespasian, and Titus. Thus, Rev. 17:9-12 was written during the reign of Domitian. This conclusion also satisfies the exegetical problems in the chapter and places the expectation of history's finale at the end of the first century. See also 4, B.

[1963]
301. Bruns, J.E. "John Mark: A Riddle within Johannine Enigma." **Scrip** 15 (1963): 88-93.

Shows how little was known about John Mark in the early church, how confusion grew within the traditions, and, how, eventually, through the work of a sixth-century monk named Alexander, John came to be associated with Ephesus (ca. A.D. 51) and later identified with John the Presbyter.

302. Sanders, J.N. "St. John on Patmos." **NTS** 9 (1962-63): 75-85.

Discusses the Johannine writings with a special concern to identify John of Patmos, author of the Revelation. S. argues that the Gospel is the product of two hands: the original author (the Beloved Disciple) and the editor, who imposed on it a new theology and dramatic order on the work. The editor of the Gospel is identified as John of Patmos. After an investigation of relevant passages in the Johannine corpus and interacting with the early church Fathers, S. concludes that the editor of the Gospel and the author of the Revelation are the same person, viz., John Mark of Jerusalem, the author of the second Gospel and the last surviving eyewitness to the Logos event.

[1962]
303. Helmbold, A. "A Note on the Authorship of the Apocalypse." **NTS** 8 (1961-62): 77-79.

Suggests that the author of the Apocryphon of John (perhaps dated late-first or early-second century) identifies himself as "John, the brother of James, these who are the sons of Zebedee." In citing Rev. 1:19 at an important revelatory section of the work, H. concludes that the author understood the writer of the Revelation to be John the Apostle. Thus the Apocryphon must be considered along with Papias and Justin Martyr as evidence for the Revelation's apostolic authorship.

304. Pierce, E.L. "Author of Revelation (an imaginary portrait)." **BrL** 7 (1962): 20-23.

Offers a creative, fanciful portrait of John, the author of the Revelation, based on internal and external biographical evidence.

[1954]
305. Valentin, A. "The Johannine Authorship of Apocalypse, Gospel and Epistles." **Scrip** 6 (1953-54): 148-150.

Discusses the pros and cons regarding the authorship of the Johanine corpus.

[1951]
306. Käsemann, E. "Ketzer und Zeuge, Zum johanneischen Verfasserproblem." **ZTK** 48 (1951): 292-311.

Discusses the problem of authorship in the Johannine corpus while engaging the current scholarship of Bultmann, Harnack, Windisch, and Bauer.

[1946]
307. Lee, G.M. "The Presbyter John." **ET** 57 (1945-46): 278-279.

Identifies the author of the Book of Revelation as John the Presbyter who is also John the Apostle.

[1943]
308. Evans-Prosser, K.F. "On the Supposed Early Death of John the Apostle." **ET** 54 (1942-43): 138.

Observes that stories recounted by Clement of Alexandria and Eusebius support a late date for the Apostle John's death, contra the primitive tradition for early martyrdom with James.

F. CANONICAL QUESTIONS

Discussions of canonical questions and problems related to the Book of Revelation are usually treated in the general survey and introductions to the NT text by scholars familiar with the discipline as a part of text transmission and history. Specific monographs and research articles are noticably absent from this period of research connected to the Revelation.

[1937]
309. Kretzmann, P.E. "The Position of the Apocalypse in the Ancient Church." CTM 8 (1937): 133-134.

Suggests, with Stonehouse, that research and history indicate strongly that the Revelation of John was apostolic in origin and also considered prophecy for the early church.

G. CULTURAL, RELIGIOUS, SOCIO-POLITICAL LIFE-SETTING

[1990]
310. Thompson, L. **The Book of Revelation: Apocalypse and Empire.** New York: Oxford University Press, 1990.

Studies the *Sitz im Leben* and genre of the Revelation in relation to the social life-settings of apocalyptic writing in general. Then, under the rubric of "script," "stage," and "play," T. analyzes 1) the linguistic unity of the book through the language of worship and John's vision of a unified world; 2) the history and rhetoric of Domitian's reign in relation to the Christians and Jews situated in an urban environment in Asia; 3) the social situation of the Revelation. Lastly, there is a concluding remark about the social order and religious language, and a discussion of recent research on the social setting of the Revelation. Concludes that the first-century Christians of Asia Minor were living rather peaceful lives at the time of the writing of the Revelation.

[1989]
311. Barnett, P. "Polemical Parallelism: Some Further Reflections on

the Apocalypse." **JSNT** 35 (1989): 111-120.

Expounds the theory that a polemical parallel existed between the Christ cult and the Emperor cult in the Revelation, especially in Rev. 12-22. This polemic is highlighted in the allusions to the Roman imperial court ceremonial and in the author's reflections on the true and false prophet.

312. Kreitzer, L. "Sibylline Oracles 8, the Roman Imperial Adventus Coinage of Hadrian and the Apocalypse of John." **JSP** 4 (1989): 69-85.

Argues that the Latin inscription of the **Adventus Augusti** coinage (Hadrian, A.D. 117-138) points to a possible linguistic connection with the NT word παρουσια. After discussing relevant historical and numismatic data, concludes that the idea of the sea beast of Rev. 13 and 17 was reinterpreted in Asia Minor during the second century to identify Hadrian as the Nero *redivivus*.

313. Hemer, C.J. **The Letters to the Seven Churches of Asia in Their Local Setting.** "Journal for the study of the NT Supplement Series 11." Sheffield, England: JSOT Press, 1986.

This revised doctoral dissertation (University of Manchester, 1969) offers an extensive exegetical study (212 pp. text, 126 pp. notes, etc.) of Rev. 2-3 in their *Sitz im Leben* while utilizing independent literary, epigraphical, archaeological, and numismatic sources. H. reassesses the work of William Ramsay while considering the evidence that gives background to the cities named in Rev. 2-3. The ideas in Rev. 2-3 have a strong OT base, but the big picture of the whole book is dependent upon our awareness of the historical setting of the book itself. Argues cogently for a rigorous commitment to the investigation of "social history" in future biblical studies. See also 4, B.

[1988]
314. Botha, P.J.J. "God, emperor worship and society: Contemporary experiences and the Book of Revelation." **Neo** 22 (1988): 87-102.

Studies emperor worship in the first century A.D. through an analysis of the cities mentioned in Rev. 2-3. Although there are obstacles to such a study, B. argues that the things of the cult, e.g., architecture, temples, statues, and rituals, suggest the power of emperor worship to integrate the life of the people. Concludes with a discussion of "confrontation" and "interiority" as two fundamental experiences of divinity.

[1987]
315. Beagley, A.J. **The "Sitz im Leben" of the Apocalypse with Particular Reference to the Role of the Church's Enemies.** "Beiheft zur Zeitschrift für die neutestamentliche Wissenschaft und die Kunde der alteren Kirche, 50." Berlin-NY: de Gruyter, 1987.

Argues contrary to the view that the "life situation" of the Revelation is to be understood against the traditional theory of Domitian persecution. The themes of suffering, martyrdom, and Jerusalem are discussed in the light of OT and Jewish thought. Concludes that Babylon is to be identified with Jerusalem in the book. Jesus Christ is shown to be the embodiment of Yahweh's blessings promised to his people; but Israel and Jerusalem should expect final judgment.

[1986]
316. Thompson, L. "A Sociological Analysis of Tribulation in the Apocalypse of John." **Sem** 36 (1986): 147-174.

Analyzes the theme of tribulation from a sociological perspective. First, T. studies several aspects of the literary theme. Second, he evaluates the sociopolitical situation of the church in Asia under the rule of Domitian. Lastly, he suggests a plan for connecting the literary and sociopolitical aspects of tribulation according to the Revelation. From John's perspective, there were a number of elements that helped him to form an opinion concerning persecution: 1) The gospel of a crucified King; 2) faithful behavior by Christians imitating their King; 3) social and political relations in the cities of Asia Minor; 4) the Christian statement against Church-Roman state relations. Those things resulted in a "feedback loop" that impacted the Church. Religious identification with the crucified Christ helped to form the Christians' psychosocial character, and that led to further, more intense, identification with the King. Throughout, Christians gain knowledge, which replicates itself in all dimensions of life to create a comprehensive world for the believer.

[1985]
317. Patterson, S.J. "A Note on an Argive Relief of Selene." **HTR** 78 (1985): 439-443, figs. 1-2.

Studies a second-century stele from Argos that portrays Selene as the universal queen of heaven. She is identified by the Zodiac about her head, seven planets around her head and shoulders, and a series of divine names in Greek in the inscription. Suggests in conclusion that there may be a possible parallel between Selene and the figure of the woman in Rev. 12.

[1984]
318. Collins, A.Y. **Crisis and Catharsis: The Power of the Apocalypse.** Philadelphia, PA: The Westminster Press, 1984.

Investigates authorship, date, historical setting, social themes, and possible meanings behind the apocalyptic language of the book using historical, literary, and psychological methods. The author (John) was probably an unknown itinerant Jewish prophet who had a strong affinity with the Jewish Sibylline tradition. The book is to be dated during the reign of Domitian, when elements of crisis for the Church were strong respecting Jewish conflict, Gentile antipathy, and the struggle over wealth. The book displays a kind of social radicalism and rhetoric against current evils resulting in "catharsis" for the Church. Concludes with a brief dialogue with several scholars (e.g., Barclay, Lawrence, Fiorenza, Ellul, Stringfellow, Metz) while upholding her own method as a proper extension of historical criticism.

319. Scherrer, S.J. "Signs and Wonders in the Imperial Cult: A New Look at a Roman Religious Institution in the Light of Rev. 13:13-15." **JBL** 103 (1984): 599-610.

Identifies a similarity between contrived ancient cultic wonders and the two signs found in Rev. 13:13-15, viz., 1) miraculous, speaking and/or moving images (statues); 2) lightening and fire signs. Insofar as it appears that the imperial cult used technology and simulation of nature in its activities, it should not be difficult to understand Rev. 13:13-15 as a description of such practices in the East.

[1983]
320. Aune, D.E. "The Influence of Roman Imperial Court Ceremonial on the Apocalypse of John." **BRes** 28 (1983): 5-26.

Analyzes the historical-political and thematic parallels between the imagery in the Revelation and the Roman court ceremonies. The title of majesty is then discussed in reference to God and the Lamb, Jesus Christ.

321. ———. **Prophecy in Early Christianity and the Ancient Mediterranean World.** Grand Rapids, MI: Wm. B. Eerdmans Publishing Co., 1983.

Reviews research on Christian prophecy, examines Greco-Roman prophecy in terms of the form and function of prophetic oracles, and discusses briefly the Revelation of John in relationship to the theme.

Concludes that the distinctiveness of early Christian prophetic speech was its supernatural origin. The decline of the so-called gift is to be understood more in terms of social influences than theological. See also 5, H, (31).

322. Beauvery, R. "L'Apocalypse au risque de la numismatique. Babylone, la grande Prostituée et le sixième roi Vespasien et la déesse Rome." **RB** 90 (1983): 243-260.

Suggests that Rev. 17 might be interpreted in light of a bronze sesterce (A. D. 71) with Vespasian (Rev. 17:10) on the obverse and the goddess Roma seated on the seven hills of Rome (17:9). John's use of the prostitute figure in Rev. 17:5 for Babylon-Rome may have developed from the figure of the she-wolf who is alongside the goddess. The term $\lambda\upsilon\pi\alpha$ ("she-wolf") might well connote a loose woman.

[1982]
323. Edgar, T.R. "Babylon: Ecclesiastical, Political, or What?" **JETS** 25 (1982): 333-341.

Argues that the Babylon mentioned in Rev. 17 is to be understood in terms of economics and not as an ecclesiastical or political entity. Babylon is an economic entity that controls local commerce from a world-center location. Thus "the great harlot" is to be identified as any activity toward an international economy or monetary control.

[1981]
324. Aune, D.E. "The Social Matrix of the Apocalypse of John." **BRes** 26 (1981): 16-32.

Describes John's careful and cautious presentation of himself as prophet in terms of the values of the local church in Asia Minor at that time so that his apocalyptic message might be more readily received. If the Revelation says little about the polity of the seven churches it is because John is trying to transcend the local character of the saints, apostles, and prophets. John was probably a member of an association of prophets who attached themselves to many of the churches named in the Revelation.

325. Collins, A.Y. "Coping with Hostility." **BT** 19 (1981): 367-372.

Argues that the life-setting of the Revelation is a crisis in which the Church in Asia Minor developed a fear of Rome and a resentment toward the disparity between the rich and the poor. This prompted the Christians to seek revenge. The book tries to deal with the feelings of Christians then by providing for an experience of catharsis. This experience, in turn, helped the readers to avoid physical violence against their foes in favor of simply releasing violent feelings. See also 5, H, (11).

326. Collins, A.Y. "The Revelation of John: An Apocalyptic Response to a Social Crisis." **CuTM** 8 (1981): 4-12.

Explains the historical background of the Revelation as follows: 1) A split with the local Jewish communities; 2) Rejection of the local Greco-Roman life and culture; 3) Hostility toward Rome and fear of its agents; 4) Resentment of the wealth of a privileged elite. C. suggests that the Revelation produced a catharsis through the narrative and structure of the writing with its pattern of persecution, judgment, and salvation. John was probably a charismatic, eschatological prophet who wanted to create a sense of community for the early Christians, focusing on their life together in the liturgy.

[1979]
327. Hill, D. **New Testament Prophecy**. Atlanta, GA: John Knox Press, 1979.

Studies the theme of prophecy through investigating the name, the Hebrew-Jewish tradition (Palestinian and Hellenistic), the place of Jesus as "a prophet mighty in Deed and Word," the book of Revelation and Prophets in the rest of the NT. Regarding Revelation, H. discusses genre, form and content, and the prophet and his community. Concludes that John's Revelation represents a particular strand of literature in the Palestinian-Jewish tradition of prophecy. John's role in his community was probably unusual within the early church. See also 6, H. (31).

328. Légasse, S. "Les chrétiens et le pouvoir séculier d'après l'Apocalypse johannique." **BLE** 80 (1979): 81-95.

Argues that John's Revelation is a statement for the Christian faith against armed revolt in favor of constancy and, possibly, martyrdom, in the face of conflict with the imperial cult. Martyrdom, then, initiates the eschaton and hastens divine judgment upon the persecutors.

[1978]
329. Lähnemann, J.; "Die sieben Sendschreiben" in **Studien zur Religion**. S. Sahin, E. Schwerlheim, *et. al.*, eds. Leiden: E. J. Brill, 1978.

Investigates the form and function of the letters to the seven churches in their historical context in Rev. 2-3.

[1977]
330. Collins, A.Y. "The Political Perspective of the Revelation to John." **JBL** 96 (1977): 241-256.

Contends that the crisis caused by Antiochus IV Epiphanes resulted in three types of resistance response: 1) Revolution (cf. Maccabees); 2) Passive Resistance (cf. Daniel); 3) Synergistic passive resistance expressed in action taken by the deity in order to avenge the deaths of the elect (cf. Assumption of Moses). The Revelation urges the early Christians not to take up arms against the enemy, but to endure persecution and hope for final salvation (Rev. 12; 2:10; 13:10). But Rev. 6:9-11 suggests that a kind of synergism was still operative and that the death of each martyr facilitated the eschatolotgical process. Thus the Book of Revelation and the Zealots, although different in their views of violent resistance, agree in terms of the possibility of synergism for the faithful martyrs and in terms of their mutual critique of Roman rule and rejection of images as a form of protest against Rome.

331. Fiorenza, E.S. "The Quest for the Johannine School: The Apocalypse and the Fourth Gospel. **NTS** 23 (1977):402-427.

Suggests that John understood his role (and his authority) to be as a Christian prophet and not an apostle. His *Sitz im Leben* saw him functioning as the head of a prophetic circle within the early church and thus, like Paul, he assumes his authority not from his relationship with Jesus, but from the revelation of the resurrected Lord. Therefore the Revelation must be discussed in cultural/political contexts that move beyond the Johannine-school tradition, e.g., the traditions of Paul, post-Paul, and Christian prophetic-apocalyptic.

332. Prigent, P. "L'Hérésie asiate et l'Église confessante de l'Apocalypse à Ignace." **VC** 31 (1977): 1-22.

Contends that the letters of Ignatius identify an active heresy in Asia Minor at the start of the second century A.D. This heresy, characterized as gnostic, dualistic, and docetic, with Judaizing tendencies, was behind the letters of Rev. 2-3. The Nicolaitans of Rev. 2:15 may be identified with such a heresy. John's Revelation and Ignatius strongly opposed the heresy. See also 5, H, (13).

[1976]
333. Müller, U.B. **Zur früchristlilchen Theologiegeschichte: Judenchristentum und Paulinismus in Kleinasien an der Wende vom ersten zum zweiten Jahrhundert n. Chr.** Gütersloh: Gerd Mohn, 1976.

Considering only the letters of Ignatius to be realistic descriptions of the church situation in Asia Minor of the first century, M. posits the theory that the prophet John, a likely emigrant from Palestine-Syria, knew very little about and had nothing in common with the Christian communities of Asia Minor in the Book of Revelation.

[1975]
334. Hemer, C.J. "Unto the Angels of the Churches. 1. Introduction and Ephesians; 2. Smyrna and Pergamum." **BuH** 11 (1975): 4-27; 56-83.

Combines the study of the literary, historical, and archaeological elements that are found in the composition of Rev. 2-3. Article 1 introduces the letters and exegetes the letter to the Ephesian church. H. offers that a massive statue of emperor Domitian excavated at the temple in Ephesus may suggest the kind of pressures the Ephesian Christians had to face. The "tree of life" mentioned in 2:7 perhaps alludes to the temple of Artemis, which at one time had the form of a tree-shrine. Article 2 treats the churches in Smyrna and Pergamum, using the tools of critical scholarship to offer explanations of the symbolism and historical allusions there. The Nicolaitans are described as a group who threatened the Church by attempting to justify compromise with the world. The references to hidden manna, white stone, and the written name are ambiguous. Both articles are accompanied by photos. See also 4, B.

335. ———. "Unto the Angels of the Churches. 3. Thyatira and Sardis." **BuH** 11 (1975): 110-135.

Argues that the importance of the local trade-guilds provides interpretative background to the letter to Thyatira (Rev. 2:18-29). Apparently the Christians there had little in their faith to guide them in a way that was contrary to the pagan society. Ps. 2 could be offered as background to this letter because God is described there as Lord of earthly powers. Regarding the letter to Sardis (Rev. 3:1-6), exegesis and critical analysis suggest that the church had fallen and its Christian reputation had become a sham. Reference to the *modus vivendi* among the Church, Judaism, and paganism identifies the problem of compromise. Other historical references are then identified in order to bring clarity to the text. See also 4, B.

336. ———. "Unto the Angels of the Churches. 4. Philadelphia and Laodicea." **BuH** 11 (1975): 164-190.

Suggests that the key to understanding the letter to Philadelphia (Rev. 3:7-13) is the earthquake of A.D. 17, with its accompanying slow recovery and fear. Respecting the letter to Laodicea (Rev. 3:14-22), every important element in the text is to be understood against the local background of that city. See also 4, B.

337. Johnson, S.E. "Asia Minor and Early Christianity" in **Christianity, Judaism and Other Greco-Roman Cults: Studies for Morton Smith at Sixty.** Vol. 2. SJLA 12. J. Neusner, ed. Leiden: E. J. Brill, 1975. Pp. 77-145.

Presents one of eleven essays in Vol. 2 on "Early Christianity" in relationship to the key cities and provinces of Asia Minor. See also 2, G.

338. Prigent, P. "Au Temps de l'Apocalypse. II. Le culte impérial au 1er siècle en Asie Mineure." **RHPR** 55 (1975): 215-235.

Suggests that historical evidence indicates that the imperial cult flourished in Asia Minor in the first century A.D. Also, inscriptions picture a group similar to the mystery cults whose context was that of a political-religious messianism and renewal (perhaps generated by the expectation of Nero's return). Concludes that the imperial cult did not have deep roots in the popular religions; but it was a demonstration of loyalty to the absolute power of the emperor.

339. ———. "Au temps de l'Apocalypse. III. Pourquoi les persécutions?" **RHPR** 55 (1975): 341-363.

Reviewing the writings of Tacitus, Suetonius, and Tertullian, P. argues that from the time of Nero there was a firm tradition of persecution of Christians. Tertullian and the records of the martyrs tell about how Christians refused to take part in Roman cultic practices, which, in turn, threatened the social stability of the time. Apparently the imperial cult itself, in particular the *Kyrios Kaisar* confession, did not play the significant role that Bousset, *et al.*, had argued. At the time of the writing of the Revelation, there was no recognizable, sustained persecution of Christians, although, as P. contends, John did foresee the inevitable future crisis between Christianity and the Roman state.

340. Saffrey, H.D. "Relire l'Apocalypse à Patmos." **RB** 82 (1975): 385-417.

Asserts John's presence on the island of Patmos by identifying a Roman presence there at the same time in the form of a temple of Artemis and a gymnasium. The Artemis cult myths no doubt influenced Rev. 12, which describes the pregnant woman, the great dragon, and the victorious child.

[1974]
341. Prigent, P. "Au temps de l'Apocalypse. I. Domitien." **RHPR** 54 (1974): 455-483.

Studies the writings of the classical historians and concludes that Domitian frequently exerted power against individuals and/or groups that threatened his authority or the state's. However, there is no record of any specific Christian victims of persecution (unless it be John at Patmos). Concludes that it was the Jewish question that seemed to occupy the thoughts of the emperor at the end of his reign, since the Jews were perceived as the real threat to Roman religion.

[1973]
342. Fiorenza, E.S. "Apocalyptic and Gnosis in the Book of Revelation and Paul." **JBL** 92 (1973): 565-581.

Questions the traditional scholarly views of apocalyptic and gnosis in the Book of Revelation: 1) That John's polemic is directed primarily against the Gnostics rather than the Roman state; and 2) That John's theology was too Jewish and apocalyptic to offer any comfort to the early, persecuted church. After analyzing the "opponents" in the Revelation and comparing them to Paul's opponents in I Cor., F. concludes that John's theology is really Christian and that the opponents are to be understood in terms of Gnosticism within the Roman state communities of Asia Minor. See also 5, H, (10), (13).

[1972]
343. Hemer, C.J. "The Sardis Letter and the Croesus Tradition." **NTS** 19 (1972): 94-97.

Defends the findings of W. Ramsay on local traditions in Rev. 2-3, suggesting that there is also a possibility of linking the Croesus traditions to Rev. 3:2-3. H. lists a number of parallels in first- and second-century A.D. Jewish and Christian literature that identify the Herodotean story and Croesus with local traditions.

344. Ρηγοπουλος, G.Ch. "*Ιησους Χριστος: Ὁ αστηρ ο λαμπρος ο πρωινος* (Symbolism in the interpretation of Apok. 22,16b today.)" [Greek original]. **DBM** 1 (1972): 224-237.

Offers an exegesis of Rev. 22:16b and a special interpretation of "The star" in relationship to Jesus Christ. Suggests, after reviewing the idea of "star" in Near Eastern, OT, and Jewish literature, that *star* as a symbol has eschatological and messianic connotations in Jewish writings. John identified Christ with the "star" in Rev. 2:28 and 22:16b to suggest the true spiritual light that has overcome the darkness (cf. Jn. 1) and the fulfillment of the Balaam prophecy of Num. 24:17. Adds that the Christ-star connection has continued among Eastern Christians in their hymnology and iconography. See also 4, B and 5, H, (4).

345. Reicke, B. "Die jüdische Apokalyptik und die johannische Tiervision." **RSR** 60 (1972):173-192.

Argues that the vision of the Beast in Rev. 17:10-11 refers to the Roman Empire and to Nero in particular, who is both the first head as well as the eighth who will return in the future. John was writing during the time of Domitian (the sixth head). Several Jewish and Jewish-Christian apocalyptic writers confirm the legend of Nero's return, which would signify Rome's collapse and the time of the final age (cf. Sibylline Oracles, 4-5; Epistle of Barnabas; Ascension of Isaiah). This literature provided general background to the NT apocalyptic understanding of the Beast. See also 3, D and 4, B.

[1969]
346. McCaughey, J.D. "Three 'Persecution Documents' of the New Testament." **ABR** 17 (1969): 27-40.

Compares Mark, the Revelation of John and I Peter as persecution documents written during the Roman persecutions at the times of Nero, Domitian and Trajan. Each writing represents a contrasting response to persecution. The Revelation especially was trying to develop a philosophy of history and an understanding of the state. The Revelation is thoroughly political in character. See also 5, H, (26).

347. Tatford, F.A. **The Patmos Letters**. Sussex, U.K.: Prophetic Witness Publishing House, 1969.

Studies the historical, geographical, political, and religious (mythological) backgrounds to the letters of Rev. 2-3 following the method of W.

Ramsey. Interprets and offers exposition of the seven messages in terms of church history and the present. Concludes that Christ is sufficient for our needs today -- as He was for the needs of the early church -- and therefore we should all trust in Him.

[1968]
348. Newman, B. **Rediscovering the Book of Revelation.** Valley Forge, PA: Judson Press, 1968.

A popular, brief study that posits the theory that the Revelation was written to oppose the teachings and influences of a gnostic group that had entered the Church in Asia Minor. John chose to use the apocalyptic form of writing because the gnostics were given to such myths. See also 5, H, (10) and (23).

[1966]
349. Satake, A. **Die Gemeindeordnung in der Johanes-Apokalypse.** "WMANT 21." Neukirchen-Vluyn: Neukirchener Verlag, 1966.

Argues that, because the church order of Rev. 2-3 differs significantly from the Church of Asia Minor in the letters of Ignatius, Revelation reflects a prophetic community similar to a Jewish apocalyptic conventicle in an otherwise Pauline missionary field.

[1964]
350. Cerfaux, L. and Cambier, J. **L'Apocalypse de Saint Jean lue aux Chrétiens.** "LD 17." Paris: Cerf, 1964.

Argues boldly that Rev. 17:9-16 was a redactor's insertion for the purpose of deliberately predating the work.

351. Giet, S. "Retour sur l' 'Apocalypse'." **RevSR** 38 (1964): 225-264.

Not seen.

[1962]
352. Wood, P. "Local Knowledge in the Letters of the Apocalypse." **ET** 73 (1962): 263-264.

Offers unique theories regarding the local allusions found in Rev. 2:13 and 3:1, e.g., the "Satan's Throne" reference in Pergamum could refer to the actual shape of the city-hill being throne-like.

[1958]
353. Bird, S.W.H. **And Unto Smyrna**. London: Clarke, n.d.

Offers an historical, political, and religious account of the development of the city of Smyrna (presently Izmir).

[1957]
354. Barclay, W. **Letters to the Seven Churches: A Study of the Second and Third Chapters of the Book of Revelation**. NY: Abingdon Press, 1957.

Directs an historical study toward a lay audience. Offers rich examples and illustrations from antiquity while doing devotional exposition and commentary. Interesting word studies taken from each text.

[1956]
355. George, A. "Un appel à la fidélité, Les Lettres aux Sept Eglises d'Asie." **BVCh** 15 (1956): 80-86.

Suggests that the seven letters of Rev. 2-3 are actual letters to historical churches during the reign of Domitian. Each letter is structured to fit the special needs of the church addressed, and is intended to encourage Christlike fidelity within a particular sociohistorical context. The themes treated in the letters are sustained throughout the whole Revelation. See also 4, B.

[1955]
356. Stauffer, E. **Christ and the Caesars: Historical Sketches**. K. and R. Gregor Smith, trans. Philadelphia, PA: Westminster, 1955.

Presents a series of historical sketches and character studies as he describes the great conflict between the emerging church and the Roman empire. Utilizes numismatics in analysis. Notes especially the persons of Augustus, Domitian, and John the author. Cf. reviews in **ET** 66 (1955): 226-227; **JR** 36 (1956): 265-266; **BF** 36 (1955): 234-238. See also 2, H.

[1952]
357. Giet, S. "La 'Guerre des Juifs' de Flavius Josèphe et quelques enigmes de l'Apocalypse." **RevSR** 26 (1952): 1-29.

Not seen.

358. ———. "Les épisodes de la guerre juive et l'Apocalypse." **RevSR**
26 (1952): 325-362.
Not seen.

[1951]
359. Blaiklock, E.M. **The Seven Churches**. London: Marshall, Morgan,
and Scott, 1951.

Analyzes the character of the seven churches in Rev. 2-3. Makes
application to the contemporary church.

[1949]
360. Kitter, P. **Die Frauen der Urkirche, nach der Apostelgeschichte,
den Briefen der Apostel und der Apokalypse**. Stuttgart: Kepplerhaus,
1949.

Not seen.

361. Knox, W.L. "Church and State in the New Testament." **JRS** 39
(1949): 23-30.

Studies the relationship between church and state in the NT writings.
Touches on the obvious tensions (political and eschatological) between
the two institutions in the Revelation of John.

[1941]
362. Ketter, P. "Der römische Staat in der Apokalypse." **TTS** (1941): 70-
93.

Not seen.

[1938]
363. Cadoux, C.J. **Ancient Smyrna: A History of the City from the
Earliest Times to 324 A.D.** Oxford, U.K.: Basil Blackwell, 1938.

Researches, analyzes, and interprets the history (including writings,
inscriptions, etc.) of this old Asian city in twelve comprehensive chapters.
I. Geographical; II. Pre-Hellenic Smyrna; III. The Old Hellenic Smyrna;
IV. The Village Period, etc. Chaps. XI and XII cover Christians and Jews
as inhabitants of the city for the period 31 B.C. to 324 A.D. The work
includes pictures, maps, and twenty-seven pages of indexes.

[1904]
364. Ramsay, W.M. **The Letters to the Seven Churches of Asia and Their Places in the Plan of the Apocalypse.** Minneapolis, MN: James Family Publishing Co., 1978 (Reprint of the 1904 A. C. Armstrong & Son edition).

Investigates the historic setting of the cities mentioned in Rev. 2-3 and uses the data as a basis for his interpretation of the text. The first half of the work (Chaps. I-XVI) treats historical and critical problems, e.g., letter transmission, symbolism, the education of John, persecution, etc. The second section (Chaps. XVII-XXXI) addresses each letter in two parts: 1) The city named (with the author's description) and 2) The interpretation. The preterist view predominates the discussion.

H. FORM-, TRADITION-HISTORY, HISTORY-OF-RELIGIONS STUDIES

[1990]
365. Aune, D.E. "The Form and Function of the Proclamations to the Seven Churches (Revelation 2-3)." **NTS** 36 (1990):182-204.

Insists that the form of the seven messages of Rev. 2-3 is that of "proclamations" associated to the literary genre of the royal or imperial edict. These proclamations, like the ancient edicts, show comparable formal and structural 1) *praescriptiones*, 2) *narrationes*, 3) *dispositiones*, and 4) *sanctiones*. In terms of content, 2) and 3) exhibit characteristics of the salvation-judgment oracles of Christian prophecy. John seems to have used the form of the royal edict in order to highlight the fact that Jesus Christ, not Caesar, was the real king. The Roman emperor was a model and tool for Satan. See also 3, B.

[1987]
366. ———. "The Apocalypse of John and Graeco-Roman Revelatory Magic." **NTS** 33 (1987): 481-501.

Discusses three clusters of religious themes: "I have the keys to Death and Hades" (Rev. 1:18), "I am coming quickly" (2:16; 3:11; 22:7, 12, 20), and "I am the Alpha and the Omega" (1:8, 11;m 21:6; 22:13) and compares them to Hellenistic magical traditions found in Greek and Demotic magical papyri. A. concludes that John used techniques, formulas and themes from pagan magical rites to develop an anti-magical polemic against those who would oppose Christian prophets.

[1983]
367. Shea, W.H. "The Covenantal Form of the Letters to the Seven Churches." **AUSS** 21 (1983): 71-84.

Argues that Rev. 2-3 coincide with the form of OT and ancient Near Eastern covenant formulas -- preamble, historical prologue, stipulations, witness, and blessing and curse. If Chap. 2-3 are understood in terms of this form, i.e., as covenant-renewal messages, then the letters are representative symbols for the Church's experience throughout history.

368. Strand, K.A. "A Further Note on the Covenantal Form in the Book of Revelation." **AUSS** 21 (1983): 251-264.

Concurs with Shea's discussion on the covenantal form (1983) and applies the structure to the whole Book of Revelation. The covenantal structure points to God's prior and continuing goodness. John's prologue (especially 1:5-6) reflects the preamble and historic prologue, while the epilogue (especially 22:6-7, 14, 16-20) reflects the covenantal call on witnesses and the blessing-curse formula. The main part of the book reflects the specifics of the covenantal stipulations.

[1982]
369. Bergmeier, R. "Altes und Neues zur 'Sonnenfrau am Himmel (Apk 12).' Religionsgeschichtliche und quellenkritische Beobachtungen zu Apk. 12:1-17." **ZNW** 73 (1982): 97-109.

Identifies the form of Rev. 12:1-17 as Jewish apocalyptic, but the interpretation of the Lamb (vss. 10-11) as Christian. Suggests that Jewish literature often borrowed from pagan, mythological sources. John modified the myth in order to connect with the idea of the remnant of Israel. Argues that John added vs. 17 as a Christian explanation for the persecution of the church that witnesses to Jesus.

[1981]
370. Reader, W.W. "The Twelve Jewels of Revelation 21:19-20: Tradition History and Modern Interpretations." **JBL** 100 (1981): 433-457.

A two-part history of tradition study identifies and evaluates 1) The relationship between Rev. 21:19-20 and Hellenistic-Jewish translations as well as the Targums, midrashic texts, and Biblical Antiquities (pseudo Philo); 2) Some modern interpretations of the passage. Concludes that the jewel motif in the Revelation of John is creatively aligned to the gem stories in Antiquities, but may contrast the jewels adorning the great whore of Rev. 17 and 18. The stones represent ideas in the Revelation related to theophany, ecclesiology, protology, and eschatology. Furthermore, they seem to contrast the corruption of the profane world and the incorruptibility of the divine promise of God. See also 1, C, (1).

[1977]
371. Collins, A.Y. "The History-of-Religions Approach to Apocalypticism and the 'Angel of the Waters' (Rev. 16:4-7)." **CBQ** 39 (1977): 367-381.

Investigates Rev. 16:4-7 as a starting point for studying the background of apocalyptic thought, arguing that vs. 4 was borrowed from the Egyptian plague tradition, but vss. 5-7 were John's composition. C. disagrees with Betz's earlier contention that John was interested in the "four elements" in Rev. 16. The negative judgments in the chapter, although sharing points with Kore Kosmou 53-70, are rooted in the religiosocial experience of a peculiar group that held to the destruction of the world and a new creation. Future scholarship regarding origins and the history-of-religions context of apocalyptic writing should be careful to note the author's own religious tradition as well as the modifications made to other ethnic and cultural traditions within the writer's environment.

[1976]
372. ———. **The Combat Myth in the Book of Revelation.** "Harvard Dissertations in Religion 9." Missoula, MT: Scholars Press, 1976.

Presents the thesis that the ancient combat myth was an organizing structure for the Revelation and a framework in which the readers of the book could understand their persecution and resolve to endure suffering and martyrdom. C. develops her study, first, by demonstrating that the Revelation has a definite and coherent structural base shown by a repeated visionary pattern that moves from persecution/threat to salvation/victory. Next, there is a discussion of the combat myth tradition found in the eastern Mediterranean world that provides the background to Rev. 12. C. argues that John has adapted this material to interpret the conflict situation of the early church. Lastly, the author indicates that the conclusions drawn in reference to Rev. 12 may also be applied to the rest of the Revelation. See also 5, H, (23) and (37).

373. Fiorenza, E.S. "Cultic Language in Qumran and in the New Testament." **CBQ** 38 (1976): 159-177.

Investigates the relationship between Qumran and the NT, especially with regard to cultic language and the interpretative category of "spiritualization" used by NT writers. Concludes that Qumran was interested in transferring Temple ideas to the community, but the NT was not. NT writers affirmed the concrete, bodily, and missionary character of true worship. That focus influenced their transference of cultic language from Qumran. See also 3, C.

374. Jenkins, F. **The Old Testament in the Book of Revelation.** Grand Rapids, MI: Eerdmans, 1976.

Suggests that since the OT texts are still extant as written "patterns" or "copies," these give the best clue to the patterns found in the Revelation. The best antecedent links are found in the prophets Ezekiel, Isaiah, and Daniel and Exodus.

[1975]
375. Glasson, T.F. "The Order of Jewels in Revelation xxi. 19-20: A Theory Eliminated." **JTS** 26 (1975): 95-100.

Argues against Charles' and Kircher's (earlier, 1602-80) theory that the order of the stones in Rev. 21:19-20 is the opposite of the order found in the ancient Egyptian zodiac pattern. Contends that Egypt offers no evidence to support the thesis and, further, that the Arabic writer, Abenephius, whom Kircher cites for authority, may never have existed.

376. Müller, U.B. **Prophetie und Predigt im Neuen Testaament: Formgeschichtliche Untersuchungen zur urchristlichen Prophetie.** "Studien zum Neuen Testament Band 10. Gütersloh: Gerd Mohn, 1975.

Studies the character of early Christian prophecy, particularly within the Corinthian church, and then identifies the forms found in Rev. 2-3 as "prophetic sermons." Discusses the function of prophetic preaching in the early church in terms of its consoling effect on the community preparing for eschatological judgment. Using the Revelation of John, the Pauline letters, along with the extrabiblical material, the author treats such themes as prophetic exhortation and preaching in Jesus' discourses and prophetic proclamation of judgment and salvation by the OT prophets. This work is a revision of the author's 1972 work entitled **Habilitationschrift**. See also 5, H, (31).

[1972]
377. Staples, P. "Rev. XVI 4-6 and Its Vindication Formula." **NT** 14

(1972): 280-293.

Critiques the work of Betz ("Zum Problem des religionsgeschichtlichen Verständnisses der Apokalyptik," 1966) and suggests that the vindication formula of Rev. 16 did not emerge from the world of Jewish-Hellenistic apocalyptic syncretism but rather (with Riddle, **The Martyrs**, 1931) it emerged from martyrological and Jewish apocalyptic materials. Concludes that Jewish nationalism caused the two genres to unite against the Roman Empire. See also 4, B and 3, D.

378. Vögtle, A. "Mythos und Botschaft in Apokalypse 12" in **Tradition und Glaube: Festgabe fur Karl Georg Kuhn.** G. Jeremias, H.-W. Kuhn, and H. Stegemann, eds. Göttingen: Vandenhoeck & Ruprecht, 1971. Pp. 395-415.

History-of-religions study concludes that the message of Rev. 12 is derived essentially from Near Eastern mythology.

[1971]
379. Gollinger, H. **Das "Grosse Zeichen" von Apokalypse 12.** SBM 11. Stuttgart: Katholisches Bibelwerk; Würzburg: Echter-Verlag, 1971.

Investigates the history-of-religions background to Rev. 12. Cf. review by A. Serra, "Una monografia su Apocalisse 12." **Mar** 38 (1976): 19-28. See also 5, H, (39) and 4, B.

380. Hahn, F. "Die Sendschreiben der Johannesapokalypse: Ein Beitrag zur Bestimmung prophetischer Redeformen" in **Tradition und Glaube: das fruhe Christentum in seiner Umwelt. Festgabe für Karl Georg Kuhn zum 65. Geburtstag.** G. Jeremias, H.-W. Kuhn, and H. Stegemann, eds. Göttingen: Vandenhoeck & Ruprecht, 1971. Pp. 357-394.

Does an in-depth form-critical study of the prophetic speech forms of Rev. 2-3. Analysis identifies the early prophetic forms in connection with Amos 1 and 2.

[1970]
381. Van Unnik, W.C. "'Worthy is the Lamb': The Background of Apoc 5." in **Mélanges bibliques en hommage au R. P. Béda Rigaux.** A. Descamps and A. de Halleux, eds. Gembloux: Duculot, 1970. Pp. 445-461.

One of thirty-five articles analyzes the "worthy" acclamation of Rev. 5 in terms of its rich historical and literary background.

[1969]
382. Betz, H.D. "On the Problem of the Religio-Historical Understanding of Apocalypticism." **JTC** 6 (1969): 134-156.

Focuses on the judgment doxology of the Revelation, suggesting that modern scholars tend to pay undue emphasis on Jewish apocalyptic and OT forms and patterns in the Revelation and in the process fail to treat adequately the milieu of Hellenisitic-Oriental syncretism surrounding the writing.

[1967]
383. Pax, E. "Jüdische und christliche Funde im Bereiche der 'Sieben Kirchen' der Apokalypse." **BL** 8 (1967):264-278.

Not seen.

384. Von der Osten-Sacken, P. "'Christologie, Taufe, Homologie' -- Ein Beitrag zur Apc Joh 1,5f." **ZNW** 58 (1967):255-266.

Studies the *Sitz im Leben* and structure of the hymn in Rev. 1:5 f., and identifies three strophes and a baptismal setting. Several expressions ("who loved us," "free from sins," etc.) suggest Pauline influence, baptism contexts, and redemption (baptism) traditions. O-S. concludes that Rev. 1:5 f. is a hymn of praise to Christ, which John had taken over from his Christian community. See also 4, B and 5, C.

[1964]
385. Halver, R. **Der Mythos im letzten Buch der Bibel: Ein Untersuchung der Bildersprache der Johannes-Apokalypse.** TF 32. Hamburg and Bergstedt: H. Reich, 1964.

Investigates the metaphorical language of the Revelation and concludes that the author drew upon (and combined) a variety of mythical traditions, patterns, and motifs.

[1963]
386. Harder, G. "Eschatologische Schemata in der Johannes-Apokalypse." **TVia** 9 (1963): 70-87.

Analyzes OT, Jewish apocalyptic, mythical, and early Christian form patterns in order to determine the eschatological scheme of the Revelation. See also 3, E.

387. Van Unnik, W.C. "A Formula Describing Prophecy." **NTS** 9 (1963): 86-94.

Argues that the phrase, "that which is, that which has been, and that which will be," is an ancient formula for prophecy described in pagan and Christian literature touching on the theme of the mystery of existence. Rev. 1:19, therefore describes the office and privilege of the prophet John, who wanted his book to be considered as a *"prophetic revelation."* See also 5, H, (31).

[1960]
388. Müller, H.-P. "Die Plagen der Apokalypse: Eine formgeschichtliche Untersuchung." **ZNW** 51 (1960): 268-278.

Analyzes the plague sections of the Revelation (Seals--6:1-17; 8:1; Trumpets--8:8-9:21; 11:15-19; and Bowls--16:1-21) and identifies the author's use of OT (E and P) patterns found in Exodus. The central figure in each section is the mediator and author of the plagues. He is also understood in the role of magician. See also 5, G.

389. Pfeiffer, C.F. "Lotan and Leviathan." **EQ** 32 (1960): 208-211.

Compares the monster Lotan of Ugaritic literature with the biblical figure of Leviathan and suggests the importance of the role they play in early-Semitic and later-Jewish thought. Sees Leviathan personified as evil in the figure of the dragon in Rev. 12.

[1959]
390. Delling, G. "Zum gottesdienstlichen Stil der Johannes-Apokalypse." **NT** 3 (1959): 107-137. Reprinted in **Studien zum Neuen Testament und zum hellenistischen Judentum**. F. Hahn, T. Holtz, and N. Walter, eds. Göttingen: Vandenhoeck & Ruprecht, 1970. Pp. 425-50.

Offers a form-critical study exploring the liturgical/worship style of the Revelation. D. analyzes the worship sections and notes the important role they play for interpretation, e.g., they are the highlight events that finalize the salvation-acts of God by means of world judgment. God and the Lamb are ascribed worth (cf.*Würdig-Rufe*) through praise and this ultimately will become actualized in the end-time events. Thus the worship/praise passages give unity and meaning to the book. See also 5, H, (19) and (41).

391. Prigent, P. **Apocalypse 12: Historie de l'exégèse.** "Beiträge zur Geschichte der Biblilschen Exegese, 2." Tübingen: Mohr-Siebeck, 1959.

Studies the complex religious history and the various scholarly interpretations of Rev. 12 and concludes with a personal interpretation. See also 1, C, (1) and 4, B.

[1955]
392. Cambier, J. "Les images de l'Ancien Testament dans l'Apocalypse de Saint Jean." **NRT** 77 (1955): 113-122.

Investigates the style of apocalypticism and the OT image patterns that influenced the writing of the Apocalypse. Concludes that John adapted traditional OT material in his own composition and that prophetic imagery was used to reflect the contemporary historical reality of the first century. See also 3, B and 3, C.

[1954]
393. Bieder, W. "Die sieben Seligpreisungen in der Offenbarung des Johannes." **TZ** 10 (1954)6:13-30.

Sets forward a theological discussion of the seven beautitudes and their theological connection to the eschatology in the Revelation. Explains the connection between Christ's prophetic role as Son of Man and the life-and-death situation of believers. See also 5, G, (1).

[1947]
394. Gaechter, P. "Semitic Literary Forms in the Apocalypse and Their Import." **TS** 8 (1947): 547-573.

Deals with the literary forms of the Apocalypse in terms of their Semitic backgrounds. Discusses Heptads, numerical symmetry, chiasm, closed forms, etc. Concludes that John used closed Semitic forms borrowed from some of the prophets and literary or oral sources. He changed and adapted the forms at will. Suggests a structural outline. See also 3, D.

[1942]
395. Michl, J. "Zu Apk 9,8." **B** 23 (1942): 192-193.

Offers a religionsgeschichtliche note investigating the literary and thematic background of Rev. 9:8. Draws a connection between the locust of the fifth trumpet passage ("*hatten Haare wie Weiberhaare,*") and the Gilgamesch Epic., Tafel 1. See also 4, B and 3, D.

I. SOURCE AND REVISION HYPOTHESES

[1972]
396. Müller, U.B. **Messias und Menschensohn in den jüdischen Apokalypsen und in der Offenbarung des Johannes.** SNT 6.
Gütersloh: Gütersloher Verlagshaus, Gerd Mohn, 1972.

Using christological criteria and data, M. identifies two types of texts in the Revelation for study: 1) Those referring to the Messiah's judgment of the nations and 2) those referring to Christ in relationship to the Church. The former are identified from Jewish sources and the latter from Christian sources. The figure of the Son of Man in Dan. 7 and I Enoch are investigated first. M. then treats the notion of a national figure while examining IV Ezra and noting the connections between IV Ezra and II Baruch respecting the Son of Man and the Messiah. Lastly, the concepts of Messiah and Son of Man in the Jewish sources of Revelation are analyzed, and an historical sketch of the two concepts concludes the work. See also 5, C.

397. Stierlin, H. **La verité sur l'Apocalypse: Essai de reconstitution des textes originel.** Paris: Buchet-Chastel, 1972.

Maintains that three separate apocalyptic works were combined by a different redactor sometime early in the second century. Presents a thorough reconstitution of the original text of the Apocalypse along with a new translation.

[1971]
398. Rousseau, F. **L'Apocalypse et le milieu prophétique du Nouveau Testament: Structure et préhistoire du texte.** Recherches 3. Théologie.
Paris and Tournai: Desclée, 1971.

Studies the broad literary plan of the Revelation through its structure and prehistory and suggests that there are five successive stages of redaction: two Jewish and three Christian. The last redaction of the work reflects the author's interaction with the Christian prophetic milieu of the period. See also 3, D and 5, H, (31).

[1969]
399. Mazzaferri, F.D. **The Genre of the Book of Revelation from a Source-Critical Perspective.** "BZNW 54." Berlin/NY: de Gruter, 1969.

Attempts to define classical prophecy and apocalypticism in terms of genre, and to decide where the Revelation fits. He argues that the book's genre is suggested by the author's primary source, viz., Ezekiel. Thus Revelation is to be differentiated from the pseudepigraphic apocalypses (like I Enoch, IV Ezra, etc.) and identified with classical prophecy.

[1960]
400. Quiery, W.H. "Opening 'The Closed Book' of the New Testament." **AER** 143 (1960): 49-56.

Offers a new and "sensible" way for Catholics to read the book of Revelation. Follows Swete's division of the book's structure into five major doxologies. See also 1, C, (1) and 5, H, (15) and (19).

[1949]
401. Boismard, M. E. "L'Apocalypse' ou 'les Apocalypses' de S. Jean." **RB** 56 (1949): 507-541.

Posits the theory that an editor combined two of his own previously written works into the final form of the Revelation. See also 3, E.

-Select Dissertations-

[1992]
402. Kraybill, J. N. "Cult and Commerce in Revelation 18." Unpublished Doctoral Dissertation. Richmond, VA: Union Theological Seminary, 1992.

[1985]
403. Morton, R. S. "A History-of-Religions Analysis of Revelations 4-5." Unpublished Doctoral Dissertation. Chicago, IL: Lutheran School of Theology, 1985.

[1983]
404. Beagley, A. J. "The *Sitz im Leben* of the Apocalypse with

Particular Reference to the Role of the Church's Enemies." Unpublished
Doctoral Dissertation. Pasadena, CA: Fuller Theological Seminary, 1983.

[1976]
405. Tengbom, L.C. "Studies in the Interpretation of Revelation Two and
Three." Unpublished Doctoral Dissertation. Hartford, CT: Hartford
Seminary Foundation, 1976.

[1975]
406. Dichot, M.E. "Les Dimensions de l'Apocalypse Medievale, Edition
et Signification du Manuscrit No. 5091 de la Bibliotheque de l'Arsenal.
[French Text]." Unpublished Doctoral Dissertation. Ann Arbor, MI:
University of Michigan, 1975.

[1939]
407. Soule, C.D. "Emperor Worship and Its Representation in the
Apocalypse of John." Unpublished Doctoral Dissertation. Boston, MA:
Boston University School of Theology, 1939.

Chapter 3

Compositional Studies

Compositional studies and literary analyses investigate the compositional and literary activity of the author who creates and brings aesthetic form and power to his work. The author's interests and intentions in composing a text to be read and to have some kind of social impact are usually the focus of this area of research.

A. GENERAL WORKS

[1990]
408. Witherup, R.D. "Visions in the Book of Revelation." **BT** 28 (1990): 19-24.

Views the literary and thematic connections of the visions in the Revelation, concluding that the book is composed of one major vision that stresses a message of hope.

[1987]
409. Duckworth, R. "Making Sense of the Apocalypse." **PP** 1 (1987): 54-56.

Offers a plain, popular discussion of the Apocalypse in terms of 1) genre, 2) theme, 3) imagery and 4) symbolism.

[1985]
410. Morrice, W.G. "John the Seer. Narrative Exegesis of the Book of Revelation." **ET** 97 (1985): 43-46.

Writes a "narrative exegesis" from the perspective of John the Elder, while treating critical matters of introduction, and the themes of emperor worship, the Hebrew Scriptures, the nature of Jesus Christ, worship in the early church, and the book as an encyclical letter within the biblical canon.

[1981]
411. Collins, J.J. "The Apocalypse -- Revelation and Imagination." **BT** 19 (1981): 361-366.

Asserts that the essential character of the Revelation is traditional apocalyptic. This assertion is based on our recognition that its language is the expressive, commissive language of poetry. The effective power of the writing is then to be understood in terms relevant to that fact. Therefore if the power of the Revelation is to be allowed, the reader should use the book sparingly so that the images may not become trivialized.

[1975]
412. Bailey, J.G. "Those four horsemen ride again." **HPR** 75 (1975): 51-56.

Compares the theological and literary features of the Revelation to the apocalyptic writings of the same time period. Suggests that the apocalyptic section, beginning at Rev. 4, is a wonderful victory song for the Church, while Rev. 21-22 represent a magnificent climax to the whole Bible. See also III, D, and 5, A.

[1954]
413. Olivier, A. **L'Apocalypse et ses Enseignements**. Paris: Librairie Orientaliste Paul Geuthner, 1954.

A general introduction considers several critical questions regarding the basic composition of the work. Commentary on the French text includes interpretation of grammar and figures of speech and focuses on Chaps. 2-3.

[1938]
414. ———. **La Clé de L'Apocalypse**. Paris: Librairie Orientaliste Poaul Geuthner, 1938.

Looks at the "keystone" element of prophecy in the composition of the Rev. Interprets the writing according to a structure of six strophy sections: I. Messages to the Churches (10 pericopes, 40 strophes, 120 stiques), etc.

B. GENRE STUDY

[1989]
415. Horine, S. "A Study of the Literary Genre of the Woe Oracle."
CBTJ 5 (1989): 74-97.

Traces the origin of the prophetic form of the woe oracle from the OT
through the book of Revelation. Concludes that this form functioned
primarily to describe and condemn sinful activity on earth. See also 3, D
and 5, G, (3).

416. Knoch, O.B. "Apokalyptische Zukunftsängste und die Botschaft der
Offenbarung des Johannes." **TPQ** 137 (1989): 327-334.

Introduces the mind of apocalypticism by investigating 1) Daniel's
interpretation of history and the future hope, and 2) early Jewish
apocalyptic writings. Then it studies the apocalyptic preaching of Jesus
and the Christian interpretation of his death and resurrection. Next, it
discusses the message of the Revelation as understood through its
statement of comfort and admonition to the persecuted church under trial.
Concludes with an examination of the current ideas of the future today, in
terms of their relationship to biblical truth.

417. Sand, A. "Jüdische und christliche Apokalyptik. Exegetische Fragen
und theologische Aspekte." **Ren** 45 (1989): 12-24.

Traces the history of the Revelation as an influential writing, indicates
how the work is like and unlike traditional apocalyptic, and discusses the
nature and interpretation of the Christian message contained in the book.
Concludes with a suggestion on how the Revelation might be read in an
apocalyptic age.

418. Thomas, R.L. "The Spiritual Gift of Prophecy in Rev. 22:18." **JETS**
32 (1989): 201-216.

Studies and explains the spiritual gift of prophecy as mentioned in Rev.
22:18. Argues that the Revelation is a product of this gift and the biblical
warning, "If any man shall add unto them [i.e., 'the words of prophecy'],
God shall add unto him the plagues." It is also an explanation of the end
of NT prophecy as a spiritual gift within the church.

[1988]
419. Lohse, E. "Wie christlich ist die Offenbarung des Johannes?"

NTSt 34 (1988): 321-338.

Identifies the connections between the Revelation and Jewish apocalyptic literature, but decides that the Christian character dominates the work. There are major differences between apocalyptic and the Revelation, in terms of form and content; but also there are similarities in form and content between the Revelation and other early Christian letters, e.g., the description of "the Christ-event," the use of christological titles, Christian hymns, and Christ as the center of its eschatology. Concludes by saying that only when we link together the apocalyptic elements of the Revelation to the "Christusbotschaft" are we able to fully understand the last book of the Bible.

420. Vorster, W.S. "'Genre' and the Revelation of John: A study in text, context and intertext." **Neo** 22 (1988): 103-123.

Develops his discussion in two parts: 1) the current debate in literary theory regarding "genre"; 2) the study of the genre of the Revelation. Concludes that scholars have two viable options open to them: One, continue to seek out an acceptable genre theory that can answer the many problems raised in connection with text interpretation. Or, two, let genre study die in favor of an intertextual methodology.

[1986]
421. Aune, D.E. "The Apocalypse of John and the Problem of Genre." **Sem** 36 (1986): 65-96.

Characterizes the apocalyptic genre of the Revelation in terms of form, content, and function, while discussing the recent research of J. Collins ("paradigmatic") and D. Hellholm ("syntagmatic"). Discusses the areas of orality and textuality and the relationship between the whole and the part in connection with literature and the cult. Apocalypticism is generally an autobiographical report of the author's personal experience of revelatory visions written in the style of prose narrative and structured in a form consistent with its central message. It reports a new eschatological and transcendent perspective in order to persuade the readers to change their minds. Apocalyptic must be understood in relation to revelatory magic and the "reveal/conceal" dialectic. The Revelation is John's replication of his original revelatory experience intended as a divinely inspired teaching for the church in public worship.

422. Hellholm, D. "The Problem of Apocalyptic Genre and the Apocalypse of John." **Sem** 36 (1986): 13-64.

Examines the problem of generic concepts from a paradigmatic perspective noting a variety of characteristics of the macrosign "apocalypse" and the need to supplement that perspective with a syntagmatic approach. There follows 1) a three-dimensional text-linguistic analysis, which includes content, form, function, and syntagmatic aspects, and 2) an investigation of how the communication levels and the hierarchial ranking of text sequences can be applied to the Revelation of John. Concludes with a six-page outline of the generic concept "Apocalypse," showing the delimitation of its macro structure into hierarchically ranked text sequences.

423. Karrer, M. **Die Johannesoffenbarung als Brief. Studien zu ihrem literarischen, historischen und theologischen Ort.** "Forschungen zur Religion und Literatur des Alten und Neuen Testaments 140." Göttingen: Vandenhoeck & Ruprecht, 1986.

This revised dissertation asserts that Revelation is essentially an epistle and not an apocalypse contained in an epistolary frame. K. reviews the history of scholarship on the book 1) as an epistle, 2) as a work within the context of Jewish apocalypticism and 3) as an early Christian epistle. Finally, there is a discussion of the Revelation in terms of its communication structure (E.g., 1:1-3, 4-8; 1:9-3:22; 4:1-22:21) and its religious and historical setting in Asia Minor. Five excursuses are included on various themes.

424. Kuykendall, R.M. "The Literary Genre of the Book of Revelation: A Study of the History of Apocalyptic Research and Its Relationship to John's Apocalypse." Unpublished Doctoral Dissertation. Fort Worth, TX: Southwestern Baptist Theological Seminary, 1986.

Explores the history of apocalyptic scholarship and reaffirms the traditional position regarding the Revelation as a part of the apocalyptic literary genre. While studying similarities and differences, K. concludes with a specific application of his research to the problem of categorizing the Revelation of John within the apocalyptic genre. See also 3, D below.

[1984]
425. Collins, J.J. **The Apocalyptic Imagination. An Introduction to the Jewish Matrix of Christianity.** NY: Crossroads, 1984.

Considers genre and surveys Jewish apocalyptic literature from early Enoch, Daniel, Qumran, Similitudes of Enoch, post A.D. 70 works (4

Ezra, etc.), and apocalyptic writings from the Diaspora (Roman).
Concludes with a discussion of the apocalyptic legacy. See also 3, D.

[1981]
426. Ladd, G.E. "New Testament Apocalyptic." **REx** 78 (1981): 205-209.

Argues that all of the major doctrines of NT theology -- the kingdom of
God, the resurrection, the Holy Spirit, etc. -- are rooted in apocalyptic.
The main theme of the Revelation is the triumphant, glorious, apocalyptic
Christ, who, behind the scenes of history and with the power of God,
battles against the power of Satan. See also 5, C.

427. Minear, P.S. **New Testament Apocalyptic.** "Interpreting Biblical
Texts." Nashville, TN; Abingdon, 1981.

Examines apocalypticism in the NT in two sections: First, M. identifies
the forces and events that gave rise to the apocalyptic movement in three
parts: 1) the gift to the prophet; 2) the gift to the congregation; and 3) the
horizons of apocalyptic prophecy. Secondly, M. highlights eight
"apocalyptic" texts from the NT, viz., Rev. 4:1-8:1 (the vision of heaven);
I Peter (the discernment of the Spirit in baptism); Rev. 11:19-14:5 (the
vision of heavenly warfare); Romans 8 (the discernment of the Spirit in
shared futility); Rev. 19:11-21:4 (the vision of the death of death); Heb.
2:1-4:13 (the discernment of victory over death); Rev. 21:9-22:9 (the
vision of the holy city, Jerusalem); and Heb. 12:1-13:25 (the discernment
of life in the city). Concludes that John's vocation was to give pastoral
guidance to the church. Worship and vision are both important to that
task, but the latter served to help translate worship into a language that
disclosed its infinite reach and range.

428. Paul, A."L'Apocalypse n'est pas la fin du monde." É 355 (1981);
515-524.

Traces the political and literary development of Jewish apocalypticism in
postexilic Diaspora in terms of its significance and character. Notes how
John writes the Revelation as a Christian adaption of apocalypticism and
concludes that the book does not designate the end of the world but
rather, following the nature of apocalypse, the Revelation reveals a new
world that will arise out of the present world crisis. The conclusion is
positive and optimistic respecting the book's message.

[1980]
429. Blevins, J.L. "The Genre of Revelation." **REx** 77 (1980): 393-

408.

Contends that the Revelation is Christian prophecy that uses traditions and language of Greek tragedy to admonish the Church and to interpret its real-life situation. Uses the form of the Ephesian stage (with seven windows), the Greek theater chorus and the structure of Greek tragedy to explain the work in seven acts: 1) The Seven Church Visions (1:9-3:22); 2) The Seal Visions (4:1-8:1); 3) The Trumpet Visions (8:2-11:18); 4) The Visions of the Lamb and the Beast in Conflict (11:19-15:4); 5) The Bowl Visions (15:5-16:21); 6) The Visions of Babylon's Fall (17:1-19:10); 7) The Visions of Victory (19:11-21:5). See also 5, H, (31).

[1977]
430. Collins, J.J. "Pseudonymity, Historical Reviews and the Genre of the Revelation of John." **CBQ** 39 (1977): 329-343.

Evaluates the traditional points of contrast between the Revelation and Jewish apocalypses (e.g., pseudonymity, absence of *ex eventu* prophecies, and epistolary framework) as superficial. Argues that these points were irrelevant at that time to the author of the book since prophecy was again accepted as authoritative and the imminence of the end was not doubted. Thus there was no need for John to utilize pseudonymity or *ex eventu* prophecies. Finally, C. points out that the so-called contrast between the "open" and "sealed" character of the two genres is only apparent. The esoteric character of Jewish literature is often a by-product of the device of pseudonymity. See also 3, D.

[1975]
431. Corsani, B. "L'Apocalisse di Giovanni: Scritto apocalittico, o profetico?" **BO** 17 (1975): 253-268.

See summary in **NTA** 22 (2, '78): #525.

432. Hanson, P. D. **The Dawn of Apocalyptic**. Philadelphia: Fortress Press, 1975.

This important study demonstrates how the beginning of apocalyptic eschatology was neither sudden nor anomalous, but follows a definite pattern of continuous development from pre-exilic and exilic prophecy. The essential character of apocalyptic literature seems to have been fully developed before any outside influences, e.g. Persian or Hellenistic, took effect. See also 2, H and 3, B.

[1974]
433. Prigent, P. **Flash sur l'apocalypse.** Paris: Delachaux & Niestlé, 1974.

Briefly considers the critical questions and then studies Rev. 4-5, 12, 20 and 21 exegetically and historically, concluding that each section displays an ancient liturgical background and this controls the meaning of the text.

[1973]
434. Comblin, J. "L'homme retrouvé: la rencontre de l'Epoux et de l'Epouse. Ap 22, 12-14.16-17.20." **AS** 29 (1973): 38-46.

Analyzes verses in Rev. 22 and identifies three genre: 1) A kerygma (vss. 12, 14), which announces the themes of coming, works, and beatitude; 2) A testimony (vss. 13, 16), which characterizes Jesus as head of the church, messianic king, and divine sovereign; 3) A dialogue (vss. 17, 20), which takes place between the groom and his bride. See also 4, B.

435. Mottu, H. "Trace de Dieu: la manifestation." **BCPE** 25 (1973): 40-55.

Introduces his study by first noting the contribution that apocalyptic thought makes to an eschatological worldview by means of adding the dramatic, the spatial, and the totality. Next, there is an attempt to connect the apocalyptist's experience with our own, viz., the experience of impotence, the night of history, the renewal of the "figurative" due to our impatience with language, preaching, explanations, and listening. Rev. 21 is then discussed in terms of God's *Erscheinung* and not the *Offenbarung*, the antithesis of two cities (Babylon and Jerusalem), new space, and the religion of the oppressed. M. concludes that Rev. 21 should be categorized as *Tagtraum* (daydream) because there the source of all thought is *desire*. See also 5, G, (1) .

436. Prigent, P. "Apocalypse et apocalyptique." **RevSR** 47 (1973): 280-299.

Identifies four characteristics of apocalyptic and then argues for the uniqueness of the Revelation of John vis-à-vis apocalyptic. The message of the Revelation recognizes the Christian martyr as one who already shares victory with Christ and can enjoy the present while waiting for the promise of eternity. Concludes that the Revelation's view of history is closer to the OT prophets than to the determinism of the apocalyptic writers. Christ is at the center of that history and his "return" is to be recognized in a realized, sacramental sense. See also 5, C and H, (21).

[1972]
437. Hill, D. "Prophecy and Prophets in the Revelation of St. John." **NTS** 18 (1971-72): 401-418.

Explores four topics: 1) The prophetic features of the book vis-à-vis apocalyptic; 2) The identity of the prophets and their place in the Church; 3) The relation of prophets and prophecy to the "testimony of Jesus"; 4) What Revelation says about the activity and contents of Christian prophecy. Concludes that the Revelation is a work of Christian prophecy, that the Christian prophets in the book are like the Jewish *maskilim*. The prophet-author is an authoritative figure (like the Teacher of Righteousness at Qumran), whose main concern is to interpret Scripture for the Church. See also 5, H, (31).

438. Sand, A. "Zur Frage nach dem 'Sitz im Leben' der apokalyptischen Texte des Neuen Testaments." **NTS** 18 (1971-72): 167-177.

Suggests that the infrequency of apocalyptic texts probably indicates that the early church was not generally inclined to apocalypticism as a genre or attitude. The Christian writers tended to change, edit, or synthesize apocalyptic writings in relation to Christian ideas. Concludes that the *Sitz im Leben* of NT apocalyptic texts may have been either 1) theological debate or 2) an apologetic against the threat of disunity and false teaching. See also 2, G.

[1971]
439. Beardslee, W.A. "New Testament Apocalyptic in Recent Interpretation." **Int** 25 (1971): 419-435.

Touches only indirectly on the Revelation of John. Reviews recent scholarship on the question of NT apocalypticism (discusses Qumran, Nag Hammadi literature), debates with Bultmann, Käsemann, Pannenberg, and Altizer. Raises important questions regarding 1) Jesus' relationship to apocalypticism; 2) Roots in prophecy or wisdom; 3) The connection with Hellenistic syncretism. See also 3, D and 5, H, (31).

440. Bratten, C.E. "The Significance of Apocalypticism for Systematic Theology." **Int** 25 (1971): 480-499.

Sketches the way systematic theology has neglected apocalypticism and concludes that systematic theologians must begin to incorporate all "thoughts of faith" into their discipline. Systematic theology has much to learn from the Revelation.

441. Rollins, W.G. "The New Testament and Apocalyptic." **NTS** 17 (1970-71): 454-476.

Attempts to clarify the idea of apocalyptic in the NT by examining Käsemann's view (1960) and interacting with several contemporary scholars while omitting any interaction with the Revelation.

442. Wilder, A.N. "The Rhetoric of Ancient and Modern Apocalyptic." **Int** 25 (1971): 436-453.

Considers the definitions and the descriptions of ancient rhetoric and concludes that early apocalyptic literature (like the Revelation) can and should be used as one norm for understanding and criticizing modern literature. See also 3, G.

[1969]
443. Snyder, G.F. "The Literalization of the Apocalyptic Form in the New Testament Church." **BRes** 14 (1969): 5-18.

Only indirectly connects with the Revelation, but argues that the form of ancient apocalypticism and the message of biblical apocalypses are not necessarily linked. Frequently the form and the message of ancient apocalypticism are dissociated. The heart of biblical theology is a "radically disjunctive eschatology," i.e., it asserts God's promise to mankind through Israel. It denies that present history or its institutions can lead to fulfillment. See also 3, D and 5, G, (1).

[1968]
444. Jones, B.W. "More About the Apocalypse as Apocalyptic." **JBL** 87 (1968): 325-327.

Refers to the study of Kallas (1967), critiques his evaluation of suffering in the Revelation and extends the point that the Revelation is not an apocalyptic book mainly because of its missing pseudonymity. This has always been important to pure apocalyptic works. See also 5, H, (26).

[1967]
445. Kallas, J. "The Apocalypse - An Apocalyptic Book?" **JBL** 86

(1967): 69-80.

Observes the character of apocalyptic thought by comparing the changing idea of suffering in Jewish and Christian literature, and concludes that the central feature of its system of ideas was its position regarding the meaning (nature), purpose and source of *suffering*. Apparently, the apocalyptist tried to answer the questions, "Is suffering ultimately good and therefore to be accepted?" Or, "Is suffering bad and a thing that God would seek to overcome?" Suggests that the apocalyptic writers held the latter view, but John's Apocalypse proposed the former. Thus, the Revelation is not an apocalyptic book. See also 5, H, (26).

[1964]
446. Russell, D.S. **The Method and Message of Jewish Apocalyptic.** Philadelphia, PA: Westminster Press, 1964.

Reviews the historical background of Jewish apocalyptic and describes how and when the genre emerged from OT prophecy. Analyzes forms and content while commenting on the psychology of the Jewish apocalyptic authors. Treats the message under the headings "Angels and Demons," "Eschatological Messiah," "Kingdom," "Son of Man," etc. Extensive bibliography included (25 pp.). See also 2, H and 3, D.

[1963]
447. Cantley, M.J. "Introduction to Apocalyptic." **BT** 1 (1963): 500-504.

Identifies the Revelation as apocalyptic writing and defines the genre in terms of its consolation for the afflicted during times of persecution. Apocalyptic helps the reader to interpret present difficulties from past experience and with a view to future redemption. See also 5, H, (26).

448. Rowley, H.H. **The Relevance of Apocalyptic: A Study of Jewish and Christian Apocalypses from Daniel to the Revelation.** London: Lutterworth, 1963. Third Revised Edition.

Discusses in two parts (four chapters) the rise of apocalyptic, tracing its historical development and enduring message. Part 1 covers Apocalyptic literature from 200 B.C. to the time of Christ. Part 2 covers the first Christian century. This revised edition adds a section on the Dead Sea Scrolls. See also 3, D.

[1962]
449. Howard, G. "Jewish Apocalyptic Literature." **RQ** 6 (1962): 77-84.

Describes the general background, place in Judaism, and later development of apocalyptic literature. Touches on several doctrinal issues (prophecy, the problem of evil, angels, etc.). Outlines the relationship between apocalyptic and Christianity with special focus on the Son of Man while connecting to the Revelation only occasionally. See also 3, D; 5, C, G, (1), H, (1), (2), and (31).

[1960]
450. Vawter, B. "Apocalyptic: Its Relation to Prophecy." **CBQ** 22 (1960): 33-46.

Studies apocalyptic literature, generally, in terms of its development and connections with the notions of eschatology and prophecy. Views the Revelation as a NT development of the "prophetic apocalyptic"genre. OT prophecy, thus, had found its fulfillment in the NT (Revelation) in a new form of the salvation prediction. See also 5, G, (1) and H, (31).

[1959]
451. Best, E. "Prophets and Preachers." **SJT** 12 (1959): 129-150.

Discusses the difference between biblical prophecy and modern preaching. Suggests that the OT prophets dealt with God's work past, present, and future; NT prophecy dealt mainly with future prediction and church order. Modern preachers, however, deal essentially with the proclamation and application of past Gospel facts.

[1957]
452. Buber, M. "Prophecy, Apocalyptic, and the Historical Hour." **USQR** 12 (1956-57): 9-21.

A chapter from his book, **Pointing the Way,** offers a general survey and analysis of the problem of connecting biblical prophecy and apocalyptic to the historical situation.

453. Ladd, G.E. "The Revelation and Jewish Apocalyptic." **EQ** 29 (1957): 94-100.

Explains why the Revelation of John has a unique distinctiveness and superiority about it that separates it from the majority of Jewish apocalyptic writings. Notes several areas of difference, e.g., Revelation's prophetic nature, its lack of pseudonymity, its optimism, its ethical character, etc. See also 3, D.

454. ———. "Why Not Prophetic-Apocalyptic?" **JBL** 76 (1957): 192-200.

Proposes that apocalyptic eschatology and prophetic eschatology are *not* mutually exclusive categories of thought. Three points establish a case for "prophetic-apocalyptic" eschatology: 1) Amos' view of history is to be understood in terms of apocalyptic eschatology. 2) Nonprophetic apocalyptic is to be contrasted with the "prophetic" in that the former is pessimistic and ethically passive. 3) Jesus taught an eschatology that was both apocalyptic and ethically prophetic. See also 5, G, (1) and H, (31).

[1949]
455. Glasson, T.F. "Jesus Christ and Christian Apocalypticism." **MC** 39 (1949): 33-42.

Considers apocalypticism in general and Christ's place in that literature in particular. Contrasts the Revelation (God's working out Christian hope in the future) with Ephesians (God's working out His purpose in the world). Calls for the Church to abandon "the gloomy mood of apocalypticism" and embrace God's plan for the earth. See also 5, C.

[1948]
456. Beasley-Murray, G.R. "Biblical Eschatology: I. The Interpretation of Prophecy." **EQ** 20 (1948): 221-229.

Discusses principles that govern the interpretation of prophetic teaching of the Day of the Lord, viz., imminence, the prophet's environment, effects governed by the subjects of prophecy, subsequent generations may modify early prophetic descriptions, and the interpreter's caution with symbolism.

457. ———. "Biblical Eschatology: II. Apocalyptic Literature and the Book of Revelation." **EQ** 20 (1948): 272-282.

Analyzes the differences between apocalyptic literature and the Book of Revelation and reviews several methods of interpretation, e.g., historicist, preterist, etc. Concludes with his own picture of the overall structure of the Revelation.

458. Rowley, H.H. "The Voice of God in Apocalyptic: Eternal Values in the Biblical Apocalypses." **Int** 2 (1948): 403-418.

Argues for the presence of "Eternal Values" in the Revelation of John, e.g., optimism of God's rule, the present realization of hope, the Day of Judgment, and the hereafter. The reader is challenged to heed God's spiritual word. See also 5, B and G, (1).

459. Scott, E.F. "The Natural Language of Religion: Apocalyptic and the Christian Message." **Int** 2 (1948): 419-429.

Describes the nature of religious language and argues for the positive relationship between apocalyptic and Christian terminology. Apocalyptic is valuable because it expresses spiritual truth. See also 3, C.

[1946]
460. McDowell, E.A. "The Message of the Book of Revelation and Prophetic Preaching." **RE** 43 (1946): 177-185.

Suggests that the Rev. is a source for great preaching today only insofar as it connects with "prophetic preaching," i.e. "forthtelling" for God and not "foretelling" the future. Touches on several relevant prophetic themes. See also 1, B and 1, C, (1).

[1944]
461. Rowley, H.H. **The Relevance of Apocalyptic: A Study of Jewish and Christian Apocalypses from Daniel to the Revelation.** London: Lutterworth, 1944.

Discusses in two parts (four chapters) the rise of apocalyptic, tracing its historical development and enduring message. Part 1 covers Apocalyptic literature from 200 B.C. to the time of Christ. Part 2 covers the first Christian century. The Revelation of John is identified within the genre and its contents are described, emphasizing the vision of the glory of Christ and His triumph over evil. The relevance is understood in terms of man's loyalty to the Lamb and the need for the Church to find life and service to Him. Excursuses discuss critical questions. See also 3, D.

[1943]
462. Chafer, L.S. "An Introduction to the Study of Prophecy." **BibSac** 100 (1943): 98-133.

Introduces the subject by linking eschatology (the last major division of systematic theology) with prophecy, i.e., the biblical predictions of the End. Underscores the importance of *chiliasm* in the study in seven areas, viz., OT, Israel, etc. Concludes with a discussion of the main ideas surrounding the millennium, including antimillennialism and premillennialism. See also 5, G, (1) and H, (31).

[1940]
463. Parker, N.H. "Jewish Apocalypse in the Time of Christ." CQ 17 (1940): 33-46.

Explains the character and development of Jewish apocalypse up to and including the time of Christ. Lists the merits and faults of the literature, concluding that this form of writing, which tended to comfort and encourage persecuted Christians, disappeared when the Church began to show victory in its life. It reemerged when the Church again began to suffer trial by fire. See also 3, D and 5, H, (26).

C. LANGUAGE, GRAMMAR, STYLE

[1990]
464. Enroth, A.-M. "The Hearing formula in the Book of Revelation." NTS 36 (1990): 598-608.

Says that the two hearing formulas, "*ο εχων ους ακουσατω*" (Rev. 2:7, 11, 17, 29; 3:6, 12, 22) and "*Ει τις εχει ους ακουσατω*" (Rev. 13:9) are addressed to the whole church in order to 1) stress the importance of hearing right and 2) encourage faithfulness and the preservation of what one possesses. The Christian is reminded that his situation has been determined by God.

[1989]
465. Delebecque, É. "'J'entendes 'dans l'Apocalypse." RevThom 89 (1989): 85-90.

Concludes that the Greek verb, "I heard," can be followed by 1) a simple substantive, 2) a participle in the accusative, and 3) a present participle (genitive). Numbers 2 and 3 must be distinguished for proper analysis and translation.

466. Rondelle, H.K. "The Etymology of *Har-Magedon* (Rev. 16:16)." AUSS 27 (1989): 69-73.

Discusses the LXX translation of the plain of Megiddo phrase in Zech. 12:11, "In the plain of the cut down [pomegranate grove]," and suggests that the Jewish translators took "Megiddo" to be related to the Hebrew root *gdd* ("cut down"). Revelation makes reference to the locations of Megiddo and Zion (Rev. 16:16; 14:1) as symbolic places and defines them theologically in relationship to Israel's history.

467. Porter, S.E. "The Language of the Apocalypse in Recent Discussion." **NTS** 35 (1989): 582-603.

Evaluates, first, Thompson's proposal that the Revelation of John was written in a Christianized Jewish Greek (See **The Apocalypse and Semitic Syntax,** 1986), and secondly, suggests some sociolinguistic elements that may have been present in the first century that may have contributed something to the language of the book. Lastly, P. argues that the language of the Revelation seems to be within the acceptable range of registers of first-century Greek usage.

468. Topham, M. "'A human being's measurement, which is an angel's.'" **ET** 100 (1989): 217-218.

Argues that the Hebrew *BN'L(W)HYM* + 144 cubits ("Son of God," Rev. 21:17) was the measure of an angel (Dan. 3:25) or of a certain human being (Rev. 2:18). There appears to be a numerical link between the number "144" of Revelation and the 153 fish of Jn. 21:11.

[1988]
469. Delebecque, É. "Je vis' dans l'Apocalypse." **RevThom** 88 (1988): 460-466.

Investigates the verb "to see" in visionary contexts of the Revelation and concludes that the verb is more receptive than active in meaning. "I saw" is used forty-four times as a part of visionary formulas with a participle or a complement. Thus John is to be identified with the other John who "saw and believed," according to John 20:8.

470. Newport, K.G.C. "Some Greek Words with Hebrew Meanings in the Book of Revelation." **AUSS** 26 (1988): 25-31.

Reviews recent research on the Greek language of the Revelation and indicates that a number of Greek words suggest an underlying Semitic concept, e.g., "ποιεω," "ονομα," "σκηνη," "πεμπω," etc. Future research on the Greek text of the Revelation would benefit greatly from the use of Hebrew and Aramaic lexicons.

[1987]
471. Deer, D S. "Whose faith/loyalty in Revelation 2:13 and 14:12?"
BTr 38 (1987): 328-330.

Argues that the grammatical constructions in 2:13 and 14:12 both reflect
objective genitives and therefore should be translated "(your) faith/loyalty
in/to me," (2:13) and "(their) faith/loyalty in/to Jesus."

472. Delebecque, É. "Où situer l'Arbre de vie dans la Jérusalem céleste?
Note sur Apocalypse XXII, 2." **RevThom** 88 (1988): 124-130.

Argues that Rev. 22:2a, εν μεσω της πλατειας αυτης και του
ποταμου εντευθεν και εκειθεν ξυλον ζωης.... should be translated,
"Between the esplanade and the river, in the middle, in the interval, a
wood (or, tree) of life. . . ."

473. Newport, K.G.C. "Semitic Influence in Revelation: Some Further
Evidence." **AUSS** 25 (1987): 249-256.

Sees Semitic influence on John's use of prepositions and prepositional
phrases, e.g., εν ("at the price of"), instrumental εν, απο, expressing
agent, etc.

474. Whale, P. "The Lamb of John: Some Myths about the Vocabulary of
the Johannine Literature." **JBL** 106 (1987): 289-295.

Debates against several NT commentaries and introductions regarding the
contrasting language found in the Revelation and the Gospel of John
based on the findings of Charles' commentary (1920). Suggests that
Charles was not always accurate nor forthright in his presentation of all
the grammatical evidence, e.g. in analyzing the words "lamb" and "call."
Regarding the former, Charles often omitted or easily explained away
contrary illustrations. Regarding the latter, the same is true with the
attracted relative.

[1986]
475. Bachmann, M. "Der erste apokalyptische Reiter und die Anlage des
letzten Buches der Bibel." **B** 67 (1986): 240-275.

Analyzes the vocabulary and grammatical structure of Rev. 6:1-8 and
argues for a positive interpretation of the first rider (vs. 2) based on the
whole structure of the book. Suggests that all the series contained in the
book are introduced by the image of a figure riding on something

positively white (E.g., 6:2-8; 14:14-20; 19:11-21). That first apocalyptic rider (*'ιππος λευκος*) is understood to be Christ.

476. Newport, K.G.C. "Semitic Influence on the Use of Some Prepositions in the Book of Revelation." **BTr** 37 (1986): 328-334.

The following Greek phrases were probably influenced by Semitic thought: *απο προσω που, μαρτυρεω επι, προφ...επι, πορνευω μετω μοιχευω μετα, ενωπιον* with *'ιστημι, and θαυμαζω οπισω*

477. _____. "The Use of *Εκ* in Revelation: Evidence of Semitic Influence." **AUSS** 24 (1986): 223-230.

Discusses the use of the Greek preposition *εκ* in the Revelation by showing the connection between *εκ, χειρος* and the verbs *μετανοεω, νικαω, μεθυω,* and *εσθιω*. Also, the same preposition functions partitively in addition to showing cause, agent (personal and impersonal), and the material out of which a thing is made. Lastly, N. argues that *εκ* usage in the Revelation may have been influenced by the Hebrew and Aramaic preposition *min.*

[1983]
478. Ellingworth, P. "'Salvation to our God.'" **BTr** 34 (1983): 444-445.

Studies the Greek term *σωτηρια* in Rev. 7:10, 12:10 and 19:1 and concludes that insofar as the word carries with it the OT concept of "victory" it should be rendered "victory" in each verse. See also 4, B.

[1982]
479. Edgar, T.R. "R. H. Gundry and Revelation 3:10." **GTJ** 3 (1982): 19-49.

Argues contra Gundry's (post-tribulation) interpretation of *τηρησω εκ* in Rev. 3:10 on grammatical and linguistic grounds, suggesting that it is grammatically impossible to separate the phrase into disparate and contradictory elements. The meaning of the terms becomes meaningless under such interpretation. The phrase *τηρησω εκ* should be interpreted literally, thus rendering it consistent with the pretribulation thought of Rev. 3:10. See also 4, B.

480. Mueller, T. "'The Word of My Patience' in Revelation 3:10." **CTQ** 46 (1982): 231-234.

The Greek phrase, "The word of my patience," in Rev. 3:10 contains a genitive noun ($\upsilon\pi o\mu o\nu\eta\varsigma$), expressing a result relationship, and a pronoun ($\mu o\upsilon$) as objective respecting the genitive noun. Thus the proper rendering should be "You have kept the word with the result of perseverance in Me." See also 4, B.

481. Osburn, C.D. "Alexander Campbell and the Text of Revelation 19:13." **RQ** 25 (1982): 129-138.

Suggests that in the Campbell-Rice debate of 1843 concerning the variant readings of Rev. 19:13, Campbell's argument for $\epsilon\rho\rho\alpha\nu\tau\iota\sigma\mu\epsilon\nu o\nu$ ("sprinkled") over $\beta\epsilon\beta\alpha\mu\mu\epsilon\nu o\nu$ ("dipped") was essentially correct. The former reading has strong attestation in the Greek manuscript traditions, the ancient versions and the patristic writings. The imagery is clearly related to Is. 63:1-6 and supports the "sprinkled" reading. See also 4, B.

482. Winfrey, D.G. "The Great Tribulation: Kept 'Out of' or 'Through'?" **GTJ** 3 (1982): 3-18.

Contends that Gundry's interpretation of the $\tau\eta\rho\eta\sigma\omega$ $\epsilon\kappa$ phrase in Rev. 3:10 calls for correction. W. offers a four-fold critique of Gundry: 1) Criticism of the use of Jn 17:15 as a help for the interpretation of Rev. 3:10; 2) Discussion of several antithetical Greek expressions that seem to support a pretribulation view; 3) Presentation of four complications to Gundry's argument; 4) Illustration of the difference between the phrase "keep out of" and "deliver out of." See also 4, B.

[1980]
483. Lancellotti, A. "Predominante paratassi nella narrativa ebraizzante dell'APocalisse." **SBFLA** 30 (1980): 303-316.

See summary in **NTA** 25 (3, '81): #1018.

484. Vanni, H. "Gli apporti specifici dell'anna isi letteraria per l'esegesi e l'attualizzazione ermeneutica dell'Apocalisse." **RivB** 28 (1980): 319-335.

See summary in **NTA** 25 (3, '81): #1021.

[1976]
485. Vanni, U. "Un esempio di dialogo liturgico in Ap 1,4-8." **B** 57 (1976): 453-467.

Discusses the liturgical dialogue found in Rev. 1:4-8. See summary also in **NTA** 21 (3, '77): #866.

[1974]
486. Minear, P.S. "The Disciples and the Crowds in the Gospel of Matthew." **ATR** Supp. Series 3 (1974): 28-44.

Suggests that the Greek term *οχλοι* in the Gospel of Matthew and John's Revelation, plays a positive role as objects of Jesus' ministry and are faithful in connection to the faithfulness of the disciples.

[1973]
487. Cassem, N.H. "A Grammatical and Contextual Inventory of the Use of *Κοσμος* in the Johannine Corpus with Some Implications for a Johannine Cosmic Theology." **NTS** 19 (1972-73): 31-91.

Offers a grammatical and contextual inventory (with charts) of the Greek word *Κοσμος* in the Johannine corpus. He finds the term used three times in the Revelation in a positive and neutral sense, suggesting that this may have implications regarding John's cosmic theology and should be studied further. See also 5, H, (40).

[1972]
488. Cain, D.W. "Artistic Contrivance and Religious Communication." **RS** 8 (1972): 29-43.

Discusses and illustrates how artistic contrivance in the Revelation communicates religious form, depth, and richness. Rev. 2-3 reveal the same structure, e.g., Christ-attribute, problem, response, and promise. This contrivance found in Chaps. 2-3 draws from Rev. 1, but also finds ongoing substantiation throughout the book.

489. Trudinger, L.P. " *'o αμην'* (Rev. III:14), and the Case for a Semitic Original of the Apocalypse." **NovT** 14 (1972):277-279.

Examines L. Silberman's note (1963) on the grammar and background of Rev. 3:14, and while agreeing with the suggestion that 3:14 may have a Hebrew antecedent, T. disagrees with the original Semitic document hypothesis. Says that *'o αμην* simply reflects a style of composition and not a translation. See also 4, B.

[1971]
490. Beardslee, W.A. "New Testament Apocalyptic in Recent

Interpretation." **Int** XXV (1971): 419-435.

After a brief review of recent scholarship, B. investigates the language and compositional style of the Revelation, concluding that the dynamic strength of the work is not to be found in its theological argument nor its historical information, but in its "evocative power," which calls Christians to imaginative participation. See also 3, B.

491. Mussies, G. **The Morphology of Koine Greek as Used in the Apocalypse of St. John: A Study in Bilingualism.** "Supplements to N.T. Vol. XXVII." Leiden: E. J. Brill, 1971.

This massive study (386 pp., 32 pp. indexes) indicates that the Koine "morphs" found in the Revelation suggest that the author was in a sense bilingual. After discussing the several cultural "problems" in the book and the history of the study of language and style of the Apocalypse, M. concludes that the great failure in morphology analysis of the Revelation is the missing systematic analysis of the use of tenses, and regarding syntax, a description of word order is also absent. There follows discussions of linguistics, orthography, phonology, morphology, substantives, adjectives, pronouns, and verbs. Concerning the use of verbs in the Revelation, M. concludes that the author's preferences are the present indicative, durative participle, aorist indicative, aorist imperative and infinitive, the future indicative and middle perfective participle. John shows a Semitic vernacular by his involuntary choices of Greek categories. Thus the Semitic color of the verb in the Revelation is mainly stylistic. The shifts of time are attributed to apocalyptic genre. But Rev. 2-3 are not apocalyptic. John probably was influenced by both Hebrew and Aramaic. Cf. also review by Birdsall in **EQ** 45 (1973): 49-53.

[1970]
492. Foerster, W. "Bemerkungen zur Bildersprache der Offenbarung Johannis," in **Verborum Veritas: Festschrift für G. Stählin zu 70. Geburtstag.** O. Böcher and K. Haacker, eds. Wuppertal: Brockhaus, 1970. Pp. 225-236.

Not seen.

493. Minear, P.S. "An Apocalyptic Adjective [*megas*]." **NovT** 12 (1970): 218-222.

Observes that 50 percent of the occurrences of the Greek adjective μεγας in the NT are found in the Revelation. John uses the term to describe the *mysterium tremendum*, i.e., the momentous activity of God toward people and events of the world. See also 3, D.

494. Peterson, E.H. "Apocalypse: The Medium Is the Message." **ThT** 26 (1969): 133-141.

Draws from McLuhan's work in interpreting the book of Revelation as a combination of voices and images. The latter seems to produce an "implosive effect." The ultimate medium for the eschatological message is understood in terms of number, as an extension of tactility, cosmos as the city, with final emphasis on the sense of smell. See also 3, B.

[1969]
495. Younce, D.R. "The Grammar of the Apocalypse." Unpublished Doctoral Dissertation. Dallas, TX: Dallas Theological Seminary, 1969.

Examines the Greek grammar of the Revelation and offers suggestions pertaining to the peculiar literary character of the work.

[1968]
496. Bartina, S. "Un nuevo semitismo en Apocalipsis 14: tierra o ciudad." **EsB** 27 (1968): 347-349.

See summary in **NTA** 14 (3, '70): #973. See also 4, B.

[1967]
497. Mussies, G. "*DYO* in Apocalypse IX 12 and 16." **NT** 9 (1967): 151-154.

Studies Rev. 9 and suggests that the grammar may be problematic for the exegete, especially in vss. 12 and 16. A clue to the numbers is found in the system of Hebrew cardinal numbers and their specific meanings, i.e., the feminine categories have a multiplicative sense. Thus Rev. 9:12 should be translated "a two-fold woe follows." Rev. 9:16 should be rendered "and their number was ten thousand and *times* ten thousand." Hebrew numbers tend to have a qualitative notion, e.g., ten = "the smallest effective group"; thousand = "clan" or "the largest component military group"; and ten thousand = "a group of such units" or "the least number for a complete fighting force." Rev. 9:16 implies an "army of armies." See also 4, B.

[1966]
498. Lancellotti, A. "L'Antico Testamento nell'Apocalisse." **RevB** 14

(1966): 369-384.

See summary in **NTA** 11 (3, '67): # 1147.

499. Stott, W. "A Note on the Word κυριακη in Rev. 1.10." **NTS** 12 (1965-66): 70-75.

Notes that κυριακη 'ημερα in Rev. 1:10 refers to "Sunday," the day of the Lord's Supper, a special day chosen and consecrated for Christ. This interpretation is confirmed by the early church who expected the return of Christ on Sunday. See also 4, B and 5, H, (20).

[1965]
500. Ozanne, C.G. "The Language of the Apocalypse." **TyHB** 16 (1965): 3-9.

Offers a critical discussion of the unique language and grammar of John's Revelation.

[1963]
501. Silberman, L.H. "Farewell to 'ο αμην (A Note on Rev. 3:14)." **JBL** 82 (1963): 213-215.

Notes an alternative interpretation of the phrase 'ο αμην based on a study of a midrash on *Bereshith Rabbah*. Concludes that αμην is a faulty translation of the Hebrew taken from Proverbs, which, in the Revelation, refers to Christ as God's advisor in creation. See also 4, B.

[1962]
502. Robb, J.D. "'ο ερχομενος ('Who Is to Come' -- N.E.B.) [Rev. 1:4, 8; 4:8]." **ET** 73 (1961-62): 338-339.

Says that the best translation of the phrase 'ο ερχομενος is "He who is coming." This translation is based upon the NT notion that the living Christ is always coming and a "constant happening" to His followers, and not some far-off future, divine event. See also 4, B.

[1959]
503. Torrey, C.C. **The Apocalypse of John.** New Haven, CT: Yale University Press, 1959.

Postulates that the Revelation is a poor Greek translation of an Aramaic original. While interacting with contemporary opinions on the origins of the final Greek text, T. argues from John's grammatical peculiarities (e.g., use of the indefinite, third-person plural of the verb in place of the passive; the constant use of εχω denoting simple possession; the frequent preference for the Aramaic participle) that the translator "faithfully" translated the Aramaic original. Concludes that a possible date for the writing of the Revelation may be A.D. 68. The book concludes with critical notes and the author's own translation. See also 1, B.

[1956]
504. Schilling, F.A. "Amen, I Say to You [Rev. 3:14]." **ATR** 38 (1956): 175-181.

Concludes the article by insisting that the use of "amen" in Rev. 3:14, 1) is taken from the literary tradition of Is. 65:16, and 2) asserts the ultimate judgment authority of Christ. See also 4, B.

[1953]
505. Burns, A.L. "Two Words for 'Time' in the New Testament." **ABR** 3 (1953): 7-22.

Offers a brief introductory analysis of the use of the Greek terms χρονος and καιρος in the NT. Suggests that, in John's Revelation, the writer did not try to make the normal Greek distinctions as in the rest of the NT, but rather used the terms in a fluid and overlapping sense. See also 5, H, (14).

[1952]
506. Brewer, R.R. "Revelation 4:6 and Translations Thereof." **JBL** 71 (1952): 227-231.

Studies Rev. 4:6 and offers that the influence of Greek drama must be seen in the text, especially in reference to the translation of the phrase εν μεσω. See also 4, B.

[1951]
507. Cope, G. "'The World' -- in the New Testament." **HibJ** 49 (1950-51): 264-270.

Examines the use of the term κοσμος in the NT and analyzes various meanings in different contexts. Concludes that in the Revelation, John uses the term to refer both to earth in a physical sense and to the eternal Kingdom of God. See also 5, H, (40).

[1948]
508. Gaechter, P. "The Role of Memory in the Making of the Apocalypse." **TS** 9 (1948): 419-452.

Illustrates the literary technique of John's disciple in editing the Revelation by suggesting (with Charles) that the disciple/editor depended entirely on his memory in hearing John speaking to audiences concerning his visions. The deficiencies and inconsistencies of the text (omissions, doublets, faulty grammar, etc.) are due mainly, but not totally, to the faulty memory and poor literary technique of the editor. See also 3, E.

509. Marcus, R. "Acrostics in the Hellenistic and Roman Periods." **JNES** 6 (2,1947): 109-115.

Posits the theory that the literary background to the Book of Revelation is a Hebrew composition arranged in the form of an alphabetic acrostic of twenty-two strophes/sections. A thesis is then developed in an attempt to support the wider usage of acrostics in general didactic, liturgical, oracular, and Gnostic literature of the period.

[1945]
510. Bretscher, P.M. "Syntactical Peculiarities in Revelation." **CTM** 16 (1945): 95-105.

In nine sections, B. presents a thorough discussion of John's peculiar writing style without classifying the oddities. Notes: I. The violation of concord (case, gender, number, person; e.g., 1:5; 2:20; 3:12; etc.). II. The resumptive pronoun (e.g., 3:8; 6:4). III. The resolution of the participle in one of the oblique cases (e.g., 1:5-6, 17-18; 2:2). Concludes that John broke traditional rules of grammar and, rightly, gave priority to Aramaic idiom, use of the LXX, and poetic freedom.

511. Gillet, L. "Amen. (Rev. 3:4)." **ET** 56 (1945): 134-136.

Studies the language of Rev. 3:4 and concludes that the term "Amen" as used by John suggested to the early church the notion of "One True Witness."

[1944]
512. Walvoord, J.F. "New Testament Words for the Lord's Coming." **BibSac** 101 (1944): 283-289.

Defines, interprets, and classifies doctrinal words such as παρουσια, αποκαλυψις, and επιθανεια. Suggests that none of the words seem to refer specifically to the Second Coming of Christ in a technical sense.

[1943]
513. Furfey, P.H. "Πλουσιος and Cognates in the New Testament." **CBQ** 5 (1943): 243-263.

Investigates the NT doctrine of "wealth" and concludes that material riches in general and the rich in particular are dangerous and potentially evil for those involved. Differentiates between the Greek notion of the πλουσιος, as a classification based on a source of income and the English idea of the "rich" as possessing great wealth. Passages in the Revelation (e.g., Chaps. 6 and 18) are then connected to the theme. See also 5, H, (28).

514. Lund, N.W. "The Significance of Chiasmus for Interpretation." **CQ** 20 (1943): 105-123.

Demonstrates the chiasmus style in the NT and in Rev. 18, where lists are given. Such passages are particularly meaningful in liturgical usage.

[1942]
515. Simpson, E.K. "The Apostle John's Diction." **EQ** 14 (1942): 81-87.

Points out the unique features of John's diction, especially the chiasmus structure and style, which compares favorably with I John.

[1941]
516. Torrey, C.C. "The Language and Date of the Apocalypse" in **Documents of the Primitive Church.**

Insists that the book is a unity from three sources: the OT, current eschatology, and the writer's creative mind. The book is both Jewish and Christian and written ca. A.D. 68. The original language was Aramaic, but was translated into Greek and imitates Semitic grammar. The work includes forty-five pages of critical notes on the text. See also 2, E and 2, G.

[1928]
517. Scott, R.B.Y. **The Original Language of the Apocalypse.** Toronto: University of Toronto Press, 1928.

Argues for the Revelation being a translation from Hebrew or Aramaic with minor editorial changes in the final Greek form of the text.

D. LITERARY AND MOTIF RELATIONSHIPS (EXTRABIBLICAL, BIBLICAL TRADITIONS)

[1990]
518. Fekkes, J. "'His Bride Has Prepared Herself': Revelation 19-21 and Isaian Nuptial Imagery." **JBL** 109 (1990): 269-287.

Shows the dependence of Rev. 19:7-8; 21:2b on Is. 61:10 and Rev. 21:18-21 on Is. 54:11-12. The vision of the bride develops in three stages: 1) Final planning and preparation; 2) Debut and covenant promise; 3) Description of the bride's dress.

519. Hall, R.G. "Living Creatures in the Midst of the Throne: Another Look at Revelation 4.6." **NTS** 36 (1990): 609-613.

Links the phrase "$εν μεσω του θρονου$" (Rev. 4:6) to Jewish tradition (cf. Josephus, Pirqe Rabbi Eliezer, and Shir Rabbah) and image of the heavenly throne on the ark. The four living creatures are seen as an integral part of the throne, as components, and not as occupants. Thus 5:6, "$εν μεσω του θρονου και των τεσσαρων ζωων$," is understood as a reference to the Lamb on the throne. See also 4, B.

520. Morton, R. "The 'One Like a Son of Man' in Daniel 7:8-13 Reconsidered in Revelation 1:13-18." **Kar** 5 (1990): 23-27.

Maintains the traditional view that John used the language of Dan. 7:8-13 (and 10:5-7) but changed it in Rev. 1:13-18 to identify Jesus as the heavenly and exalted resurrected One. See also 5, C.

521. Smith, C.R. "The Portrayal of the Church as the New Israel in the Names and Order of the Tribes in Revelation 7.5-8." **JSNT** 39 (1990): 111-118.

Observes that the peculiar order and content of the list of the twelve tribes in Rev. 7:5-8 indicates John's deliberate desire to portray the Church as the new Israel. Concludes: 1) Judah is made head of the list because Jesus descended from that tribe; 2) The advancement of the handmaid Zilpah's sons suggests the new place of the Gentiles in the new covenant; 3) Reuben represents the faithful Israelites; 4) The remaining "non-handmaid" groups are typical of those who will be saved through the Church. See also 4, B and 5, F.

[1989]
522. Ruiz, J.-P. **Ezekiel in the Apocalypse: The Transformation of Prophetic Language in Revelation 16:17-19:10.** "European University Studies, Series 23: Theology 376." Frankfurt--Bern--New York--Paris: Lang, 1989.

This revised dissertation asserts that the unity of the text of Revelation 16:17-19:10 is dependent upon a consistent metaphoric rereading of OT literature (especially Ezekiel) in order to get a meaningful picture of "Babylon the Great" in a true prophetic sense. Discusses the research on John's use of the OT, his hermeneutical methodology respecting the OT text, and, after a thorough exegesis of the passage, concludes with a synthesis of the work of John in his use of the prophetic material.

523. Trevett, C. "The Other Letters to the Churches of Asia: Apocalypse and Ignatius of Antioch." **JSNT** 37 (1989): 117-135.

Suggests that Ignatius and John in the Revelation were both influenced by the same factors of situation, language, and thought of the Asian Christians and Christianity. Contrasts and compares the letters of Ignatius to the Revelation, noting several points of contact, e.g., grammatical parallels, ideas of authority, and discontent.

524.Ulfgard, H. **Feast and Future. Revelation 7:9-17 and the Feast of Tabernacles.** "Coniectanea Biblica, N.T. Series 22." Stockholm; Almqvist & Wiksell, 1989.

This published doctoral disssertation surveys modern scholarly views of the Feast of Tabernacles in Rev. 7:9-17 and examines the literary context. The specific details of the passage are then compared to the Jewish celebration of Tabernacles at the time of the second Temple according to the traditions of the Mishna, pre-A.D. 100 writings, postbiblical literature, and archaeological evidence. Concludes that it is the pattern of the exodus tradition seen in the picture of Christian experience that holds together the aspects of the feast and the future in Rev. 7:9-17. See also 5, H, (9).

[1988]
525. Bauckham, R. "The Book of Revelation as a Christian War Scroll." **Neo** 22 (1988): 17-40.

Argues that 1QM offers evidence for the fact that there may have been a kind of militant messianic thinking operating in Jewish circles during the writing of the Revelation and that John may have been aware of it. After exegeting several passages (Rev. 5:5-6; 7:2-14; 14:1-5), B. demonstrates that John used the language of the holy war but adapted it to fit his nonmilitary purpose, viz., to show how evil is overcome. Although John states that humans do participate in the eschatological war, and this participation is described in holy-war terms, nevertheless the effect of it all is understood in terms of the "faithful witness," who participates to the death. See also 5, H, (37).

526. Downing, F.G. "Pliny's Prosecutions of Christians: Revelation and I Peter." **JSNT** 34 (1988): 105-123.

Using the correspondence between Pliny and Emperor Trajan, D. suggests that there was no great legal action against Christians in Asia Minor at the time of the writing of Revelation and I Peter. Therefore John was apparently anticipating *future* trouble and persecution for the Church.

527. Draper, J.A. "The twelve apostles as foundation stones of the heavenly Jerusalem and the foundation of the Qumran community." **Neo** 22 (1988): 41-63.

Suggests that the image of the twelve apostles as foundation stones in Rev. 21:14 has been influenced by the Qumran writings (see IQS 8:1-16; 9:3-7; 11:7-9; 4QpIsa^d). Concludes that John shared important themes with Qumran, but altered his sources at a number of points. See also 2, F.

528. Kreitzer, L. "Hadrian and the Nero *Redivivus* Myth." **ZNW** 79 (Heft 1/2, 88): 92-115.

Reviews some of the scholarly interpretations of the "myth," traces its historical and literary origins and development. Specific connections are established with the Sibylline Oracles (5, 8, and 12). Concludes that the myth was applied to certain historical situations, and Nero and Hadrian were linked as wicked and evil emperors. See also 5, H, (23).

529. Paulien, J. "Elusive Allusions: The Problematic Use of the Old Testament in Revelation." **BRes** 33 (1988): 37-53.

Probing the use of the OT by John, P. suggests that a major reason for disagreement in listing OT references is the inability of scholars to distinguish clearly between "allusions" and "echoes." Direct allusions must be determined by connecting the text of Revelation, the verbal motif and structural parallels to antecedent writings (OT, I Enoch, Jubilees) and then considering the ones John may have used. Allusions should be classified as 1) certain, 2) probable, 3) possible, 4) uncertain, and 5) nonexistent.

530. Poucouta, P. "La mission prophétique de l'Église dans l'Apocalypse johannique." **NRT** 110 (1988): 38-57.

Argues that the Jewish menorah (from the OT and other Jewish literature) stands behind the imagery of the lampstand (Rev. 1-3) and the two witnesses (Rev. 11:1-13). The lampstand symbolism describes the mission of the Church as it reflects the light of God's presence and the shining of the Lamb throughout history. See also 5, H, (22) and (31).

531. Skiadaresis, J. "Γενεση και Αποκαλυψη (Genesis and Apocalypse). **DBL** 17 (1, 1988): 48-60; (2, 1989):68-86.

This revised thesis (originally, "*The Hymns of the Apocalypse of John*") discusses the literary and thematic connections between Gen. 1-3 and John's Apocalypse, focusing on the relative schema "creation-history-eschata." Concludes that John's interpretation of the paradise, fall, renewal, and restoration motifs in Genesis was influenced by Christ and church life experiences.

[1987]
532. Feuillet, A. "Le festin des noces de l'agneau et ses anticipations." **EsV** 97 (87): 353-362.

Studies the marriage of the Lamb motif in Rev. 19:7, 9 and concludes that there are close verbal and thematic connections with the Gospel of John (see esp. Jn. 1:29, 36; 3:29). The motif is anticipated by the author in earlier sections of the book, e.g., Rev. 3:20; 7:9-17; etc.

533. Smalley, S. "John's Revelation and John's Community." **BJRL** 69 (1987): 549-571.

Investigates the relationship between the Revelation and the Gospel of John under the categories ethos, theology, tradition, language, and structure. Suggests that the Revelation belongs to the Johannine corpus as an early writing (70s) predating the Gospel and the epistles.

[1986]
534. Allison, D.C. "4Q 403 fragm. 1, col. I, 38-46 and the Revelation to John." **RQum** 12 (1986): 409-414.

Connects the Qumran fragment, which describes parts of the temple (pillars, etc.) as living beings joined in song with the heavenly hosts praising God, with Rev. 3:12 and 9:13-14 (see also I Pet. 2:4-5) and other Jewish and Christian texts that refer to the angelic destiny of the faithful. The notion of a "living" temple in Qumran helps to explain the development of the NT idea of the Church as the Temple of God.

535. Altink, W. "Theological Motives for the Use of I Chronicles 16:8-36 as Background for Revelation 14:6-7." **AUSS** 24 (1986): 211-221.

Continuing his research of 1984, A. argues for I Chr. 16:8-36 as background to Rev. 14:6-7 based on the common literary elements of the ark of the covenant (including covenant formulary), mercy seat, and Decalogue.

536. Beale, G.K. "A Reconsideration of the Text of Dan. in the Apocalypse." **B** 67 (1986): 539-543.

Studies the use of Daniel in the Revelation and concludes that John used Theodotion's Greek text of Daniel. However, five passages seem to be based on the older LXX (cf. 17:12, 14; 14:7-8; 13:5 and 1:13-14). There are no direct quotations from Daniel in the Revelation.

537. Charlesworth, J.H. "The Jewish Roots of Christology: The Discovery of the Hypostatic Voice." **SJT** 39 (1986): 19-41.

Examines the use of the phrase "the Voice" in old and contemporary Jewish and Christian apocalyptic literature and concludes that the roots of Christology are discovered in Jewish soil. The statement in Rev. 1:12, "And I turned around to see the Voice who spoke with me" was meant to be taken literally. Apparently, prior to A. D. 100 the Jews believed in the existence of a heavenly being called "the Voice." Discusses briefly the development of the idea, concluding that John reminted this tradition to fit into his understanding of Christian christology. All essential creatures are joined into one; Sophia, Logos, Memra, the Bath Qol and the Voice proclaim the fact that God has spoken. He has moved mankind to offer freedom to those trapped in slavery. See also 5, C.

538. Georgi, D. "Who is the True Prophet?" **HTR** 79 (1986): 100-126.

Compares the Revelation's eschatological program to the text of *Carmen Saeculare* by Horace, first, by describing the latter's theological, religious, political, and social dimensions and then, secondly, by demonstrating the tension between John and the prophets of Caesar's religion, viz., Horace and Virgil. John's predictions of the future decline of Rome prove to be superior to Horace. Horace's prediction of the emerging rural life, however, may have been closer to the truth of his times. See also 5, H, (31).

539. Muse, R.L. "Revelation 2-3: A Critical Analysis of Seven Prophetic Messages." **JETS** 29, 2 (1986): 147-161.

Investigates the form and literary history of Rev. 1-3, along with the motif/thematic connections with Rev. 4-22 and concludes that the book is a unity. Rev. 2-3 are not "letters," as traditionally accepted, but rather "prophetic" judgment messages of salvation and condemnation, similar to the prophetic speech forms of Amos. Chaps. 1-3 function in the context of 4-22 as 1) *general* hermeneutical preparation for Christian and Church suffering persecution in the first century and 2) *specific* warnings of judgment and promise of salvation for the Church immediately before the Parousia of Christ, the Son of Man. See also 2, H and 5, H, (31).

540. Trudinger, P. "The Apocalypse and the Palestinian Targum." **BTB** 16 (1986): 78-79.

Builds on Diaz's study referred to by J. R. Macho (1963) regarding the presence of a Palestinian Targum tradition in the NT. Examines six passages from the Revelation (1:4, 6; 2:11, 14; 7:14; 9:13a; 17:14) and argues that, although it is difficult to establish a definite proof of connection between the Revelation and the Palestinian Targum, it is appropriate to suggest that John knew of a tradition behind that Targum. Furthermore, it appears that John studied the law ("learned his Torah") within a Palestinian synagogue milieu.

[1985]
541. Beale, G.K. "The Origin of the Title 'King of Kings and Lord of Lords' in Revelation 17.14." **NTS** 31 (1985): 618-620.

Argues that the christological title in Rev. 17:14 had its antecedents in the title found in Dan. 4:37 (LXX). Suggests further that the humiliation of the King of Babylon by God in Dan. 4 may serve as a typological prophecy for God's humbling of the kings on earth during the time of John. See also 5, C.

542. ————. "The Use of Daniel in the Synoptic eschatological discourse and in the book of Revelation" in **The Jesus Tradition outside the Gospels.** "Gospel Perspectives, Vol. 5." D. Wenham, ed. Sheffield, Eng.: Sheffield Press, 1985. Pp. 129-153.

Investigates the use of the literary and theological traditions of Daniel in the composition of the eschatological discourse in the Gospels and the Revelation of John. See also review in **ET** 97 (1985):151.

543. Berger, P.R. "Kollyrium für die blinden Augen, Apk. 3:18." **NovT** 27 (1985): 174-195.

Studies the key Latin, Greek, Hebrew, and Aramaic terms connected to Rev. 3:18 and the admonition for the church in Laodicea to buy "salve" (κολλυριον) in order to heal its blindness. Further investigates relevant evidence from Jewish literature and Scripture (cf. Jer. 4:30; Mk. 8:23; Jn. 9:6, 11, 15) and concludes with a statement of the possible medicinal effects of such a procedure.

544. Dumbrell, W.J. **The End of the Beginning. Revelation 21-22 and the Old Testament.** Australia: Lancer Books. Grand Rapids, MI: Baker Book House, 1985.

Treats the conclusion of the book of Revelation (Chaps. 21-22) under five "idea" headings: "New Jerusalem," New Temple," New Covenant," "New Israel," and "New Creation," connects them to OT literature, and follows them through the other NT writings. Uses the "biblical theology" method to demonstrate how the whole Bible is moving and growing in an eschatological sense. Concludes that the schema, Creation -- the Renewal of Creation (Redemption) -- the New Creation, are to be seen as the axis for all biblical theology. See also 4, B.

545. Hurtado, L.W. "Revelation 4-5 in the Light of Jewish Apocalyptic Analogies." **JSNT** 25 (1985): 105-124.

Critiques and rejects Rowland's thesis regarding the lack of Christian influence in the Book of Revelation in general and Rev. 4 in particular. After considering a number of Jewish apocalyptic analogies, H. suggests that the vision of Rev. 4 reflects a strong Christian faith on the part of John. The central description of the twenty-four elders plus the controlling themes of God's sovereignty, the worship of His majesty, the relationship between God's throne and His elect people, and the triumph

132   *The Book of Revelation*

of the Christ the Lamb all argue for a Christian adaption of the traditional material. See also 5, H, (41).

546. Rowland, C. "A Man Clothed in Linen. Daniel 10.6 ff. and Jewish Angelology." **JSNT** 24 (1985): 99-110.

Discusses the descriptions of Christ in Rev. 1:13-16, Jaoel in the Apoc. of Abraham 11, and Michael in Joseph and Aseneth 14 in light of Dan. 10:5-6, and concludes: 1) that all three passages refer to and interpret Dan. 10:5-6 and 2) that Dan. 10:5-6 is to be linked with Dan. 7:13 through the LXX phrase 'ως παλαιος 'ημερων.

547. Vogelgesang, J.M. "The Interpretation of Ezekiel in the Book of Revelation." Unpublished Doctoral Dissertation. Harvard University. Ann Arbor, MI: University Microfilms, Inc., 1985.

Studies the interpretation of Ezekiel, which provides a key to a general understanding of the book. Argues that John probably used Ezekiel as a model (*Vorlage*) for his work; but he gives a radical reinterpretation of Ezekiel's restoration program. Revelation is an "anti-apocalyptic" book, i.e., it is not intentionally esoteric, but is created to be purposely accessible to the reader. The Christ event gives the motive for John's critical hermeneutical principle. It, therefore, remains a "sealed book" to many today only because of its usual interpretation as a normal apocalypse. It is not intended to be an apocalypse. See also 1, C, (1); 2, I and 3, B.

[1984]
548. Altink, W. "I Chronicles 16:8-36 as Literary Source for Revelation 14:6-7." **AUSS** 22 (1984): 187-196.

Analyzes and interprets the literary connections between David's psalm of praise in I Chr. 16 and the angel's proclamation in Rev. 14:6-7 respecting the linguistic, contextual, and theological evidence.

549. Beale, G.K. **The Use of Daniel in Jewish Apocalyptic Literature and in the Revelation of St. John.** Lanham, MD: University Press of America, 1984.

This 1980 dissertation examines the relationship between Daniel, the Revelation, and Jewish apocalyptic literature in four chapters and suggests that Daniel was used in Qumran literature, I Enoch, The Testament of Joseph, IV Ezra, II Baruch, and also in Rev. 1:4-5, and

Chaps.13 and 17. Concludes that John may have been familiar with both Jewish and Christian literary traditions of Daniel. The influence of Daniel on the Revelation may be seen primarily in the book's structure and theology, e.g., the structural connection with Dan.'s allusions and the use of a Danielic midrash of Mark 13, in addition to the common themes shared. Concludes that the Book of Daniel is the most important influence on the formation of the thought and structure of the Revelation. See also 3, E.

550. ————. "The Influence of Daniel Upon the Structure and Theology of John's Apocalypse." **JETS** 27 (1984): 413-424.

Suggests that OT Daniel influenced Qumran writings (esp. I Enoch, IV Ezra, II Baruch) and John's Revelation. Regarding the latter, the influence may be seen primarily in the structure and theology of the work.

551. Feuillet, A. "La Femme vêtue du soleil (Ap 12) et la glorification de l'Epouse du Cantique des Cantiques (6, 10). Réflexions sur le progrès dans l'interprétation de l'Apocalypse et du Cantique des Cantiques." **NovT** 59 (1984): 36-67.

Focuses attention on "the woman clothed with the sun" in Rev. 12:1 in two parts: Identifies the woman as Mary the mother of Jesus and the mother of the new people of the future age of grace. This is tied into Is. 7:14 and Lk. 1:26-38. Lastly, the study suggests that the mystical bride of God described in Cant. 6:10 is the OT antecedent to the passage. See also 3, F.

552. Strand, K.A. "An Overlooked Old-Testament Background to Revelation 11:1." **AUSS** 22 (1984): 317-325.

Studies Rev. 11:1 in the light of Zech. 2:1-5, Ez. 40-48 and Lev. 16 and concludes that although there is the measuring symbolism common to Rev. 11, Zech. 2, and Ez. 40-48, Rev. 11:1 appears to be closer to Lev. 16, which describes a measuring of altar and worshippers as well as the temple.

[1983]
553. Bauckham, R. "Synoptic Parousia Parables Again." **NTS** 29 (1983): 129-134.

Observes Parousia parable allusions in several extrabiblical sources: Ascen. of Is. 4:16; Sibyl. Or. 2:177-183; Symposium (Methodius); Haer.

69.44.1 (Epiphanius); and Epistle of the Apostles 43. Concludes that these allusions suggest a process he terms "deparabolization" and the history of the parabolic tradition. See also 4, B and 5, G, (2).

554. Gordon, R.P. "Loricate Locusts in the Targum to Nahum iii 17 and Revelation ix 9." **VT** 33 (1983): 338-339.

Notes that in Targum of Nahum 3:17 the Aramaic expands the original Hebrew to read, "Behold, your plates gleam like the locust." The passage compares the scaled armor of the Assyrian warriors to the scaled thoraces of the locust. John borrows the same idea in Rev. 9:9, where he describes the demonic locusts as having "breastplates like breastplates of iron."

555. Popkes, W. "Die Funktion der Sendschreiben in der Johannes-Apokalypse. Zugleich ein Beitrag zur Spätgeschichte der neutestamentlichen Gleichnisse." **ZNW** 74 (1983): 90-107.

Studies the letters to the seven churches in Rev. 2-3 and suggests that they function as hermeneutical preparation for the later apocalyptic vision in Rev. 4-22. A key to this suggestion lies in the call to "hear" (Cf. 2:7, 11, 17, 19: 3:6, 13, 22), which is rooted in apocalyptic wisdom and connects specifically to the Markan and Matthean parable tradition. Argues finally that this link between traditions helps to establish the historical-apocalyptic character of the Revelation itself as well as the later stages of the parable tradition.

[1982]
556. Geyser, A. "The Twelve Tribes in Revelation: Judean and Judeo-Christian Apocalypticism." **NTS** 28 (1982): 388-399.

Suggests that the notion of the twelve tribes is an important symbol for cosmic fulfillment and completion in the Revelation. The dominant concern of the author John is to depict a twelve-tribe kingdom restored in a renewed and purified Jerusalem under the rule of the Lion of Judah, the Root of David (Rev. 5:5; 22:16). This emphasis on the twelve-tribe kingdom reflects the faith and mind of the Judean church (See James, I Peter, Q, M, Mark's source) but contrasts the minds of Paul, the author of the fourth gospel and Acts. See also 3, E and F.

557. Ozanne, C.G. **The Fourth Gentile Kingdom (in Daniel and Revelation).** Worthing, 1982.

See summary in **NTA** 29, #216.

558. Strand, K.A. "The Two Olive Trees of Zechariah 4 and Revelation 11." **AUSS** 20 (1982): 257-261.

Argues that one lampstand of Zech. 4 refers to Zerubbabel, but Rev. 11:4 interprets the two lampstands to refer to God's word in a twofold manner: 1) the OT prophetic forecast and 2) the NT confirmatory proclamation. Thus John finds relevance in the OT image through his varied, symbolic use of the OT text. See also 3, F and 5, H, (31).

[1981]
559. Böcher, O. "Johanneisches in der Apokalypse des Johannes." **NTS** 27 (1981): 310-321.

Identifies similarities and differences between the Revelation of John and the other Johannine writings. Similarities are related to the world, God, Christology, good and evil spirits, ecclesiology, anthropology, ethics, and eschatology. Differences are noticed in the concepts of light/darkness, Logos, lamb/ram, bride/bridegroom, and mana. Concludes that the writings all reflect usage of common prophetic-apocalyptic and Jewish-Christian traditions. The Book of Revelation preserved these faithfully; but the Evangelist changed the traditions by demythologizing, intellectualizing, and gnosticizing.

560. Hanhart, K. "The Four Beasts of Daniel's Vision in the Night in the Light of Rev. 13.2." **NTS** 27 (1981): 576-583.

Suggests that because of the clue in Rev. 13:2, that the leopard of Dan. 7:6 represents Rome, the four beasts in Dan. 7 symbolize four contemporaneous kingdoms: 1) Lion=Egypt, 2) Bear=Persia, 3) Leopard=Rome, 4) Anonymous beast (elephant?)=Syria. See also 3, F and 4, B.

561. Manns, F. "Traces d'une Haggadah pascale chrétienne dans l'Apocalypse de Jean?" **An** 56 (1981): 265-295.

Reviews the scholarly discussion regarding the origin of a Passover Haggadah, noting that some of the traditions antedate A. D. 70, and suggesting that the presence of I Cor. 5:7-8 and Melito's "Paschal Homily" argue for the existence of a Christian Passover Haggadah. These writings present a christological interpretation of Passover symbols and hope for the return of the Messiah. Contends that traces of Christian Passover Haggadah are to be found in Rev. 4-5 and a comparison with the Palestinian version of the Jewish Passover Haggadah indicates several thematic connections, e.g., the gift of the Law, the power of the King of Kings, the covenant, the new song, etc. However, Rev. 4-5 remains theologically Christian and different from the Palestinian tradition. See also 4, B.

562. Morgen, M. "Apocalypse 12, un targum de l'Ancien Testament." **FV** 80 (1981): 63-74.

Suggests that a clue to the composition of Rev. 12 and its use of the OT may be discovered in the Pentateuchal Targums. In a two-part study M. first investigates the OT presentations of the dragon-serpent (ct. Gen. 3) and the woman-Israel images. Next, he illustrates how the OT Targums clarify the meaning of Rev. 12 by studying Gen. 3 and Ex. 7 in terms of the serpent image and its connection to the woman-Israel and nourishment themes. See also 4, B.

[1980]
563. Beale, G.K. "The Danielic Background for Revelation 13:18 and 17:9." **TyB** 31 (1980): 173-170.

Discusses Daniel's eschatology in Dan. 2, 9, 11, 12 as background to understanding the νους and σοφια terms in Rev. 13:18 and 17:9. John identified Christians as the Danielic *maskilim* who were being tempted by flatterers. See also 4, B.

564. McNeil, B. "Revelation 12, 5 and the History of Joseph the Carpenter." **Mar** 42 (1980): 126-128.

Criticizes the insufficiency of Bagatti's study (1978), **History of Joseph the Carpenter**, and argued for a second-century interpretation of the woman in Rev. 12:1-6 as Mary. Concludes that both works stand within a tradition that utilized the OT. See also 2, H.

565. Page, S.H.T. "Revelation 20 and Pauline Eschatology." **JETS** 23 (1980): 31-43.

Argues for a literary and imagery connection between Rev. 20 and some of the major features of Paul's eschatological teaching. In particular, there is a strong agreement between Rev. 20:4 regarding the millennium period between the first and second advents, the coming to life, and Paul's understanding of the new birth of Christian initiation. See also 4, B and 5, G, (1).

566. Parker, H.M. "The Scripture of the Author of the Revelation of John." **IR** 37 (1980): 35-51.

Discusses the seven seals cycle (Rev. 6:1-8:5) from a literary perspective and suggests that Scripture of the community that created the Revelation of John included numerous apocalyptic writings, as well as works from the Apocrypha and Pseudepigrapha. References to the noncanonical writings may be categorized as follows: Doctrinal, Supportive, and Interpretative. See also 2, H and 4, B.

567. Rowland, C. "The Vision of the Risen Christ in Rev. 1:13ff.: The Debt of an Early Christology to an Aspect of Jewish Angelology." **JTS** 31 (1980): 1-11.

Suggests that parts of the "christophany" vision are borrowed from the angelology tradition of Dan. 10:5-6, which has influenced a number of other biblical texts. Behind Rev. 1:13ff. is also a theological history connected to the call-vision of Ezekiel. This is seen especially in the trend in Jewish thought that separated the human figure from the *merkabah* in Ez. 8:2. The vision is very primitive in content. See also 5, C and H, (1).

[1979]
568. Collins, A.Y. "The Early Christian Apocalypses" in **Apocalypse: The Morphology of a Genre.** J. J. Collins, ed. Semeia 14. Missoula, MT: Scholars Press, 1979. Pp. 61-121.

This "definitional-composite" study centers on "the heavenly journey" as a primary characteristic of the apocalypse genre and concludes that the Revelation of John is an apocalypse. See also III, B.

569. Cortes, E. "Una interpretación judía de Cant 5,2 en Ap 3,19b-20." **RevCT** 4 (1979): 239-258.

See summary in **NTA** 25 (3, '81): 1026.

570. Hauret, C. "Ève transfiguré. De la Genèse à l'Apocalypse." **RHPR** 59 (1979): 327-339.

Observes that Rev. 12:1-17 is a midrashic comment on Gen. 3:15 and a statement concerning original woman emerging as the eschatological woman. Eve transfigured suggests the paradox of humanity -- triumphant in struggle and suffering. This is all accomplished through the child who conquers the "serpent-dragon" and his accomplices. Concludes that Gen.

3:15, John 19:25-27, and Rev. 12:1-17 form the triptych of a *speculum humanae salvationis*. See 4, B and 5, H, (39).

[1978]
571. Van der Waal, C. "The last book of the Bible and the Jewish Apocalypses." **Neo** 12 (1978): 111-132.

Based on an interpretation of Rev. 11:8, W. contends that the Revelation was not like the traditional nationalistic Jewish apocalypses, but was really concerned with the prophesy of the fall of Jerusalem ("the great city") as the center of the Jewish world. John used traditional Jewish symbols against the synagogue, noting that "Babylon" was the old city of the covenant, viz., Jerusalem and not Rome. See also 3, F and 5, H, (10).

[1977]
572. Bauckham, R. "Synoptic Parousia Parables and the Apocalypse." **NTS** 23 (1977): 162-176.

Analyzes the sayings of Rev. 3:3, 20; and 16:15, and suggests that they are John's attempt at metaphoric enrichment rather than creative imagination respecting the parables of watching servants and the thief (cf. Lk. 12:35-40). B. says that the sayings are a part of a process called "deparabolization," which means they are the author's attempt to use Jesus' parabolic imagery in ordinary Christian discourse, apart from its original parabolic context. In Rev. 3:3, etc., the process takes the shape of "I" sayings by Jesus. B. concludes that the effect of the interaction between the Church's paranesis and its tradition of Jesus' sayings in the synoptics is to be understood as modification rather than formulation. See also 4, B and 5, G, (2).

573. ———. "The Eschatological Earthquake in the Apocalypse of John." **NovT** 19 (1977): 224-233.

Maintains that the earthquakes in the Revelation reflect John's use of the OT tradition in order to stress the coming of God in judgment. In at least three instances (cf. 18:5; 11:19; 16:18; and perhaps 4:5) there is a clear allusion to the theophany at Mt. Sinai. Other references suggest the apocalyptic future, which includes not only judgment descriptions (like the Day of the Lord), but also pictures of the vindication of God's people. Rev. 20:11 appears to include a reference to the destruction of the old and creation of the new cosmos. See also 5, F and G, (3).

574. Fiorenza, E.S. "The Quest for the Johannine School: The Apocalypse and the Fourth Gospel." **NTS** 23 (1977): 402-427.

Analyzes the linguistic and theological relationship between the Apocalypse and the Revelation of John and suggests that the evidence does not support the common Johannine-school hypothesis in terms of authorship. Concludes that the author of Revelation probably was the leader of a prophetic-apocalyptic school that reflected those traditions; but he also had access to and dialogued with the Johannine -- and, in particular, the Pauline -- school traditions. See also 3, C and 5, H, (31).

575. Vivian, A. "Gog e Magog nella tradizione biblica, ebraica e cristiana." **RivB** 25 (1977): 389-421.

See summary in **NTA** 23 (2, '79): #615.

[1976]
576. Aus, R.D. "The Revelance of Isaiah 66:7 to Revelation 12 and 2 Thessalonians 1." **ZNTW** 67 (1976): 252-268.

Argues that Rev. 12:2, 5-6 is an illusion to Is. 66:7 and the messianic interpretation is directed to the context of the persecuted church for their encouragement. Jewish antecedents found in the writings Genesis Rabbah (85), Leviticus Rabbah (14:9), and Tg. Ps.-Jonathan on Is. 66:7 connect to the Revelation, especially with the Hebrew (cf. *hbl*, "pain") and the messianic woes. (2 Thes.1 also shows several possible allusions to Is. 66:7.)

577. Feuillet, A."Quelques énigmes des chapitres 4 à 7 de l'Apocalypse. Suggestions pour l'interpretation du langage imagé de la révélation johannique." **EsV** 86 (1976):455-459, 471-479.

Identifies some of the enigmatic figures in Rev. 4-7: 1) The twenty-four elders in Rev. 4:4 are OT saints and not angels; 2) The first rider of 6:2 is traditional divine judgment (war, famine, pestilence); 3) The 144,000 of Rev. 7:4-8 are the remnant of Israel who are sealed to distinguish them from the unbelieving synagogue. See also 3, E; 4 B and 5, G, (1).

578. Jenkins, F. **The Old Testament in the Book of Revelation.** Grand Rapids, MI: Baker, 1976.

Studies the Revelation in order to determine the frequency of John's use of the OT and how the images and symbols of the OT may provide the necessary material for doing a proper exegesis of the book. After a brief foreword by H. Hailey, J. shapes his work around chapters that treat 1) The OT background of the Revelation; 2) The place of Revelation in apocalyptic literature; 3) The OT books used most often in the Revelation; etc. Concludes that John creatively adapted OT words and images to fit his own time and purpose. See also 3, F.

579. Marconcini, B. "L'utilizzazione del T. M. nelle citazioni isaiane dell'Apocalisse." **RivB** 24 (1976): 113-136.

See summary in **NTA** 23 (2, '79): #604.

[1975]
580. Gangemi, A. "L'albero della vita (Ap. 2,7)." **RivB** 23 (1975): 383-397.

See summary in **NTA** 20 (3, '76): #904.

[1974]
581. ———. "L'utilizzazione del Deutero-Isaia nell'Apocalisse di Giovanni." **EuD** 27 (1974): 109-144; 311-339.

See summary in **NTA** 20 (1, '76): #226.

[1972]
582. Fiorenza, E.S. "Die tausendjährige Herrschaft der Auferstandennen (Apk 20,4-6)." **BL** 13 (1972): 107-124.

Offers a redaction-critical study of the millennium in the Revelation, concluding that John reworked the traditions of Ezekiel (concerning the resurrection at the start of the messianic period and the activity of Gog and Magog), and Jewish apocalyptic (concerning the millennial kingdom, the earthly rule of God's people, and final judgment according to good works). Concludes that John's listing of the final events (e.g., Parousia, crushing God's enemies, etc.) is not to be taken as a literal, temporal sequence of occurrences. See also 3, F and 5, G, (4).

583. Prigent, P. "Une trace de liturgie judéo-chrétienne dans le chapitre XXI de l'Apocalypse de Jean." **ReScR** 60 (1972): 165-172.

Compares the vice list in Rev. 21:8 with parallel lists in Rev. 22:16-20, 1 Cor. 16:20-24, Didache 10:6, 2 Cor. 6:16-18, Rev. 7:13-17, and suggests that the setting is the liturgy of baptism (like most catalogue of vices in the NT). Although there are also Eucharistic allusions to be found in some of these passages, P. says that does not argue against the baptismal liturgy because the two sacraments were frequently found together in theology and practice in the early church. See also 4, B and 5, H, (19).

584. Trudinger, P. "HO AMHN (REV. III:14), and the Case for a Semitic Original of the Apocalypse." **NovT** 14 (1972): 277-279.

Expands Silberman's study (1963) of the Hebrew background to the titles in Rev. 3:14, but does not agree regarding a Semitic original document. Thus 'ο αμην and απο του 'ο ων are "grammatical and syntactical oddities" of John's peculiar style and not his odd translation. See 3, C.

[1971]
585. Ford, J.M. "The Divorce Bill of the Lamb and the Scroll of the Suspected Adulteress. A Note on Apoc. 5, 1 and 10, 8-11." **JSJ** 2 (1971): 136-143.

Suggests that both scrolls in the Revelation reflect a connection with the nuptial relations of the Lamb in light of the marital and adultry imagery of Exodus. Several Jewish and OT texts are examined for evidence of harmony. See also 2, G and 5, H, (18).

586. Hendrick, W.K. "The Sources and Use of the Imagery in Apocalypse 12." Unpublished Doctoral Dissertation. Berkley , CA: The Graduate Theological Union. Ann Arbor, MI: University Microfilms 1971.

Investigates the imagery of Apoc. 12 by means of a two-step critical procedure: 1) Identifies the figures of the woman, child, dragon, and Michael as OT Jewish tradition; 2) Traces the "unprecedented portions" of Apoc. 12 to the Apollo myth and the slaying of the dragon. John gives the mythical characters Jewish and Christian identities with one difference: Michael replaces the Messiah as the warrior in battle. John adapted the myth in order to counter Nero's claim to be Apollo. The chapter as a whole provides a cosmological context in which the churches can better understand their persecution as a part of the struggle between evil (from the original Serpent to Rome) and God's own power. Lastly, the apparent chronological disorder of the book is John's way of combating end-time (scheduling) speculation. See also 3, F.

[1970]
587. Ford, J.M. "'He that Cometh' and the Divine Name (Apocalypse 1, 4.8; 4,8)." **JSJ** 1 (1970): 144-147.

Contends that the author (or editor) of the Revelation recognized in the
figure of "the Son of Man and the Lamb" some divine aspects, and thus
tried to communicate this theological insight by introducing the divine
name into the title "He That Cometh." Study of the Fourth Gospel and
John's use of the title (especially Jn. 3:31 and 11:27) plus several texts
from Qumran help to enlighten usage in the Revelation. There is no need
to posit a Christian adaption by John in the Revelation. See also 5, C and
H, (18).

[1969]
588. Schmidt, J.M. **Die jüdische Apokalyptik: Die Geschichte ihrer
Erforschung von den Anfängen bis zu den Textfunden von Qumran.**
Neukirchen-Vluyn: Neukirchener Verlag, 1969. Pp. 87-97.

Insists that the Book of Revelation is an apocalyptic book and therefore, if
it is to be interpreted properly, it must be read as a work of poetry, with
all the appropriate imagery and symbolism. See also 3, B and F.

[1968]
589. Rissi, M. "The Kerygma of the Revelation to John." **Int** 22 (1968):
3-17.

Explores the theological categories implied in the Revelation (God,
Christ, Holy Spirit, Church, etc.) and demonstrates how the book (seen as
a unity) interprets history according to those categories and thus may be
considered kerygmatic. See also 5, H, (14) and (17).

590. Stuhlmacher, P. "'Behold, I make all things new!'" **LW** 15 (1968): 3-
15.

Offers analysis of Rev. 21:5-8 in terms of God's direct statement of
comfort and warning for Christians. Proper understanding of the passage
is based upon Is. 43:16-21 and subsequent eschatological reinterpretations
(cf. Is. 65:17 ff.; Eth. Enoch 45:4 ff.; Baruch 44:12 ff.; 1QH iii, 19-23,
and the rest of the NT). Eschatological misinterpretations are treated by
John (against Gnosticism) and Paul (against apocalyptic Montanism), and
Paul's final warning is normative, viz., that any word of renewal must be
rooted in and focused on Christ and "him crucified" (I Cor. 2:2). See also
4, B and 5, G, (1).

[1967]
591. Boll, F. **Aus Der Offenbarung Johannis: Hellenistische Studien**

zum Weltbild der Apokalypse. Amsterdam: Verlag Adolf M. Hakkert, 1967. (Revision of 1914 work, Leipzig, Berlin.)

Investigates the literary figures of speech and imagery found in Hellenism and then tries to apply them to the Book of Revelation. Identifies prophecy, apocalyptic *Weltschaaung,* the notions of heaven, the bowl and trumpet visions, the first woe (Apoc. 9), the riders, and the queen of heaven (Rev.12) in their various connections with Hellenism and ultimate influence on the Revelation of John. See also 2, G; 3, F and 5, H, (31).

[1966]
592. McNamara, M. "A Study of Certain Themes in the Palestinian Targum and in the Apocalypse" in **The New Testament and the Palestinian Targum to the Pentateuch,** pp. 189-237. Rome: Pontifical Biblical Institute, 1966.

Chap. VII of M.'s published thesis offers a literary critical look at the symbolism of the Apocalypse related to comparative religion, texts from Apoc. 1:12, 16, and 20; PT Ex. 15, and some aspects of liturgy of the Apocalypse, Protevangelium in PT and Apoc. 12:17 f.; Jewish Sources; the Kingdom theme of the Targums to Ex. 19:6; etc. Concludes that there is a definite thematic and symbolic relationship. See also 3, F.

593. Trudinger, P. "Some Observations Concerning the Text of the Old Testament in the Book of Revelation." **JTS** 17NS (1966): 82-88.

Observes four points: (1) John used Semitic OT sources and not Greek. (2) The Semitic sources were from the Aramaic Targumim tradition. (3) The sources of "quotations and allusions" in the Revelation seem to be of several midrashim on the OT (cf. Ps. 18). (4) John knew a Hebrew text tradition other than the Massoretic. T. concludes that John was steeped in a Palestinian synagogue tradition. See also 2, C and H.

[1965]
594. Vos, L.A. **The Synoptic Traditions in the Apocalypse.** Amsterdam: J. H. Kok/N. V. Kampen, 1965.

Doctoral dissertation studies selected synoptic traditions (i.e., the literal and allusive use of synoptic words and sayings of Jesus) and their incorporation into the composition of the book of Revelation. Concludes that there is little evidence to suggest any support for the notion that John knew the written Gospels.

595. Grassi, J.A. "Ezekiel XXXVII. 1-14 and the New Testament." **NTS** 11 (1964-65): 162-164.

Suggests that the influence of Ez. 37 on Rev. 11:11 may be seen best in terms of the resurrection motif. See also 5, G, (2).

[1964]
596. Borowicz, K. "Canticum Moysi et canticum agni (Apoc. 15,3)." **RuBL** 17 (1964): 81-87.

See summary in **NTA** 9 (1, '64): #284. See also 4, B.

597. Prigent, P. **Apocalypse et liturgie.** Cahiers Théologique 52. Neuchâtel: Delachaux & Niestlé, 1964.

Investigates the literary traditions that influenced John's writing of the Revelation and argues for a Jewish-Christian liturgy structure. See also 3, E and 5, H, (19).

598. Rissi, M. 'The Rider on the White Horse. A Study of Revelation 6:1-8." **Int** 18 (1964): 407-418.

Identifies passages from Ezekiel 14, 39, Jeremiah 15, and Zechariah 1 as the source of Rev. 6. Concludes that the rider is, ironically, the Antichrist who moves through history opposing the real rider on the white horse, viz., Christ, the Ruler and Almighty Judge of history. See also 4, B.

[1963]
599. Cerfaux, L. "'L'Evangile éternel' (Apoc., XIV, 6)" **ETL** 39 (1963): 672-681.

Studies the phrase "eternal gospel" in Rev. 14:6 in light of Is. 52:7-8 and observes that scholars have developed two formulas regarding the gospel, viz., that the Revelation is clearly apocalyptic and that the Gospels and Paul apply the work and missionary work of Jesus. Both formulas are apocalyptic. "Eternal gospel" corresponds to the first formula in terms of judgment, the kingdom of God, and a new world order as set forth in the Revelation. C. rejects the noneschatological view of Joachim of Floris, insisting that it is God's intervention that brings fulfillment and that the Church's mission must be subject to that divine intervention. See also 5, H, (17) and (22).

600. Müller, H.-P. "Die himmlische Ratsversammlung:

Motivgeschichtliches zu Apc 5, 1-5." **ZNW** 54 (1963): 254-267.

Studies the heavenly council scene in Rev. 5 and suggests that because of several difficulties in the flow of the story, John must have borrowed from another source (cf. similar accounts in Is. 6:8; I Ki. 22:20-22, and the Keret myth from Ugarit) without revising the material. Rev. 5:1-5 instructs the persecuted church to focus its look and hope upon the future reign of the glorified Christ. See also 4, B.

[1962]
601. Vanhoye, A. "L'utilisation du livre d'Ezéchiel dans l'Apocalypse." **B** 43 (1962):436-476.

Discusses the use of Ezekiel in the Revelation respecting the two areas of verbal dependence and free elaboration. Although V. does not identify the specific text used by John (Hebrew or LXX), he does conclude that the author of the Rev. was not mechanical in his utilization of the OT prophet. Evidence suggests John simplified and developed Ezekiel in a very creative way. See also 2, H and 3, D.

[1961]
602. Feuillet, A. "Le Cantique des Cantiques et l'Apocalypse. Étude de deux réminiscences de Cantique dans l'Apocalypse johannique." **ReScR** 49 (1961): 321-353.

Contends that Rev. 3:20 and 12:1 are borrowings from the Canticle of Canticles, 5:2 and 6:10 respectively. Rev. 3:20 is an allegorical representation of Cant. 5:2, while 12:1 alludes directly to Cant. 6:10, with special interest shown to the symbolic woman. It appears that John interpreted the Canticle in the light of Jewish prophecy. F. offers two conclusions: 1) The two texts from Rev. have an essentially mystical meaning. 2) The Johannine circle seems to have interpreted the Canticle allegorically. See also 4, B.

[1960]
603. Leiser, B.M. "The Trisagion of Isaiah's Vision." **NTS** 6 (1959-60): 261-263.

Intimates that Walker's study of the three-fold *q{dosh* in Is. 6:3 (cf. **NTS** 5, 1959: 132 f.) was inconclusive and that the three-fold repetition was traditional and therefore original in Is. 6:3. See also 4, B.

604. Olivier, A. **Apocalypse et Evangiles.** Cahiers de littérature

Sacréel. Saint-Maurice [by the author], 1960.

Not seen.

605. Shepherd, M.H. **The Paschal Liturgy and the Apocalypse.**
Richmond, VA: John Knox, 1960.

Concludes that the model for John's literary pattern in the Revelation was
derived from a Jewish-Christian paschal liturgy.

[1959]
606. Feuillet, A. "Le Messie et sa Mère d'après le chapitre XII de
l'Apocalypse." **RB** 66 (1959): 55-86.

Investigates the three main characters of Rev. 12, viz., the woman, the
child, and the dragon, and concludes that John used a Qumran hymn and
the OT (especially Gen. 37:9; Is. 60; Cant. 6:10; and Dan. 10, 12) as
sources. The woman compares favorably to the ideal Sion of the prophets
and engenders salvation through the Messiah. The dragon echoes the
defeat of the enemy by the angel Michael in Dan. 10:13 and 12:1. Lastly,
a proper interpretation of Rev. 12 must also take into consideration the
centrality of Mary, the mother of Jesus the Messiah. See 5, F and 4, B.

607. Walker, N. "The Origin of the Thrice-Holy." **NTS** 5 (1959): 132-
133.

Discusses Rev. 4:8 in terms of its OT connection with Is. 6:3, suggesting
that the common liturgical usage influenced the author of Rev. The text in
Rev. 4:8 is a product of a number of variant interpretations, all of which
attempt to convey the notion of God's great holiness. See also 3, D; 4, B.

[1958]
608. Feuillet, A. "Essai d'Interprétation du Chapitre xi de l'Apocalypse."
NTS 4 (1958): 183-200.

Analyzes the "prophetic" chapters, Rev. 4-22, and suggests that the
section is in two parts: 4-11 and 12-22. The fall of Jerusalem and the
destruction of the Temple form the Jewish background to the first part.
Through literary fiction (identifying the time of writing as the reign of
Vespasian), John presents the theological value of Jerusalem's destruction
and, thus at a later time, makes explicit what Mk. 13 suggested earlier.
See also 4, B and 5, H, (16).

609. Giblet, J. "De visione Templi coelestis in Apoc. IV, 1-11." **ColM** 43 (1958): 593-597.

See summary in **NTA** 3 (3, '59): # 682. See also 4, B and 5, H, (16).

610. Hammer, J. "Herkunft des johanneischen 'Logos.'" **BK** 13 (1958): 116-119.

Contends that the origin of the Logos in the opening section of the Revelation is to be discovered in Rev. 19:13. The name is taken neither from Greek philosophy nor the OT wisdom writings but came as a revelation from the angel Gabriel, much like the name Jesus was revealed to Mary. Suggests further that Lk. 2:21 makes a good parallel text for Rev. 19:13. See also 4, B.

611. Kassing, A. "Das Weib, dans den Mann gebar (Apk 12,13)." **BM** 34 (1958): 427-433.

Argues that Rev. 12 depicts Christ as the Lord of history and that the notion of *Heilsgeschichte* becomes the unity of both OT and NT. OT images are echoed throughout the chapter, while the 1,260 days of Daniel (7 and 12) seem to be symbols for eschatological time in the NT when God's interim fulfillment is demonstrated in terms of persecution from the world and protection by God. The image of the Man-child, however briefly treated, suggests God's cohesive central role in *Heilsgeschichte*. See also 4, B.

612. Russell, E. "A Roman Law Parallel to Revelation Five." **BibSac** 115 (1958): 258-264.

Says that the book and seven seals of Rev. 5 may have a parallel in Roman law, corresponding to the *familiae mancipatio* (seven-witness seal) and the *familiae emptor* (the one through whom inheritance became possible). See also 4, B.

[1957]
613. Piper, O.A. "Unchanging Promises: Exodus in the New Testament." **Int** 11 (1957): 3-22.

Develops his thesis by showing how the Revelation identifies the fate of the Church, first, in terms of the "new Exodus" and secondly, in relationship to the conquest of Canaan. John's treatment of Paradise does not work backwards but forwards toward final salvation. See 5, H, (32).

[1946]
614. Beasley-Murray, G.R. "The Relation of the Fourth Gospel to the Apocalypse." **EQ** 18 (1946): 173-186.

Compares the Revelation to the Gospel of John in terms of general theological ideas (God, Holy Spirit, Christology, etc.) and eschatology in particular (Parousia, Tribulation, Judgment, etc.). Concludes that the two theologies are harmonious; however, while there may be an intimate link between the two authors, they are not the same writers. See also 5, A.

[1941]
615. Guyot, G.H. "Balaam (2 Petr 2, 15-16; Apoc. 2, 14)." **CBQ** 3 (1941): 235-242.

Addresses several questions regarding the messianic prophecy of Balaam (Num. 24:15-19) in relationship to II Pet. 2:15f. and Rev. 2:14. Two key points are made: 1) Balaam in Scripture is not considered a *Nabhi*, but a soothsayer. 2) Balaam's relationship to Yahweh was by "a hidden instinct" implanted by Yahweh Himself.

616. Rife, J.M. "The Literary Background of Revelation II-III." **JBL** 60 (1941): 179-182.

Suggests the structural model for Rev. 2-3 is not Paul's letters but rather Amos 1-2. Identifies six formula elements shared by Rev. 2-3 and Amos 1-2, and concludes that John's method is closer to the Ignatian corpus than to the Pauline. See also 4, B.

[1939]
617. Burch, V. **Anthropology and the Apocalypse**. New York: Macmillan, 1939.

Offers a new rendering of the Revelation as drama, and studies the book in connection to B.'s understanding of "anthropology" as archaeology, religious literature and ritual, folklore, and the Semitic folkmind. Disagrees with most commentators and suggests the book is a Christian transmutation of a Semitic apocalyptic Folk-Saga of *the Man*. See also 3, E.

E. STRUCTURE / PLAN OF THE BOOK

[1990]
618. Surridge, R. "Redemption in the Structure of Revelation." **ET** 101 (1990): 231-235.

Studies the imagery, structure, and redemption narrative in the Revelation, concluding that this important theme is foundational to the whole structure of the book, with Rev. 5 as the central part. Images treated are as follows: Lamb (Rev. 5), Blood, Robe, Songs, Names and Books, Scroll, etc. Suggests further that the unique contribution of the Revelation to NT theology is its presentation of the gospel beyond the parochial to a cosmic setting and concludes that "Redemption is the pervasive theme" in the Book of Revelation.

[1989]
619. Strand, K.A. "The 'Spotlight-on-Last-Events' Sections in the Book of Revelation." **AUSS** 27 (1989): 201-221.

Correlates the interludes in the Revelation (7:1-17; 10:1-11:13; 14:1-13) to vision numbers two through four (4:1-8:1; 8:2-11:18; 11:19-14:20), first, by examining the content of these bipartite "spotlight-on-last-events" interludes and then, by looking at the basic themes of prophetic warning and judgment in 10:1-11:13. Lastly, S. identifies the structural and theological interconnections between the interludes.

620. White, R.F. "Reexamining the Evidence for Recapitulation in Rev. 20:1-10." **WTJ** 51 (1989): 319-344.

Observes three arguments supporting recapitulation between Rev. 20:1-10 and Rev. 19:11-21: 1)The different events described in Rev. 20:1-3 and Rev. 19:11-21; 2) The recap of 19:11-21 in 20:7-10; 3) The theme of angelic ascent and descent in the book. Concludes that the revolts of 20:7-10 and 19:11-21 (Gog-Magog and Armageddon) are to be identified with the Second Coming; but this also supports the thesis that Rev. 20:1-6 is a sequential recapitulation of events before the Second Coming, not a simple progressive chronology.

[1988]
621. Segert, S. "Observations on Poetic Structures in the Songs of the Sabbath Sacrifice." **RQum** 13 (1988): 215-223.

Studies Sabbath Sacrifice Songs based on Newsom's publication (1985) and draws some parallels between Qumran and the hymnic material in the Book of Revelation. See also 3, D.

[1987]
622. Ford, J.M. "The Structure and Meaning of Revelation 16." **ET** 98 (1987): 327-330.

Shows the literary structure of plagues of Rev. 15-16 to be dependent upon the motifs of the Exodus tradition: 1-3) the Egyptian plagues; 4) the antithesis of the cloud by day; 5) the pillar of fire by night; 6) the antithesis of the dividing of the Red Sea; 7) the events at Sinai. John utilized ideas from magic in order to create an ironic tension to his work.

623. Hatfield, D.E. "The Function of the Seven Beautitudes in Revelation." Doctoral Dissertation. Louisville, KY: The Southern Baptist Theological Seminary. Ann Arbor, MI: University Microfilms, 1987.

Views the book as a liturgical drama while analyzing the function of the makarisms within that structure. Concludes that, due to their ecclesiological, ethical, and eschatological content, the beautitudes reiterate and intensify the major themes of worship, witness, and reward for the early church. See also 3, D and 5, H, (19).

624. Strand, K.A. "The Eight Basic Visions in the Book of Revelation." **AUSS** 25 (1987):107-121.

Identifies eight visions that compose the book: Nos. 1 and 8 (1:10b-3:22; 21:5-22:5) are a victory introduction and prophetic description. Nos. 2-7 (4:1-21:4) add an interlude and eschatological consummation to the first two elements. The first four prophetic sequences treat Christ as Alpha-Omega, and the last four visions deal with Christ's Parousia at the end of the age and the final rewards according to good works.

625. ———. "The 'Victorious-Introduction' Scenes in the Visions in the Book of Revelation." **AUSS** 25 (1987): 267-288.

Investigates the various introductions to the main visions of the Revelation (1:10b-20; 4:1-5:14; 8:2-6; 11:19; 15:1-16:1; 16:18-17:3a; 19:1-10; 21:5-11a) and notes these characteristics: 1) The emphasis on temple imagery; 2) The combination of both positive and negative highlights in the scenes; 3) The development both of the temple imagery and negative judgment symbolism after vision two (cf. 8:2-6 ff.); 4) The close similarity between Rev. 1:10b-20 and 21:5-11a, in terms of structure and content.

[1986]
626. Barr, D.L."The Apocalypse of John as Oral Enactment." **Int** 40 (1986): 243-256.

Investigates the structure and intent of the Apocalypse while developing the thesis that the "orality" of the book is an essential component of its "hermeneutic." Section one of the essay discusses and demonstrates "the signs of orality" in the book's structure by pointing up three oral techniques used by John: 1) Numbering: 7-3-2; 2) Place and Image; and 3) The Three Scrolls (Letters, Liturgy, and Heavenly Signs). Section two explains the social significance of the oral experience for the early church. Concludes that the prophet is actually the surrogate and voice for Jesus in a Eucharistic setting in the early church. The enacted story the Revelation has the power to bring into being is the reality which it describes, i.e., to transform meaning into the ultimate reality of those who worship God. See also 3, F and G.

[1985]
627. Charlier, J.-P. "The Apocalypse of John. Last Times Scripture or Last Scripture?" **LV** 40 (1985): 180-192.

Discusses 1) John's use of apocalyptic style and 2) the structure of the book, in terms of five septenary series (letters, 1:9-4:11; seals, 5:1-8:1; trumpets, 8:2-14:5; cups, 14:6-19:8; visions, 19:9-22:5). Concludes that series 1-2 are historical and 4-5 are metahistorical. Series 3 focuses on Jesus Christ at the center of history and eternity.

628. Shea, W.H. "The Parallel Literary Structure of Revelation 12 and 20." **AUSS** 23 (1985): 37-54.

Literary analysis observes that Rev. 12:1-17 and 20:1-10 exhibit the same kind of literary outline: 1) Beginning of the era (12:1-5 and 20:1-2); 2) Transitional statement (12:6 and 20:3); 3) Central statement (12:7-12 and 20:4-6); 4) Transitional statement (12:13-16 and 20:7); and 5) End of the era (12:17 and 20:8-10). These two literary units also show a connection in terms of lexical and thematic as well as the alteration of vertical and horizontal dimensions. Finally, 20:11-15 parallels 11:19, which introduces 12:1-17. Concludes his study with two structural diagrams. See also 4, B.

629. Trevès, M. "Remarques sur l'Apocalypse." **CCER** 33 (1985): 33-42.

Contends that the earliest section of the Book of Revelation was the vision of the Lamb, probably composed ca. A. D. 69-70. This created the structure of the work, and then later, when Jesus was identified as the Messiah, interpolations were made for dogmatic reasons (cf. Rev. 5:5; 11:15; 12:10; 19:11-21; 20:4, 6). Sometime in the second century (A. D.), the author republished the Lamb vision along with a personal introduction (Rev. 1-3) and epilogue (Rev. 20-22). See also 5, H, (18).

[1984]
630. Blevins, J.L. **Revelation as Drama.** Nashville, TE: Broadman Press, 1984.

Demonstrates the structure of the Book of Revelaiton as a drama in seven acts with seven scenes in each act. The book was written by the Apostle John, who used his experiences in the Ephesian theater to frame his message. B's exposition and hermeneutic develop a dramatic method, incorporating dialogue, biblical text, history, symbolism, music, and chorus into a unified message. Concludes with a "Drama Script" intended for use by local churches and drama groups. See also 6, G.

[1983]
631. Gourgues, M. "'L'Apocalypse' ou 'les trois Apocalypses' de Jean?" **ScEsp** 35 (1983): 297-323.

Identifies the structure of the Revelation as follows: Prologue (1:1-3); epilogue (22:6-21); seven letters (1:4-3:22); and three apocalyptic scenarios: 1) seven seals (4:1-8:1); 2) seven trumpets (8:2-11:19); and 3) seven bowls (12:1-22:5). The first two have the same outline (Preparation, precursory signs, delay, and final triumph). The last deals with the world of adversity, the end of the world, the end of the old and the start of the new world. Each scenario describes the same events but from different perspectives.

[1982]
632. Carnegie, D.R. "Worthy Is the Lamb! The Hymns in Revelation" in **Christ the Lord: Studies in Christology presented to Donald Guthrie.** Leicester, Eng.: Inter-Varsity Press, 1982: 243-256.

Building on the study of Jörns, C. argues that the hymns in the Revelation are not borrowed literally from the Christian worship of the early church but are John's compositions. The hymns found in 1:5b f. and in Chaps. 4-

19 function to interpret the work's visions. They are eschatological songs of praise and are an essential part of the book's structure and message, which proclaims that all things -- past, present and future -- revolve around the Lamb, the historical Jesus, who is worshipped on terms equal to God. See also 5, C, and H, (18).

633. Shea, W.H. "Chiasm in Theme and by Form in Revelation 18." **AUSS** 20 (1982): 249-256.

Expands Strand's study (in the same issue, pp. 53-60) regarding the chiastic structure of Rev. 18 by identifying the literary forms that provide the setting for Rev. 18. There are eight hymns of judgment on or lament over Babylon (cf. 18:2b-3, 4b-8, 10b-14, 16-17a, 19b, 20, 21b-24), including the prose introductions. The chiastic arrangement is ABCDD'C'B'A'. See also 3, C.

634. Strand, K.A. "Two Aspects of Babylon's Judgment Portrayed in Revelation 18." **AUSS** 20 (1982): 53-60.

Studies the thematic structure of Revelation 18 and identifies three units: descriptions of Babylon's situation (18:1-3, 21-24); interludes of appeal (18:4-8, 20); judgment mourning scene (18:9-19). Concludes that the structure places into dramatic relief the two main ideas: 1) execution of judgment on Babylon according to the main litany of vss. 9-19; and 2) investigative judgment according to the law of malicious witness that lays on Babylon (the false witness) the judgment that she unjustly laid upon God's people. See also 4, B and 5, G, (3).

[1981]
635. Goulder, M.D. "The Apocalypse as an Annual Cycle of Prophecies." **NTS** 27 (1981): 342-367.

Maintains that the Revelation follows the order of Ezekiel and should be explained in terms of the liturgical structure and not the literary structure. The book's alignment with the Jewish calendar of feast and holy days can be observed, while the Lord's prophecies and Ezekiel are seen as secondary forces. The author of the Revelation functioned as one of the OT prophets using Ezekiel as well as Isaiah, Jeremiah, and the Twelve in cycle. See also 3, D and 5, H, (19) and (31).

636. Monloubou, L. "Bulletin d'Ecriture Sainte. A propos de deux livres récents: l'Apocalypse de Jean et sa structure." **EsV** 91 (1981): 81-88.

Building on the work of Prigent (**Et le ciel s'ouvrit**, 1980) and editor Lambrecht (**L'Apocalypse johannique et l'Apocalyptique dans le Nouveau Testament**, 1980), M. argues for the structural significance of the successive themes as well as the importance of the distinction between Gentiles and Jews. The latter part of the discussion focuses on twenty-one characteristics of apocalyptic thought found in the Revelation and other writings. See also 3, B.

637. Whealon, J.F. "New Patches on an Old Garment: The Book of Revelation." **BTB** 11 (1981): 54-59.

Argues that the main part of the Revelation, between the epistolary introduction (1:-3:22) and conclusion (22:8-21) was originally a Jewish apocalypse that John preserved without editing. The original apocalypse included fourteen parenthetical Christian glosses of Jewish works comparable to 4 Ezra and 2 Baruch. See also III, D.

[1980]
638. Satake, A. "Inklusio als ein beliebtes Ausdrucksmittel in der Johannesapokalypse." **AnJBI** 6 (1980): 76-113.

Asserts that John used the literary device, *inclusio*, in structuring his text on several levels: 1) words; 2) sentences; and 3) narratives, and that this device expresses the book's dualism. See also 3, C.

[1979]
639. McNicol, A. "Revelation 11:1-14 and the Structure of the Apocalypse." **RQ** 22 (1979): 193-202.

Argues that the structure and content of Rev. 11 indicate that it is a Christian prophetic oracle against Israel set at a time of conflict between Christians and Jews, sometime after A.D. 70. The work is not to be identified as a Zealot pamphlet nor as a work of any Jewish exegetical tradition. It is clearly a Christian piece in response to the fall of Jerusalem. See also 3, D and 4, B.

640. Prigent, P. "L'Apocalypse: Exégèse Historique et Analyse Structurale." **NTS** 26 (1979): 127-137.

Presents a structural analysis of the operations and functions in the book and concludes that for John the eyes of faith understand the present as an apparent reality (not what it seems); but real life is to be found in the death of the Lamb, Jesus Christ. Argues that structural analysis alone cannot discover the message of the Apocalypse. It must be complemented by historical exegesis in order to enter into dialogue with John. Several passages are studied to illustrate the need for both kinds of investigation. See also 2, H and 5, C.

[1978]
641. Spinks, L.C. "A Critical Examination of J. W. Bowman's Proposed Structure of the Revelation." **EQ** 50 (1978): 211-222.

Reviews and critiques Bowman's 1955 monograph **(The Drama of the Book of Revelation)**, which suggested that the main part of the Revelation (1:9-22:5) was structured as seven acts, each consisting of a setting and seven comparable scenes. Discusses the contribution of R. Loenertz to the debate and concludes that Bowman has in fact discovered the author John's dramatic structure of the Book of Revelation.

642. Strand, K.A. "Chiastic Structure and Some Motifs in the Book of Revelation." **AUSS** 16 (1978): 401-408.

Criticizes the "concentric-symmetry" theory of Fiorenza (1977, "Composition and Structure") and the scholars who identify a major division between Rev. 11 and 12 in favor of a chiastic-structural analysis that places the major division of the book between Chaps. 14 and 15. S. suggests that the evidence for placing the midpoint there is based on the common themes that are counterparts in each of the historical and eschatological settings. See also 3, C.

[1977]
643. Calloud, J., Delorme, J., and Duplantier, J.-P. "L'Apocalypse de Jean: Propositions pour une analyse structurale" in **Apocalypses et Théologie de l'espérance.** "LD 95." L. Monloubou, ed. Paris: Cerf, 1977. Pp. 351-381.

Analyzes the "deep" structure of the Book of Revelation beyond surface composition and outline.

644. Ellul, J. **Apocalypse: The Book of Revelation.** George W. Schreiner, tr. "A Crossroad Book." New York: The Seabury Press, 1977.

Investigates the structure of the Revelation in relationship to its theological message and relevance to the church/world setting at the time of the writing and today. Critical of modern historical-critical scholarship, E. attempts to disclose the lasting yet "simple" message of the Revelation through an analysis of the book's "structural movement." Shows Chaps. 8:1-14:5 as "The Keystone" theological unit where the liberty of God meets the hope of man and the net result is mankind's freedom for the future. See also 1, B and C.

645. Fiorenza, E.S. "Composition and Structure of the Book of Revelation." **CBQ** 39 (1977):344-366.

Analyzes the creative literary work of John in composing the Revelation and concludes that the book is a unified work of John, who derives authority by patterning Revelation after the authoritative Pauline letter form. The letter structure plus the prophetic-apocalyptic judgment/salvation genre provide the "macro-form" of the book. Rev. 10:1-15:4 represents the center of the work, styled in the pattern ABCDC'B'A', which is a prophetic interpretation of the political and religious situation of the church at that time. See also 2, H, and 3, C.

[1976]
646. Oliver Roman, M. "El Septenario de las Cartas a las Iglesias (Apoc. 1,4-3,22)." **Com** 9 (1976): 377-439.

See summary in **NTA** 21 (3, '77): #867.

647. Strand, K.A. **Interpreting the Book of Revelation.** Worthington, Ohio: Ann Arbor Publishers, 1976.

Offers hermeneutical guidelines with a brief introduction based on a literary analysis of the Revelation, concluding that the book shows a chiastic structure, recapitulation and a two-fold theme: God's presence with His children and God's final reward to the children. See also 1, C, and 3, C.

[1975]
648. Satake, A. "Sieg Christi -- Heil der Christen. Eine Betrachtung von Apc. XII." **AnJBI** 1 (1975): 105-125.

Asserts that John inserted the Michael-tradition of Rev. 12:7-9 into the narrative of Rev. 1-6 and 13-17 and created the hymn of Rev. 12:10-12 as a transition and preparation for Rev. 13. Thus the hymn speaks to the persecution of the church and offers encouragement by suggesting that the dragon is losing power. Michael is to be identified with the child of vs. 5 (see also Ps. 2) and Michael's victory is one more indication of the decline of the dragon. See also 3, D; 4, B; and 5, C and H, (1), (2).

[1974]
649. Giblin, C.H. "Structural and Thematic Correlations in the Theology of Revelation 16-22." **B** 55:487-504.

Builds on Vanni's work (1971) by correlating structure and biblical theme and concluding that the end of the seven last plagues is the crucial point of departure for showing the decisive moment of God's judgment, which is understood both in negative and positive terms, viz., wrath against Babylon and the new creation. G. argues with Schüssler Fiorenza that this decisive moment is at the end of history. But thematic correlations of divine judgment and divine testimony are harmoniously spoken in the very literary structure of 16:17 ff., in terms of correlated narratives and disclosures, which suggest the need for a revision to S.F.'s idea of the literary structure of the Revelation. See also 3, C; 4, B; 5, A and G, (3).

[1973]
650. Davis, D.R. "The Relationship Between the Seals, Trumpets, and Bowls in the Book of Revelation." **JETS** 16 (1973): 149-158.

Argues for a sequential interpretation of the seal, trumpet, and bowl symbols and that the end of each series is parallel to the end of the other. The author seems to structure his work so that when a critical point in judgment arises the reader may look ahead and focus on the coming of the Lord Jesus Christ. In so doing John is trying to offer hope and power to the Church so that they may endure. See also 5, C and G, (3).

[1972]
651. Cain, D.W. "Artistic Contrivance and Religious Communication." **RS** 8 (1972): 29-43.

Suggests that the book gives evidence of religious communication of form, depth, and richness through artistic contrivance. Offers several examples of planned structure, e.g., Rev. 2-3 and the connections with Rev. 1 and the remainder of the book. See also 3, C.

[1971]
652. Jörns, K.-P. **Das hymnische Evangelium. Untersuchungen zu Aufbau. Funktion und Herkunft der hymnischen Stücke in der Johannesoffenbarung.** "Studien zum Neuen Testament, Band 5." Gütersloh: Gütersloher Verlagshaus Gerd Mohn, 1971.

This published dissertation critically analyzes the composition of several hymn passages in the Revelation and concludes that the hymnic elements and rest of the book were written by the same man. The theme of the preaching of the coming of God as judge of the world and savior of the Christian community, which composes most of the Revelation, is seen also in the hymnic material. Finds traditional OT and Jewish hymns behind the writing. Passages considered are Chaps. 4-5, the antiphonies in 7:10-12; 11:15b, 7 f. and 12:10b-12; etc., and Chaps. 15-16, and the "finale" in Chap. 19. J. finally considers a possible liturgical structure to the book. See also III, D and V, H, 15, 19. Cf. the review of T. Holtz in **TLZ** 97 (1972): 358-360.

653. Vanni, U. **La Struttura letteraria dell'Apocalisse.** "Aloisiana 8." Rome: Herder, 1971.

Not seen.

[1969]
654. Thompson, L. "Cult and Eschatology in the Apocalypse of John." **JR** 49 (1969): 330-350.

Defines the heavenly liturgy in terms of its relationship to dramatic events and suggests that the liturgy is the setting in which the author John narrates the events. The form of the book substantiates this claim. That is to say, the liturgy of the Revelation is included in each unfolding event in the seven-fold structure of the work. Also, each liturgical section contains conclusions that are revealed in the subsequent events. Concludes that the liturgy of the Revelation is a frame taken from the early church and used by the author to organize the events of the apocalyptic vision. See also 5, G. (1) and H, (19).

[1968]
655. Fiorenza, E.S. "The Eschatology and Composition of the Apocalypse." **CBQ** 30 (1968):537-569.

Studies the structure of the Revelation in terms of its composition while developing a morphological approach that attempts to highlight the form-content configuration of the book in relationship to its eschatological message. See also 2, H and 5, G, (1).

[1966]
656. Bandstra, A.J. "Jerusalem and Rome in the Apocalypse." **CTJ** 1 (1966): 67-69.

After briefly reviewing some contemporary scholarship on the Revelation of John, B. critiques and commends Hopkins' proposal regarding the structure of Rev. 1-11 as past history and 12-22 as future, i.e., in terms of history's relationship to Jerusalem and Rome. Concludes that this scholarship may be important for systematic preaching on the Book of Revelation. See also 5, H, (14) and (16).

657. Thomas, R.L. "John's Apocalyptic Outline." **BibSac** 123 (1966): 334-341.

Evaluates the notion that Rev. 1:19 contains the outline for the book. Regarding the key phrases, "the things seen," "the things that are," and "the things about to happen," and concludes that 1:19 is the key to the book's outline. The verse also lays out three clear consecutive time divisions: 1) The vision of the glorified Christ (aorist, past); 2) The present condition of the churches; 3) A revelation of the future. Ultimately, the study argues for a "futurist" interpretation of the Revelation. See also 1, C, (2) and 4, B.

[1962]
658. Stormon, E.J. "Austin Farrer on Image-Patterns in the Apocalypse." **ABR** 10 (1962): 21-31.

Examines the work of Farrer respecting image-patterns (cf. **The Glass of Vision**, 1948) and suggests that the author has not discovered a structure from within the book, but has imposed a systematic framework from the outside, viz., a scheme of six divisions of seven and a creation and festal pattern. Although not convinced, S. says that Farrer has opened our thinking and broadened our appreciation for the Revelation. See also 3, C and D.

[1960]
659. Hubert, M. "L'architecture des lettres aux Sept Églises (Apoc., ch. II-III). **RB** 67 (1960): 349-353.

Identifies parallels in the "letters" in Rev. 2-3: a) The letter beginnings; b) The conclusions; c) four themes in each, viz., the glorious Christ as author; the examination of each conscience; exhortation to fidelity and threat of punishment; and the promise of recompense. Thus the letters display a definite scheme for study. See also 3, C and 4, B.

660. Lauchli, S. "Eine Gottesdienststruktur in der Johannesoffenbarung." **TZ** 16 (1960): 359-378.

Offers a literary analysis of the hymnic material in the Revelation and suggests a Jewish-Christian liturgical pattern behind the writing of the book. While discussing the sequence of the hymnic passages and their connection to Hellenistic Judaism, L. concludes that the Rev. is an important source of information regarding a liturgical tradition unique to the area of Asia Minor. See also 2, G; 3, D; 5, H, (15), (19), and (41).

[1957]
661. Montagnini, F. "Apocalisse 4:1-22:5: l'ordine nel caos." **RivB** 5 (1957): 180-187.

Not seen.

[1955]
662.Bowman, J.W. "The Revelation of John: Its Dramatic Structure and Message." **Int** 9 (1955): 436-453.

Offers a literary analysis as an *apologia* for his previously published (popular) book, **The Drama of the Book of Revelation** (Westminster, 1955). Continues to argue for the Revelation as the great gospel drama in Seven Acts. See also 3, D.

[1949]
663.Gaechter, P. "The Original Sequence of Apocalypse 20-22." **TS** 10 (1949): 485-521.

Building on the "Memory" article (See 0508.), G. now deals with the sequence/order of the parts and verses in Rev. 20-22 and concludes that, due to the editor's use of his memory, he had no personal intentions respecting the final arrangement of the book. When the sequential order is suspect, scholarship will point out what kind of mistake had been made, and open the way to discover the author's intention as separate from his secretary. Concludes that where such a solution is impossible all that remains to do is simply to analyze the pieces on their own merits. See also 3, C and 4, B.

[1948]
664. Wikenhauser, A. "Doppelträume." **B** 29 (1948): 100-111.

Presents a study of the two-fold nature of apocalyptic visions, including the Revelation of John.

[1947]
665. Michael, J.H. "The Apocalypse: A Review and Revision of Vischer's Theory." **ET** 59 (1947-48): 200-203.

Reviews and critiques Vischer's earlier theory (1886) that the Revelation is a Christian adaption of a Jewish Apocalypse written in Hebrew before A.D. 70, and that the introduction (Rev. 1-3) and conclusion (22:8-21) were Christian additions. Argues for the unity of the book written by one author, John, who took over small parts of an earlier Jewish writing. See also 1, C, (1) and 3, D.

[1941]
666. Loenertz, R.J. "Plan et division de l'Apocalypse." **Aug** 18 (1941): 336-356.

Not seen.

[1939]
667. Moberly, C. A.E. **Five Visions of the Revelation**. London: Mowbray, 1939.

Studies the general content and the meaning of the Revelation in light of the five-vision structure.

[1891]
668. Brown, D. **The Apocalypse: Its Structure and Primary Predictions**. NY: The Christian Literature Co., 1891.

Insists that the artistic structure of the Revelation is the key to interpretation. Focuses on visions, especially with reference to the hymns as an important element as, e.g., a Greek chorus. Sees the millennium as a literal period of time. See also 1, B, and C, 1; 3, C.

F. SYMBOLISM AND SEMIOTICS

[1990]
669. Anonymous. "Préparation de la rencontre des Groupes Sémiotique et Bible, Brest 27-31 Août 1990." **SéB** 58 (1990): 45-57.

Offers a semiotic reading of Rev. 4-11 by the Groupe-Ardour concentrating on the interactive passages, space, and time. Concludes with D. Lombard's analysis of Rev. 6-7 and his focus on the seals and the relationship between Rev. 6:12-17 and 7:1-17. See also 4, B.

670. Manns, F. "L'évêque, ange de l'Église [Rev. 2-3]."

The angels of the churches in Rev. 2-3 are seen as symbols for bishops of the local communities based upon biblical and Jewish apocalyptic images that compare priests to angels and stars to priests (cf. Rev. 1:20). See 4, B.

671. Martin, F. "Preparation de la rencontre des groupes Sémiotique et Bible: Brest 27-31 Août 1990." **SémB** 57 (1990): 40-56.

Does a semiotic analysis of Rev. 4-5 in two sections: 1) Six pages treat the structure of the text in terms of time, space, and characters; 2) Eleven pages discuss the text according to a) entry into the vision (4:1-2a), b) first approach to the object of the vision (4:2b-8a), c) the animation of the vision (4:8B-11), and d) the apparition of the scroll and the Lamb (5:1-14).

[1989]
672. Hre Kio, S. "The Exodus Symbol of Liberation in the Apocalypse and Its Relevance for Some Aspects of Translation." **BT** 40 (1989): 120-135.

Argues that John's frequent allusions to the OT writings of Second Isaiah and Exodus suggest a strong interest in the Exodus event (with its accompanying symbols) and a close identification of the "life stance" of each of the writings. Four components of the Exodus tradition are described: 1) Judgment: The Meaning of Liberation, 2) Election: The Act of Liberation, 3) Covenant: The Seal of Liberation, 4) Tabernacle: The Presence of the Liberator. The symbolism of the Exodus is spelled out in terms of its relevance for translation (symbols used for their evocative and emotive power, cf. Schüssler Fiorenza): 1) Symbols for the Oppressor, 2) The Lamb as Liberator, 3) Judgment as the means of Liberation, and 4) Covenant and Liberated Community, sealed in Christ's blood. See also 3, C and D.

[1988]
673. Collins, A.Y. "Oppression from Without: the Symbolisation of Rome as Evil in Early Christianity." **Con** 200 (1988): 66-74.

Argues 1) that the Revelation is the most anti-Rome writing in the NT; and 2) that in referring to Rome as "Babylon," John portrays that city as the fundamental enemy of God and the Church. Concludes with the suggestion that the language of the book (which is dehumanizing, demonizing, and violent) was intended to be a restraint for negative, aggressive feelings, and a definition of the Christian identity vis-à-vis Greco-Roman culture. See also 5, H, (27).

674. Du Rand, J.A. "The imagery of the heavenly Jerusalem (Rev. 21:9-22:5)." **Neo** 22 (1988): 65-86.

Critically investigates several interpretations of the imagery of Jerusalem in Rev. 21:9-22:5 and suggests that new research on the sociocultural context in connection with the book's apocalyptic linguistic statement may provide a basis for further psychotherapeutic investigation. See also 5, H, (16).

675. Villiers, P.G.R. de. "The Lord was crucified in Sodom and Egypt. Symbols in the Apocalypse of John." **Neo** 22 (1988): 125-138.

Notes the relative lacuna in the study of symbols in apocalyptic literature and then discusses the appropriate method for studying apocalyptic symbols. Analyzes the symbols in Rev. 11:8, especially Sodom and Egypt.

676. Wojciechowski, M. "Seven Churches and Seven Celestial Bodies (Rev. 1,16; 2-3). **BN** 45 (1988): 48-50.

Says that the seven stars in the grasp of the Son of Man (Rev. 1:16, 20; 2:1; 3:1) probably represent the sun, moon, and five planets known in the first century. See also 4, B and 5, H, (4).

[1987]
677. Benson, I.M. "Revelation 12 and the Dragon of Antiquity." **RQ** 29 (1987): 97-102.

Suggests that the symbol of the dragon in Rev. 12 was familiar to Semitic, Greco-Egyptian, and Greco-Roman thought and represented the angry power of the Evil One against God's people. See also 4, B and 5, H, (2).

678. Deutsch, C. "Transformation of Symbols: The New Jerusalem in Rv. 21:1-22:5." **ZNW** 78 (1987): 106-126.

Argues that Rev. 21:1-22:5 depicts the new Jerusalem as a universal community where its inhabitants have access to God, eternal life, and final victory over chaos. The traditional Jewish symbols of bride and wife, the temple and new creation are transformed by John to extend hope to those who are being persecuted by Rome. Membership in the end-time community is open to any and all who have a relationship with God and the Lamb. See also 4, B and 5, H, (16).

679. Doll, M.A. "The Temple: Symbolic Form in Scripture." So 70 (1987): 145-154.

Examines the psychological and mystical "speakings" that are connected to the temple in Exodus and Revelation and concludes that John in the Revelation demystified and unveiled the Exodus secrets. See also 3, D.

680. Dyer, C.H. "The Identity of Babylon in Rev. 17-18. Part 1." **BibSac** 144 (1987): 305-316.

Studies the "Babylon" symbol of Rev. 17 and 18 and says that the Babylon of 17 seems to be distinguished from that of 18, due to the differences of setting, destroyer, response, and character. However, a parallel investigation seems to describe the same entity due to designation, description, deeds, and destruction. Concludes that this evidence indicates a unity and identity of one Babylon. See also 4, B.

681. ———. "The Identity of Babylon in Revelation 17-18. Part 2." **BibSac** 144 (1987): 433-449.

Concludes his study by arguing that in Rev. 17-18, John drew from Jer. 50-51 in order to show the future destruction of the actual rebuilt city of Babylon. See also 3, D and 4, B.

682. Gundry, R.H. "The New Jerusalem: People as Place, not Place for People [Rev. 21:1-22:5]." **NT** 29 (1987): 254-264.

Studies the "new Jerusalem" and relevant images found in Rev. 21:1-22:5 and suggests that John radically transformed the new Jerusalem into a new symbol for the Christian saints themselves. Concludes that John wanted to convey to the Church his vision of the new Jerusalem as the future state of believers and not as a future place of residence. See also 4, B and 5, H, (16).

683. Güttgemanns, E. "Die Semiotik des Traums in apokalyptischen Texten am Beispiel von Apokalypse Johannis 1." **LingBib** 59 (1987): 7-54.

Critiques the inadequacy of past research concerning symbols, metaphors, models, and the interpretation of dreams, then discusses a possible grammatology of apocalyptic literature while focusing on the macrosyntax of the Revelation. Suggests identifying apocalyptic literature as "fantastic literature." Sketches Freud's theories of dream interpretation while offering a personal interpretation of the dream/vision narrative of Rev. 1:9-20. See also 3, C and 4, B.

[1986]
684. Oberweis, M. "Die Bedeutung der neutestamentlichen 'Rätselzahlen' 666 (Apk 13:18) und 153 (Joh 21:11)." **ZNW** 77 (1986): 226-241.

This two-part study of the enigmatic numbers 666 and 153 focuses, first, on Rev. 13:18 and 666. The Hebrew equivalent of 666 is connected to the Hebrew root *rss-trsw* ("you should destroy") and may allude to the destruction of the "great" and "little" houses in Amos 6:11. The variant 616 is equivalent to the Hebrew *tryw,* which transcribes the Greek term "beast." Secondly, the number 153 (cf. Jn. 21:11) is the same as *qng,* "Cana in Galilee." See also 3, D.

685. Strand, K.A. "Some Modalities of Symbolic Usage in Revelation 18." **AUSS** 24 (1986): 37-46.

Studies Rev. 18:6 and 18:20 while arguing that the former verse suggests a "reversal of roles" based on allusions to Is. 40:2; 61:7; Jer. 16:18; 17:18; and Zech. 9:12. Here Babylon and not Judah is designated as the one to receive a double measure of punishment. The latter reference (Rev. 18:20) indicates a literal transmission of the conceptualization and terminology ("God has judged your judgment *out of* her"), "out of" being connected to Ez. 28:18. See also 3, D and 5, G, (3).

[1984]
686. Barr, D.L. "The Apocalypse as a Symbolic Transformation of the World: A Literary Analysis." **Int** 38 (1984): 39-50.

Suggests that John's experience of Jesus Christ led him to present a powerful message in the Revelation that helped to establish a new world where lambs conquer and suffering rules. John accomplished this by transvaluing traditional apocalyptic symbols into the idea that a faithful witness brings both salvation and judgment. In three dramatic acts (Rev. 1:1-3:22; 4:1-11:19; and 12:1-22:21), Jesus is described as 1) coming to the churches in salvation and judgment, 2) enabling the cosmic worship of God to persist, and 3) overthrowing the work of the evil one.

Concludes by insisting that the book should be interpreted in the context of public worship and in the Eucharist. L. Golden's work (1976) on catharsis as intellectual clarification is used to explain the Revelation's power as literature. See also 1, C and 3, E.

687. Giesen, H. "Das Buch mit den sieben Siegeln' Bilder und Symbole in der Offenbarung des Johannes." **BK** 39 (1984): 59-65.

Two-part symbolic study describes 1) The nature, background, and purpose of the symbolic language used by John; 2) The five symbolic expressions found in Rev. 5, 12, 13 and 17, viz., the book with seven seals (5:1-5), the "Lamb" as a title for Christ (5:6), the woman as a figure for God's people (12:1-17), the two animals as opponents of Christ (13:1-18), and the great whore Babylon (17:1-6). See also 3, E and 5, H, (33).

[1983]
688. Cothenet, E. "Le symbolisme du culte dans l'Apocalypse." **Sym** (1983/5): 223-238.

Investigates religious cult symbolism in the Book of Revelation.

[1982]
689. Moore, M.S. "Jesus Christ: 'Superstar' (Revelation xxii 16b." **NovT** 24 (1982): 82-91.

Identifies the background to the christological title for Jesus, "the bright star, the morning star" (Rev. 22:16b), as the reduplicated male Venus star of Ugarit, ancient Mesopotamia, and Syria. This extrabiblical background is further substantiated by the "water of life" reference (Rev. 22:17) and the list of the groups left outside the new city, Jerusalem, in Rev. 22:15. See also 3, D and 5, C.

[1981]
690. Aletti, J.N. "Essai sur la symbolique céleste de l'Apocalypse de Jean." **Chr** 28 (1981): 40-53.

Offers an analysis of the celestial symbols found in Rev. 4:1-2 while expounding on the heavenly scenes and characters found there. Concludes that the function of heaven and its characters in the unfolding drama of the book is liturgical. See also 4, B and 5, H, (11), (19).

691. Edwards, P. "The Signs of the Times -- or 'Here be Dragons.'" **Way** 21 (1981): 278-291.

Reviews Rev. 12:3-4 and asserts that the dragon symbol represents to the author the vulnerability of early Christians. Contemporary Christians share some of the same vulnerability of those first Christians. We must learn this from John's main message: the evil dragon is doomed. See also 4, B and 5, H, (2).

[1980]
692. Schinzer, R. "Die sieben Siegel, Posaunen und Schalen und die Absicht der Offenbarung Johannis." **TBei** 11 (1980): 52-66.

Analyzes Rev. 6:1-16:21 and suggests that the three series of sevens in the Revelation (seals, trumpets, and bowls) are basic to the structure of the work, i.e., they correspond to the three phases of the eschatological timetable: 1) persecution, 2) testing, and 3) annihilation. See also 3, E.

693. Vanni, U. "Il simbolismo nell'Apocalisse." **Gre** 61 (1980): 461-506.

Offers a critical study of symbolism in the Apocalypse.

[1979]
694. Leveque, J. "Les quatre vivants de l'Apocalypse." **Chr** 26 (1979): 333-339.

Suggests that the four living creatures that surround the throne in Rev. 4:6-8 have astral and liturgical functions. The four creatures were identified by Irenaeus as the four evangelists, viz., lion (John), ox (Luke), man (Matthew), eagle (Mark), who spoke with a single voice. See also 4, B; 5, H, (4) and (19).

[1978]
695. Feuillet, A. "Le chapitre XII de l'Apocalypse. Son caractère synthétique et sa richesse doctrinale." **EsV** 88 (1978): 674-683.

Argues that Rev. 12 synthesizes the mysterious passion and resurrection of Christ and his victory over evil based on an inspired rereading of the OT, especially the Lamb sections. Thus the woman of Rev. 12 is to be understood as the Mother of Christ (cf. Gen. 3:15) and the perfect image of the triumphant eschatological church. Contends that this chapter is the most important biblical reference to the Virgin Mary. See also 4, B; 5, H, (18) and (39).

696. Gangemi, A. "La stella del mattino (Apoc. 2, 26-28)." **RivB** 26 (1978): 241-274.

See summary in **NTA** 23 (2, '79): #612.

697. Vanni, U. "La decodificazione 'del grande segno' in Apocalisse 12, 1-6." **Mar** 40 (1978): 121-152.

See summary in **NTA** 23 (2, '79): #614.

[1977]
698. Ezell, D. **Revelations on Revelation. New Sounds From Old Symbols.** Waco, TX: Word, 1977.

Studies the symbols of the Revelation in seven chapters according to their traditional meanings and then tries to analyze the author's application and interpretation of the symbols under the light of the cross-resurrection event. Sections deal with, 1) A kingdom of priests (1:5-7); 2) One like a son of man (1:12-17); 3) Seals, trumpets, and bowls (6:1-8:1; 8:2-11:19; 16:1-21); 4) The 144,000 (7:4-10; 14:1); 5) Time, times, and half a time (11:1-3); 6) The thousand-year reign (20:6-10); 7) The new heaven and the new earth (21-22). Study questions and illustrations are included. See also 5, G, (4), H, (12) and (30).

699. Gangemi, A. "La manna nascosta e il nome nuovo." **RivB** 25 (1977): 337-356.

See summary in **NTA** 23 (2, '79): #611.

[1976]
700. Feuillet, A. "Quelques énigmes des chapitres 4 à 7 de l'Apocalypse. Suggestions pour l'interprétation du langage imagé de la révélation johannique." **EsV** 86 (1976): 455-459; 471-479.

Article one offers analysis of Rev. 4:4 and argues against the interpretation of the twenty-four *presbyteroi* as angels in favor of OT saints who were the ancestors of the Christian faith. F. bases his argument on the descriptions given in the passage (thrones, crowns, etc.), the name "elder," and the function of the elders in heaven. Article two treats two matters: 1) The first rider in Rev. 6:2 is to be identified with divine judgment expressed in the traditional forms of war, famine, and pestilence. 2) The 144,00 of Rev. 7:4-8 are neither the whole people of God nor Jewish Christians, but the remnant of Israel who are distinct from the unbelieving synagogue (cf. Rev. 7:9-10). See also 3, D and 5, G, (4).

[1975]
701. Baines, W.G. "The Number of the Beast in Revelation 13:18." **HJ** 16
(1975): 195-196.

Basing discussion on the presupposition that the Revelation was written
ca. A.D. 72-73 and that Vespasian and Titus were probably stigmatized as
the beast incarnate, B argues that Rev. 17:10 refers to emperors Augustus
to Nero (five fallen), Vespasian (currently reigning), and Titus (heir
apparent). Then, the mark of the beast (cf. Rev. 13:16-17) probably
alludes to A.D. 72 coins with the inscription, IMP CAES VESP AUG P
M COS IIII, transliterated into Hebrew as 666. Concludes that the sea
beast from Rev. 13 is Vespasian, the lesser beast is Titus, and the chapter
alludes to the Jewish War and Vespasian's rise to power. See also 2, G
and 4, B.

[1973]
702. Miguens, M. "Los 'Reyes' de Apc 17, 9ss." **EsB** 32 (1973): 5-24.

See summary in **NTA** 18 (2, '74): #619 and see also 4, B.

[1970]
703. Jart, U. "The Precious Stones in the Revelation of St. John xxi. 18-
21." **STh** 24 (1970): 150-181.

Investigates the place of precious stones in theophany and mysticism and
in the superstitions of the Greeks, Romans, and Jews. Considers modern
research into the stones of Rev. 21 (high priest's breastplate, signs of the
zodiac, etc.) and concludes that it is impossible to identify the precious
stones specifically due to the lack of agreement among the ancients
respecting the names given to particular stones. Modern catalogues of
gems may help to identify the stones of Rev. 21. See also 2, G and 4, B.

[1969]
704. Bruins, E.M. "The Number of the Beast." **NTT** 23 (1969): 401-407.

Suggests that Rev. 13:17-18 alludes to the abacus on which the market
overseer calculated the business transactions of the first century. See also
2, G and 4, B.

705. Walvoord, J.F. "Revival of Rome." **BibSac** 126 (1969): 317-328.

Argues that the wicked woman (harlot) of Rev. 17 represents an
ecumenical/worldwide church that includes Roman Catholics, Protestants,

as well as members of the Greek Orthodox church. The ecumenical movement is just another sign of the end of the world. See also 2, G and IV, B.

[1967]
706. Feuillet, A. "Les 144,000 Israélites marqués d'un sceau." **NovT** 9 (1967): 191-224.

Discusses the interpretations of the 144,000 of Rev. 7 in relationship to the destruction of the Temple (A.D. 70) and God's apocalyptic judgment, e.g., as remnant of Israel, eschatological symbol for Israel, those baptized in the name of Christ, etc. Concludes that the 144,000 is an inclusive idea and the chapter is written to focus attention on the heavenly liturgy and events that occur in heaven as they occur on earth. See also 4, B and V, H, (19).

707. Montagnini, F. "Le 'signe' d'Apocalypse 12 à la lumière de la christologie du Nouveau Testament." **NRT** 89 (1967): 401-416.

Investigates the woman and the dragon as"signs" in Rev. 12 and concludes that they show the conquest of the Messianic faith by the Church. This victory can be seen especially in John's Gospel through the disciples, who eventually come to grips with the problem of the Messiah through their growing resurrection faith. John in particular manifests this faith. The woman in Rev. 12 is both Mary and the Church, who, painfully, give birth to Christ the Messiah. Mary then becomes a type and representation of the anquished mother. See also 4, B; 5, C and H, (39).

[1966]
708. Feuillet, A. "Le premier cavalier de l'Apocalypse." **ZNW** 57 (1966): 229-259.

Agrees with most exegetes concerning the problem of the interpretation of the first rider in Rev. 6:2, viz., that he is either evil (Antichrist) or good (Christ or the Gospel). Offers a solution based on an interpretation of the "bow" carried by the first rider. In the OT, the bow and arrows usually symbolize Yahweh's chastizing judgment. Thus the first rider is to be seen as a divine messenger who brings judgment upon the world and riders two, three, and four represent his arrows. See also 4, B; 5, G, (3).

[1962]
709. Bartina, S. "El toro apocaliptico lieno de 'ojos' (Ap 4, 6-8; Ct 4,

9)." **EsB** 21 (1962): 329-336.

See summary in **NTA** 9 (1, '64): # 282. See also 4, B.

710. ————. "Los siete ojos del Coldero (Ap. 5,6)." **EsB** 21 (1962): 325-328.

See summary in **NTA** 9 (1,'64): # 283. See also 4, B.

711. Hodges, Z.C. "The First Horseman of the Apocalypse." **BibSac** 119 (1962): 324-334.

Argues contra dispensational scholars, who interpret the rider as Antichrist, in favor of an interpretation of Rev. 6:2 as reference to Christ. Concludes that this interpretation is more consistent with a prophetic dispensational system of theology. See also 1, C, (2); 4, B and 5, C and H, (2).

[1961]
712. Bartina, S. "'Una espada salía de la boca de su vestido' (Apc 1,16; 2,16; 19,15.21)." **EsB** 20 (1961): 207-217.

See summary in **NTA** 7 (1, '62): # 244. See also 4, B.

[1958]
713. Feuillet, A. "Les vingt-quatre vieillards de L'Apocalypse." **RB** 65 (1958): 5-32.

Studies the liturgy of heaven, especially respecting the "twenty-four elders" of the Revelation (Chaps. 4, 5, 7, etc.). Argues against the theories that identify the elders with 1) angels, 2) the disciples, 3) martyrs, and 4) other Christians, but prefers to identify them as OT Jewish heroes and supports this with extensive Jewish historical references. See also 3, D; 4, B and 5, H, (19).

[1953]
714. Minear, P.S. "The Wounded Beast (Apoc. 13, 3)." **JBL** 72 (1953): 93-101.

Analyzes the figure of the beast in Rev. 13:3, concluding that it probably is not referring to Nero, but rather the beast who carries out the plagues of death. See also 4, B and 5, H, (2).

[1949]
715. Murphy, R.E. "The Epistle for All Saints [7:2-12]." **AER** 121 (1949): 203-209.

Argues that the recipients of the Revelation are "all saints," based on an exegesis of Rev. 7. See also 4, B.

[1947]
716. Stauffer, E.; "666." **ConN** 11 (1947): 237-241.

Not seen.

[1946]
717. Considine, J.S. "The Two Witnesses: Apoc. 11, 3-13." **CBQ** 8 (1946): 377-392.

Examines Rev. 11:3-13, reviews literary connections with the OT, and considers the history of exegetical treatments. Concludes that the two witnesses represent the civil and religious powers among the children of God. This allegorical interpretation suggests, further, that the witnesses symbolize the universality of Christian preachers and teachers who fight against the enemies of Christ and His church. See also 3, D and 4, B.

[1944]
718. Vogt, E. "El número 666 del Apocalipsis." **RivB** 6 (1944): 192-194.

Offers a traditional interpretation of the number 666 in Rev. 13.

[1941]
719. Keller, J.E. **Das Kommen des Herrn in dem Geheimnis der sieben Sterne und der sieben Leuchter.** Teil 1. Gehlberg: Haus Geratal, 1941.

Interprets the meaning of judgment and salvation through Jesus Christ's coming to the Church in the mysterious figures of the seven stars and the seven lampstands in Revelation, Chap. 1. See also 5, C.

G. RHETORIC

[1988]
720. Kirby, J.T. "The Rhetorical Situations of Revelation 1-3." **NTS** 34 (1988): 197-207.

Suggests that Rev. 1-3 reflects three rhetorical situations: 1) The vision of Christ speaking to John (Rev. 1); 2) The vision of Christ speaking to the churches by letter (Rev. 2-3); and 3) John addressing his audience. The key, therefore, to understanding the meaning of the book is to recognize the interplay of these situations. See also 3, E.

[1986]
721. Fiorenza, E.S. "The Followers of the Lamb: Visionary Rhetoric and Social-Political Situation." **Sem** 36 (1986): 123-146.

Insists that if the Revelation is to interpreted correctly, it must be understood as a poetic-rhetorical construction of a different symbolic universe that must connect ("fit") into its own historical-rhetorical situation. Develops an argument in three parts: I. The Mytho-Poetic Language of Revelation; II. Rhetorical Strategy; III. Rhetorical Situation (characterized by "exigency and urgency"). Scholarship must investigate the language and symbols of the book in terms of their poetic-evocative power, as well as evaluate its rhetorical dynamics regarding the nature of those symbols as propositions. Concludes that the interrelationship between John's purposes and the unique construction of his symbols must be studied in terms of the question "why" the work is a "fitting" rhetorical response to the historical-rhetorical situation of that time. See also 2, A and 5, H, (18).

-Select Dissertations-

[1991]
722. Brighton, L.A. "The Angel of Revelation: An Angel of God and An Icon of Jesus Christ." Unpublished Doctoral Dissertation. St. Louis, MO: St. Louis University, 1991.

723. Rakato, M.E. "Unity of the Letters and Visions in the Revelation of John." Unpublished Doctoral Dissertation. Chicago, IL: Lutheran School of Theology, 1991.

[1990]
724. McLean, J.A. "The Seventieth Week of Daniel 9:27 as a Literary Key for Understanding the Structure of the Apocalypse of John." Unpublished Doctoral Dissertation. Ann Arbor, MI: University of Michigan, 1990.

(Apocalyptic and Jewish Literature)." Unpublished Doctoral Dissertation. Ann Arbor, MI: University of Michigan, 1990.

[1988]
726. Fekkes, J. III. "Isaiah and Prophetic Traditions in the Book of Revelation: Visionary Antecedents and Their Development." Unpublished Doctoral Dissertation. Manchester, U.K.: University of Manchester, 1988.

727. Gnatkowshi, M.W. "The Implied Reader in the Book of Revelation." Unpublished Doctoral Dissertation. New Orleans, LA: New Orleans Baptist Theological Seminary, 1988.

[1986]
728. Koester, C.R. "The Tabernacle in the New Testament and Intertestamental Jewish Literature." Unpublished Doctoral Dissertation. New York, NY: Union Theological Seminary, 1986.

729. Stanley, J.E. "The Use of the Symbol of Four World Empires to Inspire Resistance to or Acceptance of Hellenism in Daniel 2, Daniel 7, 4 Ezra 11-12, Revelation 13, and 'Antiquities of the Jews': Insights from Sociology of Knowledge and Sect Analysis." Unpublished Doctoral Dissertation. Denver, CO: The Iliff School of Theology and University of Denver, 1986.

[1983]
730. Lurvey, J.M. "For the Healing of the Nations: Psycho-therapeutic Meanings of Apocalyptic Patterns and Images Such as the Heavenly Jerusalem of Revelation 21:9-22:2." Unpublished Doctoral Dissertation. Claremont, CA: Claremont Graduate School, 1983.

[1981]
731. Casey, J.S. "Exodus Typology in the Book of Revelation." Unpublished Doctoral Dissertation. Louisville, KY: Southern Baptist Theological Seminary, 1981.

[1976]
732. Darling, C.F., Jr. "The Angelology of the Apocalypse of John as a Possible Key to Its Structure and Interpretation." Unpublished Doctoral Dissertation. Fort Worth, TX: Southwestern Baptist Theological Seminary, 1976.

[1973]
733. Barnett, M.C. "An Examination of the Applicability of Archetypal Criticism to the Johannine Apocalypse." Unpublished Doctoral Dissertation. Louisville, KY: Southern Baptist Theological Seminary, 1973.

[1971]
734. Reader, W.W. "Die Stadt in der Johannesapokalypse." Unpublished Doctoral Dissertation. Göttingen: University of Göttingen, 1971.

[1951]
735. Wolber, V.E. "A Study of the Literary Structure of Revelation as an Aid to Interpretation." Unpublished Doctoral Dissertation. Louisville, KY: Southern Baptist Theological Seminary, 1951.

[1946]
736. Mowry, M.L. "Poetry in the Synoptic Gospels and Revelation: A Study of Methods and Materials." Unpublished Doctoral Dissertation. New Haven, CT: Yale University, 1946.

[1943]
737. Summers, R. " Historical Background as a Basis for Interpreting the Book of Revelation." Unpublished Doctoral Dissertation. Louisville, KY: The Southern Baptist Theological Seminary, 1943.

Chapter 4

Exegetical / Expositional Studies

A. COMMENTARIES ON THE REVELATION

(1) Critical and/or Expository: Series

[1990]
738. Mulholland, M.R., Jr. **Revelation. Holy Living in an Unholy World.** "Francis Asbury Press Commentary." Grand Rapids, MI: Zondervan Press, 1990.

Presents an exegetical study of the Revelation in two parts: 1) Prologue suggests how visions might be interpreted; 2) Identifies the book's structure and considers the parallel biblical image of the city under these main headings: setting the stage (1:1-8); the vision of Christ (1:9-20); the good, the bad, and the ugly (2:1-3:22); deep heaven (4:1-5:14); etc. Adopts a premillennial perspective. See also 1, C, (2) and 3, E.

739. Sweet, J.P.M. **Revelation.** "Westminster Pelican Commentaries." Philadelphia, PA: Westminster Press, 1979. Reprinted 1990.

A reprint of the 1979 edition.

[1989]
740. Boring, M.E. **Revelation, Interpretation: A Bible Commentary for Teaching and Preaching.** Louisville, KY: John Knox Press, 1989.

Holds that the Revelation was written to be read aloud and heard all at once in a context of worship. Introduction (66 pp.) describes the book as a pastoral letter from a Christian prophet to Christians in a religious-political crisis in first-century Asia Minor. The language and imagery of the letter are apocalyptic. The book is composed in three sections for exposition: 1) God speaks to the city church; 2) God judges the great city; 3) God redeems the holy city. The commentary ends with a caution: Do not accept too easily John's method of "juxtaposing paradoxical pictures." Begin with faith in God's saving act in the Israel-Christ event and then "think" toward paradox rather than using paradox as an excuse for not thinking. See also 6, G.

741. Krodel, G.A. **Revelation.** "Augsbury Commentary on the New Testament." Philadelphia, PA: Fortress Press, 1989.

Using the RSV text, and acknowledging the influence of Fiorenza on his thinking, K.writes for "laypeople, students and pastors" who are interested in the book's message for study or sermon preparation. A detailed introduction discusses critical problems like misinterpretation (ancient to modern), millennialism, Jewish and Christian apocalypse, authorship, etc. The Revelation is a unity held together by the author's use of a variety of literary techniques, including "the throne" motif as its major unifying symbol. Rev. 1: 7 refers to Christ's final return and serves as a transition from realized eschatology to the book's main theme, viz., the future judgment and future salvation as cosmic events. The millennium is shown to be the beginning of the "consummated kingdom" and not a preliminary kingdom that will later be replaced by God's eternal kingdom. See 2, A.

[1988]
742. Prigent, P. **L'Apocalypse de Saint Jean/ P. Prigent.** "Commentaire du Nouveau Testament; 14. Deuxieme Serie." 2e ed. corr. Geneve: Labor et Fides, 1988.

Presents a detailed, critical translation and commentary that includes an analysis of key words and ideas. Extensive footnotes included. Concludes with 20 pages of syntheses and conclusions, including the author's evaluation of the present state of Apocalypse study, the Apocalypse in the context of the NT, composition, etc.

[1987]
743. Morris, L. **The Book of Revelation.** "Tyndale New Testament Commentaries." Grand Rapids, MI: William B. Eerdmans Publishing Company, 1987. Second Edition.

Introduction covers critical issues of interpretation, genre, author, date, and sources. Opts for an eclectic interpretative methodology and accepts Jewish symbolism as the background key for interpretation. Argues for John's reworking of the tradition. The 144,000 are identified as the Church as the "New Israel" (= the great multitude of 7:9-17). The millennium of Rev. 20 is ambiguous and is not connected to the Second

Coming of Christ. Interprets the end of the Revelation as a statement of God's free grace given to all Christians. See also 2, A and 3, D.

744. Ritt, H. **Offenbarung des Johannes.** "Die Neue Echter Bibel, Kommentar zum Neuen Testament mit der Einheitsübersetzung 21." Würzburg: Echter Verlag, 1986.

Introduces this critical commentary first, by suggesting the best approach to interpreting the Revelation (11 pages) and then, by providing the text of the "Einheitsübersetzung," marginal cross-references to other biblical texts and exhaustive notes. The outline offered is traditional: the beginning (1:1-20); the letters to seven churches (2:1-3:22); the main apocalyptic section: end-time events, the judgment, and the fulfillment (4:1-22:5); the conclusion (22:6-21).

[1986]
745. Bruce, F.F. "Revelation" in **The International Bible Commentary with the New International Version.** F.F. Bruce, Gen. Ed. Grand Rapids, MI: Zondervan Press, 1986.

Presents a very short study (30 pages of analysis) with selective exegetical and expository commentary on the literary sections according to the traditional Rev. outline: Prologue, 1:1-8; Inaugural Vision, 1:9-20; Letters, Chaps. 2-3, etc.

[1984]
746. Damerau, R. **Die Offenbarung des Johannes.** "Studien zu den Grundlagen der Reformation. Band 19." Selbstverlag, 1984.

Publishes in three volumes a commentary on a commentary by Reformed theologian J. Hagen ("de Indagine") as a contribution to Reformed theological thought and Luther's monastic theology. Xeroxed copy of a typed manuscript containing numerous errors. Extensive notes. Follows an outline of considering 1) allegorical, 2) tropological, and 3) anagogical approaches at the end of each literary section.

747. Müller, U.B. **Die Offenbarung des Johannes.** "Ökumenischer Taschenbuchkommentar zum Neuen Testament 19." Gütersloh: Mohn, 1984.

Offers a thirty-nine page critical introduction and exposition of the Book of Revelation according to the traditional outline: 1) Introduction (1:1-20); 2) Letters to the seven churches in Asia (2:1-3:22); 3) The

Apocalyptic central section (4:1-22:5); and 4) Conclusion (22:6-21). The apocalyptic main section is divided into six parts dealing with seals, trumpets, dragon and Lamb, bowls, judgment on the whore of Babylon, and the return of Christ and fulfillment. Eight excursuses are included in the study. See also 2, A.

748. Roloff, J. **Die Offenbarung des Johannes.** "Zürcher Bibelkommentare NT 18." Zurich: Theologischer Verlag, 1984.

Presents 17 pp. of introduction on the historical impact, apocalyptic, apocalypses (including critical issues) and exposition of the book according to the following outline: 1) Foreword and epistolary introduction (1:1-3, 4-8); 2) Advice for the seven churches (2:1-3:22); 3) Jesus Christ as Lord over history (4:1-11:19): 4) End-event as God's struggle with his opponents (12:1-19:10); 5) Final visions (19:11-22:5); 6) Conclusion (22:6-21). Twelve excursuses are included, e.g., Witness, the Angels of the Churches, etc.

[1983]
749. Düsterdieck, F. **Critical and Exegetical Handbook to the Revelation of John.** "Meyer's Commentary on the NT." H.E. Jacobs, trans. Peabody, MA: Hendrickson Publishers, Inc. Reprint from the 6th German Ed. of 1884, 1983.

This comprehensive commentary includes 92 pp. of critical introduction and exhaustive commentary on the Greek text (including text-critical work), chapter by chapter. Additional critical notes by the American editor follow each chapter. Argues for the unity of the book and a uniquely apocalyptic character (as Matthew is uniquely "Gospel").

750. Gilmour, S.M. "Revelation" in **Revelation and the General Epistles.** C. M. Laymon, ed. "Interpreter's Concise Commentary 8." Nashville, TN: Abindgon, 1983.

Offers a simple, critical introduction to the book and brief exposition based on literary units. Popular and thematic with little scholarly discussion and debate.

751. Grünzweig, **Johannes-Offenbarung, 2 vols.** EDITION C: Bibel-Kommentar B 24 und B 25; 2nd ed. Neuhausen--Stuttgart: Hänssler-Verlag, 1983.

Presents a brief, critical introduction (ten pages) to the Revelation, an outline of the structure, and a detailed commentary, including his own German translation of each literary unit, exposition of the text, and ideas for further study in groups. G. argues that key to interpreting the Revelation is the "Scripture interprets Scripture" principle. He outlines the book as follows: 1) The true reality during the course of world history (1:1-5:14); 2) The end-history (6:1-19:10); 3) God's revelatory activity -- the goal of God's ways (19:11-22:21).

752. Johnson, A.E. **Revelation.** "Bible Study Commentary." Grand Rapids, MI: Zondervan;; Lamplighter Books, 1983.

Introduces the book with a brief discussion of the literary character, historical background, unity, authorship, date, interpretative schemes, structure, and outline. Opts for the futurist and idealist schemes. Exposition follows literary units of the NIV text and concludes each section with a series of questions. Notes John's extensive use of OT literary traditions. Follows the traditional historic premillennial interpretation of Rev. 20.

[1981]
753. Beasley-Murray, G.R. **The Book of Revelation.** "New Century Bible Commentary." Grand Rapids, MI: Eerdmans, 1981.

This reprint of the 1978 revised edition is from the original 1974 publication (see below).

754. Johnson, A.F. "Revelation" in **The Expositor's Bible Commentary. Vol. 12.** Grand Rapids, MI: Regency Reference Library; Zondervan Publishing House, 1981. Pp. 399-603.

Introduces the book (15 pp.) with a discussion of the general critical issues, e.g., probable date, A.D. 81-96, authorship (some John), interpretative schemes. A short bibliography classifies authors under the headings Futurist, Purely Eschatological, Preterist-Futurist, etc. Commentary follows "Text and Exposition" form with brief, critical notes at the end of each literary section. Opts for a "Premilllennium" view of the Kingdom, which is thought to be historical and earthly as an eschatological reality.

755. Prigent, P. **L'Apocalypse de saint Jean.** "Commentaire du Nouveau Testament, deuxième série 14." Lausanne--Paris: Delachaux & Niestlé, 1981.

Offers a personal translation and critical-exegetical commentary on the Revelation according to the following outline: Introduction (1:1-3); Address (1:4-8); The first vision (1:9-20); The letters to the churches (2:1-3:22); The heavenly cult (4:1-5:14); The first six seals (6:1-17); The elect (7:1-17); etc. The commentary closes with three descriptions of the end (21:1-22:5), Epilogue (22:6-21), and twenty pages of syntheses and conclusions.

[1979]
756. Collins, A.Y. **The Apocalypse.** "New Testament Message 22." Wilmington, DE: Glazier, 1979.

Offers a brief introduction (6 pp.) to the Revelation by suggesting two levels of meaning in the text: A. The old story of cosmic combat and B. The new story of the confrontation between Jesus' followers and the Roman empire. Exposition of the **RSV** text follows each literary unit according to the following outline: I. The Sealed Scroll: 1) Prologue (1:1-8); 2) The inaugural vision and commission to write (1:9-3:22); 3) The vision of what is and what is to take place hereafter (4:1-8:5); 4) The plagues preparing the way for the kingdom (8:6-11:19). II. The Open Scroll: 1) The church in a cosmic conflict (12:1-15:4); 2) The fall of Babylon (15:5-19:10); 3) The destiny of the world (19:11-22:5); 4) Epilogue (22:6-21). See also 2, A and 3, A.

757. Lohse, E. **Die Offenbarung des Johannes.** "NTD, 11." Göttingen: Vandenhoech & Ruprecht. 2d ed. , 1953; 12 ed. 1979.

Presents a new translation and critical commentary based on the author's interest in the ideas of Jewish apocalypticism and Qumran literature. Twelve brief excurses ("The Lamb," "The Number of the Beast," etc.) complement and complete his research.

758. Sweet, J.P.M. **Revelation.** "Westminster Pelican Commentaries." Philadelphia, PA: Westminster Press, 1979.

Introduces the commentary with a fifty-four-page discussion of critical questions (nature of apocalyptic, contents, interpretation, date). The main commentary exegetes and explains the RSV text of Revelation according to the literary sections. Adopts a traditional outline (1:1-20; Chaps. 2-3; 4:1-8:1; 8:2-14:20; 15:1-22:5; 22:6-21) and focuses attention on John's attempt to synthesize OT and NT themes. This reprint corrects previous views toward the imperial cult in Asia Minor based on the study of S. Price (1984).

[1977]
759. Mounce, R. **The Book of Revelation**. "New International Commentary on the New Testament." Grand Rapids, MI: Wm. B. Eerdmans Publishing Co., 1977.

Introduces the critical issues (30 pp.) and presents a crisp analysis of the ASV (1901) text based on each literary unit and verse. Greek analysis relegated to footnotes. Offers an eclectic hermeneutic that mediates between a literal and a highly subjective interpretation of each literary unit. Outline of the book is based on each separate chapter, but takes into consideration the literary structure. Rev. 1:7 is interpreted as the Danielic figure who comes for judgment and salvation in the End Time. Suggests Christ's return is premillennial and that John taught a literal Millennium, but that the essential meaning of that Millennium may be realized beyond the temporal.

760. Fiorenza, E.S. "The Revelation to John" in **Hebrews, James, 1 and 2 Peter, Jude, Revelation**. G. Krodel, ed. "Proclamation Commentaries." Philadelphia, PA: Fortress Press, 1977. Pp. 99-120.

Introduces the Revelation by treating briefly the state of critical scholarship (3 pp.), structure and composition, contextual analysis, intention, and theological perspective. After noting several theological problems (especially the Nicolaitian problem) for the early church, concludes that John was trying to formulate the reality and meaning of eschatological salvation for the Church in "universal-political-human terms." The Revelation helps us to deal effectively with the "dehumanizing-oppressive powers of evil" in the world today.

[1975]
761. Ford, J.M. **Revelation**."Anchor Bible, 38." Garden City, NY: Doubleday, 1975.

Offers a new translation, extensive critical comments and analysis based on the "source" hypothesis, i.e., that the two main parts of the Revelation (4-11; 12-22) developed from the circle of John the Baptist, while Chaps. 1-3 (and part of Chap. 22) were added later by a Jewish Christian disciple of John. Rev. 4-11 in its oral form comes from a time before Jesus' ministry; Rev. 12-22 are to be dated in the mid-sixties. Rev. 1-3 are much later. Major theological themes in the Revelation (Christology, Messianism, etc.) are discussed in the Introduction (pp. 3-57).

[1974]
762. Beasley-Murray, G.R. **The Book of Revelation.** "New Century Bible." London: Oliphants, 1974.

Introduces the critical questions and identifies the form of the Revelation as epistolary, apocalyptic, and Christian Prophecy.   Using the RSV text for comments, B.-M. investigates each literary unit, pausing to interpret significant individual verses and verse groups while using a traditional outline of the book. Literary antecedents to the imagery of the Revelation are usually discovered from the OT. This is seen especially in the influence of Daniel on the Rev. 1:7 "coming" passage and Ez. 36-37 on John's understanding of the millennium to be revealed at Christ's Parousia as the culmination of what had already been revealed from Easter onwards. The one-thousand years represent the "character" (not the length) of the period as "the sabbath of history."

763. Geiger, A. **Bilder letzter Wirklichkeit. Die Offenbarung des Johannes**. "Stuttgarter Kleiner Kommentar -- Neues Testament 18." Stuttgart: Katholisches Bibelwerk, 1974.

Introduces the work with a brief discussion of some critical questions, e.g., authorship, literary character, theology, etc. The commentary proper is an exposition of the literary sections according to the following outline: 1) Foreword (1:1-8); 2) Preparation of the community (1:9-3:22); 3) The Lord and the judge (4:1-5:14); 4) Beginning of the divine plan (6:1-8:5); etc. A list of questions relevant to the study of the Book of Revelation concludes the work.

764. Kraft, H. **Die Offenbarung des Johannes.** "HNT, 16a." Tübingen: Mohr-Siebeck, 1974.

Introduces his critical commentary on the Revelation by suggesting that the redactor/author (John) revised and expanded a copy of the Revelation that was made up of a cycle of seven seals. By studying the *Sitz im Leben* of the Revelation and comparing the letters of Ignatius, K. discovered common theological and ecclesial situations. Chaps. 13 and 17 appear to have been written near the end of Emperor Nerva's rule. The final "basic document" of this creative process is a composition that brilliantly combines a variety of traditions and common ideas into a literary unity of form and theological content. Excurses on "martyrs," "the angel of the church," the form of Chaps. 2-3, Nicolaus and the Nicolaitans, etc., are included.

[1973]
765. Gollinger, H. **Die Kirche in der Bewährung. Eine Einführung in die Offenbarung des Johannes.** "Der Christ in der Welt. Eine Enzyklopädie, VI. Reihe, Band 13." Aschaffenlburg: Pattloch, 1973.

Considers some critical questions by way of introduction, then offers an exposition based on each literary unit. Commentary and exposition are developed along the following outline: 1) Foreword and inaugural vision (1:1-20); 2) The seven letters to the communities in Asia Minor (2:1-3:22); 3) The throne-vision (4:1-11); 4) The seal-vision (5:1-8:1); 5) The trumpet-vision (8:2-11:14); 6) The introduction to the eschatological battle between God and Satan (11:15-14:20); 7) The bowls-vision (15:1-16:21); 8) The final judgment (17:1-20:15); 9) The new heaven and the new earth (21:1-22:5); 10) The conclusion (22:6-21); Finally, G. identifies several points of relevant contact between the Revelation and the modern church.

[1970]
766. Brütsch, C. **Die Offenbarung Jesu Christi. Johannes-Apokalypse.** 2d ed. 3 vols. "Zürcher Bibelkommentare." Zürich: Zwingli Verlag, 1970.

Based on his earlier French commentaries (1940, 1966), B. revises his work, offering a detailed analysis of each verse within the larger literary unit while treating the text critically in terms of the exegetical, historical, literary, and theological problems. There are frequent additional comments at the end of each chapter and sixteen appendixes ("notes documentaires") on a variety of technical problems; e.g., Revelation and mythology conclude Vol. 3. See also review by A. Feuillet, **RB** 75 (1, '68): 116-126.

[1969]
767. Barclay, W. **The New Testament. A New Translation. Vol. II: The Letters and Revelation.** New York -- London: Collins, 1969.

Offers a new translation, introductions, background on NT times and an extensive glossary of NT terms. The last section comments on text of the Revelation.

768. Morris, L. **The Revelation of St. John.** "Tyndale New Testament Commentaries, Vol. 20." Grand Rapids, MI: Wm. B. Eerdmans, 1969.

Presents a conservative yet critical exegesis of the Revelation, verse-by-verse, while focusing on the relationship of each literary unit. Treats critical introductory problems, e.g., Christological interpretation, apocalyptic literary parallels, authorship (John the Apostle), date (ca. A.D. 90-95), sources (John's work is original), etc. Interprets the symbolism in light of the OT and, finally, applies the message of the Revelation to contemporary problems.

769. Pohl, A. **Die Offenbarung des Johannes**. 1. Teil. Kapitel 1 bis 8; Wuppertaler Studienbibel. Wuppertal: Brockhaus, 1969.

Offers an introduction that deals with a discussion of occasion, date (end of Domitian's reign), recipients, author (John of Zebedee), OT and apocalyptic background, eschatology, etc. Suggests that it is Jesus Christ who is the *leitmotiv* for the book, but the commentary concludes at Rev. 8:1. Several appended notes, e.g., the structure and teaching of the letters, the victory of the lamb, and the white rider as the antichrist, conclude the work.

[1968]
770. Dominguez, N. **Apocalypsis Jesu Christi Commentarium ecclesiologicum**. Madrid: Palma, 1968.

See summary in **NTA** 13 (2, '69): 276.

771. Preston, R.H. and Hanson, A.T. **The Revelation of Saint John the Divine.** London: SCM Press, 1968. Reprint of 1949 edition.

Treats critical problems (including "Leading ideas," "Devotional Use"), while identifying the author simply as John, a Jewish Christian who thought in Aramaic and wrote in unusual *Koine* Greek. Dates the work ca. A.D. 95-96. The commentary is a nontechnical exposition of each literary section. Explains the millennium as a "problematic" symbol providing reward for the martyrs. Although some sections of the Revelation are admittedly sub-Christian, P. and H. argue strongly for the Christian faith and character of the book.

[1967]
772. Kiddle, M. **The Revelation of St. John.** "The Moffatt New Testament Commentary." New York -- London: Harper & Row, 1967.

Another unchanged reprint of K.'s 1940 edition, including introduction and verse-by-verse commentary.

773. Moffatt, J. "The Revelation of St. John the Divine" in **The Expositor's Greek Testament**. W. Robertson Nicoll, ed. Grand Rapids, MI: Wm. B. Eerdmans, 1967, V: 279-494.

Outlines and comments section-by-section on the Greek text of the Revelation. Exegetical orientation. Draws frequent authority from the early Church fathers.

[1966]
774. Caird, G.B. **A Commentary on the Revelation of St. John the Divine**. "Harper's New Testament Commentaries." New York: Harper & Row, 1966.

Views the book as "profoundly" Christian, written by a first-century pastor to encourage ordinary men and women to hear what "the Spirit" was saying to the persecuted church. Offers a personal translation of the Greek text, which is set off in bold print, and then makes critical commentary and interpretation on each literary unit. Much of the commentary suggests a contemporary application. The symbols of the book may be interpreted by past, present, or future experiences of the readers. The "coming" one in 1:7 is a reference to Christ, who is *always* coming to believers, but the end-time Parousia is not a preoccupation for John. The Parousia holds importance only for the faithless. The real crisis for John was not the imminent Parousia but the persecution of the Church. The idea of millennium is symbolic and futuristic. Concludes his work with a short "Theology" section. (A second edition was published in 1984 by A. & C. Black, London, Eng.)

[1965]
775. Glasson, T.F. **The Revelation of John**. "The Cambridge Bible Commentary, NEB." Cambridge, U.K.: University Press, 1965.

Presents a brief introduction (14 pp.) considering critical questions related to genre, authorship, structure, etc. Full NEB text is followed by short comments on the main verses and sections of the book. Suggests that Rev. 20 refers simply to the Jewish notion of a limited Messianic reign.

[1959]
776. Wikenhauser, A. **Die Offenbarung des Johannes.** "Regensburger Neues Testament, 9 Band." Regensburg: Verlag Friedrivh Pustet, 1959.

Presents a revision of the author's earlier commentary published by Gregorius-Verlag (1947). Examines the text of the Apocalypse from an historical-critical perspective. The introduction (25 pp.) identifies the peculiarity of the book as one born of an ecstatic experience by the prophet John, who reinterprets Jewish apocalyptic in Christian terms and offers a revelation about the future destiny of Christianity until the End of world-time and the final establishment of God's Kingdom on a new earth with the Messiah (Jesus) as the central figure. Verse-by-verse exegesis follows along W.'s translation of literary units. Chaps. 2-3 are letter-forms with prophetic speech formulas. The interim millennium is an OT idea but in the Revelation it is at the End. It is not political . A detailed outline of the book concludes the volume.

[1957]
777. Rist, M. "The Revelation of John" in **The Interpreter's Bible**, Vol. 12. G.H. Buttrick, Gen. Ed. New York and Nashville: Abingdon-Cokesbury Press, 1957.

Contributes the exegetical section of the **Interpreter's** commentary. After treating the critical issues and the differences between apocalyptic and prophecy, R. discusses the early church's use of the book. The outline of the Revelation is shown to be an elaborate septiform logically arranged, viz., seven big divisions with each having seven subdivisions under each. The exegesis and commentary, following Lohmeyer, maintains the preterist position, while stressing the Jewish, Iranian, Egyptian, and Greek sources for John's symbolism. The millennium of Rev. 20, according to R., is a puzzle to modern interpreters since John seemed to maintain a literal meaning. See also 3, D.

[1953]
778. Ketter, P. **Die Apokalypse.** 3d unchanged ed. "Die Heilige Schrift für das leben erklärt, Herders Bibel Kommentar." Freiburg: Herder, 1953. Original, 1942.

Offers an introduction (18 pp.), text, and commentary on the literary units of the text in Old German script. Revision of 1942 original.

[1951]
779. Bonsirven, J. **L'Apocalypse de S. Jean. Traduction et Commentaire.** Vol. 16. "Verbum Saluti Commentaire du Nouveau Testament." Paris: Beauchesne, 1951.

Discusses (70 pp.) preliminary issues, e.g., genre, visions, symbolism, plan, and composition, principles of interpretation. Book is divided into two parts: I. Apocalypse to John and II. Prophetic Part. Text and analytic commentary follow according to literary units.

[1948]
780. Behm, J. "Die Offenbarung des Johannes" in **Das Neue Testament Deutsch, 9-12**. P. Althus and J. Behm, eds. Revised from the 1937 ed. Göttingen:Vandenhoeck & Ruprecht, 1948.

Sets forth a brief introduction and commentary (114 pp.) on the Greek text in German. Exegesis and exposition of the literary units follows the traditional outline.

[1947]
781. Wikenhauser, A. **Offenbarung des Johannes**. "Das NT, 9." Regensburg: Gregorius-Verlag, 1947.

Offers a critical introduction and carefully balanced commentary on the book following literary units of study. Basically traditional in its conclusions.

[1940]
782. Kiddle, M. and Ross, M.K. **The Revelation of St. John.** "Moffatt New Testament Commentary, 17." London: Hodder and Stoughton, 1940.

Presents a balanced commentary based on the assumption that the author's interest in writing is essentially pastoral and intentionally cryptic (due to the threat of persecution for the early church). The identity of John is unknown; however he was a Christian prophet who creatively adapted old apocalyptic material to communicate his message concerning the immediate future. The main threat against the Church was seen to be Evil embodied in a poisonous civilization. The abiding value of the book is seen in its eternal, spiritual principles.

[1928]
783. Hadorn, D.W. **Die Offenbarung des Johannis**. "THKNT 18. Leipzig: Deichert, 1928.

Prolegomena treats the Revelation (in view of the Church), plan and structure, literary character, the problem of genuineness of its prophetic testimony, speeches, artform, and text criticism. Offers a fresh German translation of the Greek and comprehensive critical commentary and exposition. Excellent word studies included, along with extensive explanation of literary and religious influences behind the writing.

[1926]
784. Lohmeyer, E. **Die Offenbarung des Johannes.** "Handbuch zum Neuen Testament,16." Tübingen: J.C.B. Mohr-Siebeck. 10th ed., 1971.

Gives a balanced, insightful introduction to the critical questions and offers a historical-critical analysis of the text of the Revelation according to each literary unit. Follows a traditional outline of the contents, while analyzing in-depth the theological and religious antecedents. Includes several excursuses for expanded commentary and discussion.

[1920]
785. Charles, R.H. **The Revelation of St. John: A Critical and Exegetical Commentary.** "The International Critical Commentary." 2 vols. Edinburgh: T. & T. Clark, 1920.

Sets out a fresh translation and critical and exegetical analysis based on twenty-five (!) years of study. The work is grounded in C.'s intense interest in apocalypticism, grammatical and textual scholarship. He proposes that the final redaction of the work was undertaken by a well-meaning (but ill-equipped) disciple of the Seer. The parallelism of Hebrew poetry seems to characterize major portions of the book to the extent that C. refers to the Apocalypse as "a Book of Songs." Martyrs, kings of the earth, and the Seer all sing an apocalyptic tune concerning the struggle between good and evil. The battle against sin and darkness must go on indefinitely until the kingdom of this world has become the Kingdom of God and of His Christ. An extensive critical introduction (171 pp. -- treating a number of grammatical and textual problems in addition to the standard questions), detailed historical and exegetical verse-by-verse analysis of the Greek text. Suggests that Rev. 1:7 draws language and motifs from Dan. 7 and Zech. 12 to describe the book's theme regarding fulfilled prophecy of Christ's return. The work is essentially amillennial.

[1906]
786. Bousset, W. **Die Offenbarung Johannis.** "Meyer Kommentary, 16." Göttingen: Vandenhoeck & Ruprecht, 1906.

Develops an exhaustive study including a critical introduction (178 pp.) and historical survey of literature that attempts to interpret the book. German commentary follows the Greek text according to B.'s structural outline. Extensive historical and compositional analysis.

(2) Critical and/or Expository: Individual

[1990]
787. Horton, S.M. and Flokstra, G.J. **The New Testament Study Bible Revelation**. Springfield, MO: The Complete Biblical Library, 1990.

Offers a unique Bible-Commentary, which includes 1) Expanded interlinear text on the left-hand page and 2) commentary plus "various versions" on the right-hand page with KJV in bold print. Indexes include a list of manuscripts, early Fathers with dates, brief bibliography, and version acknowledgements.

788. Hughes, P.E. **The Book of the Revelation.** Grand Rapids, MI: Wm. B. Eerdmans Publishing Co., 1990.

Translates, discusses, and interprets the significance and symbolism of the Greek text of the Revelation. The message is held to be relevant to the first century and every subsequent age. Using the method of interpreting Scripture with Scripture, H. does a verse-by-verse exposition that he terms "popular" and "free" from the normal academic technicalities, linguistic notes, and critical argument about theories. The genre is apocalyptic but the message, which concludes the Revelation, as well as the canon, is a prophetic announcement that the lost paradise of Genesis will be regained in Christ. Presents an amillennial position while concluding that Ch. 20 describes an undetermined (symbolical) period of time between the two comings of Christ.

789. Mulholland, M.R., Jr. **Holy Living in an Unholy World: Revelation.** "A Francis Asbury Press Commentary." Grand Rapids, MI: Zondervan Press, 1990.

Building on the ideas of Stover ("The American Liberation of European Religious Consciousness," 1981) and Palmer (**To Know as We Are Known**, 1983), M. argues that most Revelation interpreters have been "one-eyed," i.e., oblivious to the reality and nature of the *vision* and thus have forced "rational, logical, left-brained, objective, analytical control" of the book. What is needed is a hermeneutic that is fully aware of the nature, communicative activity, and interpretative method of visions. Working from Rev. 17:1-22:9 (the key visionary part), it is suggested that John's book is both mystical and numinous. Language and structures are disjointed because that is the nature of vision. Various visions within the larger vision are shown to be synchronomous. The Revelation's content is really "a tale of two cities," fallen Babylon (Rome) and New Jerusalem.

The work is done exegetically, verse-by-verse. The millennium begins with Christ's resurrection and ends with Christ's Parousia (the number 1,000 relates not to calendar years, but to an era in history). Concludes with an appeal to readers to recover a deeper vision of the reality of Christ.

[1987]
790. Boesak, A.A. **Comfort and Protest: Reflections on the Apocalypse of John of Patmos**. Philadelphia, PA: Westminster Press, 1987.

Introduction (22 pp.) addresses several critical problems and then proposes to do "biblical exegesis with the black church in South Africa in mind." Rev. 1:9 ("I John, your brother, who share with you in Jesus the tribulation and the kingdom and the patient endurance. . . .") is the key to a proper historical interpretation of the book. Concludes that the Revelation is really protest literature against oppressive power structures. See also 2, G.

791. Kealey, S.P. **The Apocalypse of John, Message of Biblical Spirituality 15**. Wilmington, DE: Michael Glazier, 1987.

Describes John's Revelation as a "modern" book and then discusses the critical questions of interpretation and life-setting. Commentary treats each literary section with the purpose of underlining the spiritual meaning of each. The following themes outline the book: 1) An invitation to happiness (1:1-3); 2) Introduction to the vision on Patmos (1:4-20); 3) Seven letters to a very human church (2:1-3:22); etc. Concludes with a survey of the ways the Revelation has been treated through the ages: Millenarianist, recapitulation, world history. See also 1, C, 1.

[1985]
792. Becler, S.W. **Revelation, the distant triumph song**. Milwaukee, WI: Northwestern, 1985.

See summary in **Conc. Journal**, 11, 1985.

793. Tresmontant, G. **Apocalypse de Jean**. Paris: O.E.I.L., 1984.

Offers an exegetical commentary and (on facing pages) a fresh French translation that follows sense-lines, but without capitalization or punctuation. Suggests in conclusion, and simply, that someone named John composed the Revelation before A. D. 70.

[1983]

794. Corsini, E. **The Apocalypse: The Perennial Revelation of Jesus Christ.** F. J. Moloney, trans. "Good News Studies, 5." Wilmington, DE: Glazier, 1983.

Discusses the ongoing, present revelation of Christ based on his theological meditations on the Book of Revelation. Offers a continuous reading of the text that focuses on Jesus in history -- especially his death and resurrection -- as the great event that shaped the thought and expression of the Revelation. The translator suggests that C. has resolved the major problems in the Revelation by extracting them from the traditional eschatological context of the writing and inserting them onto the plane of the ever-contemporary, perennial revelation of Jesus Christ.

795. Cowley, R.W. **The Traditional Interpretation of the Apocalypse of St John in the Ethiopian Orthodox Church.** Cambridge, Eng.: Cambridge University Press, 1983.

Describes "the traditional Biblical and patristic Amharic commentary material of the Ethiopian Orthodox Church" and presents in translation "a sample of the Amharic and also the Geez commentary material so as to define its character." Divides commentary into three parts: 1) general introduction, 2) annotated translation of a Geez commentary, and 3) annotated translation of an Amharic commentary. The text of the Revelation is studied under the last two sections of the book. See also 1, C, (1).

796. Graham, B. **Approaching Hoofbeats.** Waco, TX: Word Books, 1983.

Offers a popular exposition of Rev. 1-6 focusing on the four horsemen and their symbolic warning to contemporary readers. See also 3, F and 5, G, (1).

797. Jeske, R.L. **Revelation for Today. Images of Hope.** Philadelphia, PA: Fortress, 1983.

Offers a critical introduction (26 pp.) and an exposition of the literary units of the Revelation. Suggests that the key to the interpretation and application of the book is related to understanding the author's intention in writing. Outlines the literary structure of the Revelation under fourteen major categories, e.g., 1) Prologue (1:1-8); 2) Prophetic call (1:9-20); 3) Letters to the seven churches (2:1-3:22); 4) Liturgy (4:1-5:14), etc.

[1981]
798. Fiorenza, E.S. **Invitation to the Book of Revelation. A Commentary on the Apocalypse with Complete Text from the Jerusalem Bible**. Garden City, NY: Image Books/Doubleday, 1981.

Introduces (21 pp.) the Revelation, first, by describing its deep political-theological character and, second, by suggesting how the author formulated his understanding of the reality and meaning of eschatological salvation for the people of God. F. discusses critical issues, e.g., language, mythological imagery, composition and structure, and theological perspective before offering her exposition according to the following concentric outline: 1) Prologue and epistolary greeting (1:1-8); 2) The prophetic messages to the churches (1:-3:22); 3) Christ as the eschatological liberator and regent (4:1-9:21); 4) The prophetic community and its oppressors (10:1-15:4); 5) The trial and sentencing of Babylon/Rome (15:5-19:10); 6) Eschatological judgment and salvation (19:11-22:9); 7) Epilogue and epistolary frame (22:10-21).

799. Vögtle, A. **Das Buch mit den sieben Siegeln. Die Offenbarung des Johannes in Auswahl gedeutet**. Freiburg: Herder, 1981.

Offers a popular treatment of the text through an exposition of each literary unit according to the following traditional outline: 1) Foreword (1:1-3); 2) Epistolary introduction (1:4-8); 3) The introductory vision of Christ (1:9-3:22); 4) The heavenly overture to the end-event visions (4:1-5:14); 5) The opening of the seven seals (6:1-7:17); 6) The seventh seal and the seven trumpets (8:1-11:19); 7) The severe persecution of the Church (12:1-13:18); etc.

[1980]
800. Prigent, P. **"Et le ciel s'ouvrit." Apocalypse de saint Jean**. "Lire la Bible 51." Paris: Editions de Cerf, 1980.

Presents a popular exposition of each literary unit of the Revelation based on the French text. While intending to recover the meaning of the words and images and to identify the structure and internal logic of the text, P. argues that the letters to the churches, the inaugural vision, and other changes to the main text were made in a second edition of the book. This material first appeared as a series of articles in **Le christianisme au XXe siècle** (1977-79). See also 3, C and E.

[1979]
801. Boer, H.R. **The Book of Revelation.** Grand Rapids, MI:

Eerdmans, 1979.

Presents a popular exposition of the main points of the teaching of the Revelation in thirteen sections. Section I introduces the work with "How to Read Revelation" and treats several critical issues. Holding to the unity of the book, B. follows the traditional outline of each literary unit and ends each segment with a practical section called "Meaning for Today." Rev. 2-3 refer to the Church at all times. Rev. 20, studied in light of other biblical traditions, is interpreted as teaching a reward for the faithful martyrs. See also 1, C, (1).

802. Hailey, H. **Revelation. An Introduction and Commentary**. Grand Rapids, MI: Baker, 1979.

Introduction (42 pp.) treats critical questions, including symbolism, history of interpretation, theme, purpose, and outline. The Revelation is then set in its historical context by means of a chapter on Roman history. H. develops his exposition according to literary units under two major headings: 1) Conflict and judgment within and without the Church (Rev. 1-11) and 2) War and victory (Rev. 12-22). Concludes that John addresses the issue of the conflict between good and evil mainly through symbols.

803. Mounce, R. **What Are We Waiting For? The Book of Revelation. A Layman's Commentary and Study Guide**. Elgin, IL: David C. Cook, 1979.

Offers a popular exposition of the NIV text chapter-by-chapter with commentary on major themes and their relevance for today's Christians.

804. Quispel, G. **The Secret Book of Revelation. The Last Book of the Bible**. P. Staples, trans. New York--San Francisco--St. Louis: McGraw-Hill, 1979.

Suggests that much can be learned if a study of the Revelation considered two important things: the character of Jewish Christianity and the notion that the East would some day return to world prominence. Comments on the King James Version, including 400 illustrations and using a traditional outline (1:1-3:22; 4:1-8:5; 8:6-11:19; 12:1-14:20; 15:1-18:24; 19:1-20:10; 20:11-22:21). The work concludes with a discussion of the relevance of apocalyptic and the heritage of John. See also 2, A.

[1978]
805. Efird, J.M. **Daniel and Revelation. A Study of Two**

Extraordinary Visions. Valley Forge, PA: Judson, 1978.

Introduces study by suggesting that both Daniel and Revelation are the same apocalyptic literary type and therefore should be interpreted according to that fact. Revelation is interpreted further as a series of religious symbols and images that focus on people in distress and not as a description of the end of the world. Exposition intended for nonspecialists follows according to each literary unit and questions for further study are included. See also 3, B and D.

[1976]
806. Franzmann, M.H. **The Revelation to John. A Commentary**. St. Louis, MO: Concordia, 1976.

After a brief introductory critique of Martin Luther's personal criticism of the Revelation, F. argues that the book presents the gospel of the crucified Christ in visionary language. Beyond this, there is a verse-by-verse exposition of the literary units according to the following outline: 1) Introduction (1:1-8); 2) The three visions of Christ's church and the powers of this world (1:9-11:19); 3) The four visions of Christ and the powers of darkness (12:1-22:5); 4) Epilogue (22:6-21).

807. Prieur, J. **L'Apocalypse. Révélation sur la vie future**. Paris: Éditions Fernand Lanore, 1976.

Argues against a strict symbolic interpretation of the Revelation in favor of a hermeneutic that accepts the book as an important statement regarding our own invisible (future) world. Provides a new French translation, verse-by-verse commentary along with an explanation of the seven laws of the spiritual world: 1) Incorruption; 2) Fullness; 3) Personality; 4) Liberty; 5) Responsibility (i.e., cause and effect); 6) Substantiality; and 7) Vibration. See also 5, G, (3).

[1975]
808. Burgbacher, B. **Die Offenbarung des Johannes. Nach der Auslegung von Johann Albrecht Bengel**. Metzinger/Württ.: Ernst Franz, 1975.

Presents an edited commentary on the Revelation based on the thought and interpretation taken from three of the main works of J. A. Bengel (1687-1752). The exposition of the text moves verse-by-verse according to literary units and acknowledges that the most prominent idea behind Bengel's hermeneutic is to be discovered in the symbols of the Beast

(Rev. 13) and the harlot Babylon (Rev. 17). Provides several excursuses throughout in order to clarify the historical and/or theological perspective of Bengel.

809. Genton-Sunier, N. **Exégèse spirituelle de la Bible. Apocalypse de Jean.** Boudry-Neuchatel: Baconnière, 1975.

Explains the nature and method of "spiritual exegesis" as investigation of a transcendent vision leading to knowledge of the absolute. Next G.-S. discusses the nature of John's vision in the Revelation and the content of the vision under the separate categories of 1) God, son, and the angel; 2) The imminence and immediacy of the resurrection in each person; 3) The divine message; etc. The author concludes that the Book of Revelation is really a mirror of the ongoing process of the Church, viz., the gathering of all people and the gathering of the self within each person. See also 6, D.

810. Lafont, L. **L'Apocalypse de Saint Jean. Texte intégral, annotations et références bibliques.** Paris: Téqui, 1975.

Presents a translation and commentary on the Revelation based on each literary unit and according to the following traditional outline: 1) Prologue (1:1-3); 2) "What is" (1:4-3:22); 3) "What will be" (4:1-22:16); 4) Conclusion (22:17-21).

[1974]
811. Barsotti, D. **L'Apocalypse.** E. de Solms, trans. Paris: Téqui, 1974.

This French translation of Barsotti's earlier work, **Meditazione sull'Apocalisse** (1966), first, treats some basic critical questions, along with the questions of history and prophecy. Next, there is a presentation of a combined meditation and commentary on Revelation along the following outline: 1) The glory of Christ (Chaps. 1-3); 2) The judgment (Chaps. 4-11); 3) Creation in glory (Chaps. 12-22). Concludes his work with an extended discussion of authorship (opts for the apostle, author of the Gospel), genre, John's visionary experience as the norm of Christian mysticism, audience, theology, and the mystery of Christ and the Church. See also 6, D.

812. Parnell, C.C. **Revelation Systematically Studied.** Cleveland, TN: Pathway Press, 1974.

Presents a premillennial exposition of the Revelation to the "Layman" using a strict literal approach according to a three-fold structure: 1)

Introduction (Rev. 1); 2) "The Things Which Are" (Rev. 2-3); 3) "The Things Which Shall Be Hereafter " (Rev. 4-22). See also 1, C, (2).

[1973]
813. Lahaye,T. **Revelation: Illustrated and Made Plain**. Grand Rapids, MI: Zondervan, 1973.

Publishes a literal translation and popular commentary with extensive charts and illustrations on various themes in the book. There is neither discussion of critical questions nor dialogue with contemporary scholarship.

814. Lindsey, H. **There's A New World Coming**. Santa Ana, Cal.: Vision House Pub., 1973.

Offers a literal, dispensational interpretation of the Revelation with popular language and contemporary analogies and illustrations.

[1972]
815. Ladd, G.E. **A Commentary on the Revelation of John**. Grand Rapids, MI: William B. Eerdmans Publishing Co., 1972.

Offers a conservative yet critical exposition of the Revelation based on the book's literary outline, arguing that the Revelation is "prophecy" that reflects the situation of the first-century church *and* the situation of the future church at the time of God's ultimate consummation. After a brief introduction (8 pp.) and analytical outline of the book, L. proceeds verse-by-verse, using a combined preterist and futurist method of interpretation. Chapters are about equal in length. The book's symbolism is to be understood through OT antecedents. The theme is stated in 1:7 in relationship to the Second Coming of Christ, which precedes the millennium (Ch. 20) and underscores the work as a "prophecy of the destiny of the church." Very short (3 pp.) bibliography and Scripture index.

816. Orr, R.W. **Victory Pageant. A commentary on the book of Revelation based on the Revised Standard Version**. Glasgow--London: Pickering & Inglis, 1972.

Suggests that the Revelation of John is "the pageant of the Lamb's victory" in his revision of an earlier work (1967) in Urdu for readers in India and Pakistan. This English translation stresses the importance of the doctrine of salvation while offering an exposition of each literary unit of the RSV text.

817. Cooper, D.L. **An Exposition of the Book of Revelation.** O. J. Siemens, ed. Los Angeles, CA: Biblical Research Society, 1972.

Argues for a literal, premillennial, "futurist" view of the book while accepting the historical significance of Chaps. 1-3. C. omits all discussion of critical issues, views the term "apocalyptic" as, simply, the "unveiling" of future prophecy and develops a personal exposition based on his chart of the chronological future from the "Christian age" to the "Eternal order." See also 1, C, (2).

[1971]
818. Barnhouse, D.G. **Revelation: An Expository Commentary.** Grand Rapids, MI: Zondervan, 1971.

Presents a popular devotional, dispensational, premillennial exposition of the Revelation based on the author's free translation of the Greek text. Interprets OT imagery and symbolism in the light of current events. Compiled and published posthumously by R. L. Keiper, who adds an appendix arguing for a literal millennium. See also 1, C, (2).

819. Cohen, G.G. and Kirban, S. **Revelation Visualized.** Huntingdon Valley, PA: Salem Kirban, Inc., 1971.

Offers a literal interpretation and exposition based on the KJV of the Revelation. Charts, outlines, and vivid photographs demonstrate a kind of futuristic message from the book based on a premillennial commentary. See also 1, C, (2).

820. Cox, C.C. **Evangelical Precepts of the Revelation. With a Verse-by-Verse Interpretation.** Cleveland, TN: Pathway Press, 1971.

Develops a literal interpretation as he give popular titles to the traditional literary units in the book. Appendix includes a verse-by-verse paraphrase of the author's renderings called "a companion to the Authorized KJV."

821. Hobbs, H.H. **The Cosmic Drama: An Exposition of the Book of Revelation.** Texas: Word Books, 1971.

Outlines and explains the Revelation based on its so-called dramatic structure. A brief initial discussion argues for a date within Domitian's reign and the "Historical Background School" of interpretation. His exegesis and exposition attempt a serious explanation of Greek and Hebrew terms and OT thought forms. The judgment of the "Seals" (Ch. 6) are not literal but symbolic of a number of principles of judgment that God enacts. The 144,000 are Christians still on earth in the End Time. Concludes that the Millennium is a symbol for a complete period of time of indefinite length. The cryptic number 666 probably refers to Domitian.

[1969]
822. Harrington, W.J. **Understanding the Apocalypse.** London: Geoffrey Chapman; Washington, D.C.: Corpus Books, 1969.

Introduces his historical interpretation of the Revelation by addressing the standard critical questions. Argues for a dating at the close of the reign of Domitian and a literary form that is both traditional (prophetic and apocalyptic) and original to John. The unity of the book is accepted, while major doctrinal themes are discussed. The "Relevance" of the Revelation is discussed (13 pp.) at the end of the Introduction. Says the book really answers Paul's question, "Who can separate us from the love of Christ?" John's answer is, "Nothing and no one can separate us." An exegetical and historical commentary follows after the translation of each literary unit. Brief select bibliography at the end. See also 1, C, (1).

823. Minear, P.S. **I Saw a New Earth: An Introduction to the Visions of the Apocalypse.** Washington, D.C.: Corpus Books, 1969.

Following a (strangely) negative "Foreword" by CBA President Bourke, M. provides a new translation of the Revelation along with a commentary and interpretation in two parts: The Visions (I) and The Issues in Interpretation (II). The vision section treats literary analysis, questions for reflection and discussion, and items for further study. The commentary is intended for practical use in the college/seminary classroom. Part II interacts with the scholarly debate on issues such as "The Significance of Suffering," "The Prophets' Motives," etc. Argues, with Caird, that John's idea of imminent crisis pointed not to the Parousia, but to the persecution of the Church. The last section (III) provides the full English text of the Revelation with M.'s annotations. Good bibliography. See also reviews by J. Kallas, **JBL** 89 (4, '70): 510-511; J. M. Ford, **CBQ** 31 (4, '69): 592-594; R. Kugelman, **TS** 30 (4, '69): 698-700.

824. Morant, P. **Das Kommen des Herrn. Eine Erklärung der Offenbarung des Johannes.** Paderborn: Schöningh; Zurich: Thomas, 1969.

Argues as insufficient the commentaries that take purely symbolic, eschatological, or church-history approaches to interpretation of the Revelation. A flexible combination of these methods is the best way to approach the book. Introduction touches on critical problems related to literary characteristics, structure and unity, author (unknown), and theological message. Offers a verse-by-verse analysis and exposition based on literary units. A brief discussion of the relationship between the Revelation and Teilhard de Chardin concludes the work.

[1968]
825. Newman, B. **Rediscovering the Book of Revelation**. Valley Forge, PA: Judson, 1968.

Argues that the Revelation was written to refute a Gnostic teaching group that had entered the churches of Asia Minor as "a more perfect form of Christianity." Offers a thematic exposition based on his previous dissertation work and research on the dating of the Revelation by Irenaeus. See also 5, H, (10).

[1966]
826. Brütsch, C. **La Clarté de l'Apocalypse**. 5th ed.; Geneva: Labor & Fides, 1966.

Continuing work on the Revelation, based on his original **L'Apocalypse de Jésu-Christ** (1940), B. offers a massive study and commentary that includes a translation (based on L. Segond's '62 version) and critical, verse-by-verse commentary on each literary unit. Additional notes (in small type) on various problems, e.g., exegetical history, literary criticism, etc., are included in each section. The work concludes with sixteen "note documentaires" and a short dictionary of the Revelation of John. The commentary is based on the author's emphatic Christology.

827. Läpple, A. **Die Apokalypse nach Johannes. Ein Lebensbuch der Christenheit**. Munich: Don Bosco, 1966.

Introduces his work with a study of the literary form, Jewish sources, and OT inspiration for the Revelation. Comments on the verses within each literary unit, emphasizing the scriptural echoes of the language and the imagery. Concludes with a brief outline of the theology (basically, a Christology) of the book.

828. Rissi, M. **Alpha und Omege. Eine Deutung der Johannesoffenbarung**. Basel: F. Reinhardt, 1966.

Offers a popular exposition and commentary on the Revelation from an historical and eschatological perspective. R. investigates the book under three major sections: 1) Introduction and personal letters (Rev. 1-3); 2) Middle, including various strange figures (Rev. 4:1-19:10; 3) Conclusion, including Jesus' return, condemnation, and new creation of the world (19:11-22:21).

829. Walvoord, J.F. **The Revelation of Jesus Christ. A Commentary**. Chicago: Moody Press, 1966.

Offers a strict, literal and premillennial reading of the Revelation. W. identifies Rev. 1:9 as the hermeneutical key to the book, and Chap. 4 as the dividing line between present and future interpretation. Chaps. 4-22 are awaiting future fulfillment, while the whole book is to be taken literally and chronologically (unless the text itself says otherwise). See also 1, C, (2).

[1964]
830. Farrer, A. **The Revelation of St. John the Divine**. Oxford: At the Clarendon Press, 1964.

Expands an earlier work (**A Rebirth of Images**, 1963) based on his correction of traditional English versions of the text. An introduction (58 pp.) places the writing in the early second century. The Revelation is structured around the number seven ("week") in a liturgical scheme. The setting of the apocalyptic drama is a frame of divine service rendered by celestial beings in the temple of heaven. The main liturgical themes stated are: "The Lord's Day" (Rev. 1-3), "The Lion of Judah" (4-8:12), "Woes of the Eagle," and "The Heavenly Man." These draw heavily on OT imagery and symbolism. The exposition develops from a religious-history perspective, while the notion of the millennium was taken over by John from rabbinic theology. See the review by E. Siegman, **CBQ** 27 (1965): 160-162.

[1963]
831. Firebrace, A. **The Revelation to John**. London: Peter Owen Ltd., 1963.

Studies the book from a general and specific design perspective while offering conservative expository comment. Unique page set-up shows two columns: left for text and right for interpretation and commentary. Grand design views four phases: 1) The Word Phase; 2) The Christ Phase (4:1-

11:19); 3) The Christianity Phase (12:1-20:15); and 4) The Science Phase (21:1-22:5).

[1962]
832. Heidt, W.G. **The Book of the Apocalypse.** "New Testament Reading Guide, 14." Collegeville, MN: The Liturgical Press, 1962.

After a brief discussion of a few critical questions and the theology of the Apocalypse, H. shows the text (according to literary units) and then follows with short comments. The "two apocalypse" literary theory is suggested as background to the visions of Chaps. 4-22. The millennium symbolizing the messianic area on earth was intended as John's stand against the "peace and prosperity" millennarianism of his day. Most of the imagery surrounding the end-time events are derived from OT antecedents. Includes lectionary readings from the Apocalypse as well as three pages of review aids and discussion topics.

[1961]
833. Niles, D.T. **As Seeing the Invisible.** New York: Harper and Brothers, Publishers, 1961.

Introduces his book, first, with a discussion of questions related to occasion, authorship, address, apocalypse; then treats 1) the drama of the book and 2) the plan of its contents. The main body of the work is a presentation of thirty-three brief theological and expositional meditations on some text of the Revelation. Concludes with a discussion of the seven beautitudes of Rev. 22:6-21.

[1959]
834. Barclay, W. **The Revelation of John.** "The Daily Study Bible." 2 Vols. Edinburgh: The Saint Andrew Press, 1966. Fourth Impression.

Proposes to make the results of modern scholarship available to nonspecialists and to make the teaching of the New Testament books relevant to life and work today. Drawing from the religious, social, literary history, and language of the time preceeding (and including) the writing of the New Testament, B. offers a personal translation and very readable exposition of each literary unit in the Revelation. Vol. 1 treats general introductory matters, e.g., the nature of Jewish apocalyptic, authorship (an unknown Jew from Palestine), and Chaps. 1-5. Vol. 2 treats Chaps. 6-22. The volumes are rich in anecdotes, stories, and word studies that illustrate the theme(s) of each section. Approach is preterist and amillennial.

835. Torrance, T.F. **The Apocalypse Today.** Grand Rapids, MI: Eerdmans, 1959.

Offers sixteen Christological expositions of the Revelation in hortatory form taken from a series of sermons intended for the "ordinary" church member. Identifies the central message of each chapter and applies it to a contemporary context. Purposely avoids critical problems by emphasizing the power of the gospel of Christ.

[1957]
836. Lilje, H. **Last Book of the Bible.** Olive Wyon, trans. Philadelphia, PA: Muhlenberg Press, 1957.

This English translation of L.'s German original (Berlin, 1940) presents an eschatological exposition of the literary (thought) units of the book after a brief discussion of several critical issues (e.g., Biblical Doctrine of the End; Form of the Apocalypse; Apocalyptic Numbers and Symbols). The first edition was completed while L. was a Nazi prisoner. Only "faith" helps the reader to interpret the Revelation properly, and to understand that we are in the last days. But there is *hope* for the future.

[1956]
837. Wernecke, H. **The Book of Revelation Speaks to Us.** Philadelphia: Westminster Press, 1956.

After dealing briefly with some critical questions, W. adopts a nonmillennial and nondispensational method of interpretation of the Revelation, while offering exposition on each chapter. Suggests that "seven" sections (seals, trumpets, etc.) are to be understood in time in terms of parallelism. See also 1, C, (1).

[1955]
838. Bowman, J.W. **The Drama of the Book of Revelation.**
Philadelphia, PA: Westminster Press,
1955.

Develops a structural interpretation based on the dramatic "Acts" of the book. Paraphrases the text while offering an exposition of each (literary) unit of the drama. Literary allusions and symbolism dominate the author's presentation. See also 3, B, and E; 1, C, (1).

[1954]
839. Durousseau, C. "The Commentary of Oecumenius on the Apoc. of

John: A lost chapter in the history of interpretation [600 A.D.; found 1901 in Messina]." **BRes** 29 (1954): 21-34.

Discusses the character and content of the newly discovered Oecumenius Commentary on the Revelation and notes its place in the history of Revelation interpretation. See also 2, C.

[1953]
840. Frey, H. **Das Ziel aller Dinge**. Stuttgart: Calmer Verlag, 2nd ed., 1953.

Presents a German commentary and interpretation of the book based on a traditional outline of the literary units. Two afterwords (15 pp.) discuss historical-critical themes and problems.

[1951]
841. McDowell, E.A. **The Meaning and Message of the Book of Revelation.** Nashville, TN: Broadman Press, 1951.

Explains the Revelation as "The Drama of the Sovereignty of God" that emerged from a crisis period of the Church (ca. A.D. 95-96) to meet specific problems. Literary units are interpreted historically and theologically (not verse-by-verse). Rev. 1:7 describes the eschatological Second Coming, but this theme does not dominate the whole book. The "seven churches" of Chaps. 2-3 are "representations" of all the churches in Asia, and, ultimately, the universal Church. The Millennium is interpreted as the "spiritual reign" of Christ and his saints that began with his exaltation. This will continue until the end of history.

842. Summers, R. **Worthy is the Lamb.** Nashville, TN: Broadman Press, 1951.

Analyzes the historical background of the Revelation in order to apply that knowledge to an interpretation of the work. The key to his thesis is that God's redeeming Lamb is the same person who dominates the lives of his people and the activity of this book, i.e., the Revelation. Preliminary material covers the nature of apocalyptic literature, methods of interpretation and history. S. adopts principles related to the "Preterist" and "Philosophy of History" schools of interpretation and suggests a date ca. A.D. 94-96. Chaps. 2-3 describe the "conditions" of the Church of every age. The "Seals" (Ch.6) represent God's forces in dealing with those who oppress his people. The 144,000 and "multitude" (Ch.7) represent the universal (true) Church on earth and in heaven respectively. The number

666 represents Domitian. The Millennium means "completeness," i.e., referring not to a specific time period but to the restraint of the devil in the End Time. See also 5, C and H, (18).

[1950]
843. Amiot, F. **Gestes et textes des Apôtres. Acts, épitres, Apocalypse. Traduction et notes**. Paris: Fayard, 1950.

Provides translation and brief commentary notes on the Book of Revelation as a concluding part of a work that includes the Acts and the Epistles.

[1947]
844. Loenertz, R.J. **The Apocalypse of St. John**. H. J. Carpenter, trans. London: Sheed & Ward, 1947.

Presents the "authentic plan" of the book with brief comments based on Allo's commentary work. Suggests a two-fold division with two "ecstasies" included. Extensive notes on formal structure and A-B-A¹ scheme conclude the work.

845. Maycock, A.L. **The Apocalypse, with Foreword and Notes**. Westminster: Dacre Press, 1947.

Focuses on the Revelation's universal meaning and primary mysteries of the Christian faith. Suggests that the book is nonpredictive and not a chronicle of actual events, but sums up the teaching of the whole Canon. Includes a seven-fold plan outlining the text along traditional lines. Expository and devotional comments follow the Revised Version text.

846. Olivier, A. **Les premières strophes de l'Apocalypse. Introduction, text, traduction et commentaire**. Paris: Geuthner, 1947.

Outlines the main structure of the Rev. in terms of the composition of strophes.

847. Schellenberg, D. **Die Offenbarung des Johannes**. Gladbeck: Volksmiss. Amt der evangelische Kirche von Westfalen, 1947.

Not seen.

848. Tatford, F.A. **Prophecy's Last Word**. London: Pickering & Ingles, 1947.

Offers a plain, popular exposition of the book underlining the glories of Christ. T. exegetes literary sections chapter-by-chapter, then discusses foundational doctrines, and draws attention to all the OT allusions and connections. Views the millennium as strictly future.

849. Tolzien, G. **Die Offenbarung des Johannes für bibellesende Gemeindeglieder erklärt**. Hamburg: Agentur des Rauchen Hauses, 1947.

Not seen.

850. Venable, C.L. **A Reading of Revelation**. Philadelphia: Muhlenberg Press, 1947.

Presents a brief introduction (14 pp.) and simple "continuous reading" (really a paraphrase) of the biblical text.

[1945]
851. Hendricksen, W. **More than Conquerors: An Interpretation of the Book of Revelation**. Grand Rapids, MI: Baker, 1945.

Offers an exposition of the book using the "synchronistic or parallelistic" system of interpretation. Stresses the importance of the historical setting and the unity of the book. Literary units are given popular titles, while the millennium is considered to be John's figurative expression over a glorious time of missionary thrust for the Church. See also 1, B.

[1942]
852. Harrison, N.B. **The End. Rethinking the Revelation**. Minneapolis: The Harrison Service, 1942.

Offers a fresh overview and brief commentary of the Book of Revelation. See also 1, B.

853. Sickenberger, J. **Erklärung der Johannesapokalypse**. 2nd ed. Bonn: Hanstein. 1st ed., 1940.

Discusses the eschatological interpretation of the Revelation and comments critically on the text.

[1941]
854. De Benoit, P. **Was der Geist den Gemeinden sage. Ein**

Kommentar zur Offenbarung. Vennes über Lausanne: Verlag Emmaus, 1941.

Presents a short critical introduction and section-by-section commentary on the literary units. Main verses are highlighted for more comprehensive analysis.

855. Von der Ropp, Fr. **Die Besiegung des Satans. Die Offenbarung des Johannes im heutigen Deutsch wortgetreu übersetzt**. Bad Blankenburg: Harfe-Verlag, 1941.

Not seen.

[1940]
856. Hartenstein, K. **Der wiederkommende Herr. Eine Auslegung der Offenbarung des Johannes**. Stuttgart: Evangelische Missionsverlag Je Doppelheft, 1940.

Emphasizes the Second Coming theme to the church of the Revelation while dividing the commentary in three parts: 1) The Mystery of the Community; 2) The Way of the Community between the Times of God; and 3) The community in the End Time. Offers a strong Christocentric interpretation of the book.

[1939]
857. Richardson, D.W. **The Revelation of Jesus Christ. An Interpretation**. Richmond, VA: John Knox Press, 1939.

Introduces this brief commentary by discussing 1) the apocalyptic method and 2) the author's purpose, i.e., to write a philosophy of history in which God is shown to be in control of the events. The last four chapters treat the seven visions of the book following Calvin's method of letting the true meaning emerge on its own. Dispensationalism is called heresy. The millennium is interpreted to mean the perfect binding of Satan.

858. Scott, E.F. **The Book of Revelation**. London: SCM Press, 1939.

Treats 1) Origin and Purpose, 2) The Drama of Revelation (Exposition), 3) Doctrine in Revelation, 4) Permanent Message, and 5) Revelation as Literature. Identifies the work as Christian prophecy dated during the reign of Domitian and views the millennium of Rev. 20 as a symbol of Christ's reign. The message is intended for Christians in crisis in every age.

[1935]
859. Kuyper, A. **The Revelation of St. John.** John Hendrik de Vries, trans. Grand Rapids, MI: Wm. B. Eerdmans Publishing Co., 1964. Reprint.

This work is a separate publication of the largest part of the fourth (last) volume of K's "The Consummation of the World." It discusses Revelation's motifs in forty-two chapters. Concludes that the book is apocalyptic (i.e., it uses "heavenly" things to describe the present), the numbers are symbolic, and the full meaning shall only be understood "when all has come to pass." Nevertheless, the Revelation is a book for the Church of all time. The Millennium is symbolic for the "fullness of divine action." Rev. 1:20 suggests the structure of the book in four parts.

[1933]
860. Allo, E.-B. **Saint Jean l'Apocalypse.** 4th ed. aug. Paris: Gabalda, 1933.

Presents an exhaustive introduction (264 pp.) covering the historical milieu, characteristics of the author, destination, apocalyptic form, symbolism, and annotated bibliography. Does a comprehensive study of the Greek text, while adding extensive cross-references. Brief excursuses follow each section (34!) and the work concludes with a detailed outline of the book.

[1926]
861. Zahn, T. **Die Offenbarung des Johannes.** 2 vols. Leipzig: Deichert, 1924-26.

Presents a German translation of the Greek text and historical-critical notes (130 pp.), including discussion of relevant literature associated with the Revelation. Text-critical remarks included. Commentary enriched by historical, theological, and OT and apocalyptic literary influence on the writing.

[1923]
862. Loisey, A. **L'Apocalypse de Jean.** Paris: E. Nourry, 1923.

Explores the meaning of the Apocalypse of John through a brief treatment of some of the critical issues and extended analysis and commentary on the literary units. Key verses and sections are set out for special discussion. Religious traditions (including OT) are considered in terms of their influence on the final text of the book.

[1922]
863. Peake, A.S. **The Revelation of John.** New York: Doran, 1922.

Revised exposition of the Revelation in two parts: 1) General critical, history, interpretation, and theology; and 2) Exposition of each section. P. says the book has permanent value, but rejects the "continuous-historical" interpretation. Opts for a straightforward and nonliteral interpretation.

[1919]
864. Beckwith, I.T. **The Apocalypse of John: Studies in Introduction with a Critical and Exegetical Commentary.** New York: The MacMillan Co., 1919.

Directs his work primarily to seminary and college students, beginning with an extensive introduction (416 pp.) to the critical problems (incl. "Eschatological Hope," "Apocalyptic Literature," "Theology," etc.). Notes the value of the historical and literary context for proper interpretation. Arguing for the unity of the book, B. proposes that John's theology is consistent with OT thought and, thus, the preferred interpretation of the book is in line with the "Contemporary-Historical" or "Apocalyptic-Prophetic" schools, i.e., in both form and content the prophecy is apocalyptic. Commentary moves verse-by-verse from the author's translation of the Greek text. The Beast is considered to be a symbol for the Emperor, the Antichrist, and, more specifically, "Nero reincarnated." The Millennium is interpreted literally as a temporary, earthly kingdom.

[1911]
865. Swete, H.B. **The Apocalypse of St. John.** 3rd ed. London: Macmillan and Co., 1911. (Originally published in 1906.)

An extensive introduction (219 pp.) precedes a thorough analysis and exposition of the Greek text. Included in the standard grammatical-critical discussion regarding language, authorship, date, etc., are sections on "Unity," "Symbolism," "Doctrine," "Commentaries," and "History and Methods of Interpretation." S. tells us that he plans to use several of the traditional methods, while holding to the unity of the book itself. Variant readings are immediately beneath the Greek text found at the top of each page. Two-column pages include a detailed discussion of each verse within the literary unit. S. makes good use of current scholarly and patristic (Greek and Latin) commentaries. Chaps. 2-3 are shown to be pastoral "messages" (λογοι) to seven historical churches. The Millennium of Rev. 20 is shown as a great epoch revealed in human history at the End

Time. Amillennial approach. Includes Index of Greek Words found in the Revelation and an Index to the Introduction and Notes.

B. STUDIES OF SPECIFIC SECTIONS

Chap. 1

[1973]
866. Coune, M. "Un royaume de prêtres. Ap 1,5-8." **AS** 20 (1973): 9-16.

Studies Rev. 1:5-8, suggesting that John's work has the form of a book (1:1-3) and a letter (1:4-8) and the letter section contains essentially kingdom and priestly titles in relationship to Christ, the Son of God. Vs. 7 in particular, announcing the imminent coming of the Son of Man, uncovers the Christian meaning of history, while vs. 8 is God's literal confirmation that Jesus has come and will come.

[1970]
867. Ford, J.M. "'He That Cometh' and the Divine Name (Apocalypse 1,4.8; 4,8)." **JSJ** 1 (1970): 144-147.

Investigates the phrase "He that cometh" (Rev. 1:4, etc.) and concludes that it is a title given by the author or redactor to attribute divinity to the Son of Man and the Lamb.

868. Pesch, R. "Offenbarung Jesu Christi: Eine Auslegung von Apk 1,1-3." **BL** 11 (1970): 15-29.

Does a literary-critical study of Rev. 1:1-3, suggesting that the passage is a three-strophe unit. Concludes that John was using an apocalyptic form in making his prophetic statement concerning the revelatory coming of Jesus at the time of the End. This message also concerns the Church of today as well as the first-century church. See also 5, G, (2).

[1967]
869. Strand, K.A. "Another Look at 'Lord's Day' in the Early Church and in Rev. I.10." **NTS** 13 (1966-67): 174-181.

Critiques W. Stott's work on the Lord's Day (1965), which, according to S., fails to consider the evidence in favor of an Easter interpretation of Rev. 1:10. See also 5, H, (20).

[1965]
870. Thomas, R.L. "The Glorified Christ on Patmos." **BibSac** 122 (1965): 241-247.

Examines the appearance of the glorified Christ to John on Patmos and suggests that the appearance forms the basis of the book's prelude and later allusions. See also 5, C.

[1961]
871. Wuest, K.S. "The Absolute Control of the Spirit." **BibSac** 118 (1961): 122.

Notes that the biblical writers were controlled by the Spirit and unique. See also 5, D.

[1960]
872. Ramlot, L. "Apparition du Ressuscité au déporté de Patmos (Apoc. 1, 9-20)." **BVCh** 36 (1960): 16-25.

Not seen.

[1959]
873. Gelston, A."The Royal Priesthood." **EQ** 31 (1959): 152-163.

Presents an exegesis of Ex. 19:6 in relation to Rev. 1:6; 5:10; etc., while emphasizing the "Royal Priesthood" theme. Concludes that, in applying the texts to the Church, all Christians are privileged to share in the Lord's mediatorial work and glorious reign.

874. Scott, R.B.Y. "'Behold, He Cometh With Clouds.'" **NTS** 5 (1958-59): 127-132.

Explores the Hebrew background of Dan. 7:13a as it relates to Rev. 1:7 and "the coming son of man." Concludes that clouds are a theophanic symbol and the Son of Man is a supernatural being in the text.

Chaps. 2-3

General Research

[1988]
875. Wilkinson, R.H.; "The *STULOS* of Revelation 3:12 and Ancient Coronation Rites." **JBL** 107 (1988): 498-501.

Suggests that the Greek term *STULOS* (Rev. 3:12) relates to the "King's pillar" in Solomon's Temple and is associated with Jewish coronations. John used the metaphor to connect the Christian with an active symbol of royalty and kingship.

[1985]
876. Knowles, J.H. "Gloryland from Revelation. Letters to the Seven Churches (Rev. 2-3)." **BT** 23 (1985): 173-181.

Presents archaeological and textual material relevant to Rev. 2-3 in order to clarify the various messages of Rev. 2-3.

[1969]
877. Brunk, M.J."The Seven Churches in Revelation 2-3." **BibSac** 126 (1969): 240-246.

Presents the argument that the seven churches represent seven periods of church history.

[1964]
878. Repp, A.C. "Ministry and Life in the Seven Churches." **CTM** 35 (1964): 133-147.

Describes Rev. 2-3 as a basis for the visions of Rev. 4-22, and a source of power for living. The churches represent Christianity in general, while God supplies ministries through the community, gifts to carry them out, along with the time to do them and opportunities. Chaps. 2-3 indicate that no two churches carry out their assigned tasks the same way. In fact, some even proved to be careless and indifferent. See also 5, F and H, (22).

[1962]
879. Fenasse, P. "Les lettres aux églises d'Asie." **BTS** 43 (1962); 2-3.

Not seen.

880. Leconte, R. "Les 7 églises de l'Apocalypse." **BTS** 43 (1962): 6-14.

Not seen.

881. Potin, J. "Pour lire l'Apocalypse." **BTS** 43 (1962): 2-3.

Not seen.

882. Wood, P. "Local Knowledge in the Letters of the Apocalypse." **ET** 73 (1961-62): 263-264.

Demonstrates how local references to Pergamum and Sardis validate the historicity and meaning of Rev. 2-3.

[1957]
883. Smith, P.K. "The Apocalypse of St. John and the Early Church." **JBR** 25 (1957): 187-195.

Discusses the situation of the early Asian church (Rev.2-3) and the function of the Revelation among those churches respecting the aim and technique of apocalyptic eschatology. Concludes that the book helped to keep a tension between the complex nature of apocalyptic myth and the worshipping congregation in order to offer the faithful hope.

[1956]
884. George, A.; "Un appel à la fidelité, Les Lettres aux Sept Eglises d'Asie." **BVCh** 15 (1956): 80-86.

Dates the Revelation during Domitian's reign, while suggesting several structural and thematic similarities between the seven letters. Demonstrates how several themes connect the chapters to the main theme of the book. The churches named are real Christian congregations in whom Christ is deeply interested and to whom He will bring judgment when He finally appears, according to their faith and charity. Lastly, the letters are a general call to the Church for greater fidelity and love. See also 5, F and H, (35).

[1943]
885. Nash, C.A."The Scriptural View of Church History." **BibSac** 100 (1943): 188-198.

Argues in favor of a four-fold "prewritten pattern" containing a prophetic outline for church history based on a literal reading of John's Revelation. In the end, all ecclesiastical organization is doomed to hopeless destruction. See also 5, F, G, (3), and H, (14).

[1940]
886. Heitmüller, F. "Die Sendschreiben des erhöhten Herrn (Apk 2-3)."

AW 37 (1940): 58-60, 77-80, 87-89, 102-105, 117-122, 132-135, 145-147.

Investigates the primary themes of the letters of Rev. 2-3 with a view to the author's emphasis on the status of Christ as the exalted Lord.

Ephesus

[1979]
887. Carson, D.A. "A Church that Does All the Right Things, But . . . ." **ChT** 23 (1979): 994-997.

Offers an exposition of Rev. 2:1-7 and concludes that the Ephesians were commended for a number of things (disciplined and persevering labor, vigilance, dislike of the Nicolaitans). But the Church is also open to reproach because she has let her initial love diminish and wither. The Church (then and now) is urged to remember earlier heights, to repent, and to return to first works of love. See also 5, F.

[1973]
888. Mackay, W.M. "Another Look at the Nicolaitans." **EQ** 45 (1973): 111-115.

Reviews several interpretations for the name "Nicolaitans" in John's Revelation and then offers the suggestion that names given in Rev. 2, viz., Balaam, Jezebel and Nicolas, all apply to church defections that were characterized by worldliness, false doctrine, and ritualism. See also 5, H, (13).

[1965]
889. Brox, N. "Nikolaos und Nikolaiten." **VC** 19 (1965): 23-30.

Not seen.

890. Sokolowski, F. "Notes and Observations: A New Testimony on the Cult of Artemis of Ephesus." **HTR** 58 (1965): 427-431.

Offers a note on recent archaeological work in Ephesus, especially relating to the shrine of Artemis, and concludes that account in Acts 19 probably describes some trouble caused by a resistance to the infiltration of a foreign cult.

[1962]
891. Maigaret, J. "Saint Paul. Le discours aux anciens d'Éphèse." **BTS** 43
(1962): 4-5.

Not seen.

[1956]
892. Janzon, P. "Nikolaiterna i Nya Testamentet och i fornkyrkan." **SvEA**
21 (1956): 82-108.

See summary in **NTA** 3 (1, '58): # 178. See also 5, H, (13).

[1955]
893. Tenney, M.C. "The Light that Failed." **BibSac** 112 (1955): 39-45.

Suggests that Rev. 2-3 are letters for every age and, in particular, Rev.
2:4-5 offers a critique of the modern evangelical church based on a
comparison with the church in Ephesus. See also 5, F.

Smyrna

[1988]
894. Schrage, W. "Meditatiion zu Offenbarung 2,8-11." **EvT** 48 (1988):
388-403.

Ponders the message directed to the church in Smyrna in her *Sitz im
Leben*, considering the fact that this phrase may have applied to the
Jewish community. Concludes by offering ideas regarding the appropriate
interpretation of the text in light of the above analysis.

[1962]
895. Dalmais, I.-H. "Saint Polycarpe de Smyrna." **BTS** 43 (1962): 4-5.

Not seen.

[1940]
896. Shepherd, M.H. "Smyrna in the Ignatian Letters: A Study in Church
Order." **JR** 20 (1940): 141-159.

Studies the Ignatian letters to determine the inner life and organization of
the early church in Smyrna of Asia Minor. Notes the character of church
order and authority, which was considered to parallel the monarchial

authority of the bishops, but not absolute at that time. It was simply developing.

Pergamum

[1957]
897. Daniélou, J. "L'Étoile de Jacob et la mission chrétienne à Damas." **VC** 11 (1957): 121-138.

Discusses the Star of Jacob and its connection of the Christian mission to Damas in Asia Minor.

Sardis

[1983]
898. Fuller, J.W. "'I Will Not Erase His Name from the Book of Life' (Revelation 3:5)." **JETS** 26 (1983): 297-306.

Analyzes Rev. 3:5 in order to clarify the problem related to erasing the "name" from "the Book of Life." Argues that 1) It is the Christian "overcomer" who, because of his/her faithfulness during persecution, enjoys the special benefits in eternity; 2) It is "the Book of Life" that contains the names (written from eternity) and deeds of the elect; and 3) The Revelation gives a word of caution to the church in Sardis: be careful, or else your name (i.e., "title" or "nickname") will remain on earth after death.

[1973]
899. Hemer, C.J."The Sardis Letter and the Croesus Tradition." **NTS** 19 (1972-73): 94-97.

Discusses the traditions behind Rev. 3:2-3 with special focus on the traditions of Croesus. See also 2, D and G.

Laodicea

[1987]
900. Porter, S.E. "Why the Laodiceans Received Lukewarm Water (Revelation 3:15-18)." **TB** 38 (1987): 143-149.

The reference to "lukewarm" water in Rev. 3:15-18 describes the local situation in that part of Asia Minor, where the Laodiceans were forced to drink a kind of warm water that was detestable. This historical reality was a reflection of the poor spiritual condition of that church.

[1958]
901. Rudwick, M.J.S. and Green, E.M.B. "The Laodicean Lukewarmness." **ET** 69 (1957-58): 176-178.

Expands an earlier article while supporting the conclusions of W. Ramsay concerning the local color in each of the letters, especially in Laodicea. Suggests that the traditional interpretations of the Greek words for "hot," "cold," and "lukewarm" are problematical in light of traditional Greek literature. The answer is to be found in local references to water, viz., *cold* suggests spiritual refreshment, *hot* suggests spiritual healing, and *lukewarm* implies uselessness, i.e., not in terms of temperature but in terms of the emptiness of their works. See also 5, F.

[1957]
902. Rudwick, M.J.S. "The Lukewarmness of Laodicea (Rev. iii.16)." **THB** 3 (1957): 2-3.

Investigates the local references and the social context of Laodicea in connection to Rev. 3:16 and the warnings given to the Church there.

[1952]
903. Wasson, M. "Revelation 3:20." **BTh** 3 (1952): 18-19.

Examines the text of Rev. 3:20 exegetically in reply to a criticism of a previous article. Concludes that the theme of holy judgment is dominant in the passage.

[1942]
904. Todd, J. "Laodicea and Its Eyesalve." **MC** 31 (1941-42): 558-562.

Investigates the local allusions in the last letter in Rev. 3. Concludes that the following words/phrases give insight into the text for exegetical interpretation: 1) Lukewarm insipidity regarding the water; 2) gold refined by fire; 3) white garments; and 4) eyesalve. See also 2, G.

Chap. 4

[1963]
905. Rinaldi, G. "La Porta Aperta nel Cielo (Ap 4,1)" **CBQ** 25 (1963): 336-347.

See summary in **NTA** 8 (1, '63): #276.

[1959]
906. Walker, N. "The Origin of the 'Thrice-Holy.'" **NTS** 5 (1958-59): 132-133.

Writes a short note on the "Trisagion" in Rev. 4:8 and its Hebrew source found in Is. 6:3. The original meaning was "Holy, exceeding holy."

907. Mowry, L. "Revelation 4-5 and Early Christian Liturgical Usage." **JBL** 71 (1952): 75-84.

Traces the literary and historical development of Rev. 4-5 and suggests that the four hymnic utterances were probably used in early Christian eucharistic worship liturgies. Rev. 4-5, therefore, are ancient pieces that bridge the gap between synagogue and church. See also 5, H, 15 and 19.

Chap. 5

[1971]
908. Ford, J.M."The Divorce Bill of the Lamb and the Scroll of the Suspected Adulteress. A Note on Apoc. 5,1 and 10, 8-11." **JSJ** 2 (1971): 136-143.

Studies two passages in the Revelation (5:1 and 10:8-11) and suggests that the two scrolls are connected to the marriage relationship of the Lamb and are also seen in relation to the marriage and adultery imagery of the Exodus. See also 5, H, 8.

[1958]
909. Russell, E. "A Roman Law Parallel to Revelation Five." **BibSac** 115 (1958): 258-264.

Identifies the similarities between the court scene and sealed document in Rev. 5 and the Roman legal transaction of *mancipatio* and the principle of substitution. Connections are made with Christ as the one who is over all men, nations, and creation. See also 5, C.

Chap. 6

[1967]
910. Van den Eynde, P. "Le Dieu du désordre. Commentaire synthétique d'Apocalypse 6, 9-11." **BVCh** 74 (1967): 39-51.

Studies Rev. 6:9 ff. and concludes that the cry of martyrs is to be understood in light of the OT as well as the eschatological situation of the primitive church. See also 3, D.

[1947]
911. Michael, J.H. "The Position of the Wild Beasts in Revelation vi.8b." **ET** 58 (1946-47): 166.

Answers the question, "Why are the wild beasts positioned last in the series in Rev. 6:8b," by stating that John knew of and used the order from Ps. of Sol. 13:2-3. See also 3, D; 4, B and 5, G, (3).

[1944]
912. Considine, J.S."The Rider on the White Horse (Apocalypse 6:1-8)." **CBQ** 6 (1944): 406-422.

Argues that Rev. 6 is a "new revelation" to John because, contrary to traditional opinion, the first rider is identified as the Lord Jesus who preaches the gospel. After this appearance the final judgment can begin. See also 4, B and 5, G, (3).

Chap. 7

[1989]
913. Winkle, R.E. "Another Look at the List of the Tribes in Revelation 7." **AUSS** 27 (1989): 53-67.

Discusses the list of the tribes recorded in Rev. 7 and suggests that a counterclockwise reversal reading of the list in Ez. 48:31-34 provides the proper background for the best interpretation of the passage. This brings the tribe of Judah into the place of prominence and that is consistent with John's theology. Lastly, W. argues that the omission of Dan is best explained from the association of Judas Iscariot with the tribe of Dan. See also 3, D.

[1973]
914. Comblin, J. "Le rassemblement du peuple de Dieu. Ap 7, 2-4. 9-14." **AS** 66 (1973): 42-49.

Focuses on the gathering of the people of God in Rev. 7, suggesting that God's suspended judgment is about to be concluded. Now God Himself gathers and seals those gathered from all the nations (real Israel) in order to celebrate the cosmic liturgy of Tabernacles. Suggests that the people of

God are really the martyrs (cf. 7:13-14); but God does not form them finally until the very end. Until that time, the gathering is in the process of being gathered. See also 5, H, (19) and (21).

[1967]
915. Feuillet, A. "Les 144,000 Israélites marqués d'un sceau." **NovT** 9 (1967): 191-224.

Directs attention to Rev. 7:4-8 as it pertains to the number 144,000 and says it is a word of consolation for Christians since the number itself symbolizes those who opposed the unbelieving Jews. They are not the unnumbered host of the saved nor the Judaeo-Christians. See also 3, F.

Chap. 11

[1988]
916. Robinson, B.P. "The Two Persecuted Prophet-Witnesses of Rev. 11." **ScripB** 19 (1988): 14-19.

Reviews the entire Book of Revelation in terms of its message and then presents an exposition of Rev. 11, suggesting that Rev. 11, with the theme of "witness," contains the central message of the whole Revelation. Thus John begins (cf. Rev. 1:2, 5) and ends (22:20) his work by focusing on one idea, viz., witness. See also 5, H, (21) and (31).

[1981]
917. Strand, K.A. "The Two Witnesses of Rev. 11:3-12." **AUSS** 19 (1981): 127-135.

Studies the literary context, symbolism, and thematic background of Rev. 11:3-12, concluding that the "two witnesses" are to be interpreted as "the word of God" and "the testimony of Jesus Christ." In contemporary terms this may be taken to mean 1) the OT prophetic message and 2) the NT apostolic witness. See also 5, H, (21).

[1965]
918. Vaucher, A.-F. "Les 1260 jours prophétiques dans les Cereles Joachimites." **AUSS** 3 (1965): 42-48.

Discusses interpretations of the 1,260-day prophetic period among the thirteenth century Joachim circles relevant to Dan. 7 and Rev. 12:14. Variations of the numbers are also considered in terms of their eschatological implications. See also 5, H, (31).

[1958]
919. Feuillet, A."Essai d'interprétation du chapitre xi de l'Apocalypse."
NTS 4 (1957-58): 183-200.

Offers a thorough exegesis and interpretation of Rev. 11 according to its
literary units: vss. 1-2, 3-13, and 14-19. Concludes that the crisis of A. D.
70 and the separation between the Church and the Synagogue serve as
historical background to the writing.

[1950]
920. Munck, J. **Petrus und Paulus in der Offenbarung Johannis. Ein
Beitrag zur Auslegung der Apokalypse.** Copenhagen: Rosenkilde &
Bagger, 1950.

Identifies the Elijah and Moses tradition as the basis for the two witnesses
in Rev. 11:3-13. But, M. contends, John reworked that tradition in light of
his theology of Christian martyrdom and, insofar as the author's intention
was to portray Christian suffering and the glorification of the Church, the
two witnesses symbolize Peter and Paul. See also 5, H, (21).

[1946]
921. Considine, J.S. "The Two Witnesses: Apoc. 11:3-13." **CBQ** 8
(1946): 377-392.

Offers a careful exegesis of Rev. 11:3-13 and suggests that the image of
the two witnesses is John's personal creation. The passage is to be taken
allegorically and the two witnesses are to be understood as the
representations of civil and religious powers among the children of God.
See also 5, H, (21).

Chap. 12

[1976]
922. Pikaza, J. "Apocalipsis XII. El nacimiento pascual del Salvador." **Sal**
23 (1976): 217-256.

See summary in **NTA** 21 (1, '77): #202.

[1973]
923. Montagnini, F. "La Chiesa alla ricerca di Cristo." **BO** 15 (1973): 27-
32.

See summary in **NTA** 18 (2, '74): #618.

[1971]
924. Gollinger, H. **Das "Grosse Zeichen" von Apokalypse 12.**
"Stuttgarter Biblische Monographien 11." Stuttgart: Katholisches
Bibelwerk, 1971.

This revised dissertation analyzes Rev. 12 as follows: 1) Discusses
general and critical problems; 2) Critiques several interpretations of Rev.
12; 3) Offers a thorough exegesis of the passage; 4) Examines the history
of the religious traditions behind the chapter; 5) Analyzes the meaning of
the birth of the child (Rev. 12:5); and, lastly, 6) Interprets the "great sign"
of Rev. 12 as the Church in heaven and on earth. See also 2, H.

[1966]
925. Montague, G.T."Eschatology and Our Lady." **MS** 17 (1966): 65-85.

Not seen. .

[1955]
926. LeFrois, B.J."The Theme of the Divine Maternity in the Scriptures."
MS 6 (1955): 102-119.

Not seen.

[1953]
927. Smith, E.J. "The Scriptural Basis for Mary's Queenship." **MS** 4
(1953): 109-117.

Not seen.

[1952]
928. LeFrois, B.J. "The Woman Clothed with the Sun." **AER** 126 (1952):
161-180.

Offers a critical and exegetical study of Rev. 12, noting the dramatic
structure of the chapter. The central figure of the woman is, at the same
time, Mary the mother of Jesus and the symbol of the ideal church. See
also 5, H, (39).

929. May, E. "Scriptural Basis for Mary's Spiritual Maternity." **MS** 3
(1952): 111-141.

Not seen.

[1950]
930. Unger, D.J."Cardinal Newman and Apocalypse XII." **TS** 11 (1950): 356-367.

Responds to an article by R. Murphy (**TS** 10 ['49], below 5, H) respecting Cardinal Newman's comments on Rev. 12. Offers further analysis concerning Newman's identification of the place and person of Mary in Rev. 12. Concludes the additional thought that Mary is alluded to in the chapter in a truly biblical sense and is living surrounded by the glory, in body and soul, of her Divine Son.

[1948]
931. Bruce, F.F. "The Crooked Serpent." **EQ** 20 (1948): 283-288.

Identifies Leviathan, "the crooked serpent," with the great dragon of Rev. 12:9. Discusses OT ideas and images relevant to this monster (serpent) as background to the Book of Revelation. Concludes that the book is really a record of the conflict between God and evil; but all is ultimately resolved in Christ.

Chap. 13

[1977]
932. Prete, B. "Il testo di Apocalisse 13, 9-10: una minaccia per i persecutori o un'esortazione al martirio?" **SBFLA** 27 (1977): 102-118.

See summary in **NTA** 22 (3, '78): #889.

[1973]
933. Brady, D. "The Number of the Beast in Seventeenth- and Eighteenth-Century England." **EQ** 45 (1973): 219-240.

Investigates the various interpretations of the symbolic number "666" as it applies to the seventeenth- and eighteenth-century English tyrants who persecuted the Christian church.

[1963]
934. Birdsall, J.N."Rev. XIII.6." **JTS** 14NS (1963): 399-400.

Notes that the variants found in p[47] regarding Rev. 13:6 should not be included in the apparatus of the text since they are not original.

935. Hillers, D.R."Revelation 13:18 and a Scroll from Murabba'at."
BASOR 170 (1963): 65.

Compares studies done on the number of the beast and disagrees with the opinion that forces the Hebrew spelling "*nrwn qsyr*" for the emperor Nero. An analysis of an Aramaic document from the second year of Nero's reign; the name "*nrwn qsyr*" is clearly indicated. See also 3, C and 4, B.

[1959]
936. Barclay, W. "Great Themes of the New Testament. V. Revelation XIII." **ET** 70 (1958-59): 260-264, 292-296.

Describes the view of the state in Rev. 13, where, apparently, Caesar worship had assumed its character. John addressed the emperor as the embodiment of satanic power and Caesar worship in his own time, and that power culminated in the return of Nero Revivus, the antichrist. See also 5, H, (2).

[1958]
937. Scharlemann, M.H."The Roll of Apocalyptic Thunder." **CTM** 29 (1958): 137-138.

Criticizes the Communist ceremony of rededication (*Jugendweihe*), i.e., the confirmation of youth for the party, and then compares the whole Communist movement with the Beast of Rev. 13. See also 3, F.

Chap. 14

[1952]
938. Boismard, M.E. "Notes sur l'Apocalypse [ch. 14, etc.]." **RB** 59 (1952): 161-181.

Discusses various interpretations of Rev. 14 regarding the 144,000 and the new Israel and OT connections. Studies further Rev. 22:6-21 in relationship to contemporary exegetical scholarship within the context of the whole book.

[1946]
939. Hanson, A.T."[Revelation 14:20]." **Th** 49 (1946): 141-144.

Examines the text of Rev. 14:20, noting the influence of Is. 63:3 and the connection between "without the city" and the crucifixion of Christ in relationship to God's judgment. Concludes that this refers to a loving God whose wrath and judgment are seen most clearly in the act of taking mankind's sin upon Himself. See also 5, G, 3.

Chap. 16

[1989]
940. Loasby, R.E. "'Har-Magedon' according to the Hebrew in the Setting of the Seven Last Plagues of Revelation 16." **AUSS** 27 (1989): 129-132.

Studies the Greek term *'Αρμαγεδων* in Rev. 16:16 and its connections with the Hebrew *'har mô'ed* ("mountain of assembly"). Concludes that the Revelation passage should be interpreted as Mt. Zion. It is from this place that Christ will render judgment against the wicked at the End Times. See also above 3, C.

[1977]
941. Eybers, I.H. "*Shephelah* and *Armageddon* -- what do they signify?" **TE** 10 (1977): 7-13.

Studies the two key terms in Rev. 16:16 -- *Shephelah* and *Armageddon* -- concluding that 1) *Shephelah* in the OT Hebrew did not include the coastal plain of Philistia and thus should not be translated "lowland." It is best to leave the word untranslated. 2) *Armageddon* most likely refers to the area of Megiddo; but the meaning of the prefix (*H*)*ar* is uncertain. Since the original readers of John's Revelation probably did not know Hebrew, E. concludes that the term *Armageddon* was just a meaningless proper name to the early Christians. See also 5, H, (3).

[1972]
942. Staples, P. "Rev. XVI 4-6 and Its Vindication Formula." **NovT** 14 (1972): 280-293.

Argues against Betz (1969) concerning the rise of apocalyptic from the context of Jewish-Hellenistic syncretism. Contrary to Betz's form study, S. exegetes Jer. 12:1; II Chr. 12:6; Dan 9:14; Tobit 3:2; Est. IV:17; and III Mac. 2:3 and concludes that the "vindication formula" probably originated in Christian martyrological material.

[1951]
943. Arndt, W.F. "Armageddon." **CTM** 22 (1951): 465-471.

Discusses the term "Armageddon" as used in the context of Rev. 16:16

and identifies the place geographically as the "Hill of Megiddo." A. sees this place as a field of decision for Jewish-Christian history, like Waterloo. Rev. 16:16 points to a time and occasion of the last great conflict between Christ and the forces of evil. The Church must be ready for this conflict by repenting.

Chap. 18

[1975]
944. Conzelmann, H. "Miszelle zu Apk 18:17." **ZNTW** 66 (1975): 288-290.

Exegetes Rev. 18:17 and Ez. 27:27-30, concluding that it is impossible to identify all the maritime professions from these passages due to the ambiguity of the terms. However, according to ancient usage, C. suggests that a good translation might be, "all captains, sea merchants, sailors, all who ply the sea as a profession." See also 3, C.

Chap. 19

[1975]
945. Ford, J.M. "For the Testimony of Jesus is the Spirit of Prophecy (Rev. 19:10)." **ITQ** 42 (1975): 284-291.

Argues that Rev. 19:10d is to be interpreted that "the spirit of prophecy" (subject of the sentence) is the witness of the genuine authenticity of Jesus Christ ("Jesus," in the objective genitive, is the predicate of the sentence). Thus prophecy, or the prophetic gift, is considered to be normative for the early Christian and operates in a way comparable to the gifts of the Spirit in Luke-Acts and I Corinthians. Sums up the article by suggesting that John inserted 19:10d as a gloss in the doublet to 22:8-9 because he thought that the churches would make a connection with Pentecost and/or the re-introduction of prophecy at that point in history. See also 5, H, (21) and (31).

Chap. 20

[1973]
946. Hughes, J.A. "Revelation 20:4-6 and the Question of the Millennium." **WTJ** 35 (1973): 281-302.

Addresses the question of the millennium in Rev. 20:4-6, evaluates Jewish traditions and relevant scholarship, and concludes that the passage refers to a single, disembodied (soul) resurrection and reign in heaven. Proposes an amillennial position. See also 1, C, (2) and 5, G, (4).

947. Smith, D.C. "The Millennial Reign of Jesus Christ: Some Observations of Rev. 20:1-10." **RQ** 16 (1973): 219-230.

Observes that the notion of a millennium in the Revelation is similar to Jewish and early Christian expressions of similar ideas. Reviews this literature and suggests that Ez. 37-48 is the most significant background to the book. Concludes with a structural analysis for setting the context of the millennium in a chronological framework. See also 5, G, (4).

[1961]
948. De Santo, C. "God and Gog." **RL** 30 (1960-61): 112-117.

Discusses the theme God vs. Gog, the final conflict as found in Ez. 38-39. Surveys relevant Jewish and early Christian literature and concludes with the affirmation that through Christ's sacrificial death the final battle against Gog has already been won. See also 5, G, (3), (4); H, (3), and (37).

[1960]
949. Ladd, G.E. "Revelation 20 and the Millennium." **RE** 57 (1960): 167-175.

Considers Rev. 20:1-4 as the locus for millennial doctrine. Suggests a two-stage Resurrection for believers, and the Kingdom as the interval between the Parousia and the "telos"; but the redeemed already live in the present and future (Heb. 6:5). Concludes that the victory of the Kingdom over Satan has already begun. See also 5, G, (2), (3), and (4).

[1956]
950. Kik, J.M. **Revelation Twenty: An Exposition**. Philadelphia, PA: Presbyterian and Reformed Publishing Company, 1956.

Offers a postmillennial, Augustinian interpretation (contra pre- and a-millennialists) of Rev. 20. K. views the statement in Rev. 21:11 as a reflection of the present Messianic kingdom, which is calling the universal Church to vanquish the enemies of God in a present, vigorous manner. Does not interpret Rev. 20 as treating the theme of the future finality of the world at large but suggests that John's interest is historical.

[1954]
951. Tenney, M.C. "The Importance and Exegesis of Revelation 20:1-8." **BibSac** 111 (1954): 137-148.

Studies Rev. 20:1-8 as it pertains to the relative importance of eschatology and surveys those various systems of thought. Concludes that the millennium is important because (1) it is the "long Day of the Lord" (p.147) when Christ administers judgment and justice; and (2) a fulfillment of prophecy (Zech. 14; Is. 11). See also 1, C, (2).

[1952]
952. Michael, J.H. "A Vision of the Final Judgment." ET 63 (1951-52): 199-201.

Analyzes the final vision of judgment based on Rev. 20:11-15. See also 5, G, (3).

[1950]
953. ———. "Gog and Magog in the Twentieth Century." ET 61 (1949-50): 71-73.

Examines Rev. 20:7-10 in light of Ez. 37-38 and the historical contexts. Concludes, with Swete, that in the end the forces of evil (especially Communism) will be subjugated and possibly annihilated. See also 5, G, (3).

[1946]
954. Arndt, W.F. "The Interpretation of Difficult Bible Passages." CTM 17 (1946): 181-197.

Presents an introductory description of biblical hermeneutics and then does an exegesis of Rev. 20:4-6 as an example of a "difficult passage." Concludes that the millennial period is understood to be a nonliteral long period of time. See also 1, C, (1) and 5, G, (4).

[1943]
955. Walvoord, J.F. "Is Satan Bound?" **BibSac** 100 (1943): 497-512.

Discusses "Biblical Prophecy" with respect to Satan's place in the prophetic program. Special attention is given to Rev. 20:1-3 as W. concludes that Satan will be literally bound and the righteous will rule on earth coincidentally with the return of Christ.

Chap. 21

[1991]
956. Sharkey, S.A. "A Vision of Hope [Rev. 21:1-22:5]." **BT** 29 (1991):
25-31.

Explains that the vision of the new Jerusalem (Rev. 21:1-22:5) is John's
last, two-part attempt to edify the suffering saints by: 1) proclaiming the
new creation (21:1-8) and 2) describing the glory of the new city,
Jerusalem (21:9-22:5).

[1989]
957. Topham, M. "The Dimensions of the New Jerusalem." **ET** 100
(1989): 417-419.

Studies Rev. 21:15-17 and contends that the exaggerated size of the holy
city there is out of proportion as compared to John's tendencies for
proportion in the rest of the book. Posits that the only way around the
problem is to read "cubit" for "stade" and therefore conclude that the total
perimeter of the city is 12,000 cubits or about 5.5 kilometers (3.5 miles).

[1968]
958. Stuhlmacher, P."'Behold, I Make All Things New.'" **LW** 15 (1968):
3-15.

Explores Rev. 21:5-8 and the central idea, "Behold, I make all things
new!" Suggests that this is the only direct word from God in the book and
it brings both comfort and warning. Possible sources are Is. 43; 65; Enoch
45:4; Baruch 44:12; and Qumran IQH iii,19-23. The phrase reflects the
Christian community's confession of Jesus' death and resurrection as it
pertains to renewal. See also 5, H, (6).

[1960]
959. Davis, C. "The End of the World: New Heavens and a New Earth."
Wor 34 (1959-60): 305-308.

Suggests that in the End the present world will not be annihilated, but
transformed, along with believers, who will have their own glorified,
risen bodies. References to Rev. 21:1-2 indicate that there will be a
"community" of the blessed after all, in accordance with the new
Jerusalem symbol. See also 5, H, (12) and (16).

[1953]
960. Marx, M.J. "The City of God." **Wor** 27 (1952-53): 136-137.

Gives homiletic instruction on Rev. 21:4 regarding the City of God as the ultimate victory and perfect manifestation of God's plan for creation and the Church. See also 5, H, (16).

[1942]
961. Burrows, E. "The Pearl in the Apocalypse." **JTS** 43 (1942): 177-179.

Details in a posthumous paper the character of the pearl in Rev. 21:21, suggesting that pearls and jewels are considered to be lights of the world to come, and relevant to Messianic exegesis. See also 6, G, (1).

Chap. 22

[1989]
962. Aune, D.E. "The Prophetic Circle of John of Patmos and the Exegesis of Revelation 22.16." **JSNT** 37 (1989): 103-116.

Exegetes Rev. 22:16 and concludes that John was part of a prophetic circle that existed late in the first century. A. summarizes his findings as follows: 1) Analysis of the syntax of Rev. 22:16 suggests that 'υμιν and ταις εκκλησιαις do not refer to the same group or entity. 2) The Greek 'αι εκκλησιαι probably refers to the seven churches addressed in Rev. 2-3 but 'υμεις must refer to a different yet overlapping group. 3) The reference to the "prophets" in Rev. 22:9 probably connects with the 'υμεις of vs. 16. 4) Since Judaism and early Christianity record the existence of certain prophetic groups, it is reasonable to suggest that a prophetic circle existed at the time of John's writing.

[1945]
963. Wilmot, J. "'The Revelation of Jesus Christ' Considered as His Endorsement of the Entire Scriptures." **EQ** 17 (1945): 211-220.

Investigates the opening and closing of the Revelation and suggests that these ideas reveal John's reliance on the whole of the Scriptural record. Discusses the connections between OT themes and the Book of Revelation.

-Select Dissertations-

[1950]
964. Saunders, F.B. **The Seven Churches of the Apocalypse.**
Unpublished Doctoral Dissertation. Louisville, KY: Southern Baptist
Theological Seminary, 1950.

Chapter 5

Theological / Thematic Studies

A. GENERAL WORKS

[1988]
965. Rowland, C. "Keeping Alive the Dangerous Vision of a World of Peace and Justice." **Con** 200 (1988): 75-86.

Argues that from the earliest time the Revelation of John has been a poem of hope for oppressed Christians and still serves as a resource for the poor in their ongoing struggle against evil and injustice. The hopeful message of the Revelation presents a dream of rapture and deliverance for the saints and that offers a legitimate escape from political struggle. Many Christians may be uneasy with this kind of interpretation of the book, but, R. says, that is not reason enough to avoid wrestling with our own apocalyptic/millennial tradition. We have a responsibility to rescue the Revelation from the literalists and others who dehumanize fanaticism and thereby render the book irrelevant to the human condition. See also below H, (21) and (27).

[1987]
966. Kealy, S.P. "'At a Loss When Faced with Apocalyptic.'" **ITQ** 53 (1987): 285-302.

Discusses general reasons for the neglect of the Revelation in the past (the gospel is inadequate, the work is cryptic, and there is little pastoral interest) and concludes that the book needs to be appreciated for what the author intends to do and what it accomplishes. Thus, the Revelation is best understood in terms of its limitations and its practical word for the world today.

[1986]
967. Boring, M.E. "The Theology of Revelation: 'The Lord Our God the Almighty Reigns.'" **Int** XL (1986): 257-269.

Observes the broad outline of John's theology in light of the impact of two basic contexts: 1) the Roman world and 2) the OT understanding of God as the Lord of history. The second context is the key to understanding the author's theological purpose. The OT prophet addressed the concrete historical situation like that of the early church with the prophetic word of the Almighty God. John, an "apocalyptic theologian," functioned as a Christian prophet. Choosing not to flee into future fantasy, he lived as an interpreter of the present, accepting both the reality of radical evil in history and the reality of the Almighty God. He helped the early church to cope by explaining "The *Heilsgeschichtlich* Context" of their experience. Ultimately the author is concerned with setting up a "Transcendent Context of Salvation History" that is expressed in both "Diachronic" (between creation and eschaton) and "Synchronic" (between heaven and the abyss) terms. Concludes that the summary of John's theology is seen in the "prophetic hymnic word" written as a word from heavenly worship in terms of "Alleluiah! The Lord our God the Almighty reigns." See also 5, C and H, (15).

[1984]
968. Mickelsen, A.B. **Daniel and Revelation: Riddles or Realities?**
Nashville, TN: Thomas Nelson Publishers, 1984.

Compares and contrasts theological themes in Daniel and Revelation by focusing on key questions, e.g., "How Big Is Your God?" The last chapter is titled "Fitting Our Short Lives into God's Big Plan." It attempts to resolve some of the tensions caused by the content of each book. The simplistic and repetitive approach sustains M.'s attempt to bridge a difficult gap between past and present by means of contemporary applications and popular language.

[1983]
969. Corsini, E. **The Apocalypse. The Perennial Revelation of Jesus Christ.** F. J. Moloney, trans. and ed. "Good News Studies 5."
Wilmington, DE: Michael Glazier, 1983.

The English translation of **Apocalisse prima e dopo** (1982). In this work the author offers a "continuous" reading of the Revelation of John and, also, focuses on the death and resurrection of Jesus as the ultimate event of history. Editor Moloney maintains that C. has eliminated most of the difficulties in the book by separating the (eschatological) critical problems from the (historical) perennial revelation of Jesus Christ in history. See also 5, C.

[1982]
970. Prigent, P. "L'étrange dans l'Apocalypse; une catégorie théologique."
LV 31 (1982): 49-60.

Discusses the nature of the Revelation in terms of its "strangeness" and
maintains that some of this is due to the readers' unfamiliarity with OT
and apocalyptic language and literature. However the general strangeness
of the book is due to the author's creative use of traditional images, novel
treatment of time and place, and fresh witness to the new creation.

[1981]
971. Fischer, K.M. "Die Christlichkeit der Offenbarung Johannes." **TLZ**
106 (1981): 165-172.

Contends that the historical notion of "already but not yet" in the
Revelation is the thing that identifies the book as Christian. Also other
themes identify the Christian character of the Revelation: 1) The idea of
God and his throne; 2) The Complex Christology (e.g., Jesus as coregent,
highest archangel, Son of Man and Judge, the Lamb); 3) The idea of the
community struggling toward final triumph; 4) The ethic of faith and
patience.

[1975]
972. Wilcock, M. **I Saw Heaven Opened. The Message of Revelation**.
"The Bible Speaks Today." Downers Grove, IL: InterVarsity, 1975.

A brief introduction and an exposition of the RSV text according to eight
scenes in the book: 1) The Church in the world (1:9-3:22); 2) Suffering
for the Church (4:1-8:1); 3) Warning for the world (8:2-11:18); 4) The
drama of history (11:19-15:4); 5) Punishment for the world (15:5-16:21);
6) Babylon the whore (17:1-19:10); 7) The drama behind history (19:11-
21:8); and 8) Jerusalem the bride (21:9-22:19).

[1968]
973. Nikolainen, A.T. "Über die theologische Eigenart der Offenbarung
des Johannes." **TLZ** 93 (1968): 161-170.

Investigates four basic themes surrounding the apocalyptic perspective of
John: 1) Prophet and prophecy. N. suggests that the Rev. is an example of
early prophetic-apocalyptic piety. 2) The Spirit. In the Rev. there is no
connection between gifts and the Spirit. He resembles the intercessor of
Rom. 8:26 and the Paraclete of John's Gospel. 3) Martyrs and confessors.

There is a difference between "martyrs," who die proclaiming the Word, and "confessors," who are simply Christians. 4) Saints and conversion. There is no special group of Christians called saints. Saints are just Christians living on earth. Also, conversion is a continuing experience for Christians because the Church is always in a state of repentance. Concludes that the Rev. is an example of very primitive Christian theology.

[1964]
974. Ladd, G.E. "The Theology of the Apocalypse." **GR** 7 (1963-64): 73-86.

Describes John's theology as moderately futuristic based on, first, his interpretation of Rev. 2-3 as letters addressed to seven historical churches (representatives of the whole Church) and, second, his contention that Rev. 7 ff. reflects a future orientation when God works out his redemption in history until the End. Concludes with a systematic theological summary of the Book of Revelation under three categories: 1) The Problem of Evil, 2) The Visitation of Wrath, and 3) The Coming of the Kingdom. See also 1, C, (2).

[1958]
975. Féret, H.M. **The Apocalypse of St. John.** Elizabethe Corathiel, trans. London: Blackfriars Publications; Westminster, MD: Newman Press, 1958.

A translation of **L'Apocalypse de St. Jean** (1943). The work is taken from a series of theological lectures on such themes as "Historic Context and Literary Style," "The Kingdom of God," "On the Mystery of Christ," "The Christian View of History According to the Apocalypse," "The Activity of Satan in History," "The Church in History and the Holy Jerusalem," "The Evolution of History and the End of Time." Concludes that the Book of Revelation synthesizes the NT and suggests a theology of history that offers eschatological "victory" to the Christian. See also 5, G and H, (14).

B. GOD

[1976]
976. Vögtle, A. "Der Gott der Apokalypse: Wie redet die christliche Apokalypse von Gott?" in **La notion biblique de Dieu.** J. Coppens, ed.

"BETL 41." Leuven: Leuven University Press: Gembloux: Duculot, 1976. Pp. 377-398.

Asserts that Revelation's portrayal of God has been shaped essentially by OT imagery and theology, but the final composition owes its character to the Christian tradition of John.

[1973]
977. Kallas, J. **Revelation: God and Satan in the Apocalypse.** Minneapolis, MN: Augsburg Publishing House, 1973.

A popular examination of the origins and place of the themes of God and Satan in the Book of Revelation. Asserts that life has meaning; and we are not to despair in the face of evil, because God is always present. Themes treated are, 1) Four Views (K. opts for the traditional view, "In That History"); 2) Revelation -- What the Word Means; 3) John, Domitian, Patmos; 4) Letters to Seven Churches; 5) Four Horsemen. Concluding chapter ("God and Satan -- Some Biblical Views Compared") takes the perspective of Jeremiah and Ezekiel and suggests that John's message is one of hope and comfort. The last word is this: God loves His children. A Six Session Study Guide for small groups by Knudsen is included. See also 5, H, (2).

C. JESUS CHRIST

[1987]
978. Hultgren, A.J. **Christ and His Benefits.** Philadelphia, PA: Fortress Press, 1987.

Considers the general theme of Christology and Redemption in the NT. Explains that the Revelation of John is an example of "Redemption won by Christ" and that redemptive Christology is both received tradition and the result of the conflict facing the early Christian community. See also 5, H, (32).

979. Wojciechowski, M. "Apocalypse 21.19-20: Des Titres Christologiques Cachés dans la Liste des Pierres Précieuses." **NTS** 33 (1987): 153-154.

Notes that a proper interpretation of the twelve stones adorning the foundation walls of Jerusalem in Rev. 21 begins by using the first letters of the list of gems as a reference to christological titles, e.g., *Iησους Χριστος, Σωτηρ*, etc.

[1985]
980. Beale, G.K. "The Origin of the Title 'King of Kings and Lord of Lords' in Rev. 17:14." **NTS** 31 (1985): 618-620.

Studies the literary history of the two phrases and concludes that this Christological title originates in the divine title of Dan. 4:37 from the LXX. This suggests Christ's sovereign defeat of the foe who is associated with eschatological Babylon. See also 3, D.

981. —————. "The Problem of the Man from the Sea in IV Ezra 13 and its Relation to the Messianic Concept in John's Apocalypse." **NT** 25 (1983): 182-188.

Compares the portrait of Christ shown in Rev. 4:6 and 5:6-7 to IV Ezra 13 and Dan. 7:2-3, 13, and concludes that John adapted the images from the common apocalyptic tradition found in Ezra and Daniel to portray Christ as the Messianic Lamb. Since the "sea" gives the nuance of evil in the pseudepigraphical works, John's adaption suggests the chaotic powers of the sea being calmed by the Lamb who now brings cosmic peace. See also 3, D.

[1984]
982. Giesen, H. "Christusbotschaft in apocalyptischer Sprache. Zugang zur Offenbarung des Johannes." **BK** 39 (1984): 42-53.

Discusses Jewish apocalypticism, first, in I Enoch and Daniel, then identifies certain features of Jewish apocalyptic writings: 1) Pseudonymity, 2) symbolic language, etc. G. concludes by placing the Revelation during Domitian's reign, outlining the book's structure, and reflecting on the similarities and differences with respect to Jewish apocalyptic works. See also 3, B and D.

[1982]
983. Edwards, S.A. "Christological Perspectives in the Book of Revelation" in **Christological Perspectives: Essays in Honor of Harvey K. McArthur.** Robert Berkey and Sarah Edwards, eds. N.Y.: Pilgrim Press, 1982: 139-154.

Studies the source and structure of the Revelation and concludes that in the two-part framework Christ is the central figure. Part 1 (4:1-22:7) is a Jewish (non-Christian) apocalypse depicting Jesus as a thoroughly Jewish Messiah. Part 2 (1:1-3:22; 22:8-21) is a Christian writing that sets out messianic titles that reflect a development of Palestinian, Hellenistic, and Jewish stages of Christian thought. The Book of Revelation finds unity in the themes of eschatololgical expectancy. See also 3, D.

[1981]
984. Bauckham, R. "The Worship of Jesus in Apocalyptic Christianity." **NTS** 27 (1981): 322-341.

Compares the Revelation and the Ascension of Isaiah respecting the worship of Jesus Christ and concludes that, although the apocalyptic traditions, which include both Revelation and the Ascension, insist on strict monotheism and prohibit "angelolatry," nevertheless, both works recognize that Jesus Christ is on the divine side of the line that the notion of monotheism must draw between God and His creatures. See also 3, D and 5, H, (41).

985. Guthrie, D. "The Lamb in the Structure of the Book of Revelation." **VE** 12 (1981): 64-71.

Argues that most of the twenty-nine references to the Lamb in the Revelation appear in worship settings and emphasize the motifs of sacrificial death, triumph, and the judgment of the Lamb. See also 5, H, (18).

[1977]
986. Leardi, J.C. "El Cristo-Total en el Apocalipsis." **RevB** 39 (1977): 253-281.

See summary in **NTA** 22 (3, '78): #887.

[1976]
987. Gehardsson, B. "Die christologischen Aussagen in den Sendschreiben der Offenbarung (Kap. 2-3)," in **Theologie aus dem Norden.** Albert Fuchs, ed. "Studien zum Neuen Testament und Seiner Umwelt 2." Freistadt: Plochl Verlag, 1976. Pp. 142-166.

Translates the Swedish article (1965) and concludes that the Christology of Rev. 2-3 emphasizes Christ as the Son of Man who will come and demonstrate a zeal against sin, false teaching, and the worship of Caesar.

Notes, further, that this "zeal" motif has antecedents in OT texts and traditions. See also 3, D.

[1975]
988. Lohse, E. "Der Menschensohn in der Johannesapocalypse" in **Jesus und der Menschensohn: Für Anton Vögtle.** R. Pesch and R. Schnackenburg, eds. Freiburg: Herder, 1975. Pp. 415-420.

Focuses on Rev. 1:13 and 14:14 for the Son of Man references and concludes that John's usage is independent of the gospel tradition and borrows from Dan. 7:13 respecting Jesus' authority for judgment. See also 3, D.

[1972]
989. Bovon, F. "Le Christ de l'Apocalypse." **RTP** 21 (1972): 65-80.

Connects the riches of the tree of life (Rev. 22:2) to John's description of Christ in the rest of the book. These riches seem to appear at different levels: 1) Grandeur (Rev. 1, 5, 12, 22); 2) Liturgical (1:4-6; 22:20-21); 3) Titles and figures (Cf. lamb, lord, Word, etc.). Further, Christ is described in relationship to the Church, the world, God, and the Spirit, and functions as the Lamb who reveals *apokalypsis* to the Church. Concludes that the Christ of the Apocalypse makes an authoritative political statement concerning the present and the future. See also 5, H, (27).

990. Sabugal, S. "El titulo *Christos* en el Apocalipsis." **Aug** 12 (1972): 319-340.

See summary in **NTA** 17 (3, '73): #1079.

[1971]
991. Holtz, T. **Die Christologie der Apokalypse des Johannes.** "Deutsche Akademie der Wissenschaften zu Berlin, 85; 2nd Ed." Berlin: Akademie Verlag, 1971.

This major study compares the christological titles used in the Revelation with their usage elsewhere in the NT and suggests that they reflect an OT background, but in a unique Johannine way. After examining passages on the Lamb, Christ's death, exaltation, and Parousia, H. concludes that through the death and resurrection of Christ the Christian community has been redeemed from sin and given priestly and royal dignity. Ultimately the whole cosmos will be placed under Christ's lordship, and, at his Parousia, heaven and earth will be renewed. See also 3, D and 5, G, (1).

992. Lohse, E. "Apokalyptik und Christologie." **ZNW** 62 (1971): 48-67.

Argues for the kingship of Christ as the major theme of the Revelation through a discussion of John's Christology against the backdrop of Jewish "apocalyptic." See also 1, C, (2).

[1970]
993. Dunphy, W. "Maranatha: Development in Early Christology." **ITQ** 37 (1970): 294-308.

Considers the grammatical aspects of the Greek term *maranatha* and concludes that if it is to be understood properly, Rev. 22:20 must be read in light of Did. 10.6 and I Cor. 16:22. It is an expression of hope for the community for the coming kingdom in a liturgical setting. See also 3, C, D and 5, H, (19).

[1967]
994. Hillyer, N. "'The Lamb' in the Apocalypse." **EQ** 39 (1967): 228-236.

Analyzes various motifs in the Revelation, e.g., Redeemer, ruler, judge, and pastor, and concludes that the Lamb imagery found in the Revelation is pervasive and, probably, is drawn from the Jewish notion of the Passover Lamb and Isaiah 53. See also 3, D.

995. Von der Osten-Sacken, P. "Christologie, Taufe, Homologie -- Ein Beitrag zur Apokalypse John 1,5 f." **ZNW** 58 (1967): 255-266.

Studies Rev. 1:5-6, and concludes that the passage is a Christian hymn of praise to Jesus Christ that John took from the Church and incorporated into his work. After commenting on the Christological statements, O.-S. suggests that the hymn probably originated in a baptismal and praise setting that reflected the Christian community at large. See also 5, H, (15).

[1965]
996. Comblin, J. **Le Christ dans l'Apocalypse.** "Bibliotheque de Theologie, Theologie Biblique 3/6." Paris: Desclée, 1965.

Studies the Christology of the Revelation based on his treatment of the themes Lamb/Servant of God, He Who is to come, Witness, the Christ, and the Living One, and concludes that a Jewish background sets the stage for the ideas in the book.

997. Gerhardsson, B. "De kristologiska utsagorna i sändebreven i Uppenbarelseboken (kap. 2-3)." **SvEA** 30 (1965): 70-90.

See summary in **NTA** 12 (3, '68): #1001.

998. Thomas, R.L. "The Glorified Christ on Patmos." **BibSac** 122 (1965): 241-247.

Investigates the initial vision of the glorified Christ in Rev. 1:13-16 and illustrates the language and imagery connections with subsequent christophanies in the book. Concludes that Rev. 1:13-16 is a prelude to the whole book. See also 4, B, (1).

[1964]
999. Boyd, W.J.P. "'I Am Alpha and Omega' (Rev. 1:8; 21:6; 22:13)" in **SE 2/1.** F. L. Cross, ed. "Texte und Untersuchungen 87." Berlin: Akademie Verlag, 1964. Pp. 526-531.

Studies the "Alpha-Omega" phrase and shows how John uses the Hebrew of Is. 44:6 (cf. also 48:12) in Rev. 1:8, etc., in order to demonstrate the divine relationship between God and Christ. Christ is identified as the "Alpha and Omega" because 1) He "predestinates and recreates" God's people and 2) He, Himself, is the gift of eternal life and ultimate sanctification to all who believe. See also 3, D,

1000. Schlier, H. "Jesus Christus und die Geschichte nach der Offenbarung des Johannes" in his **Besinnung auf das Neue Testament: Exegetische Aufsätze und Vortrage II.** Freiburg: Herder, 1964. Pp. 358-375.

Investigates the place of Christ in the Revelation in relationship to the historicity of the book. Christ's present and future victories are noted. See also 5, H, (14).

[1963]
1001.Fenasse, J.-M. "Terme et début, voilà ce que je suis." **BVCh** 54 (1963): 43-50.

Contends that Christ is the beginning and eschatological termination of all being, life and biblical revelation, based on an analysis of Rev. 22:13. See also 3, D.

[1962]
1002. Davies, P.E. "Experience and Memory: The Role of the Exalted Christ in the Life and the Experience of the Primitive Church." **Int** 16 (1962): 181-192.

Studies the role of the exalted Christ in the life and experience of the primitive church, with particular focus on Acts, I Peter, Hebrews, and the Revelation. Shows the development of Christology within the Church based on the resurrection faith and the cherished memory of the historical Jesus. Concludes that both are important in recognizing how primitive Christology grew from earliest times.

[1961]
1003. Virgulin, S. "Recent Discussion of the Title 'Lamb of God.'" **Scrip** 13 (1961): 74-80.

Discusses scholarship (1950-60) on the concept of "The Lamb" in John's Gospel. Concludes that the eschatological sense is secondary to the idea of redemption in the Johannine title, "The Lamb." See also 5, H, (18).

[1960]
1004. Schmitt, E. "Die christologische Interpretation als das Grundlegende der Apokalypse." **ThQ** 140 (1960): 257-290.

Translates the Greek term *aggelos* in Rev. 1:1 as "messenger," which is taken to refer to Christ himself, who mediates the whole book to John. Concludes that the title of the work, "A revelation of Jesus Christ" is intended to identify the Revelation's real messenger, viz., Jesus. See also 4, B, (1) and 5, H, (1).

[1959]
1005. Feuillet, A. "Le Messie et sa Mere d'apres l'chapitre XII de l'Apocalypse." **RB** 66 (1959): 55-86.

Analyses Rev. 12 and concludes that the "child" in the allegory is the Messiah and the "woman" is the mother of the Messiah, viz., the people of God. See also 5, H, (39).

1006. ————. "The Messiah born of the people of God." **TD** 11 (1963): 10-11.

Offers a condensed version of an earlier article based on a study of Rev.

12. Cf. **RB** 66 (1959): 55-86.

1007. Scott, R.B.Y. "'Behold, He Cometh with Clouds.'" **NTS** 5 (1958-59): 127-132.

Discusses Rev. 1:7 as John's adaption of Dan. 7:13 and concludes that John identified Jesus with Yahweh and the eschatological Son of Man who come "with" (translates the Greek term μετα) the clouds for final judgment. See also 3, C and D.

[1958]
1008. Giblet, J. "De revelatione Christi gloriosi in Apoc. I, 9-20." **ColM** 43 (1958): 495-497.

See summary in **NTA** 3 (2, '59): #423. See also 4, B, (1).

1009. Stanley, D.M. "'Carmenque Christo Quasi Deo Dicere . . . .'" **CBQ** 20 (1958): 173-191.

Offers the opinion that the Christological hymns of the NT employ three principal symbols for Christ's divinity, viz., suffering and glorification of the Servant, enthronement, and the Son of Man as second Adam. A part of this article points to Rev. 5:9-10, 12, and 13 as a liturgical example of the first symbol. There the Servant motif is fused with John's notion of "the Lamb of God." See also 5, H, (18) and (19).

1010. ———. "John the Witness." **Wor** 32 (1957-58): 409-416.

Identifies various aspects to John's witness/testimony to Jesus Christ as Lamb, Suffering Servant, Messiah, etc. Includes the Revelation as one part of the total Johannine statement. Concludes that Christian redemption in John's witness is viewed consistently as divine judgment. See also 5, G, (3) and 5, H, (21).

[1957]
1011. Brownlee, W.H. "Messianic Motifs of Qumran and the New Testament." **NTS** 3 (1956-57): 195-210.

Examines several messianic motifs identifying Christ as the "Amen" in Rev. 1:12 ff.; 2:7; etc. See also 3, D.

[1951]
1012. Gutzwiller, R. **Herr der Herrscher: Christus in der Geheimen Offenbarung**. Einsiedeln: Benziger, 1951.

Discusses the form and content of the Rev. as introduction to the secrets of the work in three sections.

[1948]
1013. Skehan, P.W. "King of Kings, Lord of Lords (Apc. 19:16)." **CBQ** 10 (1948): 398.

Explains the title "King of Kings, Lord of Lords" in contrast to the Beast, identified as 666 in Rev. 19. Concludes that the letters in the title in Aramaic add up to the numbers 777! See also 3, D and 4, B, (2).

[1943]
1014. Tribble, H.W. "The Christ of the Apocalypse." **RE** 40 (1943): 167-176.

Offers a practical survey of the titles for Christ in the Revelation and connects those titles to the major themes in the book. See also 3, D.

[1942]
1015. Beck, D.M. "The Christology of the Apocalypse of John" in **New Testament Studies: Critical Essays in New Testament Interpretation with Special Reference to the Meaning and Worth of Jesus.**Edwin P. Booth, ed. New York: Abingdon-Cokesbury Press, 1942. Pp. 253-277.

Studies the various Christological sections of the Revelation, and suggests that John characterizes Jesus primarily by means of allusive figures and unique ideas but not by traditional NT titles. See also 3, D.

D. THE HOLY SPIRIT

[1985]
1016. Jeske, R.L. "Spirit and Community in the Johannine Apocalypse." **NTS** 31 (1985): 452-466.

Argues that the Greek references to the Spirit, $εν$ $πνευματι$, (cf. Rev. 1:10; 4:2; 17:3; and 21:10) are not technical terms for ecstasy. They are to be taken as a relational symbolic code for life in the community of the

Spirit. Thus being "in the Spirit" suggests identification, reception, prophetic responsibility, and participation in relationship to the Church. The phrase also is a sign of the book's topical structure. See also 5, F.

[1980]
1017. Bauckham, R. "The Role of the Spirit in the Apocalypse." EQ 52 (1980): 66-83.

Suggests that the Holy Spirit moved John's normal senses to view visions and hear auditions. This is the meaning of Rev. 1:10 (εν πνευματι). The Spirit of prophecy carried the word of the exalted Christ to the Church. He also gave affirmation to John's revelations and guided the prayers of the Church on earth to the Lord in heaven. The "seven spirits" (Rev. 1:4; 3:1; etc.) appears to be a symbol for the Spirit of God. Finally, the Spirit's role is to direct generally the Church to focus on the Parousia and to interpret the present in light of the future when the Lord returns. See also 5, H 31.

[1973]
1018. Bruce, F.F. "The Spirit in the Apocalypse" in **Christ and Spirit in the New Testament: In Honour of C. F. D. Moule.**B. Lindars and S. S. Smalley, eds. Cambridge: University Press, 1973. Pp. 333-344.

Discusses the nature of the Spirit in John's Apocalypse under four categories: I. "The Seven Spirits," II. "The Spirit of Prophecy," III. What the Spirit Says to the Churches," IV. "The Responsive Spirit." The central role of the Spirit in the Revelation is seen in Section II (cf. Rev. 19:10) in relationship to prophecy (see Ez. 37:1). The "Responsive Spirit" is connected to the *Maranatha* cry and the Lord's presence in communion and worship. See also 5, F.

[1952]
1019. Schweizer, E. "Die sieben Geister in der Apokalypse." EvT 11 (1951-52):502-512.

Studies "the seven spirits" in the Revelation beginning with the theological situation of Jewish anthropology as problematic and then tracing the notion of the spirit through the NT, through the Revelation itself, and in relationship to Gnostic thought. The phrase connects with the author's view of the seven angels. See also 4, B and 5, H, 1.

[1942]
1020. Walvoord, J.F. "The Eschatology of the Holy Spirit." BibSac 99

(1942): 418-427.

Discusses the work of the Holy Spirit in the eschatological context of Salvation and in terms of the believer's place in the Tribulation and in the Millennium. See also 5, G, (4).

E. THE TRINITY

There is very little literature available at this time that focuses on the trinity as a clear element of theology in the Revelation of John. There are however some commentaries that identify a primitive allusion to the trinity in the introductory salutation, "Grace to you and peace, from him who is and who was and who is to come; and from the seven Spirits [Holy Spirit?] that are before his throne; and from Jesus Christ...." (See R. H. Mounce, **The Book of Revelation,** "The New International Commentary on the New Testament," p. 69.)

F. THE CHURCH

[1981]
1021. Keegan, T.J. "Revelation: A Source of Encouragement." **BT** 19 (1981): 373-377.

Studies Rev. 7 and suggests that this chapter puts into perspective the crises of the day. The church on earth (7:1-8) is protected in the present (symbolized by the "sealing") and the future (symbolized by the throng emerging from tribulation in white robes, 7:9-17). This knowledge should encourage the church of every age. See also 4, B.

1022. Wolff, C. "Die Gemeinde des Christus in der Apokalypse des Johannes." **NTS** 27 (1981): 186-197.

Argues that in the Revelation the most essential thing for the Christian community is to wait for the final consummation of its salvation, which is already in effect and is moulding its life. What salvation means is sharing with Christ in community, i.e., in his present suffering and future glory. This fullness in Christ is understood under the sign of *pro nobis*, while the community already begins to celebrate God's salvation. See also 5, H, 32.

[1979]
1023. Trevijano Etcheverria, R. "La misión en las iglesias de Asia

(Apoc 2-3)." **Sal** 26 (1979): 205-230.

See summary in **NTA** 24 (2, '80): #571.

[1973]
1024. Montagnini, F. "L'Eglise à la recherche du Christ. Ap. 11, 19a; 12, 1-6.10ab." **AS** 66 (1973): 22-27.

Compares apocalyptic birth-pang imagery to the sufferings of Christ in Rev. 11-12 and concludes that John intentionally presented the picture of suffering to the Church for encouragement. Suggests further that the woman of Rev. 12 is to be identified with the Church, which must be purified through suffering, and Mary the suffering mother of Jesus. See also 5, H, 26 and 39.

[1966]
1025. Aune, D.E. "St. John's Portrait of the Church in the Apocalypse." **EQ** 38 (1966): 131-149.

Analyzes John's figures of speech (figurative language, metaphor, and allegory) regarding the Church in four catetgories: 1) Language stressing God's direct initiative respecting man; 2) Language expressing the human response to God's initiative; 3) Language taken from human life; and 4) Extended metaphors and allegories of the Church, which John hopes to encourage in the midst of hostility. Concludes that John is expressing the antithesis and exclusiveness between the Church and the world, while stressing the faithfulness and ultimate victory of the Church.

1026. Minear, P.S. "Ontology and Ecclesiology in the Apocalypse." **NTS** 12 (1965-66): 89-105.

Traces the relationship between ontology (reality) and ecclesiology (the Church) in the Revelation through analysis of selected passages under four headings: 1) John and his readers; 2) John's method regarding space-time realities; 3) John's notion of the two cities; and 4) John's understanding of the boundaries between the two cities. Concludes that John is neither pure Catholic nor Protestant.

[1964]
1027. Ryrie, C.C. "Apostasy in the Church." **BibSac** 121 (1964): 44-53.

Attempts to identify modern "ecclesiasticism" with the picture of the apostate church in Scripture. See also 5, H, 13.

[1963]
1028. Nikolainen, A.T. "Der Kirchenbegriff in der Offenbarung des Johannes." **NTS** 9 (1962-63): 351-361.

Argues that the Book of Revelation reveals an ecclesiogy that is relevant to current ecumenical considerations and consistent with general NT ecclesiology. Divides the study into four basic sections : 1) Rev. 2-3 identify the historical church as $εκκλησια$ and ever present among individual communities that take $μετανοια$ seriously; 2) Rev. 7 and 14 show a unified church militant and victorious in the eschatological 144,000; 3) Rev. 12 describes the dualism of salvation-history in the dragon's hostility against the Church; 4) The Church in opposition to Babylon and the Harlot (Rev. 17-18) and triumphant as the Bride of the Lamb and new Jerusalem (Rev. 21-22) argues for its Christological nature. See also 5, H, 26.

[1960]
1029. Best, E. "Spiritual Sacrifice: General Priesthood in the New Testament." **Int** 14 (1960): 273-299.

Analyzes the idea of "Priesthood" in the NT, while arguing that I Peter and the Revelation make explicit statements in favor of a general priesthood in the Church. See also 5, H, 30.

[1959]
1030. Brownlee, W.H. "The Priestly Character of the Church in the Apocalypse." **NTS** 5 (1958-59): 224-225.

Investigates Rev. 2-3, in particular the phrase "angel of the church," and concludes that John borrowed from Mal. 2:7 and Dan. 12:3 in order to describe the priestly role of bishops. Although the Qumran documents indicate that the term for bishop stresses a teaching function, the "angel" in the phrase probably points to the churches themselves with a priestly emphasis. See also 4, B.

[1957]
1031. Trabucco, A. "La 'Donna ravvolta di sole' (Apoc 12). L'interpretazione ecclesiologica degli cattoliici dal 1563 alla prima metà del secolo XIX." **Mar** 19 (1957): 1-58.

See summary in **NTA** 2 (2, '58): #358.

[1952]
1032. Muirhead, I.A. "The Bride of Christ." **SJT** 5 (1952): 175-187.

Examines "Bridal Theology" in the OT and the NT (including the Revelation, Chaps. 19, 21, and 22). Says that the symbols of Lamb, Messiah, and Bride suggest eschatological ideas of the relationship between Christ and his Church. See also 5, C.

[1946]
1033. Sickenberger, J. "Die Messiasmutter im 12. Kap. der Apokalypse." **TQ** 126 (1946): 357-427.

Suggests that the woman in Rev. 12 is Mary, the mother of Messiah. See also 5, H, (39).

[1942]
1034. Bonnefoy, J.B. "Les interprétations ecclésiologiques du chap. 12 de l'Apocalypse." **Mar** 9 (1942): 208-222.

Not seen. See also 4, B and 5, H, 39.

[1940]
1035. Heitmüller, F. "Das Geheimnis der Gemeinde Jesu (Apk 1,9-20)." **AW** 37 (1940): 298-302.

Not seen. But see 5, C.

G. ESCHATOLOGY

(1) General Research

[1989]
1036. König, A. **The Eclipse of Christ in Eschatology: Toward a Christ-Centered Approach.** Grand Rapids, MI: Eerdmans Publishing Co., 1989.

Develops a Christocentric (practical) eschatology in order to show that since Jesus was "the last" and "the end" (Rev. 22:13), his entire life's history (and ours!) is the description of "eschatology." Initial chaps. present Christ in relationship to "the end" and "eschatology." Consideration is then given to explaining how Jesus realizes that goal for us, in us, and with us.

1037. Strand, K.A. "The 'Spotlight-On-Last-Event' Sections in the Book of Revelation." **AUSS** 27 (1989): 201-221.

Presents analysis and exposition of Rev. 7, 10:1-11:13, and 14:1-3 as important end-time activity periods for God and Jesus Christ in judgment and salvation. Concludes with words of assurance for the faithful.

[1980]
1038. Günther, H.W. **Der Nah- und Enderwartungshorizont in der Apokalypse des heiligen Johannes**. "Forschung zur Bibel 41." Würzburg: Echter, 1980.

This revised dissertation studies the eschatology of the Revelation in three main parts: 1) Surveys recent hermeneutical trends and proposes an alternate "dialectical" methodology. 2) Analyzes passages that suggest an imminent eschaton, the eschatological horizon in the three plagues (5:1-8:1; 8:2-11, 18 [19]; 15:5-16:21), the symbol "three and a half" times (12:14). 3) Concludes that recognizing the dialectical character of eschatology may be the best (appropriate) horizon for interpreting the book. John seems to demonstrate this by describing the End Time as the period that continues from the Christ-event through the present into the parousia.

[1977]
1039. Bauckham, R. "The Eschatological Earthquake in the Apocalypse of John." **NovT** 19 (1977): 224-233.

Discusses John's description and use of the earthquake as an important background symbol in the Rev. Concludes that the earthquake has theological significance regarding the End and God's Last Judgment.

[1974]
1040. Mounce, R. "Pauline Eschatology and the Apocalypse." **EQ** 46 (1974): 164-166.

Asserts that Rev. 13, 17, 19, and 20 compare favorably with I Thes. 4 and II Thes. 2, in terms of reflecting a common source of apocalyptic concepts and imagery. See also 3, D.

[1972]
1041. Rissi, M. **The Future of the World: An Exegetical Study of**

Revelation 19:11-22:15. "SBT 2/25." Naperville, IL: Allenson, 1972. Revised from **Die Zukunft der Welt** (Basel, 1966).

Expands and revises the edition of **Die Zukunft der Welt** ('66) and incorporates sections of previous studies on "the Kerygma of the Revelation" and **Time and History** ('66). R. argues for an eschatological interpretation while focusing on Rev. 19-22 as the key eschatological section in the book. There are two stages of eschatology for the Church and the world: I) Events between Parousia and end of the world (including last judgment); II) Creation of the new world. Conclusion states that, 1) Salvation for believers has already appeared in Jesus; 2) Salvation for all reality is for the present disclosed only to the faithful and thus remains a promise for the future; 3) History is to be understood as the area of promise and fulfillment with God in the center; 4) OT images for hope become transparent in the present because of faith in the victorious Lamb. See also 4, B, 2.

1042. Roberts, J.W. "The Meaning of Eschatology in the Book of Revelation." **RQ** 15 (1972): 95-110.

Argues against the views that identify the end of the world with the destruction of Rome. Suggests that these scholars make two errors in method: 1) They make all apocalyptic eschatology one unit and, then, assume that John was controlled by this unity. 2) They say that all references in the book that can have ultimate eschatological significance do in fact refer to the end of the world. Both assumptions are faulty. See also 1, C.

1043. Walther, F.E. "Vollendung (Offenbarung 21,9--22,5)." **TBei** 3 (1972): 145-151.

Discusses this section of the Revelation under three headings: 1) The final consummation of the blessed; 2) The heavenly world in which they live; and 3) The type of life they live. The faithful are best described by the two images of a bride and those who reflect God's glory and bear His name on their foreheads. Their world is depicted as a glorious city descending from heaven and as a paradise free from suffering and sadness. Concludes that the life of the "blessed" may be described in three actions: beholding the Lord, serving the Lord, and reigning with Him. See also 5, H, 12.

[1969]
1044. Wood, A.S. "The Eschatology of Irenaeus." **EQ** 41 (1969): 30-41.

Examines the character of the eschatological thought of Irenaeus and touches briefly on his millennial interpretation of Rev. 20-21. See also 1, C, (2) and 5, G, (4).

[1968]
1045. Fiorenza, E.S. "The Eschatology and Composition of the Apocalypse." **CBQ** 30 (1968): 537-569.

Argues for *eschatology* and not *zeitgeschichte* as the key to the interpretation of the Revelation, i.e., the in-breaking of God's kingdom and the destruction of evil powers. The eschatological expectation and thematic structure of the composition of the book are carefully investigated and point to the author's basic thesis. See also 3, E.

[1962]
1046. Bartina, S. "La Escatologia del Apocalipsis." **EsB** 21 (1962): 297-310.

See summary in **NTA** 9 (1, '64): # 278.

[1961]
1047. Newport, J.P. "Biblical Interpretation and Eschatological Holy History." **SWJT** 4 (1961): 83-110.

Identifies four principles for Bible interpretation, viz., 1) Linguistic, 2) Historical, 3)Theological, and 4) Homiletical. The theological method is best expressed in the "Eschatological-Holy History," the key to all Bible interpretation. Traces the history and application of this principle from Pietistic circles (Bengel) to the present.

[1960]
1048. Hamilton, N.Q. "The Last Things in the Last Decade." **Int** 14 (1960): 131-142.

Offers a general review of recent studies dealing with the significance of eschatology for theological scholarship. Touches briefly on the publications of Bowman, Richardson, and Lilje, while noting the methodological value of the reinterpretation of apocalyptic as the word of God. See also 3, B.

[1956]
1049. Colunga, A. "El Milenio (Apoc. XX, 1-6)." **Sal** 3 (1956): 220-227.

Not seen.

[1955]
1050. Cannon, W.R. "Eschatology in the Light of Current Theological Discussions." **RL** 24 (1955): 524-536.

Surveys the literature on the concept of eschatology in relationship to Methodist doctrine of the last things. Occasional references to the Book of Revelation. See also 1, A.

[1953]
1051. Torrance, T.F. "The Modern Eschatological Debate." EQ 25 (1953): 45-54, 94-106, 167-178, 224-232.

Offers an extended discussion of the modern scholarly debate on eschatology treating three time periods: First Century, Reformation, and Present Day. Draws in relevant references to the Revelation.

[1949]
1052. Flack, E.E. "Some Aspects of Christian Eschatology." **LQ (LThS)** 1 (1949): 369-393.

Investigates aspects of eschatology in light of modern theological research and renewed interest, especially in terms of new Luther research (e.g., Holl, Heim, Nygren, Althus). Some themes include, The Paradox and Purpose of the Parousia, Resurrection of the Dead, Rejection of Universalism and Chiliasm, etc. Concludes that Luther is Paul's ablest interpreter and saw superbly the return of Christ for judgment and hope as help for the Church. Occasional allusions to the Rev.

[1944]
1053. Beasley-Murray, G.R. "The New Testament Doctrine of the End." EQ 16 (1944): 202-218.

Treats major themes relevant to general NT eschatology: Apostasy, Antichrist, Great Distress, the Parousia, the Resurrection, the Judgment, the Kingdom. Identifies the important role the Book of Revelation plays in terms of its contribution to NT eschatological doctrine.

[1941]
1054. Grant, F.C. "Eschatology and Reunion." **RL** 10 (1941): 83-91.

Studies the relationship between the biblical notions of eschatology and reunion.

(2) The Parousia, Rapture, Resurrection

[1980]
1055. Townsend, J.L. "The Rapture in Revelation 3:10." **BibSac** 137 (1980): 252-266.

Presents a paraphrase of Rev. 3:10 as follows: "Because you have held fast the word which tells of my perseverance, I also will preserve you in a position outside the hour of testing . . . ." Concludes that the phrase *τηρησω εκ* identifies the position and status of the Church during the tribulation period, i.e., "the hour of testing." Thus, Rev. 3:10 may be taken to refer to the pretribulational rapture of the Church. See also 4, B.

[1977]
1056. Hughes, P.E. "The First Resurrection: Another Interpretation." **WTJ** 39 (1977): 315-318.

Discusses the general theme of resurrection in the Revelation (especially Rev. 20:5 f.) and suggests that both first and second resurrections are bodily resurrections. The "second" resurrection is identified with the general (universal) resurrection at the end of the age; but the first resurrection is to be identified with Christ's resurrection. God's faithful witnesses, therefore, are presently sharing in Christ's resurrection and await their own personal ("second") resurrection at the End. See also 5, C.

[1976]
1057. Michaels, J.R. "The First Resurrection: A Response." **WTJ** 39 (1976): 100-109.

Argues against M. Kline's conclusions (**WTJ** 37 ['75]: 366-375) regarding the first resurrection of Rev. 20 as the intermediate state. Also contests the view that the second resurrection is "metaphorical," the parallelism between "first" and "second" (Rev. 20) and "first" and "new" (Rev. 21), the paradoxical interpretation of resurrection in Rev. 20:5-6, and the place of literal future resurrection. The singular basis of argument for "rest" for the Christian dead is the expectation that their bodies will be raised at the Second coming (see 6:11; 14:13). [Note that Kline responds to Michaels' critique on pp. 110-119 of this issue.]

[1975]
1058. Kline, M.G. "The First Resurrection." **WTJ** 37 (1975): 366-375.

Argues contextually that πρωτος in Rev. 20:5 (in "the first resurrection") should be interpreted according to amillennial exegesis. Based on an analysis of Rev. 21, Hebrews, and I Cor. 15, the term suggests the opposite of "new," "second," or "last," referring to a transient experience of the present world. Concludes that the first resurrection is nonbodily and a metaphor for the death of the faithful Christian.

[1974]
1059. Shepherd, N. "The Resurrection of Revelation 20." **WTJ** 37 (1974): 34-43.

Using the "Scripture interprets Scripture" hermeneutic, S. argues that if Rev. 20 is read in light of I Cor. 15:23 and Jn. 5:24-29 and 11:24-25, the conclusion should be reasonably obvious: 1) The first resurrection refers to the baptism experience; and 2) The second resurrection refers to the resurrection of the body at the Second Coming of Christ. The main contrast between the two resurrections is between personal and cosmic salvation. The former is a resurrection experience by means of baptism into and resurrection with Christ. The latter is a cosmic reconciliation, which also includes as an integral part bodily resurrrection. See also 4, B.

[1971]
1060. Aldrich, R.L. "Divisions of the First Resurrection." **BibSac** 128 (1971): 117-119.

Studies the term "first resurrection" and suggests that it means the "chief" or "best" resurrection. This contrasts the other, dreadful resurrection for the wicked in the end. The notion of any one-stage first resurrection is rejected as unbiblical.

[1968]
1061. Mason, C.E., Jr. "The Day of Our Lord Jesus Christ." **BibSac** 125 (1968): 352-359.

Touches briefly on the Revelation of John among the NT writings while considering "the last day" (including translation of the Church, the close of the millennium, etc.). Suggests that all combination of phrases for that Day can be united into the one title, "The Day of Our Lord Jesus Christ." See also 1, C, (2).

[1967]
1062. Walvoord, J.F. "The Resurrection of Israel." **BibSac** 124 (1967): 3-15.

Argues for a literal reading of the Revelation and for a literal and separate resurrection for the nation of Israel in the End Time.

[1965]
1063. Rissi, M. "Die Erscheinung Christi nach Off. 19, 11-16." TZ 21 (1965): 81-95.

Identifies the Parousia of Christ in Rev. 19:11-16 in terms of a diptych that shows Christ on the white horse (heavenly and eschatological color) as the antithesis of the first horseman of 6:2. There are, accordingly, seven traits that will characterize the coming Lord for the Church: 1) "Faithful and true," 2) "Judge," etc. Seven is synonymous with the fullness of the Spirit. To the nonbeliever, Christ will appear in terms of four negative, punitive activities, viz., 1) Sharp sword of judgment from His mouth (suggests a sentence of condemnation); 2) Iron rod; 3) Treading the winepress; and 4) His absolute lordship in the end. See also 4, B and 5, C.

[1964]
1064. Smalley, S. "The Theatre of Parousia." SJT 17 (1964): 406-413.

Addresses two questions: 1) What is the manner of the Second Coming? 2) Where will it occur? First, Jesus will appear in a form comparable to his resurrection body. Second, the stage for the event will be, in part, the renewed and transformed earth. See also 5, H, (12) and (40).

[1960]
1065. Moule, C.F.D. "A Reconsideration of the Context of Maranatha." NTS 6 (1959-60): 307-310.

Reconsiders the "Maranatha" cry in light of its context. While connecting I Cor. 16:22; Did. 10:6; and Rev. 22:20, M. concludes that John used the term, not in a eucharistic sense, but primarily as a sanction for the ban on anyone who tampers with the book's integrity. At the same time the cry echoes the main theme of the Rev., viz., the eschatological coming of Jesus and the End.

[1959]
1066. Cummings, J. "How Many Bodies Are There in Heaven?" Wor 33 (1958-59): 367-370.

Argues, according to Rev. 20:1-7, that there will be many "bodies" in heaven after the first resurrection--in addition to Jesus and Mary. This will make all the more meaningful the celestial liturgy.

1067. Payne, J.B. "The Imminent Appearing of Christ." **BETS** 2 (1959): 8-13.

Sketches the leading historical interpretations of the Church in relationship to the Second Coming, the rapture, and, further, purposes a reconstruction of the classical viewpoint. Opts for an "imminent post-tribulationism" by synthesizing preterist, historical, and futurist positions. See also 1, C, (2).

[1958]
1068. Harrison, W.K. "The Time of the Rapture as Indicated in Certain Scriptures: The Time of the Rapture in the Revelation." **BibSac** 115 (1958): 201-211.

Determines the time of the Rapture in the Revelation to be before the great Tribulation, coincidental with the resurrection and identical to the same found in I & II Thes. and Mat. 24.

[1957]
1069. ————. "The Time of the Rapture as Indicated in Certain Scriptures." **BibSac** 114 (1957): 316-325.

Looks at I Thes. 5:1-11 and select passages from the Rev. (esp. Chaps. 15 & 16) to determine a pre-Rapture position for the Church.

1070. Wuest, K.S. "The Rapture -- Precisely When?" **BibSac** 114 (1957): 60-69.

Investigates relevant texts in the Revelation and in Paul's letters and concludes that the Rapture is always imminent and prior to the Tribulation. Also, it is to be a time of joy for Christians.

[1951]
1071. Beasley-Murray, G.R. "The Second Coming in the Book of Revelation." **EQ** 23 (1951): 40-45.

Presents a case for the Second Coming as the dominant background and theme of the Book of Revelation. The accompanying themes of judgment and the Kingdom of God substantiate the thesis.

1072. Ford, A. R. "The Second Advent in Relation to the Reign of Christ." **EQ** 23 (1951): 30-39.

Presents a postmillennial view based on I Cor. 15 and argues that this is supported by Rev. 20.

[1950]
1073. Echternach, H. **Der Kommende: Die Offenbarung**. St. Johannes-- für die Gegenwart ausgelegt. Gütersloh: C. Bertelsmann Verlag, 1950.

Suggests that the Rev. is really a "dialogue with history and the church through chorale, liturgy, and action." The German text is given along with extensive exposition. Very little interaction with contemporary scholarship.

[1947]
1074. Smith, R.F. "The Promise of His Coming." **RL** 16 (1947): 84-96.

Maintains through a study of Jewish, apocalyptic, and early Christian literature that primitive Christian hope and expectancy of Jesus' return can be maintained today. This interpretation is eternally valid and proven especially in Johannine literature. See also 5, C.

[1945]
1075. Whiting, A.B. "The Rapture of the Church." **BibSac** 102 (1945): 360-372, 490-499.

Discusses ideas, terms, and key NT passages (e.g., I Thes. 4 and Rev. 20) related to the premillennial Second Coming of Christ and the rapture of the Church. See also 5, F.

[1943]
1076. Robinson, W. "'The First Resurrection' and 'the Second Death' in the Apocalypse." **Th** 46 (1943): 97-102.

Discusses the problematical phrases, "the First Resurrection" and "the Second Death" (cf. Rev. 2:11 and Rev. 20) and submits that the former means the period of historical baptism and the latter the period of the consummation of history and final judgment.

(3) Death, Judgment and Eternity

[1985]
1077. Fiorenza, E.S. **The Book of Revelation. Justice and Judgment.**
Philadelphia, PA: Fortress Press, 1985.

Surveys the current state of research on the Revelation (21 pp.) and then
presents seven revised, previously published articles on 1) Eschatology
and Compostion; 2) Redemption as Liberation (Rev. 1:5-6; 5:9-10); 3) the
Quest for the Johannine School (cf. the Fourth Gospel and the
Revelation); 4) Apocalyptic and Gnosis in the Revelation and Paul; 5)
Apokalypsis and *Propheteia*; 6) Composition and Structure of Revelation;
and 7) The "followers of the Lamb" -- visionary rhetoric and the
sociopolitical situation.

1078. Von Balthasar, H.U. "Die göttlichen Gericht in der Apokalypse."
IKZC 14 (1985): 28-34.

Argues that the author of the Revelation, the beloved disciple John,
summarized and interpreted the gospel in the visions of God's judgment
in the book. Focuses on three aspects of divine judgment: 1) judgment of
the Lamb, 2) the opponents, and 3) the times of judgment.

[1982]
1079. Glasson, T.F. "The Last Judgment -- in Rev. 20 and Related
Writings." **NTS** 28 (1982): 528-539.

Surveys judgment scenes in Rev. 20 and a wide range of apocalyptic
literature (especially IV Ezra, II Baruch, Sibylline Oracles, I Enoch,
Psalms of Solomon, Assumption of Moses, and Jubilees), and suggests
that the term "judgment" means different things in different contexts.
Concludes that the so-called last judgment is an apocalyptic picture of
some transcendent reality. See also 3, D and 4, B.

[1976]
1080. Gangemi, A. "La morte seconda (Ap. 2, 11)." **RivB** 24 (1976): 3-
11.

See summary in **NTA** 23 (2, '79): #610.

[1974]
1081. Beasley-Murray, G.R. "The Contribution of the Book of Revelation
to the Christian Belief in Immortality." **SJT** 27 (1974): 76-93.

Points out that Rev. 2-3 offer promises to the Christian community that are ultimately fulfilled in the kingdom described later in Rev. 21-22. Life within the new Jerusalem is a blessed relationship and happy fellowship between God and man through Christ the Redeemer. But before all this can take place, there must be divine judgment within and beyond history. Rev. 19:11-21:5 describe the events caused by the Second Coming of Christ at the End Time.

[1971]
1082. Boulgarŋs, C.S. "῾Ο χρονος της Κρισεως και ῾η φυσις αυτης κατα το βιβλιον της Αποκαλυψεως." **DBM** 1 (1971): 13-33.

Discusses the "time" and "character" of judgment in the Revelation, noting the importance of the notions of imminence, signs preceding, the centrality of Christ's coming, and the earthly millennial kingdom. Judgment has both negative and positive aspects, viz., either death and destruction or cosmic renewal. Christ's role during the first phase of judgment is that of the Lamb who is eschatological judge. But the last, universal judgment is kept for God Himself. See also 5, B, C and H, (18).

[1969]
1083. Fiorenza, E.S. "Gericht und Heil: Zum theologischen Verständnis der Apokalypse" in **Gestalt und Anspruch des Neuen Testaments.** J. Schreiner, ed. Würzburg: Echter-Verlag, 1969. Pp. 330-348.

Discusses the motifs of judgment and salvation as keys to understanding the theological focus of the Revelation of John. Through compositional analysis the author traces the traditional theological connections with OT and Jewish literature. Concludes by identifying the judgment vision that precedes salvation for the Christian community in the image of the new Jerusalem.

[1968]
1084. Thüsing, W. "Die theologische Mitte der Weltgerichtsvisionen in der Johannesapokalypse." **TTZ** 77 (1968): 1-16.

Argues that the book is relevant for the modern reader because its structure discloses a fundamental theme that God is the Lord of the world and He takes control over all creation. Although the imagery is often shocking and exaggerated, the work is consistent with NT thought, viz., the mystery of God is revealed against those who would mock Him. God's judgment (as seen clearly in Rev. 2-3) is relevant for today; but this judgment idea is to be balanced by the promise of the new creation for the faithful.

[1967]
1085. McDermott, T. "Hell." **NBF** 48 (1966-67): 186-197.

Evaluates and analyzes the idea of hell in Rev. 20:1-3 as "Tartarus." Excludes the notions of Sheol, Hades, and Gehenna in reference to the text. See also 4, B.

[1965]
1086. Creager, H.L. "The Biblical View of Life After Death." **LQ(LThS)** 17 (1965): 111-121.

Suggests that the positive idea of life after death, in terms of the personal self without the Greek exclusion of the body, may be seen in such passages as Rev. 6:9 and 20:4.

[1961]
1087. Summers, R. "The Johannine View of the Future Life." **RE** 58 (1961): 331-347.

Examines the Revelation (briefly) among the Johannine writings in discussing the afterlife. Suggests that the key symbols of tabernacle, city, and garden make up the components of the idea and these places and ideas are exclusive of the wicked and indicate the call for a choice by mankind before the end.

[1953]
1088. Bollier, J.A. "Judgment in the Apocalypse." **Int** 7 (1953): 14-25.

Argues for a strong judgment theme in the Revelation through a discussion of "The Necessity of Judgment," "The Agent of Judgment," "The Mode of Judgment," and "The Consequences of Judgment." Criticizes modern "prophetic literature" for failing to see the implications of judgment in terms of its effect on the Church, its educational value, and its Christocentric character.

1089. Campbell, P.E. "The Last Judgment and the Dies Irae." **HPR** 53 (1952-53): 267-278.

Compares the Roman Catholic hymn "Dies Irae" to the theme of last judgment and the biblical evidence for the theme. Concludes that the Church should take heart in this highly liturgical experience.

[1948]
1090. Smith, T.C."The Wrath of God." **RE** 45 (1948): 193-208.

Traces the origin and development of the phrase, "The wrath of God," beginning with the ideas of R. Otto and the so-called *mysterium tremendum*. Discusses OT and NT literature and notes the emphasis in the Revelation as future retribution mainly (cf. Rev. 6:16-17; etc.).

(4) The Kingdom / Millennium

[1984]
1091. Du Preez, J. "Peoples and Nations in the Kingdom of God according to the Book of Revelation." **JTSA** 49 (1984): 49-51.

Understands the Greek term "εθνη" ("nations") in Scripture, generally, and in the Revelation, particularly, in the sense of religion and ethics within the context of salvation history, but not in the sense of ethnic nationality. Thus the one renewed people of God will exist on a new earth as a people with unique harmony in diversity. See also 5, H, (7).

[1972]
1092. Fiorenza, E.S. **Priester für Gott: Studien zum Herrschafts-und Priestermotiv in der Apokalypse.** "NTAbh 7." Münster: Aschendorff, 1972.

This published dissertation examines the theme of God's people as priests in relationship to the sovereign rule and priest themes in the Revelation. The introduction summarizes Roman Catholic and Protestant interpretations of the notion of a general and ordained priesthood. Presents the thesis in three parts: 1) Text analysis of 1:6; 5:10; and 20:6 in light of Ex. 19:6 and Is. 61:6; 2) Motif study of priesthood and Kingship of the redeemed in light of the present; 3) The relationship between priesthood and the eschatological future (Apoc. 20:4-6; 22:3-5). Concludes that both the priesthood and the royal status of believers are an eschatological gift for all the redeemed. See also 5, H, (30) and 3, D. Cf. the review of D. Harrington in **CBQ** 34 (1972): 496-497.

[1970]
1093. Brütsch, C. "Das Tausendjährige Reich. Versuch einer (vorläufigen) Deutung." **KRS** 126 (1970): 162-163.

Investigates Rev. 20:4-6 in terms of the theological interpretation and relevance of the thousand-year kingdom. Concludes that the thousand-year period is a symbol for the eschatological reign of God on earth. See also 4, B.

[1967]
1094. Hofbauer, J. "'. . . et regnabunt cum Christo mille annis' (Apc 20,5)." **VerD** 45 (1967): 331-336.

Studies Rev. 20:5 as a "millenarist" text, which points to the invisible reign of Christ before the end of time. See also 1, C, (2).

[1946]
1095. ———. "Sie werden mit Christus herrschen tausend Jahre (Offb. 20,5)." **SKZ** (1946): 106-108.

Not seen.

[1948]
1096. Kromminga, D.H. **The Millenium**. Grand Rapids, MI: Eerdmans, 1948.

Investigates and describes the nature and function of the Millennium in Scripture. Explains the relationship between the Millennium and the Resurrection and Judgment. Occasional allusions to Rev. 20 as an important text.

H. OTHER THEMES

(1) Angels

[1955]
1097. Chilvers, G. "Angels." **EQ** 27 (1955): 108-112.

Argues for the importance of angels (spiritual beings) in the Bible and says that the Revelation of John alone makes seventy-five references to angels. Gives angels characterizations such as holy, untiring, numerous, powerful, bearers of spiritual messages, etc.

[1942]
1098. Chafer, L.S. "Angelology." **BibSac** 99 (1942): 6-25.

Explores the topic of angels from OT and NT, especially in the Book of Revelation. Concludes with a study of the "career of Satan" and a relevant interpretation of Ez. 28:11-19.

(2) Antichrist, Demons, Satan

[1986]
1099. Bovon, F. "Possession ou enchantement. Les institutions romaines selon l'Apocalypse de Jean." **CS** 7 (1986): 221-238.

Not seen.

[1983]
1100. Bousset, W. **Die Antichrist in der Überlieferung des Judentums, des neuen Testaments und der alten Kirche. Ein Beitrag zur Auslegung der Apokalypse.** Reprint of the 1895 edition. Hildesheim--Zurich--New York: Olms, 1983.

Traces the history of the Antichrist tradition in two parts: I. Sources and II. History of the Antichrist Legend. B. first surveys a large variety of Jewish and Christian literature in different languages. Draws a characterization by identifying the name, the connection with the devil, the first victories, and the signs and wonders. The appendix studies the Antichrist in Rev. 12 and concludes by discussing an "Old Armenian Form of the Antichrist Saga." A postscript investigates some late-Byzantine apocalypses. See also 3, D.

[1967]
1101. McDermott, T. "The Devil and His Angels." **NBF** 48 (1966-67): 16-25.

Discusses the Scriptural doctrine of the Devil and his angels and critiques the Church's teaching on the subject.

[1962]
1102. Ling, T. "Satan Enthroned." **SEAJT** 3 (1961-62): 41-53.

Studies John's references to Satan in the Revelation and concludes that the figure is a central part of the book's message and very relevant to the contemporary world. See also 5, H, (24).

[1949]
1103. Drach, G. "Antichrist." **LQ(LThS)** 1 (1949): 455-462.

Analyzes the idea of Antichrist in Scripture and Christian history with occasional references to the allusions found in Rev. 9, 13.

[1943]
1104. Milner, G. "Antichrist and the Scarlet Woman." **MC** 32 (1942-43): 227-232.

Analyzes the images of Antichrist and the woman in connection with Rev. 17:18. Concludes that John's allusion was to Rome the city, but not to the Roman church, which was in the main a force for good in the ancient world. See also 5, F.

[1942]
1105. Graebner, T. "Extra-Lutheran Witnesses for the Papacy as the Anti-Christ." **CTM** 13 (1942): 699-704.

Names and discusses several non-Lutheran writers who identify the papacy as the Antichrist in Rev. 13:16f.; 14:9-11; etc.

1106. Gruenthaner, M.J. "Antichrist in the Scriptures." **HPR** 42 (1941-42): 448-460.

Traces the notion of the Antichrist (as a total Johannine contribution to NT thought) from the OT (Ezekiel first) through the NT. The Rev., though not naming Antichrist specifically, alludes to the Antichrist in the two beasts of 11:7, which may parallel "the lawless one" in II Thes. 2. Concludes that Antichrist is personal and individual.

(3) Armageddon

[1985]
1107. LaRondelle, H.K. "The Biblical Concept of Armageddon." **JETS** 28 (1985): 21-31.

Examines exegetically   Rev. 16:16 with an eye to the word "Armageddon" and concludes that the term carries with it the concept of destruction for Babylon. God's holy wrath of destruction is seen as a retaliation for the city's unholy war against the saints of God and His Son, Jesus Christ. Armageddon stands in the OT tradition of Yahweh's victory over Egypt and the ultimate fall of historical Babylon. See also 4, B.

[1980]
1108. Shea, W.H. "The Location and Significance of Armageddon in

Rev. 16:16." **AUSS** 18 (1980): 157-162.

Exegetes Rev. 16:16 in light of 16:12 and suggests that the analogy of drying up of the great river Euphrates (during the battle for Babylon, ca., 539 B.C.) in preparation for the kings from the East (vs. 12) refers to the coming of a messianic figure who will deliver God's people. Geographical considerations along with historical and textual analogies indicate that John 's reference to "the mountain of Megiddo(n)" in vs. 16 identifies the eschatological mountain as Mt. Carmel, the place of Elijah's contest with the prophets of Baal (I Ki. 18). See also 4, B.

(4) Astrology

See commentaries that expand discussion of Rev. 1:12-16 and especially vs. 16 on "the seven stars."

(5) Character and Ethics/Morals

[1989]
1109. Collins, T. "Moral Guidance in the Apocalypse." **Em** 95 (1989): 502-509.

Argues that John's Revelation is a vision of the exalted Christ who is seen in relationship to God's eternal plan, i.e., as Lord of all and in contrast to the world's powers that are nothing in his presence. Therefore Christian behavior in the world will be one of two things: 1) compromised with a materialistic society that will not last; or, 2) faithful to Christ the Lord who rules all and who will judge each of us at the end of time.

[1983]
1110. Weborg, C. "The Eschatological Ethics of Johan Albrecht Bengel: Personal and Ecclesial Piety and the Literature of Edification in the Letters to the Seven Churches in Revelation 2 and 3." Unpublished Doctoral Dissertation. Evanston, IL: Northwestern University. Ann Arbor, MI: University Microfilms, 1983.

Presents a critical exposition of Bengel's thoughts on the major ethical motifs in Rev. 2-3 as taken from that author's work, **Sixty Edifying Speeches on the Revelation of John or Much More of Jesus Christ**.

(6) Creation (Old and New)

[1973]
1111. Coune, M. "L'univers nouveau. Ap 21,1-5." **AS** 26 (1973): 67-72.

Surveys Rev. 21:1-22:5 and identifies the key eschatological themes, e.g., the new Jerusalem, new creation, new dwelling, and new life, as the creative word of God concerning the new world. See also 5, H, (12) and (16).

[1967]
1112. Hammerton, H.J. "Unity of Creation in the Apocalypse." **CQR** 168 (1967): 20-33.

Studies the Revelation and identifies within the book a certain unity, dignity, and functions of creation that, if applied to modern life, lead to a condemnation of sinful crimes like nuclear warfare and cruelty to animals. See also 5, A.

(7) Elect/Saints

[1965]
1113. Rewak, W.J. "The 'Reign of the Saints,'" **BT** 1 (1965): 1345-1350.

Suggests that the author exhorts and assures the persecuted Christians to recognize that they will reign over history as the new Israel and the Church. However they will reign as priest-mediators and intercessory prayer will be the authoritative means whereby they maintain the connection between the visible and invisible kingdoms. See also 4, B, and 5, G, (4).

(8) Exodus

[1987]
1114. Casey, J. "The Exodus Theme in the Book of Revelation against the Background of the New Testament." **Con** 189 (1987): 34-43.

Argues that John's understanding of the exodus event was non-Jewish; that "exodus" referred to hope fulfilled in Jesus Christ and God's continuing activity on behalf of His people. Although the author used apocalyptic language and images of a universal, cosmic battle, there is evidence of an ongoing relevance of the exodus for believers, e.g., God is still the Redeemer of His people, the judge of His people's enemies, and the assurance of future, eternal reward.

(9) Feasts

[1989]
1115. Ulfgard, H. **Feast and Future. Revelation 7:9-17 and the Feast of Tabernacles.** "Coniectanea Biblica, NT Series 22." Stockholm: Almqvist & Wiksell, 1989.

This four-part revised doctoral dissertation first reviews contemporary scholarship respecting the idea of the feast of Tabernacles in Rev. 7:9-17 and makes several general observations about the interpretation of the book. Secondly, the author examines literary context of the passage, identifying the following: 1) the heavenly scene; 2) the series of seven seals, trumpets, and bowls; 3) the exodus pattern in the passage; and 4) the portrayal of the people of God. Thirdly, U. studies the details of Rev. 7:9-17 against the context, noting the relationship between the unnumbered multitude and the 144,000, the great tribulation, the white robes, and palms. Lastly, U. describes the Jewish feast of Tabernacles in various times and traditions in history (e.g., Second Temple according to the Mishna, the pre-A. D. 100 sources, the post-biblical witnesses, and archaeological research) and suggests that it is the pattern of the *exodus tradition* that holds together the Christian life, in terms of "feast and future" according to Rev. 7:9-17. See also 4, B.

[1983]
1116. Draper, J.A. "The Heavenly Feast of Tabernacles: Revelation 7:1-17." **JSNT** 19 (1983): 133-147.

Discusses Rev. 7 as the fulfillment of Zech. 4:1-21 and a depiction of the Feast of Tabernacles. Rev. 7 describes the final eschatological pilgrimage of the surviving Gentiles and restored Israel in terms that are consistent with that Jewish feast. Concludes that some groups of Christians may have continued to keep the Feast of Tabernacles because of its eschatological meaning and the connection with Rev. 7:1-17. See also 3, E and 4, B.

(10) Gnosticism

[1977]
1117. Prigent, P. "L'hérésie Asiate et l'église confessante de l'Apocalypse à Ignace." **VC** 31 (1977): 1-22.

Discusses the Gnostic "heresy" and the church of the Apocalypse during the time of Ignatius.

(11) Hatred/Vilification/Vengeance

[1986]
1118. Collins, A.Y. "Vilification and Self-Definition in the Book of Revelation." **HTR** 79 (1986): 308-320.

Contends that the Book of Revelation contains strong vilification of Jews (Rev. 2:9-10), Roman leaders and allies (2:13), and Christian rivals (2:14-15, 20-23), and that vilification was a part of the survival tactic for Christians as they tried to establish an identity as legitimate heirs of Israel. This attitude of vilification may be understood in terms of apocalyptic hatred that expresses an awareness of one symbolic universe over against another, different one. It also serves to provide a definition and identity for a new group and to neutralize the other.

[1966]
1119. Klassen, W. "Vengeance in the Apocalypse of John." **CBQ** 28 (1966): 300-311.

Considers the prayers for vindication and vengeance in the Revelation and shows that there is a progression of thought toward fulfillment of these prayers. The difference between Jewish apocalyptic writings and the Revelation is noted. The so-called militant and vengeful attitude is not readily apparent in the text. Rather, the key to Christian victory over the enemy is found in the example of Jesus. This material is all consistent with NT theology. Lastly, the literary device that holds the entire book together is not a series of curses against the enemies of the Church, but rather a series of seven beautitudes. See also 5, G, (3) and 5, H, (11).

(12) Heaven and Earth

[1981]
1120. Aletti, J.-N. "Essai sur la symbolique céleste de l'Apocalypse de Jean." **Chr** 28 (1981): 40-53.

Exegetes Rev. 4:1-2 and then discusses John's teaching on heaven and the activities of those who live there. A. suggests that these activities may be categorized as 1) Centripetal (liturgical) and 2) Centrifugal (punitive and salvific), and this is explained further by discussing the symbolism and the imagery of the book in relationship to heaven. See also 3, F.

(13) Heresy/Apostasy

[1973]
1121. Mackay, W.M. "Another Look at the Nicolaitans." **EQ** 45 (1973): 111-115.

Studies Rev. 2: 12-17 and suggests that the Nicolaitans of Pergamum are distinct from the heresies connected with Balaam and Jezebel. This unique NT heresy seems to have been characterized by erroneous religious practices that resulted in perverted truth and excessive ritualism.

(14) History/Time

[1983]
1122. Böcher, O. **Kirche in Zeit und Endzeit. Aufsätze zur Offenbarung des Johannes.** Neukirchen-Vluyn: Neukirchener, 1983.

Offers eleven previously published articles on the Revelation in one volume. Various subjects are treated, e.g., Johannine elements in the Revelation; Israel and the Church in Revelation, water and Spirit (1970); the Iconography of the Lamb among the beasts (1975); the thousand-year reign, the significance of the precious stones in Revelation 21 (1979); citizens of the city of God according to Revelation 21-22.

[1968]
1123. Karner, K. "Gegenwart und Endgeschichte in der Offenbarung des Johannes." **TLZ** 93 (1968): 641-652.

Discusses the notion of the present and final period of history in the Rev. and concludes that John was not following   traditional Jewish apocalypticism because the *Gegenwart* and the *Endgeschichte* are now connected and under the lordship of the glorified Christ. The notion of a delayed Parousia is the creation of the early community but is not supported by the Revelation.

1124. Orna, M.V. "Time and History in the Apocalypse." **CC** 20 (1968): 184-200.

Argues that it is Jesus' appearance that separates the ideas of time and history between the OT and the Revelation. John's Revelation is the prototype of a new theology of history that is neither Greek ($\chi\rho o\nu o\varsigma$) nor Hebrew ($\kappa\alpha\iota\rho o\varsigma$). John offers a kind of "process eschatology" that seems to be understood in terms of human values transferred into a total "new creation." Of course this new creation also includes "time" as an essential element. O. offers the following texts as examples: Rev. 2:17; 3:12; 5:9; 14:3; 21:1, 4-5.

[1967]
1125. Murdock, W.R. "History and Revelation in Jewish Apocalypticism." **Int** 21 (1967): 167-187.

Discusses the theological problem of history and revelation in relationship to the Bultmannian distinction between *Historie* and *Geschichte* that limits revelation to the existential or *geschichtliche*. Interacts with a number of scholars (e.g., Pannenberg and Rössler) and a wide variety of writings on both themes. Concludes that Jewish apocalypticism viewed history and revelation in terms of the eschatological dualism and not as continuous events ("hiddenness over against revelation"). The continuity between the evil present and the future (time and eternity) was constituted by the esoteric and gnosticizing revelation that apocalypses mediated. The implications for the Revelation of John are merely suggested. See also 3, B and 5, H, (10).

1126. Schwank, B. "Der Zeitbegriff der Apokalypse." **EA** 43 (1967): 279-293.

Studies the "time" motif in the Rev. and concludes that the concept is OT and prophetic, i.e., the Rev. follows the Oriental line, which connects the past and the future with the present, which identifies certain times as they relate to salvation-history, which points to all time since Jesus as "end" time, and which suggests that Jesus Himself holds together all time forever.

[1966]
1127. Rissi, M. **Time and History: A Study on the Revelation.** G. Winsor, trans. Richmond, VA: John Knox Press, 1966. Reprint of 1952 original.

Discusses the literary structure of the Revelation relevant to time and history as the integrative and unifying theme. Biblical notions of time, the End Time, and the consummation as reported by John are the main areas of discussion. See also 1, C, (1).

[1965]
1128. Hopkins, M. "History in the Apocalypse." **BT** 1 (1965): 1340-1344.

Attempts to show that Rev. 4-11 is John's historical statement offering assurances that Rome will ultimately receive the judgment of God and Christianity will win out over Judaism. The latter notion is represented by the destruction of Jerusalem and the Temple. See also 5, G, (3)

1129. Hopkins, M. "The Historical Perspective of Apocalypse 1-11." **CBQ** 27 (1965): 42-47.

Proposes the idea that Rev. 1-11 is the historical portion of the book, and a sequel to the Acts of the Apostles. Rev. 4-11 develop an authentic interpretation of Mk. 13, and Rev. 12 begins the apocalyptic section that centers on Rome. Concludes that there is a definite literary and thematic parallelism between Rev. 1-11 and 12-20. See also 3, D and 3, E..

1130. Rissi, M. **Was is und was geschehen soll danach. Die Zeit- und Geschichtsauffassung der Offenbarung des Johannes.** Zurich-- Stuttgart: Zwingli Verlag, 1965.

Argues that the Revelation is not concerned to develop a theology of history, but rather a prophetic interpretation of history. The "history" under scrutiny is that between the first and second coming of Christ. Considering the historical structure of the book, while using a modified recapitulation hermeneutic, R. presents his thesis under the headings of structure, understanding time, the End Time, and the consummation.

[1964]
1131. Giet, S. "Retour sur l'Apocalypse." **RevSR** 38 (1964): 225-264.

Responds to those who criticized his **L'Apocalypse et l'histoire** (1957) and offers further clarification of his thesis. Says that Rev. 4:1-19:9 reveals a structure of four septenaries that refer to a continuous sequence of events from Christ's ascension to the destruction of Rome (Babylon). This section of John's work was composed during the time of Vespasian, and Chaps. 12-19 describe the Church battling emperor worship. See also 3, E.

[1956]
1132. Schlier, H. "Zum Verständnis der Geschichte nach der Offenbarung des Johannis" in **Die Zeit der Kirche: Exegetische Aufsätze und Vorträge.** Freiburg, Basel, und Vienna: Herder, 1956. Pp. 265-274.

Argues that the author John's intention with the use of history in the Revelation was more ontological than historical. See also 5, H, (24).

[1945]
1133. Féret, H. M. "Apocalypse, histoire et eschatologie chrétienne." **DV** 2 (1945): 117-154.

Not seen.

[1939]
1134. Duplessis, J. **Le sens de l'histoire. Les derniers temps d'apres l'histoire et la prophétie.** 2: L'Apocalypse de S. Jean. Téqui, 1939.

Not seen.

(15) Hymns

[1980]
1135. Coleman, R.E. **Songs of Heaven.** Old Tappan, NJ: Revell, 1980.

Lifts the songs of the Revelation from the text after seeing them in context and analyzes the messages of each. Thematic discussion and practical application conclude the work.

[1979]
1136. Prigent, P. "Pour une théologie de l'image: Les visions de l'Apocalypse." **RHPR** 59 (1979): 373-378.

Suggests that the transcendent reality disclosed by the visions and the images of the Revelation is just approximate and calls out for further interpretation. Concludes that the hymns are the key to understanding the existential implications of the visions.

[1968]
1137. O'Rourke, J.J. "The Hymns of the Apocalypse." **CBQ** 30 (1968): 399-409.

Offers a grammatical and theological analysis of the hymns of the Revelation in order to compare and contrast the contents and meaning of each. Concludes that several passages are reinterpretations of pre-existing hymns using Christological methods. Examples are given to link the non-Christian hymns with those found in the Revelation. See 3, C and 5, C.

(16) Jerusalem and Temple

[1984]
1138. Läpple, A. "Das neue Jerusalem. Die Eschatologie der Offenbarung des Johannes." **BK** 39 (1984): 75-81.

Investigates the phrase "The New Jerusalem" in the Revelation as a reworked OT image by John. See also 5, G, (1).

[1982]
1139. Du Brul, P. "'Jerusalem' in the Apocalypse of John." **Tantur Yearbook** [Jerusalem] (1981-82): 57-77.

Analyzes the Jerusalem vision in Rev. 21:9-22 in terms of time, place, characters, plot, imagery, motif, and the message. The city Jerusalem is the one unifying image of the book. It joins the visionary and the vision in a singular complex act.

1140. Riley, W. "Temple Imagery and the Book of Revelation. Ancient Near Eastern Temple Ideology and Cultic Resonances in the Apocalypse." **PIBA** 6 (1982): 81-102.

Argues that locus of God's majesty in the Revelation of John is found in the Jerusalem temple. This reflects Near Eastern thought respecting the ideas of safety and security, and in the Revelation these are connected with the earthly and the eschatological temples. All of God's power, victory, and kingly enthronement come from the eschatological (heavenly) temple. Concludes that all the temple imagery in the Revelation may be seen as evidence for an enthronement festival at Mount Zion that influenced OT and NT times. See also 2, G.

[1968]
1141. Thüsing, W. "Die Vision des 'Neuen Jerusalem' (Apk 21, 1-22, 5) als Verheissung und Gottesverkündigung." **TTZ** 77 (1968): 17-34.

Analyzes Rev. 21:1-22:5 and concludes that the New Jersualem exists within the new heavens after the final coming of Christ. The city is both a place where God dwells with mankind and the perfected people of God. There is both continuity and discontinuity between the present world and the New Jerusalem. John uses the OT prophets to describe the city; but he sublimates them to his own purposes, i.e., to show in Rev. 21 God's proclamation of the "new" and the glorification of all mankind.

[1965]
1142. Comblin, J. "La ville bien-aimée, Apocalypse, 20, 9." **VS** 112
(1965): 631-648.

Contends that the notion of the "city" (secular, biblical and, in particular,
Jerusalem) reveals that nature of the Church. Rev. 20 is a classic example
of this notion. See also 4, B and 5, F.

[1961]
1143. Wulf, H. "Das himmlische Jerusalem." **GL** 34 (1961): 321-325.

Offers a brief description and analysis of the heavenly Jerusalem in Rev.
21. See also 6, E.

[1959]
1144. Van Bergen, P. "Dans l'attente de la nouvelle Jérusalem." **LuVS** 45
(1959): 1-9.

Argues that the Revelation points to the new Jerusalem at the end of
history as the ultimate symbol for the new Covenant as the hope for all
Christians. John's use of prophetic terms and ideas in Rev. 21:1-22:5
serves to offer assurance of a new intimacy with God in the end. See also
4, B.

[1953]
1145. Comblin, J. "La Liturgie de la Nouvelle Jérusalem (Apoc. 21, 1-22,
5)." **ETL** 29 (1953): 5-40.

Describes and interprets the liturgical patterns in connection with John's
use of the new Jerusalem imagery. See also 5, H, (16) and 5, H, (19).

(17) Kerygma/Gospel

[1968]
1146. Rissi, M. "The Kerygma of the Revelation to John." **Int** 22 (1968):
3-17.

Discusses the book in terms of its literary unity, interpolations (e.g., Rev.
17:9b-17), and John's prophetic role in interpreting history, both present
and future. The most important (kerygmatic) statement is found in (cf.
1:6; 2:28; etc.) the confession that God is the "father" of Jesus Christ and
God speaks and works out His will through Christ. The role of the Spirit,
the world, the Church and Israel, and the healing Redeemer are studied in

relationship to God's ultimate healing of every creature and the inclusion of Israel in the final triumph. See also 5, H, (31).

(18) The Lamb

[1985]
1147. Bergmeier, R. "Die Buchrolle und das Lamm (Apk 5 und 10)." ZNTW 76 (1985): 225-242.

Offers a critical and exegetical study comparing the literary and theological connection between Rev. 5 and 10. Suggests that Rev. 5 is John's Christian interpretation of the Lamb figure and preparation for the Jewish apocalyptic vision of Rev. 10. The Lamb is shown to be a prophetic figure and the Scroll (βιβλιον) of 5:2 is the scroll of end-time prophecy.

[1984]
1148. Läpple, A. "Das Geheimnis des Lammes. Das Christusbild der Offenbarung des Johannes." BK 39 (1984): 53-58.

Discusses the portrayal of Jesus (especially in Rev. 19:7, 9; 21:1-22:21) and argues that these pictures are foundational and the unifying principle of the Revelation. The climax of the book is identified as the marriage of the Lamb (Jesus) with the people of God. See also 5, C.

[1981]
1149. Guthrie, D. "The Lamb in the Structure of the Book of Revelation." VE 12 (1981): 64-71.

Identifies twenty-nine passages where the Lamb is mentioned in the Revelation (e.g., 5:6-14; 7:9-17; etc.) and the worship context of most. Suggests that the slain yet triumphant Lamb is the central figure in heavenly worship and that judgment is closely connected to Christ's victory as the Lamb.

[1980]
1150. Hohnjec, N. 'Das Lamm-" το αρνιον " in der Offenbarung des Johannes. Eine exegetisch-theologische Untersuchung. Rome: Herder, 1980.

This 1979 dissertation analyzes the Lamb theme in the Revelation in three sections: I. State of research; II. Exegetical and theological discussion of the αρνιον passages in the book; III. Theological results, viz., 1) The

Lamb as bearer of salvation; 2) The Lamb imagery in representation and liturgy; 3) The Lamb as a leading idea of the Revelation.

(19) Liturgy

[1987]
1151. Gangemi, A. "La struttura liturgica dei capitoli 4 e 5 dell' Apocalisse di. S. Giovanni." **EcO** (Rome) 4 (1987): 301-358.

Investigates the liturgical structure of Rev. 4-5 by identifying and discussing the hymns to God and to the Lamb (4:11; 5:9-10) and the heavenly songs (5:11-12, 13). Concludes that Rev. 4-5 reflects a three-part structure of praise in heaven.

[1986]
1152. Grassi, J.A. "The Liturgy of Revelation." **BT** 24 (1986): 30-37.

Describes, first, the socioreligious and liturgical settings, then, second, defines liturgy in terms of six characteristics of the word of God found in the Revelation: 1) It is apocalyptic; 2) It is accompanied by silence and prayer; 3) It unites the speaker and the spoken; 4) It emphasizes God's presence and energy in the universe; 5) It is endowed with discernment; and 6) It has the quality of utmost urgency.

[1980]
1153. Etcheverria, R. "El lenguaje bautismal del Apocalipsis." **Sal** 27 (1980): 165-192.

Not seen.

[1976]
1154. Vanni, U. "Un esempio di dialogo liturgico in Ap 1, 4-8."

Not seen.

[1968]
1155. Williams, R.B. "Liturgy and the New Testament." **Wor** 42 (1968): 450-465.

Alludes to the Revelation and other NT writings as he suggests that some relevant literary units found in the NT were probably shaped and preserved in liturgical activity in the early church, e.g., confessional formulas, Christological hymns, baptismal and Eucharistic forms. See also 5, H, (15) and 5, H, (19).

[1964]
1156. Prigent, P. **Apocalypse et Liturgie.** Neuchâtel Suisse, eds. Delachaux et Niestlé, 1964.

Part one investigates the Revelation (specifically Chaps. 2-3 and 4-5) in terms of ideas, imagery, OT and apocryphal connections, and the liturgical structure. Part two regards Rev. 4-5 as Jewish liturgy adapted to early Christianity and concludes that the book makes a presentation of and commentary on the paschal liturgy of the early church. See also 3, D and 3, E.

[1959]
1157. Delling, G. "Zum Gottesdienstlichen Stil der Johannes-Apokalypse." **NT** 3 (1959): 107-137.

Holds that the worship passages of the Rev. pre-interpret the events that follow. These passages seem to carry the action forward as well as give it unity and theological undertone. The worship in the Rev. contains within it the ability to define God in terms of his future actions, which are primarily defined as eschatological judgment and salvation. See also 5, H, (41) and 3, C.

[1957]
1158. Torrance, T.F. "Liturgie et Apocalypse." **VerC** 11 (1957): 28-40.

Compares and contrasts the OT liturgy with the liturgy found in the Revelation and asserts that the Revelation uses "this age and the age to come" theology for the purpose of describing the setting of ecumenism and timelessness. The Revelation contrasts OT ideas, that some catastrophy would end the present age, by including all ages and all people. Thus the Resurrection of Christ is shown in all time periods and the reader is encouraged to envision the heavenly liturgy as an interaction with historical events. See also 3, D and 5, G, (1).

[1956]
1159. Vawter, B. "The Johannine Sacramentary." **TS** 17 (1956): 151-166.

Discusses John's general interest in sacramentalism, including notes on the *gyne* ("woman") of Rev. 12 and her connection to Jesus' Mother and the Church (incl. Rev. 19:7, 9; 21:2, 9 ff., etc.). See also 5, H, 39.

[1952]
1160. Cabaniss, A. "A Note on the Liturgy of the Apocalypse." **Int** 7 (1952): 78-86.

Investigates the liturgical framework of the Revelation beginning with the early writing of Justin and then the book itself. Suggests a strong eucharistic form that is eventually confirmed by the Church's practical use of the book. See also 3, E.

[1947]
1161. Tyciak, J. **Maranatha. Die Geheime Offerbarung und die kirchliche Liturgie.** "Die religöse Entscheidung." Warendorf: Schnell, 1947.

Focuses on the Greek term "*Μαραναθα*" in connection with the early church's liturgy as key to understanding the secret of the Revelation. See also 3, D.

[1946]
1162. Hammenstede, A. "The Apocalypse and the Mystery of the Eucharist." **OF** 20 (1945-46): 104-110.

Offers two "faith supports" for Christians in the midst of contemporary world catastrophes: 1) The Catholic liturgy and 2) John's Apocalypse. Outlines the thematic connections between the Mass and the work of John as seen mainly in his major visions, which focus on God and the glorified Savior Jesus. Christians should all take heart in the light of this.

(20) Lord's Day/Sabbath

[1987]
1163. Johnston, R.M. "The Eschatological Sabbath in John's Apoc.: A Reconsideration." **AUSS** 25 (1987): 39-50.

Explains that the idea of eschatological "rest" in the Revelation is taken from the Jewish tradition, which stresses that the ultimate reward of the faithful is timeless rest. The notion of "timelessness" following after the Sabbath millennium is consistent with traditional seventh-day and -year paradigms of first-century Judeo-Christian thought.

[1978]
1164. Vanni, U. "Il 'Giorno del Signore' in Apoc. 1, 10, giorno di purificazione e di discernimento." **RivB** 26 (1978): 187-199.

Not seen.

[1967]
1165. Strand, K.A. "Another Look at 'Lord's Day' in the Early Church and in Rev. i. 10." **NTS** 13 (1967): 174-181.

Offers criticism of W. Stott (**NTS** 12 [1965]: 70-75) for not taking seriously the suggestion of Dugmore (1962) that the phrase refers to Easter. Raises some doubt respecting the relevance of Stott's use of Ignatius' Magnesians 9 and the uncertainty of the translation. Rev. 1:10 may have been influenced by a Quartodeciman context where neither Easter nor Sunday is relevant. The use of the phrase there is also questionable.

1166. Fenasse, J.-M. "Le jour du Seigneur, Apocalypse 1, 10." **BVCh** 61 (1965): 29-43.

Not seen.

(21) Martyrdom/Witness

[1990]
1167. Ellingworth, P. "The μαρτυρια Debate." **BTr** 41 (1990): 138-139.

Reviews the debate between Vassiliadis (1985) and Mazzaferri (1988) concerning the use of this Greek term and similar words in the Revelation. The issue is whether or not these words maintain the sense of "witness" or have shifted toward the idea of "martyrdom." The author leans slightly toward the latter idea.

[1988]
1168. Reddish, M.G. "Martyr Christology in the Apocalypse." **JSNT** 33 (1988): 85-95.

Argues that John sustains the image of Christ as a martyr figure even as he (John) shows him as the conquering warrior or the glorified Lord. The intention of the book was to motivate Christians to take their witness seriously. See also 5, C.

1169. Mazzaferri, F.D. "Μαρτυρια Iησου Revisited." **BT** 39 (1988): 114-122.

Suggests that the phrase "*Μαρτυρια Ιησου*" in Rev. 19:10 is meant to characterize the whole book. Thus the Church is called upon to listen to John's writing as Jesus' personal testimony, the voice of the Spirit.

[1985]
1170. Vassiliadis, P. "The Translation of *Μαρτυρια Ιησου*" in Revelation." **BTr** 36 (1985): 129-134.

Argues that the six occurrences of *μαρτυρια Ιησου* (cf. Rev. 1:2, 9; 12:17; 19:10; 20:4) have martyrological nuance and should be translated as an objective genitive, viz., "witness (unto death) to Jesus." The term *μαρτυρια* was in the last stage of becoming a technical term. (See also the article in **DBM** 13 [1984]: 41-51.)

[1980]
1171. Reicke, B. "The Inauguration of Catholic Martyrdom according to St. John the Divine." **Aug** 20 (1980): 275-283.

Argues that the Book of Revelation describes a period of persecution under the Roman emperor Domitian (ca. A.D. 95) and suggests strongly that the experience of the seven churches (Rev. 2-3) was representative of the whole church during the period of transition when religious tolerance was being replaced by increased persecutions in Asia Minor.

[1977]
1172. Feuillet, A. "Les martyrs de l'humanité et l'Agneau égorgé. Une interprétation nouvelle de la prière des égorgés en Ap 6, 9-11." **NRT** 99 (1977): 189-207.

Interprets the references in Rev. 6:9 to those slain "for the word of God" and "for the witness they had born" to refer to all those who died for the cause of moral and religious truth before the Christian era (see Mat. 23:31-35). This is substantiated by the prayer of the martyrs in Rev. 6:10-11 and suggests that these martyrs prefigured Jesus' death, but, nevertheless, received the redemptive effects from the Cross. Draws final attention to Heb. 11:4; 12:24; and Luke's writings for similar ideas.

[1976]
1173. Bauckham, R. "The Martyrdom of Enoch and Elijah: Jewish or Christian?" **JBL** 95 (1976): 447-458.

Investigates twenty-four relevant texts in terms of their relationship to the origin of the Christian tradition of the martyrdom of Enoch and Elijah, arguing that the traditional view of the return of Enoch and Elijah provides no evidence for a Jewish (pre-Christian) tradition concerning their martyrdom. Concludes that Rev. 11:3-13 probably provides the innovative idea for the Enoch/Elijah martyrdom based upon the martyrdom of Jesus Christ. See also 3, D.

[1973]
1174. Trites, A.A. "*Μαρτυς* and Martyrdom in the Apocalypse: A Semantic Study." **NovT** 15 (1973): 72-80.

Discusses the logical process whereby the Greek term *μαρτυς* (witness) came to mean "martyr" in the Rev. Uses the diachronistic semantic method and concludes that *μαρτυς* had just begun to mean a martyr's death in John's book. See also 3, C.

1175. Pollard, T.E. "Martyrdom and Resurrection in the New Testament." **BJRL** 55 (1972-73): 240-251.

Presents a critical examination of the two ideas of martyrdom and resurrection as found in the NT, generally, and then suggests that the martyr is granted immediate and special resurrection and, consequently, admission to the presence of Christ, e.g., Rev. 20:4ff. See also 4, B and 5, G, (2).

[1964]
1176. Grillmeier, A. "'Ihre Werke folgen ihnen nach' (Offb 14,13)." **GL** 37 (1964): 321-324.

Explains that "good works" follow after those who die within God's peace (Rev. 14:13), but how that applies to today is a matter for careful interpretation and application by serious Christians. See also 4, B and 5, G, (3).

[1960]
1177. Schwarz, O.J.R.A. "Die zwei Zeugen: 'Kirche' und 'Israel.'" US 15 (1960): 145-153.

Discusses the figures, Church and Israel, as two important symbols for witnesses in the Rev. See 5, F.

[1947]
1178. Fischel, H.A. "Martyr and Prophet." **JQR** 37NS (1946-47): 265-280, 363-386.

Presents an extensive critical study of the literature and scholarship (Holl, Reitzenstein, Schlatter, et al.) on the relationship between the biblical ideas of the martyr and the prophet. Observes that the view of the early church regarding the messianic prophet as martyr may reflect its connection with the tannaitic Jewish belief. However, F. says that Hellenistic influence is difficult to prove.

(22) Mission / Ministry

[1988]
1179. Poucouta, P. "Mission-témoignage dans l'Apocalypse." **Sp** 29 (1988): 397-405.

Argues that in the Revelation, the term "witness" is to be interpreted as "mission" and vice versa. This mission demands living as a witness, being involved in the process of history, and being saved.

[1970]
1180. Du Preez, J. "Mission Perspective in the Book of Revelation." **EQ** 42 (1970): 152-167.

Expands on his article (in Afrikaans) in **NGTT** 10 (1969): 20-32.

[1947]
1181. Barrett, J.O. **The Book of the Revelation.** London: The Carey Press, 1947.

Investigates the themes of mission and ministry in the Revelation and concludes that the book is really John's call to the contemporary church to continue to take its missionary task seriously in these "last days" of crisis. The warfare themes in the Rev. highlight the critical nature of the world situation, both then and now.

(23) Myth

[1989]
1182. Bodinger, M. "Le myth de Néron. De l'Apocalypse de saint Jean au Talmud de Babylone." **RHR** 206 (1989): 21-40.

Argues that the "myth" of Nero's return arose immediately after his death and continued on until the Middle Ages. The Talmudic edition of the Rev. (ca. A.D. 68-69) identifies Nero (cf. Antiochus IV) as a new avatar of the great persecutor of the Jews and one who attempted to place himself on

God's throne. John edited the text in a Christian spirit but in order to present a comparable anti-Roman, Jewish eschatological-messianic message.

[1982]
1183. Hooker, M.D. "Myth, Imagination and History." **EpR** 9 (1982): 50-56.

Defines "myth" as the expression of human experiences of the world in terms that humans can understand. The Revelation uses ancient myths and symbols to communicate the message that, in spite of historical appearances to the contrary, God is still in control of all things. See also 3, D.

[1979]
1184. Court, J.M. **Myth and History in the Book of Revelation.** Atlanta, GA: John Knox Press, 1979.

Concentrates on combining a serious study of the Rev.'s historical background with a critical analysis of the traditional mythology used by John. After listing the possible interpretative approaches to the work, e.g., "Chiliastic," "Alexandrian -- spiritual or allegorical," etc., C. focuses on the two prominent areas of history and myth as the best possible keys to interpretation. Seven topical studies lead to the conclusion that the Rev. is not anti-Jewish, but is merely angry against those Jews who sold out to the Imperial cult. The Rev. is seen as the product of an apocalyptic party within Judaism (perhaps Qumran), but the writing was altered through its contact with the Christian Gospel. See also 5, H, (14).

(24) Ontology

[1966]
1185. Minear, P.S. "Ontology and Ecclesiology in the Apocalypse." **NTS** 12 (1966): 89-105.

Studies the conjunction of ontology (reality) and ecclesiology (church) in the Revelation by means of the analysis of selected passages from the book. Organizes his work under four sections: 1) The author's situation in relationship to his readers, viz., shared κοινωνια in eschatological tribulation and historical endurance. 2) John's grasp of space-time realities, shown especially in the symbol of the two olive trees (Rev. 11). 3) John's idea of the two cities. 4) John's understanding of the boundary between the two cities. Concludes that his study has implications for hermeneutics, ethics, ecclesiology, and ontology. In particular, the view of the Church in Revelation does not fit neatly into traditional church patterns. See also 5, F and 5, H, (14).

(25) Peace

[1984]
1186. Ford, J.M. "Shalom in the Johannine Corpus." **HBT** 6 (1984): 67-89.

Considers the general Johannine notion of peace and suggests that in the Revelation, specifically, we find an example of quietist or pacifist apocalyptic ideas in the tradition of the writings of Daniel and the Assumption of Moses. Although John does highlight the myth of the Divine Warrior in his treatment of such motifs as threat, battle-victory, theophany, banquet, he does not announce a literal, physical battle preparation or call to arms. His idea of warfare is taken up completely by God's divine intervention. Concludes that the figure in Rev. 19 is not the incarnate Christ, but the *Memra* or Word. In the Johannine writings, generally, the new age of *Shalom* comes with the Holy Spirit. See also 5, D and 5, H, (37).

(26) Persecution/Tribulation/Suffering

[1990]
1187. Ford, J.M. "Persecution and Martyrdom in the Book of Revelation." **BT** 28 (1990): 141-146.

Argues that there is little textual support in the Rev. for the view that the term "martyr" should be interpreted as one who dies for faith in Christ. Being a "witness" for God and Christ meant witnessing in the daily experiences of life, viz., at home, in trade guilds, public service, entertainments, and in the practices of religion. Thus, persecution against Christians did not have its roots in political situations or general imperial oppression. See also above 5, H, (21).

[1966]
1188. Brown, S. "'The Hour of Trial' (Rev. 3:10)." **JBL** 85 (1966): 308-314.

Reasons that the πειρασμος ("trial") of Rev. 3:10 is used differently from the rest of the NT. Here it refers to the testing of "the inhabitants of the earth," i.e., the enemies of the Church (cf. 6:10; 8:13; etc.). The key to

John's unique usage is to be found in Dan. 12:1. Ultimately, the "trial" of Rev. 3:10 has a double effect, viz., it tests and purifies Christians, but also punishes the enemies of the Church. Therefore, the Church is not untouched by πειρασμος but is kept from it, while being led through it. See also 4, B.

(27) Politics/State

[1987]
1189. Pippin, T. "Political Reality and the Liberating Vision: The Context of the Book of Revelation." Unpublished Doctoral Dissertation. Louisville, KY: Southern Baptist Theological Seminary. Ann Arbor, MI: University Microfilms, 1987.

Presents a "rereading" of the history of Asia Minor from the perspective of the oppressed Roman subjects and suggests that the rereading was part of a liberation hermeneutic of the Book of Revelation. Using Marxist language in order to examine the class struggle and Marxist literary criticism to reread the narrative of the book (especially Rev. 12, 13, 17, and 18), P. concludes that the Rev. is actually radical political "resistance literature." See also 2, G.

[1986]
1190. Bovon, F. "Possession ou enchantement. Les institutions romaines selon l'Apocalypse de Jean." **CS** 7 (1986): 221-238.

Argues that although the Roman empire threatens the world and the Church, the Lord, the Lamb, and the prophetic Spirit prevail in the end. This is expressed in Rev. 18 at the fall of Babylon (Rome). Still, in the final analysis, as John expressed deep opposition to Rome, he also seems to display a secret admiration of the demonic triad in the Roman state.

1191. O'Donovan, O. "The Political Thought of the Book of Revelation." **TyB** 37 (1986): 61-94.

Argues that much of the Revelation is essentially antipolitical based on the following points: 1) The paradigm of politics is described in terms of imperial conquest. 2) The city (Babylon) sustains and develops the exploitation of imperial dominion by means of commercialism. 3) When the Word of God moves the believer to exercise freedom, he is moved into conflict with the organized community. 4) The imperial power (empire) becomes the instrument of the Antichrist in the "last days." 5) The Church fails to provide the needed social life that qualifies God's judgment on these affairs. Therefore, 6) Any true social order, in which love is to be the basis of all relationships, must be the clear revelation of God's justice.

[1977]
1192. Collins, A.Y. "The Political Perspective of the Revelation to John." **JBL** 96 (1977): 241-256.

Insists that the political crisis begun by Antiochus IV Epiphanes provided models of resistence for Christian believers and in the Rev. we see best the model of "synergistic passive resistence" whereby the martyrs' deaths bring to completion the eschaton. Thus, the Zealots and John share similar ideas of synergism and the critique of the Roman government.

1193. Garrett, J.L., Jr. "The Dialectic of Romans 13:1-7 and Revelation 13. Part Two." **JCS** 19 (1977): 5-20.

Reviews the history of interpretation of Rev. 13 and discusses contemporary scholarly interpretation along four main lines: Preterist, Continuous-Historical, Futurist, and Idealist (Philosophy of History). There are six themes common to all lines of interpretation, e.g., 1) The state may become a persecutor of Christians. 2) The persecuting civil state is authorized and empowered by Satan. 3) The civil state can force its subjects to worship it; and so forth. Concludes that although Rev. 13 does not deal with such issues as Christians in public office, military service, revolution, or the welfare state, Christians should accept the dialectical obligations to obey or disobey the state according to the teachings of Rom. 13:1-7 and Rev. 13. See also 1, C, (1) and 4, B.

1194. Fiorenza, E.S. "Religion und Politik in der Offenbarung des Johannes" in **Biblische Randbemerkungen: Schülerfestschrift für R. Schnackenburg.** Würzburg: Echter-Verlag, 1974. Pp. 261-271.

Critically investigates the interconnection between religion and politics in John's Revelation and the implication for the early church. See also 2, G.

[1973]
1195. Agouridηs, S. "*Δραμα και ποιησις την Αποκαλυψι του Ιωαννου.*" **DBM** 2 (1973): 3-28.

Considers John's use of drama and poetry in the Revelation to address the questions, Can the power and authority of the state be higher than Jesus Christ? And, can that state demand obedience and at the same time ignore man's humanity? Concludes that scenes of destruction are not expressions of vengeance, but poetic expressions of the triumph of God's government over the false powers of the world. See also 3, C and 3, D.

[1959]
1196. Barclay, W. "Great Themes of the New Testament: V. Revelation xiii." **ET** 70 (1959): 260-264; 292-296.

Contends that John's attitude toward the state in Rev. 13 is unlike the rest of the NT. The background to the problem in Rev. is Caesar-worship, and Rome is understood to be an instrument of Satan. The ultimate manifestation of evil is seen in the return of Nero, the wounded head, who comes as Antichrist to re-establish evil worship. See also 4, B.

[1954]
1197. Héring, J. **A Good and a Bad Government According to the New Testament**. Springfield, Ill.: Charles C. Thomas, 1954.

Compares Rev. 13 and Rom. 13 as he analyzes the Christian view of government. Concludes that Rev. 13 defines the evil quality of the government, while Rom. 13 describes the relationship in terms of Christian obedience and disobedience. See also 4, B.

(28) Poverty

[1982]
1198. Roffey, J.W. "On Doing Refection Theology: Poverty and Revelation 13:16-17." **Col** 14 (1982): 51-58.

Defines "Biblical reflection-theology" as that which calls for personal involvement in the examination and interpretation of any text, as well as praxis and reflection from beneath. Rev. 13:16-17, therefore, suggests that poverty is the inevitable price one pays for not worshipping the state. Yet, it is also the necessary sacrifice that helps to usher in the new age. See also above 4, B.

(29) Prayer

[1969]
1199. Thomas, R.L. "The Imprecatory Prayers of the Apocalypse." **BibSac** 126 (1969): 123-131.

Considers the altar and incense themes along with the imprecatory prayers and concludes that the nature of God's future wrath will be dependent upon the prayers of His saints. See also 5, H, 19.

(30) Priesthood

[1975]
1200. Feuillet, A. "Les Chrétiens prêtres et rois d'après l'Apocalypse. Contribution à l'étude de la conception Chrétienne du sacer doce." **RevThom** 75 (1975): 40-66.

Studies John's notion of priesthood by Christ and relative ministerial implications, in light of Rev. 1:5-6 and 5:9-10, where Christ is shown to be priest, king (Rev. 1), and suffering servant "victor" (Rev. 5). Argues against Fiorenza's **Priester für Gott** (1972) respecting the sociopolitical dimensions of redemption. The Christian life is shown to be liturgical in character; but baptism is not an underlying motif here as in I Peter. See also 4, B.

(31) Prophecy/Prophets

[1985]
1201. Bultema, H. **Maranatha: A Study of Unfulfilled Prophecy**. C. Lambregtse, trans. Grand Rapids, MI: Kregel Publications, 1985.

Originally a Dutch work, this translation examines five major themes, e.g., Prophecy, the First Resurrection, Believers, etc., and comments on their unfulfilled nature. A section on the Rev. (12 pp.) offers a "chiliastic look" into the book, which includes traditional structure and literal translation and interpretation. Appendices survey the history of interpretation from the early fathers to the present. Champions chiliasm.

[1975]
1202. Dauzenberg, G. **Urchristliche Prophetie. Ihre Erforschung, ihre Voraussetzungen im Judentum und ihre Struktur im ersten Korintherbrief.** "Beiträge zur Wissenschaft vom Alten und Neuen Testament 104." Stuttgart: KohlHammer, 1975.

Offers a detailed analysis of early Christian prophecy, first, through an introduction to the relevant source literature and recent critical questions. Part one considers the background and milieu of early Christian prophecy by studying the language of interpretation and understanding in Daniel, Wisdom Literature, the LXX, as well as the exposition and interpretation of revelation in the literature of Qumran, I Enoch, the prophecy of 4 Ezra

and 2 Baruch. Part two deals extensively with the form and function of
early Christian prophecy in I Cor. 12-14 and concludes by showing the
complex literary and theological connection between I Cor. 12-14, the
Revelation of John, and Jewish apocalyptic. See also 3, D.

[1965]
1203. Siegman, E.F. "John the Prophet." **BT** 1 (1965): 1334-1339.

Argues that John the Prophet follows the lines of traditional prophecy in
the Revelation in terms of offering a whole book of inspired preaching
and Christological applications of OT texts. See also 3, D and 5, C.

[1956]
1204. Ordonez, V. "El Sacerdocio de los fieles (Sentido escrituristico
textual)." **RevET** 64 (1956): 359-379.

Studies the priestly role of the faithful in Rev. 1:6; 20:6; I Pet. 2:4-9; etc.
See also 5, H, (30).

[1952]
1205. Langenberg, H. **Die prophetische Bildsprache der Apokalypse**.
Matzinger: Franz, 1952.

Investigates and evaluates the prophetic imagery in the Revelation and its
traditional connections. See also 3, C and 3, D.

[1944]
1206. Smith, U. **The Prophecies of Daniel and the Revelation**. Revised
and newly illustrated. Nashville, TN: Southern Pub. Association, 1944.

Discusses the literary and theological relationships between the OT Book
of Daniel and John's Revelation, especially in terms of their prophecies.
Identifies historical references, exposition of themes, and pictures. See
also 3, D.

(32) Salvation/Redemption

[1989]
1207. Pilgrim, W.E. "Universalism in the Apocalypse." **WW** 9 (1989):
235-243.

Suggests the possibility that the Apocalypse does not present an exclusive
notion of salvation but rather offers a redemptive vision that includes all

humankind. Studies relevant passages from the text and concludes that the Apocalypse allows a "possibility" of God's redemptive goal for everyone. In the final analysis, however, that reality is left up to God and God alone. See also 5, G, (3).

[1982]
1208. Giesen, H. "Heilszusage angesichts der Bedrängnis. Zu den Makarismen in der Offenbarung des Johannes." **SNTU** 6-7 (1981-82): 191-223.

Offers a critical analysis of the seven makarisms in the Rev. (Cf. Rev. 1:3; 14:13; 16:15; 19:9; 20:6; 22:7, 14), and suggests that they are promises extended to believers who persevere against persecution. Concludes that the makarisms are paraenetic statements that advance the message of John, viz., there will be rewards for those who persevere courageously until the End.

[1974]
1209. Fiorenza, E.S. "Redemption as Liberation: Apoc. 1:5f. and 5:9f." **CBQ** 36 (1974): 220-232.

Suggests that the literary form and theological perspective of the Revelation come from John's authority derived from his revelation of Jesus Christ and therefore approximate the authoritative perspective of the Pauline epistles. Redemption means liberation from everything that enslaves and this gives new dignity to the redeemed. The terms that best describe this new liberation are βασιλεια and ʽιερεις. Analyses of 1:5-6 and 5:9-10 suggest that redemption and/or salvation is understood by John in political-social categories, ultimately expressed as the "new world." See also 4, B and 5, H, (27).

[1957]
1210. Crouzel, H. "Le Dogme de la Rédemption dans l'Apocalypse." **BLE** 58 (1957): 65-92.

Argues that the book presents the notion of redemption in a dramatic confrontation between Jerusalem and Babylon. Each city has its protagonists, characters, and ideas of existence. After the battle, redemption is shown to be the victory of Christ and His elect. Thus, in military language, the story is told and Christ, the center and Lord of history, assures victory. The elect, like good soldiers, are sent into action. Concludes that all this represents the struggle of the Church in the midst of a hostile world. See also 5, F.

[1953]
1211. Marx, M.J. "The Tree of Life." **Wor** 27 (1952-53): 185-186.

Discusses the tree-of-life image as a symbol of redemption for the Christian. Connects the image with the latter part of the Rev. of John. See also 3, D.

[1952]
1212. Goppelt, L. "Heilsoffenbarung und Geschichte nach der Offenbarung des Johannes." **TLz** 77 (1952): 513-522.

Explores the meaning of revealed salvation and history in the Revelation in relationship to the contemporary church. Draws an analogy with Dan. 7:1-14. Interprets Rev. 6-20 in light of Christ's exaltation in Chaps. 4-5. Concludes that salvation as revealed in the Apocalypse is in God's hands "*in der Geschichte.*" The cross of Christ is crucial to this interpretation. See also 5, H, (14).

[1951]
1213. Lehmann, P. "Deliverance and Fulfillment: The Biblical View of Salvation." **Int** 5 (1951): 387-400.

Discusses the biblical view of salvation as found in the OT and NT, expecially under the notion of "Deliverance and Fulfillment." Subsequently, L. answers the questions, 1. "How Salvation Operates?" 2. "Where Salvation Ends?" and "Who Is Included?" Concludes that the Bible tends toward a view of universalism, but in the final analysis the author is uncertain as to "who" will be saved. Occasional references made to the Rev. in the course of analysis.

(33) Seals

[1973]
1214. Davis, D.R. "The Relationship Between the Seals, Trumpets and Bowls in the Book of Revelation." **JETS** 16 (1973): 149-158.

Observes the series of judgments in the book as primarily sequential to the earlier one(s), but the end of each series is parallel to the conclusion of the others. John's purpose is to focus attention on the coming Lord in the hope that from the vision those on earth may discover new power to endure. See also 5, G, (2) and 5, G, (3).

[1940]
1215. Heitmüller, F. "Die ersten sechs Siegelgerichte (Apk 6)." **AW** 37 (1940): 338-341.

Analyzes Rev. 6 in reference to the nature of the first six seal-judgments of the book. See also 5, G, (3).

(34) Sin

[1978]
1216. Vanni, U. "I peccati nell'Apocalisse e nelle lettere di Pietro, di Giacomo, di Giuda." **ScC** 106 (1978): 372-386.

Not seen.

(35) Victory/Overcoming/Fidelity

[1982]
1217. Rosscup, J.E. "The Overcomer of the Apocalypse." **GTJ** 3 (1982): 261-286.

Offer an exegetical study of the "overcomer" (*'o νικων*) passages in Rev. 2-3 and concludes that the promises of blessing and subsequent rewards are intended for Christians, i.e., those who are saved. See also 4 B.

(36) Virgins/Believers

[1964]
1218. Devine, R. "The Virgin Followers of the Lamb." **Scrip** 16 (1964): 1-5.

Judges that the term "virgins" (cf. Rev. 14:4) suggests the "elite" of Christ who have not given themselves to idolatry. Also, there is some hint of sexual perfection, which is the objective of all those who dwell in the Kingdom of heaven. See also 4, B.

(37) War

See (25) above for comparisons and contrasts.

(38) Water

[1961]
1219. Morris, H.M. "Water and the Word." **BibSac** 118 (1961): 203-215.

Analyzes Rev. 21:1 to understand why there will be "no more sea (water)" on the new earth. Concludes that although water is crucial to life on the "old" earth, it is also, according to John, a symbol for God's spiritual refreshment. In the millennium the only water necessary will be symbolic, like the first river in Eden and living waters, viz., the word of God. See also 5, H, (17).

[1953]
1220. Marx, M.J. "Living Water." **Wor** 27 (1952-53): 242-243.

Traces the biblical water motif in terms of its "life" connotations. Concludes with references to Rev. 22: 1, 17, "living water," as a fitting conclusion for the Christian community.

(39) Woman/Mary/Mother

[1990]
1221. Keller, C. "Die Frau in der Wüste: ein feministisch-theologischer Midrasch zu Offb 12." **EvT** 50 (1990): 414-432.

Discusses the notion of "open apocalyptic" concerning the text while developing a theological midrash from Rev. 12 for feminists and others not hindered by partiarchial restrictions. Other themes relevant to eschatology are discussed, e.g., creation, anthropology, and hope. The "Frau" of Rev. 12 is identified as Wisdom.

[1978]
1222. Bagatti, B. "L'interpretazione mariana di Apocalisse 12, 1-6 nel II secolo." **Mar** 40 (1978): 153-159.

Not seen.

1223. Feuillet, A. "Der Sieg der Frau nach dem Protoevangelium." **IKZC** 7 (1978): 26-35.

Argues from Gen. 3:15 that God's promise of victory over sin by mankind is seen in the typological connection between Eve, the first woman (and type of Mary), and Mary, the mother of the Messiah (and the new Eve). The description of the woman in Rev. 12 is really a Christian transposition of the *protoevangelium*. See also 3, D and 5, H, (17).

[1968]
1224. Ernst, J. "Die 'himmlische Frau' im 12. Kapitel der Apokalypse."
TG 58 (1968): 39-59.

Offers an exegetical study of Rev. 12, while evaluating the ecclesiological
and Marian interpretations. Suggests that both views have problems, but
prefers an interpretation (held by many Catholic scholars) wherein the
woman represents the Church as first, the people of God, and second,
Mary. See also 4, B.

[1965]
1225. Pétrement, S. "Une suggestion de Simone Weil á propos
d'Apocalypse xii." **NTS** 11 (1965): 291-296.

Argues that Jewish-Christian literature suggests a connection between the
woman, the Church, and the Holy Spirit in Rev. 12. This interpretation
has connections with the research of Lohmeyer and the intuition of
Simone Weil. See also 4, B and 5, D.

[1964]
1226. Bruns, J.E. "The Contrasted Women of Apocalypse 12 and 17."
CBQ 26 (1964): 459-463.

Argues that the woman of Rev. 12 seems to be the Church, primarily, and
Mary, secondarily. II Ki. 11:1-3 is helpful toward this interpretation. The
woman of Rev. 17 appears to portray imperial Rome, generally, and
Empress Messalina particularly. See also 3, D.

[1963]
1227. Hopfgartner, L. "La Sacra Scrittura e il soggiorno di Maria a Efeso
nell'interpretazione esegetica di alcuni brani dell'Apocalisse." **RivB** 11
(1963): 367-378.

Studies the place and interpretation of the woman in Rev. 12 and her
connection to Mary, the mother of Jesus.

[1962]
1228. Gahan, S. "'The Woman Clothed with the Sun' According to St.
Lawrence of Brindisi." **AER** 147 (1962): 395-402.

Considers Rev. 12:1 as a reference to the mother of Jesus through a
glorious and special apparition to John, the author of the book. See 4, B.

[1960]
1229. James, P.P. "Mary and the Great Sign." **AER** 142 (1960): 321-329.

Investigates the woman figure in Rev. 12:1 and suggests that she signifies the Blessed Virgin and also the Church. The sign is understood to be inclusive of all God's statements regarding the Incarnation. It is becoming clear that there is a moral identification between the woman, Mary, and the Church. See also 3, F and 4, B.

1230. Kassing, A. "Das Weib und der Drache (Apk 12, 1-6, 13-17)." **BK** 15 (1960): 114-116.

Studies the figures of the woman and the dragon in Rev. 12 as dynamic symbols for the struggle of the Church against the Roman empire. See also 3, F.and 4, B.

1231. O'Donoghue, N.-D. "A Woman Clothed with the Sun." **F** 11 (1960): 445-456.

Studies Rev. 12:1 and concludes, with LeFrois, that the figure of the woman is a symbol for the virgin Mary and the Church. See also 4, B.

1232. Peinador, M. "El problema de María y la Iglesia. La interpretación de Apocalipsis XII, 1 ss." **EpM** 10 (1960): 161-194.

Not seen.

[1958]
1233. LeFrois, B.J. "The Mary-Church Relationship in the Apocalypse." **MS** 9 (1958): 79-106.

Examines the figure of Mary in the Revelation of John in terms of her relationship to the Church and her struggle to bring into life a regenerated people. Her struggle, like that of the Church, is against the powers of darkness in order to bring the Church into perfection (the Marian ideal). When the Church realizes in herself the "Marian prototype," then the Lord will come again. See also 5, F.

[1956]
1234. Stefaniak, L. "Mulier amicta sole (Apok 12, 1-17)." **RuBL** 9 (1956): 244-261.

Not seen.

[1951]
1235. Bissonnette, G. "The Twelfth Chapter of the Apocalypse and Our Lady's Assumption." **MS** 2 (1951): 170-177.

Argues that Rev. 12 depicts the assumption of the Virgin Mary. See also 4, B.

[1950]
1236. Unger, D.J. "Did St. John See the Virgin Mary in Glory?" **CBQ** 11 (1949): 249-262; 392-405; 12 (1950): 75-83; 155-161; 292-300; 405-415.

Summarizes the content of Rev. 12 in a series of articles and reviews that offer several scriptural and traditional arguments for regarding the woman in the chapter as the Virgin Mary. Concludes that even though John does not say explicitly that this is Mary who is assumed into glory, it is clearly implied in the "literal" and "explicit language." See also 4, B.

[1949]
1237. Murphy, R.E. "An Allusion to Mary in the Apocalypse." **TS** 10 (1949): 565-573.

Critiques Cardinal Newman's statement on Rev. 12 that this chapter makes an "allusion" to Mary's sanctity and dignity but does not refer to this in a true "biblical" sense. Concludes that there is a connection to the assumption of Mary in the passage, but it is understood in terms of her "glorious privilege" as the mother of God.

[1941]
1238. Böckeler, M. **Das grosse Zeichen. Apok. 12,1. Die Frau als Symbol göttlicher Wirklichkeit**. Salzburg: O. Müller, 1941.

Examines Rev. 12:1 respecting the appearance of the woman in the text as a symbolic figure for heavenly and spiritual truth. See also 3, F and 4, B.

1239. Rösch, K. "Die himmlische Frau und der Drache in Apk 12." **Pastor Bonus** (Trier) 52 (1941): 17-21.

Not seen.

(40) World

[1988]
1240. Collins, A.Y. "The Physical World in the Book of Revelation." **BT** 26 (1988): 156-159.

Contends that in the Revelation of John, the physical world has its source and foundation in the spiritual world. The physical world is the expression of the spiritual in terms of creation, personal salvation, and the ultimate evolution of our physical and social contexts.

[1975]
1241. Eller, V. "How the Kings of the Earth Land in the New Jerusalem: 'The World' in the Book of Revelation." **Kat/B** 5 (1975): 21-27.

Notes that John tends to divide things in the Revelation into two categories: First, Christianity (worship of the Lamb) and, second, worldliness (worship of the Beast). Although "the kings of the earth" are identified in the worldly category (see 6:9-17; etc.), they land in the new Jerusalem (Rev. 21:24). How? E. explains that "the kings" are a theological category, the first rank of the enemies of God. Hence, 1) in the new humanity there is no place (as in the OT) for second-class Gentile citizens. And 2), because of the resurrection, all history must pass away. Therefore, God will claim a place for the "the kings of the earth" in His new Jerusalem. See also 5, H, (12).

[1955]
1242. Braun, F.-M. "La Femme vêtue de soleil (Apoc. XII)." **RevThom** 55 (1955): 639-669.

Evaluates the work of Le Frois and Cerfaux on Rev. 12, who interpret the chapter as referring to the Church personified in Mary. Identifies several problems related to the debate, and attempts to solve them by the use of Moeller's concept of individual and common vocation (cf. **Mentalité moderne et évangélisation**). Connects Rev. 12 with Gen. 3:15, while noting the Eve-Mary association. Concludes that the woman in Rev. 12 is symbolic and does imply Mary and the Church fused inseparably. See also 4, B.

(41) Worship

[1988]
1243. Peterson, D.G. "Worship in the Revelation to John." **RTR** 47 (1988): 67-77.

Insists that the main message of the Revelation is that "worship" is offered to Christ daily on earth as Christians keep the faith and resist the temptation to idolatry and apostasy. Encouragement for Christian living is best discovered in the hymns that focus on the sovereign God and the victory of the Lamb. See also 5, H, (19).

[1960]
1244. Quiery, W.H. "Opening 'The Closed Book' of the New Testament." **AER** 143 (1960): 49-56.

Offers a practical, nontechnical exposition of the five major doxologies found in the Revelation (1:6; 4:9; etc.).

-Select Dissertations-

[1990]
1245. Carlson, S.W. "The Relevance of Apocalyptic Numerology for the Meaning of CHILIA ETE in Revelation 20." Unpublished Doctoral Dissertation. Iowa: Mid-America Baptist Theological Seminary, 1990.

1246. Moore, H. "Revelation as an 'Apocalypse' in the Context of Jewish and Christian Apocalyptic Thought." Unpublished Doctoral Dissertation. Belfast, Ireland: Queen's University of Belfast, 1990.

[1985]
1247. Hre, Kio, S. "Exodus as a Symbol of Liberation in the Book of the Apocalypse." Unpublished Doctoral Dissertation. Atlanta, GA: Emory University, 1985.

[1984]
1248. Marty, W.H. "The New Moses." Unpublished Doctoral Dissertation. Dallas, TX: Dallas Theological Seminary, 1984.

[1983]
1249. Cesar, E.E.B. "Faith Operating in History: New Testament Hermeneutics in a Revolutionary Context." Unpublished Doctoral Dissertation. Atlanta, GA: Emory University, 1983.

1250. Warren, W.L. "Apostasy in the Book of Revelation." Unpublished Doctoral Dissertation. Louisville, KY: Southern Baptist Theological Seminary, 1983.

[1982]
1251. Kempson, W.R. "Theology in the Revelation of John."
Unpublished Doctoral Dissertation. Louisville, KY: Southern Baptist
Theological Seminary, 1982.

1252. Reddish, M.G. "The Theme of Martyrdom in the Book of
Revelation." Unpublished Doctoral Dissertation. Louisville, KY:
Southern Baptist Theological Seminary, 1982.

[1981]
1253. Engelbrecht, J.J. "The Christology of the Revelation to St. John"
(Afrikaans Text). Unpublished Doctoral Dissertation. Pretoria, S. A.:
University of South Africa, 1981.

[1978]
1254. Melton, L.D. "A Critical Analysis of the Understanding of the
Imagery of City in the Book of Revelation." Unpublished Doctoral
Dissertation. Louisville, KY: Southern Baptist Theological Seminary,
1978.

[1975]
1255. Haag, H.J. "The Concept of Death in the New Testament."
Unpublished Doctoral Dissertation. Waco, TX: Baylor University, 1975.

[1960]
1256. Kusche, R.W. "The Concept of the Community of Believers in the
Apocalypse of John: A Study of the Doctrine of the Church."
Unpublished Doctoral Dissertation. Nashville, TN: Vanderbilt University,
1960.

[1948]
1257. McCall, J.G. "The Eschatological Teaching of the Book of
Revelation." Unpublished Doctoral Dissertation. Louisville, KY:
Southern Baptist Theological Seminary, 1948.

[1944]
1258. McGinnis, J. "The Doctrine of the Lamb of God in the
Apocalypse." Unpublished Doctoral Dissertation. Louisville, KY:
Southern Baptist Theological Seminary, 1944.

[1943]
1259. Poirier, L. "Les sept églises, or le premier septénaire prophétique

de l'Apocalypse." Unpublished Doctoral Dissertation. Washington, D. C.:
The Catholic University of America, 1943.

Chapter 6

The Revelation
in the Life of the Church

A. GENERAL WORKS

[1991]
1260. Charlier, J.-P. **Comprendre l'Apocalypse**, Vol. 1, Lire la Bible 89. Paris: Cerf, 1991.

Presents some popular ideas regarding apocalyptic literature, a brief survey of the content of the Book of Revelation, and, an extended exposition of Rev. 1:1-14:5 based on the outline of 1:1-8 (Introduction); 1:9-4:11 (Letters); 5:1-8:1 (Seals: Living as a Christian in the world); 8:2-14:5 (Trumpets: history of humanity and the incarnation of God). See also 1, B.

[1990]
1261. Kuhn, C.L. "The Fine Line: The Relevance of Apocalyptic Today." **BT** 28 (1990): 267-269.

Suggests that the Revelation is relevant to our time because it reminds us that, in spite of the appearance of disorder and chaos in the world, God is still in control of all principalities and powers.

1262. Rowland, C. "Revelation: Mirror of Our Passion, Goal of Our Longing." **Way** 30 (1990): 124-134.

Declares that the whole of the Revelation (including "the less tasty parts") is helpful for the Christian identity today, for it mirrors the reality of evil and destruction in the world. It also reminds us of the continuation of certain values and actions that we should not tolerate. See also 5, A.

[1988]
1263. Martin, G.M. "Wie die Offenbarung des Johannes in

apokalyptischen Zeiten zu Leben und zu lesen ist." **US** 43 (1988): 139-145, 155.

Suggests several ways that the Revelation of John may be read and applied to our apocalyptic times. See also 5, H, 14.

[1987]
1264. Guthrie, D. **The Relevance of John's Apocalypse.** Devon, Eng.: The Paternoster Press; Grand Rapids, MI: Wm. B. Eerdmans Publishing Company, 1987.

Discusses issues of practical relevance for the Church such as content and meaning, Christology and the modern challenge, the Church (past, present, future), and the conflict and its consummation. Conclusions suggest, 1) Christians should be "open" to the contents of the book because the Rev. is a communication from God for those who are listening; 2) the exalted image of Jesus in the book offers the "unshakable conviction" that the Lamb will triumph in the end; 3) the risen Christ still sustains the Church, and He must be worshipped in the context of the Church; 4) The end vision of the New Jerusalem offers positive hope to all who embrace the Christian gospel.

[1984]
1265. Geiger, A. **Apokalypse heute: Zeichen der Zeit.** Stuttgart: KBW, 1984.

Writes a popular interpretation of primary themes in the Revelation, e.g., heaven and earth, the author and End redaction, prophecy, Christ, etc. The second part of the work (100 pages) offers a short commentary on the major literary sections and concludes with sixty pages of color and black-and-white pictures along with interpretations and Scripture references.

[1981]
1266. Maier, G. **Die Johanesoffenbarung und die Kirche.**
"Wisssenschaftliche Untersuchungen zum Neuen Testament 25."
Tübingen: Mohr-Siebeck, 1981.

Examines the place of the Revelation of John in the history of the Christian church. Divides his work into five parts: 1) The struggle of the early church (Papias and the presbyters, Gaius and the Alogi, Dionysius and Eusebius); 2) The reinterpretation in the West (Ticonius and Augustine); 3) The Reformation (The Baptist movements and Luther); 4) The age of Pietism (pre-Spener, Spener and early German Pietism,

Württemberg before Bengel, Bengel and beyond Bengel); 5) The Enlightenment to the present (the breakthrough of historical criticism, Schleiermacher and Baur, the "after-hold" of the nineteenth century, liberalism, dialecticalism, biblicism [1885-1935], further historical criticism). Concludes that the Book of Revelation in every period of church history has proven to be a touchstone of eschatological ideas and hermeneutical positions. See also 1, C.

[1962]
1267. Bratsiotis, P. "L'Apocalypse de saint Jean dans le culte de l'Eglise Grecque Orthodoxe." **RHPR** 42 (1962): 116-121.

Contends that the life of the Greek Orthodox Church, with its two-fold emphasis on Christ's eschatological Resurrection and on end-time expectation, is maintained by the mystery of the Book of Revelation.

B. ART/MUSIC

[1975]
1268. Oberhuber, O. **Apokalypse.** Illustrated. Klosterneuburg: Österreichisches Katholisches Bibelwerk, 1975.

A. Stöger introduces the German text, "*Einheitstext der Heiligen Schrift*," while Oberhuber offers color and black-and-white illustrations.

[1964]
1269. Snyder, J. "The Reconstruction of an Early Christian Cycle of Illustrations for the Book of Revelation -- the Trier Apocalypse." **VCh** 18 (1964): 146-162.

Investigates codex Stadtbibliothek of Trier (MS 31) regarding the medieval art cycles for the Revelation. See also 2, C.

C. SECULAR AND DEVOTIONAL LITERATURE

[1984]
1270. Patrides, C.A. and Wittreich, J., eds. **The Apocalypse in English Renaissance Thought and Literature: patterns, antecedents, and repercussions.** Ithaca, NY: Cornell University Press, 1984.

This collection of thirteen essays treats the subject in four major sections: I. Background -- McGinn, Reeves. II. The Apocalypse in Renaissance England and Europe -- Pelikan, Capp, Murrin. III. The Apocalypse in Renaissance English Literature -- Sandler, Wittreich, Patrides. IV. The Aftermath -- Korshin, Stein, Carpenter and Laudow, Tureson, Abrams. An excellent seventy-two page bibliography follows. Abrams' essay, "Apocalypse: theme and variations," offers insight into how the Apocalypse helped to shape 1) views of history, including millennialism, meliorism, revolution, chiliasm, and; 2) the meaning of the relationship between the apocalyptic writer's view of himself as both "seer and bard." See also 2, B.

[1981]
1271. Quitslund, S.A. "Revelation: A Springboard to Prayer." **BT** 19 (1981): 380-385.

Suggests that a "spiritual" approach to the Revelation of John may mean using the book as a springboard to prayer. This can help the reader to become conscious of the reality of sin; but he can also find reassurance that God is in control. Insists that such an approach aids us in entering into the author's experience and also gives us strength and confidence in God's ultimate victory.

[1973]
1272. Scott, N.A., Jr. "'New Heavens, New Earth' -- the Landscape of Contemporary Apocalypse." **JR** 53 (1973): 1-35.

Discusses the parallels between Judeo-Christian apocalypticism (with reference to the Revelation and other biblical writings) and American "secular radicalism." Notes points of comparison and contrast.

[1966]
1273. Gilmour, S.M. "The Use and Abuse of the Book of Revelation." **ANQ** 7 (1966): 15-28.

Discusses the current debate over the relative value of the Book of Revelation with a focus on the persons and "fringe groups" who have misinterpreted the book to fit their own millennial programs. The Jehovah's Witnesses are singled out for careful critique and criticism. Attempts to draw the reader toward the historical and literary intentions of the author.

1274. Newbold, F. "The Millennium [A Poem]." **HibJ** 64 (1965-66): 155.

Creates a three-stanza poem about the expected final day of "Doom" which, at last, did not come. The responses of the people left on earth are noted. See also 1, C, (2) and 5, G, (4).

[1957]
1275. Bock, E. **The Apocalypse of St. John.** London: Christian Community Press, 1957. Translated from the 1951 German edition.

Offers a devotional study of the Revelation in twelve chapters in order to direct the present-day persecuted community to sources of inward security and strength. Introductory observations describe the character and structure of the book as the authoritative work on "intuitive spiritual experience." The main theme is the Second Coming of Christ, the Son of Man. Rev. 2-3 represent the great human epochs in history. The millennium simply signifies an undefined epoch designed to help mankind struggle against evil.

[1954]
1276. Fritsch, C.T. "The Message of Apocalyptic for Today." **TT** 10 (1953-54): 357-366.

Discusses the location of apocalyptic thought among modern Christians in terms of its nature, value, and proper place within Christian hope. Treats the genre and idea in relationship to the unity of history, divine determinism, and its relevance to human need. See also 5, A.

[1953]
1277. Harkness, G. "Eschatology in the Great Poets." **RL** 22 (1953): 85-99.

Explores six types of eschatology to be found in the world's great poets. Only resurrection of the body is missing from eschatological categories in these writers. Concludes with an analysis of Whittier, Tennyson, and Browning regarding the "Personal immortality and the forward look."

[1895]
1278. Rossetti, C.G. **The Face of the Deep: A Devotional Commentary on the Apocalypse.** London: Society for Promoting Christian Knowledge, 1895.

Weaves a profound poetic and meditative exposition of the literary units of the Book of Revelation. Exhortations to the reader encourage personal application of the various themes.

D. HOMILETICS

General

[1990]
1279. Rogers, C. "Images of Christian Victory: Notes for Preaching from the Book of Revelation." **QR** 10 (1990): 69-78.

Offers some ideas for preachers concerning the scholarly caution surrounding the Revelation and, then, a discussion of the relationship between the book and modern culture, the apocalyptic genre and symbolism, and methods of homiletic communication.

[1986]
1280. Craddock, F.B. "Preaching the Book of Revelation." **Int** XL (1986): 270-282.

Addresses two questions: First, is the careful study of Revelation a good stewardship of time for the local pastor? Second, what clues are available to help with the hearing and the proclaiming of the messages of the text? The author's answer to the first is affirmative, especially to those who are prepared to take the time to see its seven-fold relevance. Suggests that Revelation is basically a liturgical book that invites its readers to sing, to pray, and to praise God. Those who attempt to preach or teach the themes of the book apart from a liturgical setting rob it of much of its power. Regarding the second question, C. offers nine "Procedural Suggestions for Preaching Revelation," Examples include: 1) Be prepared to accept and regard positively the distance between oneself and the text; 2) Be immersed in the whole text; 6) Be clear about imagery and visions; 9) Let the whole liturgy itself bring the Revelation to the congregation. The essay concludes with a list of suggested readings.

[1985]
1281. Kelly, J.F.T. "Early Medieval Evidence for Twelve Homilies By Origen on the Apocalypse." **VC** 39 (1985): 273-279.

Investigates the available data from the Medieval period that testify to twelve sermons on the Revelation of John by the early church Father, Origen.

[1984]
1282. Blevins, J.L. **Revelation.** "Knox Preaching Guides." Atlanta, GA: John Knox Press, 1984.

Offers homiletic suggestions to "preachers" of the Revelation. Introduction deals with the work's apocalyptic, theological, and dramatic background along with the outline of the seven visions. Each literary/dramatic unit is given a preaching theme/title, e.g., Rev. 2:1-7, "Fallen from First Love" or Rev. 8:5-11:18, "Destruction." Practical preaching ideas are included in each section.

1283. Collins, A.Y. "'What the Spirit Says to the Churches': Preaching the Apocalypse." **QR** 4 (1984): 69-84.

Asserts that the keys to interpreting and preaching the Rev. are related to understanding the book's unified composition, historical setting (ca. A.D. 95-96), social situation (including marginality and alienation), apocalyptic genre, and "depth" language. The message of the Rev. should remind the reader that the Kingdom of God involves a transforming experience for people, as individuals or church, regardless, including the social and political dimension.

[1969]
1284. Jochen, V.B. "Preaching Values in the Book of Revelation."
Unpublished Th.M. Thesis. Philadelphia, PA: Eastern Baptist Theological Seminary, 1969.

Offers various ways that the Revelation may be used in contemporary preaching to proclaim the Gospel to modern society. After discussing the nature of evangelical preaching and the nature of apocalyptic, the author suggests passages that are particularly relevant to preaching for today's world.

[1959]
1285. Tenney, M.C. "Eschatology and the Pulpit." **BibSac** 116 (1959): 30-42.

Discusses the importance of including eschatological themes in preaching, especially in terms of motives, content, and method. Includes ideas from the Revelation.

[1957]
1286. Farris, A.L. "The Preacher's Use of the Book of Revelation." **CJTh** 3 (1957): 102-110.

Urges preachers to preach from the Book of Revelation and to take the privilege away from fanatics. Suggests the preaching approach as

Christocentric with knowledge of the historical situation of the writing, the theology (e.g., church-state conflict), etc. Concludes that Revelation sounds a theology of hope and a note of triumph and confidence for Christians. See also 2, G and 5, C.

[1951]
1287. Davies, P.E. "Crisis Preaching." **McQ** 4 (1950-51): 11.

Asserts the thematic value of the Book of Revelation for contemporary crisis preaching.

[1948]
1288. Calkins, R. "Militant Message: How to Preach from the Apocalyptic Message of the Bible." **Int** 2 (1948): 430-443.

Places the origin of apocalyptic in the "dark days" and suggests that this is the basis for preaching from the Revelation today, since the days of today are dark. Revelation should be used as a message of assurance to an age of pessimism.

[1947]
1289. Burnet, A.W. **The Lord Reigneth. A Preacher's View of the Book of Revelation**. London: Hodder and Stoughton, 1947.

Addresses pastors regarding the Revelation, while identifying John as the Elder who writes with an apocalyptic style but from a prophetic point of view in a time of stress for the Church. The book is a kind of moving picture intended to give heart and help to Christians of the first century and to modern Christians in a war-torn world.

1290. Wishart, C.F. "Patmos in the Pulpit." **Int** 1 (1947): 456-465.

Presents hints for the preacher who may be trying to preach on the Revelation. After suggesting the value of knowing John's visionary structure and dismissing the chronological approach, W. analyzes the genre, key symbols, etc., noting the symbol of the Lamb as the key to the mystery of life at the end of time. See also 3, E and 5, C.

[1945]
1291. Menzies, R. "The Apocalyptic Note in Modern Preaching." **EQ** 17 (1945): 81-90.

Traces several apocalyptic themes in modern preaching with occasional references to the Revelation of John. Concludes that the abiding message of apocalyptic may be seen in its application to the sphere of history, moral struggle, message of comfort, and the new social hope.

[1940]
1292. Rigg, W.H."The Apocalypse: The Book for Today." **ET** 51 (1939-40): 503-505.

Writes a general, homiletical exposition of the whole book of Revelation according to a traditional outline and stressing the need for today's world to yield to the Lordship of Jesus Christ. See also 1, C, (1).

[1935]
1293. Russell, D. **Preaching the Apocalypse**. NY: Abingdon Press, 1935.

Exhorts "working preachers" regarding preaching values in the Revelation. Exposition treats the major units of thought and concludes each section with a detailed sermon outline.

[1909]
1294. Vangorder, J.J. **A B C's of the Revelation**. Grand Rapids, MI: Zondervan, 1909.

Sermon notes follow an acrostic approach, A-Z: A=Apocalypse; B=Backslidden church; C=Commended church, etc. Expository writing.

Specific Sermons

Chap. 1

[1969]
1295. Small, R.L. "A Sermon for Bible Sunday [Rev. 1:3]." **ET** 80 (1968-69): 47-48.

Offers a sermon for Bible Sunday based on Rev. 1:3. Urges all Christians to read the Scriptures regularly.

[1962]
1296. Jarvis, P. "Jesus, the First and the Last [Rev. 1:17-18]." **ET** 73 (1961-62): 219-220.

Gives a post-Easter homily based on Rev. 1:17-18 regarding Christ as the answer to every Christian's fears.

[1961]
1297. Barr, A."Christ the Lord [Rev. 1:16]." **ET** 72 (1960-61): 23-25.

Affirms the powerful presence of Christ as Lord among Christians based on an exposition of Rev. 1:16.

[1958]
1298. Riach, J.L. "Where Are We to Live [Rev. 1:8]?" **ET** 69 (1957-58): 90-91.

Gives a New Year's message from Rev. 1:8 respecting the importance of living in the new year in terms of the Christian past, present, and future.

[1954]
1299. Johnston, G. "God's Last Word [Rev. 1:8]." **ET** 65 (1953-54): 310-312.

Suggests, according to Rev. 1:8, that although the early church asserted that the end of the world was near and the "last things " were present, the last word from God is a name, even Jesus Christ, who promises reward and assurance to the faithful.

[1949]
1300. Schlep, A.W. "The True Spirit of Thanksgiving Day [Rev. 1:5-6]." **CTM** 20 (1949): 779-781.

Outlines a sermon presentation on Rev. 1:5-6 for Thanksgiving Day. Christians are called to focus not on material blessings but on God's love and pardon in Jesus Christ.

[1947]
1301. Tillich, P. "Behold, I Am Doing a New Thing [Rev. 1:1-5]." **USQR** 2 (1946-47): 3-9.

Presents a sermon from passages in Is. 43, 65, Ecc. 1, Mat. 9, and Rev. 21 on old and new contrasts, respecting the personal and the secular world for Christians. Applies his conclusions to the current critical situation of the world, suggesting that God is indeed doing His "new thing."

[1945]
1302. David, A.A. "The Living One [Rev. 1:17-18]." **ET** 56 (1944-45):

161-162.

Submits an Easter sermon based on Rev. 1:17-18 calling people to accept the eternal guarantee that at the end of time . . . "Life wins!" See also 4, B.

Chap. 2

[1957]
1303. Bannon, R. "Let a Privileged Church See to Its Life [Rev. 2:1-7]." **CTM** 28 (1957): 760-761.

Submits a sermonic interpretation of the message to Ephesus in Rev. 2 in two parts: I. Remember Jesus' love; II. Remember His Gospel and His communion.

1304. Rudnick, M.L. "Faithful Unto Death [Rev. 2:8-11]." **CTM** 28 (1957): 761-763.

Provides Rev. 2:8-11 as the text for a three-point sermon: I. The Devil uses suffering to make us falter. II. Faith leads to the "Crown of Life." III. Christ wins our Crown of Life for us.

[1941]
1305. Bonniwell, W.R. "The After-Life [Apoc. 2:10]." **HPR** 41 (1940-41): 102-105.

Suggests ideas for Christians from Rev. 2:10 on immortality, heaven and hell, purgatory, and preparations (by prayer, love, etc.) for the afterlife.

Chap. 3

[1968]
1306. Bridge, W.H. "The Challenge of the Two Doors [Rev. 3:8]." **ET** 79 (1967-68): 118-120.

Announces that passing through the two doors of Christ (cf. Rev.. 3:3 and Jn. 10:7) provides the final answer for the human predicament.

[1967]
1307. Kolb, E.J. "[Untitled Homily on 3:15-17]." **CTM** 38 (1967): 610-612.

Challenges listeners to evaluate their lives with an ear to the judgment promised in Rev. 3:15-17 and to answer two questions: 1) Are you *passing* (judgment by Rev. 3)? And, 2) Are you *passionate* (contra lukewarmness)?

[1965]
1308. Parsons, N.C. "God on the Doorstep [Rev. 3:20]." **ET** 76 (1964-65): 190-191.

Offers a sermon for the third Sunday in Lent warning Christians against idolatry and counseling them to open the door of life and society to God.

[1964]
1309. Rouner, A.A., Jr. "The Man at the Door [Rev. 3:20]." **USQR** 19 (1963-64): 231-236.

Presents a short sermon on Rev. 3:20 and the effects of closing and opening the symbolic "door" to Christ.

[1961]
1310. Friedrich, E.J. "The Door No Man Can Shut [Rev. 3:7, 8]." **CTM** 32 (1961): 330-333.

Submits a chapel sermon manuscript based on Rev. 3:7-8 that emphasizes the Scriptural "door" open to God's future and its consequent blessings, viz., spiritual growth, theological maturity, service, and fellowship with God.

[1960]
1311. Matthews, H.F. "'Opsed' [Rev. 3:15]." **ET** 71 (1959-60): 340-341.

Challenges the church to become "hot" in response to the statement of Rev. 3:15: "I would that you were hot or cold."

[1957]
1312. Caemmerer, R.R. "What Is the Church That Is Truly Rich [Rev. 3:14-22]?" **CTM** 28 (1957): 766-768.

Answers the rhetorical question posed by the sermon title by suggesting that the truly "rich" church must be the church of Jesus Christ, must be zealous, and must use its zeal to keep faith against idolatry.

1313. Kienberger, V.F. "God's Idea of a King [Apoc. 3:21]." **HPR** 57

(1956-57): 1125-1128.

Offers a homily for "Feast of Christ the King" based on Rev. 3:21. St. Stephen was a king among men and Saint before God. He shall sometime rule indeed. Concludes that it was difficult for men to see Christ as King because He did not measure up to their ideas of a king.

1314. Mueller, E.E. "A Dying Church [Rev. 3:1-6]." **CTM** 28 (1957): 763-766.

Clarifies the problems of the church at Sardis in Rev. 3:1-6 and draws parallels to the contemporary church.

[1953]
1315. Sheerin, J.B. "The Lukewarm Don't Care [Rev. 3:15]." **HPR** 53 (1952-53): 313-317.

Discusses the character of lukewarm Catholics based on Rev. 3:15. Calls the people back to love for and through Christ.

[1952]
1316. Bouman, W.H. "Is Ours a Congregation Patterned After Philadelphia [Rev. 3:7-13]?" **CTM** 23 (1952): 759-761.

Sets forth a preaching outline for Rev. 3:7-13 based on three questions: I. Does it merit the Lord's praise? II. Does it heed the Lord's admonition? III. Does it cherish the Lord's promise? Conclusion: God crowns missionary churches.

1317. Louttit, W. "The King's Troup [Rev. 3:12]." **ET** 63 (1951-52): 246-247.

Considers the analogy and encourages the application of the notion of Christ writing his name on the martyr (Rev. 3:12), and King George VI giving the name "King's Troop" to a group of Royal Artillery soldiers.

[1944]
1318. Bethune, R. "The Things That Remain [Rev. 3:2]." **ET** 55 (1943-44): 48-50.

Offers an Advent sermon on the abiding values that Christ gives in light of Rev. 3:2.

[1940]
1319. Fritz, J.H.C. "Eine rechte Philadelphia = Gemeinde (Offenb. 3, 7-13)." **CTM** 11 (1940): 839-843.

Advances a three point sermon on "the righteous" Christian community in Philadelphia, according to Rev. 3:7-13. The key ideas are 1) *Lob* (Praise), 2) *Ermahung* (Admonition), 3) *Verheißung* (Promise). See also 4, B.

Chap. 4

[1970]
1320. Stancliffe, M. "Light and Colour [Rev. 4:3]." **ET** 81 (1969-70): 237-239.

Considers Rev. 4:3 for Trinity Sunday and suggests that the absence of colors in the Bible is due to the brightness of the light of God in the context of the world.

[1965]
1321. Jarvis, D.E. "A Throne in Heaven [Rev. 4:2]." **ET** 76 (1964-65): 261-262.

Says that the truth of the Trinity may be based on John's vision of God as depicted in Rev. 4:2.

Chap. 5

[1986]
1322. Achtemeier, P.J. "Revelation 5:1-14." **Inter** XL (1986): 283-288.

Arguing that the climax of the book is found at chap. 5 (with a second at chap. 21), A. concludes that the rest of the Revelation is a working out of the implications of the seven seals being opened and the role of the lamb in the events to follow. Sermons on this passage should seriously consider the themes of "the new creation which redemption will bring" (including one's faith in the "second coming"), "the nature of our own reality, and hope," and "the contradiction" of the lion and the lamb, viz., salvation through defeat and redemption through death. Lastly, the Book is shown to be "good news of comfort" for all those who suffer.

[1972]
1323. Glover, F.C. "Unworthy [Rev. 5:2]." **ET** 83 (1971-72): 114-115.

Describes three biblical characters (centurion, rich young ruler, prodigal son) in reference to the question of Rev. 5:2 and the worthiness of each. Makes personal application in conclusion.

[1962]
1324. Caird, G.B. "The Kingship of Christ [Rev. 5:7]." **ET** 73 (1961-62): 248-249.

Explains the reign of Christ as the Lamb from Cross to final judgment according to Rev. 5:7. See also 5, C.

[1961]
1325. Wright, J.W. "The Transformed Prophet [Rev. 5:9]." **ET** 72 (1960-61): 283-285.

Draws a clear connection between Ps. 137:4 and Rev. 5:9 regarding the motif of singing a new song of transformation through the cross and the resurrection. See also 5, H, (32).

[1958]
1326. Stewart, R.W. "A Comparison and a Contrast: An Address for Holy Communion [Rev. 5:12]." **ET** 69 (1957-58): 375-377.

Declares that communion is at once a mystery, a word, and the gospel, based on Rev. 5:12. It is a human and divine event that elicits for the believer both sadness and joyful love.

[1957]
1327. Good, E.M. "Who is Worthy [Rev. 5:1-7]?" **USQR** 12 (1956-57): 41-43.

Sets forth a devotional study of Rev. 5:1-7, answering the question with an emphatic, "The conquering Christ." See also 4, B.

1328. Hohenstein, H.E. "It's Indeed a Good Friday [Rev. 5:1-14]." **CTM** 28 (1957): 204-207.

Offers an exposition of Rev. 5:1-14 in terms of our "good day" in three points: I. The Book is opened; II. A Lamb has been slain; III. Therefore, sing a "new song."

[1956]
1329. Stewart, D. "The Communion of Saints [Rev. 5:11; 7:9]." **ET** 67

(1955-56): 23-24.

Considers the ideas of large numbers, vastness and unity in love in connection with the afterlife of the Christian.

[1954]
1330. Manz, J.G. "The Heavenly Victor [Rev. 5]." **CTM** 25 (1954): 225-227.

Offers an Easter sermon from Rev. 5 on the impact of Christ's resurrection victory for the church today.

[1951]
1331. Coffin, H.S. "To Him That Overcometh [Rev. 5:5]." **Int** 5 (1951): 40-45.

Presents a chapel meditation on Rev. 5:5, noting 4 principles for guidance and encouragement in our own personal historical situation. Concludes with the idea that the consummation of history is the heavenly commonwealth and this happens in and through Jesus Christ. See also 5, G, (1).

[1940]
1332. Bernthal, A.F."[Untitled homily on Rev. 5:8-14]." **CTM** 11 (1940): 188-190.

Submits an exposition of Rev. 5:8-14 calling the faithful to offer praise for the Lamb who was slain. This praise should resound from 1) The whole Christian church, 2) All the holy angels, and 3) All creatures. See also VI, H, 18 and 41.

Chap. 7

[1986]
1333. Kelly, B.H. "Revelation 7:9-17." **Inter** XL (1986): 288-295.

Because Revelation appeals to "the sense of hearing" as much as sight, K. considers the hymnic character of the passage as he studies the inner structure, details of language, the context and possible lines of interpretation for the preachers and teachers of the contemporary church. Elements of ch. 7 may have been drawn from liturgical sources, martyrological hymns, or apocalyptic literature that connect with a coming period of great tribulation described in the vision(s) of chap. 7.

Suggests relevant themes for today, e.g., victory, ultimate triumph and the final security of believers. Is. 49 provides the theological foundation for the passage. By resisting the temptation to literalize or spiritualize the imagery of this vision and by letting the "mythic flavor" stand, the intepreter gives opportunity for others to bring their own thoughts and ideas to the vision for new insight.

[1972]
1334. Senior, G.R. "One Knot Is Sunday [Rev. 7:9]." **ET** 83 (1971-72): 269.

Considers a knot of rope as an object lesson for children and explains the object in terms of the Penan calendar.

[1971]
1335. Ford, D.W.C. "A People Sealed [Rev. 7:4]." **ET** 82 (1970-71): 16-17.

Suggests that "sealed" (Rev. 7:4) alludes to security, consolation, communion, and comprehensiveness for believers.

[1967]
1336. Ford, D.W.C. "Lift Up Your Hearts [Rev. 7:9]." **ET** 78 (1966-67): 26-27.

Proclaims that small churches need to be reminded on All Saints Day that they are a vital part of "a great multitude" beyond their local walls and should lift up their hearts in praise.

[1966]
1337. Williams, H. "All Sorts [Rev. 7:9]." **ET** 77 (1965-66): 16-17.

Contends for "variety" in the church through the promise of unity.

[1965]
1338. Ford, D.W.C. "The Lamb Is the Shepherd [Rev. 7:16-17]." **ET** 76 (1964-65): 34-35.

Utilizes Rev. 7:16-17 for a message on All Saints Day concerning the afterlife for the Christian and the assurance that Jesus, the Shepherd, will continue his work in our own personal afterlife.

[1961]
1339. Rumble, L. "The Communion of Saints [Apoc. 7:9]." **HPR** 61
(1960-61): 59-61.

Pronounces a meditation on Rev. 7:9 for the "Feast of All Saints" as a
tribute to all saints, witness to the power of Christ, and a statement about
our ultimate home in heaven.

[1956]
1340. McCorry, V.P. "We Can -- Because They Did [Rev. 7:9]." **HPR** 56
(1955-56): 46-48.

Submits a sermon for "The Feast of All Saints" on Rev. 7:9. Suggests that
Christians are called to take courage from the Saints as well as take them
for their models.

[1954]
1341. Cassidy, J.H."All Saints: Our Unnamed Friends [Apoc. 7:9]." **HPR**
54 (1953-54): 55-57.

Shares a message on Rev. 7:9 concerning canonized saints and the
"multitude" of 7:9. Concludes that others have joined the great band of
Saints, so too, should we join.

[1953]
1342. Crock, C.H. "[Untitled homily on Apoc. 7:9]." **HPR** 53 (1952-53):
51-53.

Gives a message from Rev. 7:9 making five points: 1) Everyone loves a
hero. 2) Our saints are heros. 3) Heavenly joys are difficult to
comprehend. 4) Beatific Vision is the Saints greatest joy. 5) We are all
destined to become Saints.

[1947]
1343. Scharrer, J.F. "The Vast Number of Saints [Apoc. 7:9]." **HPR** 47
(1946-47): 59-61.

Submits a sermon for the "Feast of All Saints" based on Rev. 7:9.
Discusses 1) the magnificence of John's vision. 2) Sainthood for every
human being. 3) Many Saints were not extraordinary. 4) Saints must cling
to faith. 5) Sainthood is in within reach of all. 6) Aspire to be one of the
Saints.

[1945]
1344. Ross, J.E. "Known and Unknown Saints [Rev. 7:4]." **HPR** 45 (1944-45): 62-65.

Presents a homily for the "Feast of All Saints" based on "144,000 were signed from every tribe of the children of Israel" (Rev. 7:4). Suggests that a day be set aside to honor all Saints known and unknown and that the Mass prayers should be studied from this angle. "All Saints" refers to all canonized and uncanonized persons in heaven. Only unforgiven, serious sin will bar anyone from heaven.

[1943]
1345. Hanrahan, D.U. "Partisan Christianity [Apoc. 7:9]." **HPR** 43 (1942-43): 76-80.

Offers a homily for "The Feast of All Saints" based on Rev. 7:9. Suggests that John gives insight into the future in four areas: 1) It is error to say that God reserves the future for a favored people. 2) This writing refutes the error. 3) From Paul to Pius the Church has opposed the notion. 4) We must earnestly refute this teaching. Concludes that Christians should be "one in Christ."

[1942]
1346. Arndt, W.F. "The People That Reach Heaven and Their Bliss [Rev. 7:13-17]." **CTM** 13 (1942): 298-299.

Outlines and presents his theme under four major points: I. They are the true believers; II. They have come out of the great tribulation; etc. See also 5, H, (21).

1347. Mennicke, V. "The People That Reach Heaven and Their Bliss [Rev. 7:13-17]." **CTM** 13 (1942): 298-299.

Announces the identity of the true believers as those who have come out of tribulation. They are the ones who ultimately reach their heavenly rewards, which are listed in Rev. 7, viz., in the presence of God, heavenly service, without thirst, etc.

Chap. 8

[1960]
1348. Small, R.L. "A Remembrance Day Sermon [Rev. 8:1]." **ET** 71 (1959-60): 27-29.

Presents a Remembrance Day sermon to offer silent remembrance for the war losses based on Rev. 8:1.

Chap. 11

[1962]
1349. Routley, E. "'All the Kingdoms' [Rev. 11:15]." **ET** 73 (1961-62): 156-157.

Contributes a Lenten sermon comparing the temptations of Jesus (Mat. 4:8f.) with the exclamation that "Christ shall reign forever and ever" in Rev. 11:15. Concludes that Lent is a season of shed burdens and refreshment through self-denial.

Chap. 12

[1963]
1350. Flynn, D.J. "Ancient Belief Newly Stated [Rev. 12:1]." **HPR** 63 (1962-63): 890-892.

Provides a homily on Rev. 12:11 for the "Feast of Assumption." Focuses on "a great feast in heaven," while discussing events preliminary to the assumption, evidence of the traditional belief, and definition of the assumption. Reaffirms the assumption of Mary as "divinely revealed truth."

[1953]
1351. Murphy, W.R. "The New Eve [Apoc. 12:1]." **HPR** 53 (1952-53): 919-922.

Reflects on Rev. 12:1, "the woman clothed with the sun" in terms of Mary, the mother of Jesus. Gives a brief account of the history and meaning of the dogma, the reason for the proclamation, a tree, a man, a woman. Concludes that there is no surer way to Jesus Christ than through His mother who stands by His side now.

Chap. 13

[1948]
1352. Baldinger, A.H. "A Beastly Coalition: An Expository Sermon on The Revelation 13:1-18." **Int** 2 (1948): 444 450.

Considers the book to be a mirror of the past and a prophecy of the future, i.e., a super-view of the direction of human history. The "coalition" is thought to be the uniting of civil and religious authority into one hand. Notes examples from history and concludes that Christians must beware of this "beastly" situation as they wait patiently for future judgment.

Chap. 14

[1953]
1353. Selwyn, E.G. "The Life After Death [Rev. 14:13]." **Th** 56 (1953): 13-19.

Presents a theological reflection on Rev. 14:13, suggesting that the text means more than the traditional survival or immortality of the soul. Opts for the ideas of Eternal Life and Resurrection as the best expressions of the NT themes in this connection. Concludes that life after death means entering into fellowship with God and one another in the church. See also 5, G, (3).

Chap. 19

[1967]
1354. Schreiner, J.; "Sonntag nach Christi Himmelfahrt. Homilie zu Apg 19.1-7." **BL** 8 (1967): 68-70.

Offers a message on the heavenly marriage scene between Christ and his bride, the Church.

[1960]
1355. Kent, J.L."The Lord God Omnipotent Reigneth [Rev. 19:6]." **ET** 71 (1959-60): 26-27.

Reflects on how Jesus the omnipotent reigns through washing feet, praying in the garden, and dying on the cross.

[1959]
1356. Cowan, A.A. "The Right Sequence in Christian Experience [Rev. 19:4]." **ET** 70 (1958-59): 280-281.

Affirms that the true "order of progression" in authentic Christian experience and worship is found in Rev. 19:4: Amen! and then, Hallelujah! The progression states, first, accepting God's purpose and, second, offering praise to Him as you discover future victory.

[1953]
1357. Stewart, J.S. "The Relevance of Worship to Life [Rev. 19]." **USQR** 8 (1952-53): 3-9.

Uses Rev. 19:4 as his text and develops a three point sermon on the essential relevance of worship: First, acceptance of the will of God. Second, commitment to the purpose of God. Last, joy in the fellowship of God. Concludes with a general call to join the Church triumphant in worship.

Chap. 20

[1968]
1358. MacDonald, H.R. "A Christian Faces Guilt [Rev. 20:11-12]." **ET** 79 (1967-68): 188-190.

Offers a Palm Sunday sermon based on Rev. 20:11-12 touching the problem of judgment for the Christian and suggesting that Christ's sacrificial work provides the solution.

Chap. 21

[1986]
1359. Raber, R.W. "Revelation 21:1-8." **Int** XL (1986): 296-301.

From the terrible chronicling of woes, plagues, calamities, and disasters there emerges a new heaven and a new earth, which informs the reader that "the funeral" has been terminated and now the wedding for the faithful is to begin. The bride is a beautiful city -- but not old Jerusalem -- and the action is to be interpreted as being presently *in process*. The newness of the event is God's present residence with generic humanity, which, by the way, coincides with the manifestation of the church as the new Jerusalem, the people of God. The focus of Rev. 21:1-8 is the intimacy between God, his people and the world in that end time. Although there are some sinful "types" who will be condemned, still all alienation from God is finally over. He is now dwelling with his Bride and "with men."

[1972]
1360. Gray, J.R. "Pain [Rev. 21:4]." **ET** 83 (1971-72): 143-144.

Describes the mystery of pain in relationship to the promise of Rev. 21:4: "...no more pain."

[1971]
1361. Moellering, R.L. "Isaiah 24:1-6 and Revelation 21:1-5a." **CTM** 42 (1971): 177-182.

Brings forward an inspirational message comparing Is. 24:1-6 to Rev. 21:1-5a in terms of the environment and the need for Christian accountability and political action. Concludes by noting that God's judgment is promised against those who continue to violate His laws.

[1970]
1362. Gray, J.R. "The Holy City [Rev. 21:2]." **ET** 81 (1969-70): 212-213.

Affirm that the Holy City in Rev. 21:2 means for the believer reality present contrasted to reality to come and the two must be held in tension.

[1968]
1363. Gray, J.R. "No Road Back [Rev. 21:2, 25; 22:2]." **ET** 79 (1967-68): 90-91.

Issues a sermon for the first Sunday after Christmas, asserting that one cannot turn back to Eden but, rather, should press forward to the City of God.

1364.Wulf, F. "'Siehe, ich mache alles neu!' Meditation zu Apk 21, 5-8." **GL** 41 (1968): 391-393.

Presents a brief homily on "making all things new" according to Rev. 21:5-8.

[1967]
1365. Rosin, W.L. "Going Home [Rev. 21:5-7]." **CTM** 38 (1967): 612-614.

Expresses interest in the "heavenward" way of the Christian in the phrase "Going Home." Insists that the Christian must continue to carry on with his present duties; but he must also find new zeal for his tasks as he acknowledges the absolute certainty of his security in Christ.

[1966]
1366. Gray, J.R. "Compensations [Rev. 21:5]." **ET** 77 (1965-66): 373.

Identifies the various practical "compensations" for Christians related to God's proclamation in Rev. 21:5, that He makes "all things new."

[1965]
1367. Bornemann, G.W."The Church -- A Triumphant Church [Rev. 21:7]." **CTM** 36 (1965): 652-653.

Proclaims a triumphant church based on Rev. 21:7, noting three main points: I. The Victor offers a Heritage; II. The Church continues in Triumph and Conquest; and III. The Triumphant Church has a Heritage, viz., "Eden to heaven--not death but life" (p.653).

1368. Matthews, H.F. "Three Wonders [Rev. 21:5]." **ET** 76 (1964-65): 221.

Talks to children regarding three wonders in life, but offers a fourth, the resurrection, which is the greatest wonder of all.

[1961]
1369. Matthews, H.F. "All Change [Rev. 21:5]." **ET** 72 (1960-61): 375.

Illustrates the theme "all things new" from Rev. 21:5 by means of a bus ride in Birmingham, England and references to constructive, creative work.

[1951]
1370. Rhys, T.T. "Festival of the Redeemed [Rev. 21:21]." **ET** 62 (1950-51): 375-376.

Explains the heavenly festival for the redeemed in three areas: The way to it; the warfare for it; and the wonder of it.

[1949]
1371. Hartner, H.G. "The New Heaven and the New Earth [Rev. 21:1-8]." **CTM** 20 (1949): 781-782.

Contrasts the old and the new in terms of death and eternity (heaven). Concludes by stressing the Alpha-Omega theme from Rev. 21, suggesting that the best in life is in the future. God always keeps His promises.

[1945]
1372. MacQueen, H.Q. "The Message of a Church Bell [Rev. 21:5]." **ET** 56 (1944-45): 319.

Presents a sermon using an analogy of a bell and the call of Christ based on the text of Rev. 21:5. See also V, B, 20.

[1942]
1373. Smukal, G.H. "That Happy Moment Which Dissolves Into Eternity [Rev. 21:1-8]." **CTM** 13 (1942): 861-862.

Provides the reader with a two point homily on Rev. 21:1-8: I. In which the former things are passed away; and II. For which we prepare by faith in Jesus Christ. Concludes with a warning and a promise to the church.

1374. Thomson, R.W. "A Happy New Year! [Rev. 21:5]." **ET** 53 (1941-42): 138-139.

Contends for Rev. 21:5 as a New Year's message for change and improvement in the future.

Chap. 22

[1962]
1375. Poellot, L. "A Homiletical Study of Revelation 22:12-21." **CTM** 33 (1962): 738-742.

Submits a brief sermon for New Year's eve based on Rev. 22:12-21. Responds to the three notions, 1) Who the coming One is, 2) When He will come, and 3) Why He will come.

[1954]
1376. Lillie, W. "Finis [Rev. 22:21]." **ET** 65 (1953-54): 83.

Presents a note on Rev. 22:21 and suggests that it might be interpreted as a new year's good wish and promise of blessing.

[1953]
1377. Price, A.W."The Name on the Gate [Rev. 22:4]." **ET** 64 (1952-53): 305.

Suggests that each Christian should live according to the "name" label that he/she carries.

[1945]
1378. Wilson , J.B. "Criss-Cross-Row [Rev. 22:13]." **ET** 56 (1944-45): 212.

Considers Rev. 22:13 as a text for his homily on Jesus as the alphabet of life. See also V, B, 21.

[1944]
1379. Hellriegel, M.B. "Final Day After Pentecost [Apoc 22:20]." **OF** 18 (1943-44): 536-537.

Presents a brief homily based on the parousia and its implications for the Church. Concludes with the cry, "*Maranatha!*"

[1940]
1380. Smukal, G.H. "Das Schlusswort der Heiligen Schrift: 'Die Gnade unseres Herren Jesu Christi. . . .'" **CTM** 11 (1940): 846-848.

Offers a two point sermon in German on the praise of Jesus Christ: I. At the close of time; and II. At the end of the church year.

E. LITURGY

[1970]
1381. Bourke, M.M. "The New Testamant and the State of the Liturgy." **Wor** 44 (1970): 130-142.

Discusses the Catholic litrugy in relation to suggested changes. Offers a comparison of several NT liturgical texts in order to evaluate current eucharistic celebrations. Touches briefly on the hymns of Rev. (cf. 5:9) and their reflection of the ideas of suffering within the worship experience.

[1955]
1382. Lew, T.T. "A New Jerusalem We Seek." **TT** 11 (1954-55): 158-159.

Offers a five stanza hymn on the future coming "New Jerusalem" of the Rev. See also 5, H, (16), and (19).

[1952]
1383. Mowry, L. "Revelation 4-5 and Early Christian Liturgical Usage." **JBL** 71 (1952):75-84.

Investigates the throne scenes of Rev. 4-5 as an example of early Christian liturgy. See also 3, D and 5, H, (19).

[1951]
1384. Piper, O.A. "The Apocalypse of John and the Liturgy of the

Ancient Church." **CH** 20 (1951): 3-14.

Suggests that the liturgical character of the Revelation helps to explain the historical development of Christian liturgy in general. Names such features as "Eucharistic Parousia," "Angelic Worship," "Spiritual Battle," etc. as contributing factors. Concludes that the Revelation presupposes a definite type of worship in the churches to whom John wrote. The author, who viewed heavenly and earthly worship combined, borrowed largely from Jewish Temple and Synagogue worship practices. See also 3, D and 5, H, (19).

F. PEDAGOGY

[1987]
1385. Grimsrud, T. **Triumph of the Lamb: A Self-Study Guide to the Book of Revelation.** Scottdale, PA: Herald Press, 1987.

A brief introduction precedes an inductive study and passage-by-passage exposition following a traditional outline. G. concludes by suggesting applications for the church today.

[1986]
1386. Van Daalen, D.H. **A Guide to the Revelation.** "TEF Study Guide 20." London: SPCK, 1986.

This World Council of Churches project offers an ecumenical, practical, and inclusive study guide with non-western and second-language English students in mind. After a brief critical introduction to the book, V. treats each literary unit of the Revelation according to a three-fold method: 1) Summary, 2) Exegetical notes, and 3) Interpretation. Excellent study suggestions and questions follow each section. Specific "Notes" in such subjects as "The Angels," "The Letters," etc. are included.

[1983]
1387. Neall, B.S. **The Concept of Character in the Apocalypse with Implications for Character Education.** Washington, D.C.: University Press of America, 1983.

Argues in this published dissertation that John's description of "righteous character" is founded upon a vertical relationship with God that expresses itself in mission to the world's needs. This message is needed in education today if students are to discover their origin, identity, and destiny.

Develops his thesis by studying the concept of character in the Rev. in connection with the humanistic philosophy of Plato and Aristotle, especially in terms of their ideas of 1) the norm of character, 2) the nature of the person, 3) the nature of good and evil, and 4) the method of character development.

[1979]
1388. Prager, M. **Das neue Jerusalem. Ein Arbeitsheft zur "Offenbarung des Johannes" (Apokalypse). Mit besonderer Berüksichtigung des Kirchenbildes dieser Schrift des Neuen Testaments.** "Gespräche zur Bibel 8." Klosterneuburg: Österreichisches Katholisches Bibelwerk, 1979.

Presents a study guide and methodology for group leaders, catechists, and readers on ten selected texts from John's Revelation: 1) 1:1-3; 2) 1:9-20; 3) 2:1-7; 4) 2:8-11; etc.

[1978]
1389. Stegner, W.R. "From the New Testament: On Teaching the Book of Revelation." **Expl** 4 (1978): 79-86.

Presents ideas on teaching the Rev. based on the presupposition that the book originated in a crisis of persecution and cultural seduction. John has composed a work of mixed (often fluid) language and literary forms, with the focus on the sovereignty of God.

[1947]
1390. Guyot, G.H. "The Apocalypse in the Seminary Scripture Course." **CBQ** 9 (1947): 471-478.

Offers a method for teaching the Rev. which focuses on the needs of both the priest and the scholar by stressing the spiritual and the intellectual value of the book. Proposes that the course should not get bogged down in details, but should offer a general and universal mindset. The instructor must not feel the need to cover all interpretations, but rather to demonstrate his own best exegesis and interpretation.

[1946]
1391. Gettys, J. M. **How to Study the Revelation.** Richmond, VA: John Knox Press, 1946.

Presents a practical handbook for the thematic and practical study of the Revelation.

-Select Dissertations-

[1989]
1392. Smith, S.O. "Milton and the Book of Revelation: Attaining the 'Prophetic Strain' in 'Paradise Regained'." Unpublished Doctoral Dissertation. Newark, DE: University of Delaware, 1989.

[1988]
1393. Fredericks, R.L. "A Sequential Study of Rev. 1-14 Emphasizing the Judgment Motif: With Implications for Seventh-Day Adventist Apocalyptic Pedagogy." Unpublished Doctoral Dissertation. Berrien Springs, MI: Andrews University, 1988.

[1987]
1394. Stevens, M. "Apocalyptic Literature: 'The Mother of Justice Education,' A Design of the Use of the Book of Revelation in Religious Education." Unpublished Doctoral Dissertation. Boston, MA: Boston College, 1987.

1395. Hodder, A.D. "Emerson's Rhetoric of Revelation: Nature, the Reader, and the Apocalypse Within." Unpublished Doctoral Dissertation. Cambridge, MA: Harvard University, 1987.

[1985]
1396. Petersen, R.L. "Preaching in the Last Days: The Use of the Theme of 'Two Witnesses,' as Found in Revelation 11:3-13, with Particular Attention to the Sixteenth and Early Seventeenth Centuries." Unpublished Doctoral Dissertation. Princeton, NJ: Princeton Theological Seminary, 1985.

[1984]
1397. Adams, H.A. "A Homiletical Approach to Revelation." Unpublished Doctoral Dissertation. Dallas, TX: Dallas Theological Seminary, 1984.

1398. Bachmann, S.M. "Narrative Strategy in the Book of Revelation and D. H. Lawrence's Apocalypse." Unpublished Doctoral Dissertation. Buffalo, NY: SUNY, 1984.

[1983]
1399. Frontain, R.-J. "John Donne's Poetic Uses of the Bible."

Unpublished Doctoral Dissertation. West Lafayette, IN: Purdue University, 1983.

[1982]
1400. Kempson, W.R. "Theology in the Revelation of John." Unpublished Doctoral Dissertation. Louisville, KY: Southern Baptist Theological Seminary, 1982.

1401. Van Dixhorn, L.J. "Preaching and Teaching from Revelation." Unpublished D.Min. Dissertation. Deerfield, IL: Trinity Evangelical Divinity School, 1982.

1402. Neall, B.S. "The Concept of Character in the Apocalypse with Implications for Character Education." Unpublished Doctoral Dissertation. Berrien Springs, MI: Andrews University, 1982.

[1980]
1403. Pitts, B.A. "The Apocalypse in Medieval French Verse." Unpublished Doctoral Dissertation. Bloomington, IN: Indiana University, 1980.

1404. Taylor, R.D. "A Conceptual Model for the Professional Practice of Seventh-Day Adventists Educational Administration Based on the Proclamation of the Three Angels of Revelation 14." Unpublished Doctoral Dissertation. Berrien Springs, MI: Andrews University, 1980.

1405. Wellman, S.E. "Symphony of the Apocalypse" [Original Composition]. Tallahassee, FL:Florida State University, 1980.

[1978]
1406. Morrill, M.F. "Apocalyptic Art." Unpublished Doctoral Dissertation. New York City, NY: Columbia University Teachers College, 1978.

[1975]
1407. Mauck, M.B. "The Apocalypse Frescoes of the Baptistery in Novara, Italy." Unpublished Doctoral Dissertation. New Orleans, LA: Tulane University, 1975.

Index of Authors

Achtemeier, P.J., 316
Adams, H.A., 331
Agourides, S., 288
Aldrich, R.L., 37, 41, 256
Aletti, J.N., 166, 270
Allison, D.C., 129
Allo, E.-B., 26, 209
Altink, W., 129, 132
Amiot, F., 206
Arndt, W.F., 32, 33, 226, 229, 321
Aune, D.E., 76, 77, 87, 102, 231, 248
Aus, R.D., 139
Bachmann, M., 115
Bachmann, S.M., 331
Bagatti, B., 295
Bailey, J.G., 100
Baines, W.G., 169
Baldinger, A.H., 322
Bandstra, A.J., 23, 158
Bannon, R., 313
Barclay, W., 85, 185, 203, 225, 289
Barnett, M.C., 175
Barnett, P., 73
Barnhouse, D.G., 199
Barr, A., 312
Barr, D.L., 2, 151, 165
Barrett, C.K., 9
Barrett, J.O., 284
Barsotti, D., 197
Bartina, S., 120, 170, 171, 253
Bauckham, R., 126, 133, 138, 239, 246, 251, 282

Beagley, A.J., 75, 96
Beale, G.K., 129, 130, 132, 136, 238
Bear, J.E., 45
Beardslee, W.A., 107, 118
Beasley-Murray, G.R., 8, 14, 21, 111, 148, 181, 184, 254, 258, 260
Beauvery, R., 77
Beck, D.M., 245
Beckwith, I.T., 210
Becler, S.W., 192
Bell, A.A., 69
Bellamy, H.S., 18
Bellshaw, W.G., 37
Benson, I.M., 163
Berger, P.R., 131
Bergmeier, R., 88, 277
Bernthal, A.F., 318
Best, E., 110, 249
Betancourt, P.P., 63
Bethune, R., 315
Betz, H.D., 92
Bieder, W., 94
Bietenhard, H., 29
Bird, S.W.H., 85
Birdsall, J.N., 52, 54, 224
Bissonnette, G., 298
Blaiklock, E.M., 86
Blevins, J.L., 104, 152, 308
Bloom, H., 50
Böcher, O., 5, 135, 271
Bock, E., 307
Böckeler, M., 298
Bodinger, M., 284
Boer, H.R., 194

Boesak, A.A., 192
Boismard, M.E., 96, 225
Boll, F., 142
Bollier, J.A., 262
Bonnefoy, J.B., 250
Bonniwell, W.R., 313
Bonsirven, J., 188
Boring, M.E., 177, 233
Bornemann, G.W., 326
Borowicz, K., 144
Botha, P.J.J., 74
Boulgares, C.S., 261
Bouman, W.H., 315
Bourke, M.M., 328
Bousset, W., 190, 265
Bovon, F., 240, 265, 287
Bowman, J.W., 40, 160, 204
Boyd, R., 17
Boyd, W.J.P., 242
Boyer, J.L., 20
Brady, D., 3, 224
Bratsiotis, P., 305
Bratten, C.E., 107
Braun, F.-M., 299
Bretscher, P.M., 123
Brewer, R.R., 122
Bridge, W.H., 313
Brieger, P.H., 53
Brighton, L.A., 173
Brown, D., 161
Brown, S., 286
Browne, G.M., 52
Brownlee, W.H., 244, 249
Brox, N., 215
Bruce, F.F., 179, 224, 246
Bruins, E.M., 169
Brunk, M.J., 36, 213
Bruns, J.E., 70, 71, 296
Brütsch, C., 185, 201, 263
Bube, R.H., 30
Buber, M., 110
Bultema, H., 290
Burch, V., 148

Burgbacher, B., 196
Burkhardt, H., 20
Burnet, A.W., 310
Burns, A.L., 122
Burrows, E., 231
Cabaniss, A., 280
Cadoux, C.J., 86
Caemmerer, R.R., 314
Cain, D.W., 118, 157
Caird, G.B., 15, 187, 317
Cairns, E.E., 28
Calkins, R., 310
Calloud, J., 155
Cambier, J., 84, 94
Campbell, P.E., 262
Cannon, W.R., 254
Cantley, M.J., 109
Carlson, S.W., 300
Carnegie, D.R., 152
Carson, D.A., 215
Case, S.J., 26
Casey, J.S., 174, 268
Cassem, N.H., 118
Cassidy, J.H., 320
Cerfaux, L., 84, 144
Cesar, E.E.B., 300
Chafer, L.S., 45, 112, 264
Charlesworth, J.H., 129
Charlier, J.-P., 151, 303
Chilvers, G., 264
Claudel, P., 14, 18
Clayton, R.H., 26
Clymer, D., 6
Coffin, H.S., 318
Cohen, G.G., 199
Coleman, R.E., 274
Collins, A.Y., 3, 69, 76, 77, 78, 79, 89, 137, 162, 182, 270, 288, 299, 309
Collins, J.J., 16, 100, 103, 105
Collins, T., 267
Colunga, A., 253

Colwell, E.C., 58
Comblin, J., 106, 220, 241, 276
Considine, J.S., 172, 220, 222
Conzelmann, H., 227
Cooper, D.L., 199
Cope, G., 122
Corsani, B., 105
Corsini, E., 193, 234
Cortes, E., 137
Cosmades, T., 60
Cothenet, E., 166
Coune, M., 211, 268
Court, J.M., 285
Cowan, A.A., 323
Cowley, R.W., 193
Cox, C.C., 199
Craddock, F.B., 308
Creager, H.L., 262
Crock, C.H., 320
Crouzel, H., 292
Crutchfield, L.V., 34
Cummings, J., 257
Dalmais, I.-H., 216
Damerau, R., 179
Daniélou, J., 29, 217
Danner, D., 9
Darling, C.F., Jr., 174
Dauzenberg, G., 290
David, A.A., 312
Davies, P.E., 243, 310
Davis, C., 230
Davis, D.R., 157, 293
De Benoit, P., 207
De Santo, C., 228
Deer, D. S., 115
Deere, J.S., 35
Delebecque, É., 113, 114, 115
Delling, G., 93, 279
Delorme, J., 155
Deutsch, C., 163
Devine, R., 294

Dichot, M.E., 97
Doll, M.A., 164
Dominguez, N., 186
Downing, F.G., 127
Drach, G., 265
Draper, J.A., 127, 269
Du Brul, P., 275
Du Preez, J., 263, 284
Du Rand, J.A., 163
Duckworth, R., 99
Dumbrell, W.J., 131
Dunphy, W., 241
Duplantier, J.-P., 155
Duplessis, J., 274
Durousseau, C., 204
Düsterdieck, F., 180
Dyer, C.H., 164
Ebor, W., 18
Echternach, H., 259
Edgar, T.R., 77, 116
Edwards, P., 166
Edwards, S.A., 238
Efird, J.M., 195
Ehlert, A.D., 44, 45
Eller, V., 13, 299
Ellingworth, P., 116, 281
Elliott, J.K., 51
Ellul, J., 155
Engelbrecht, J.J., 301
Enroth, A.-M., 113
Ernst, J., 296
Etcheverria, R., 278
Evans-Prosser, K.F., 72
Eybers, I.H., 226
Ezell, D., 168
Fannon, P., 16
Farrer, A., 202
Farris, A.L., 309
Fekkes, J., 125
Fekkes, J. III., 174
Fenasse, J.-M., 242, 281
Fenasse, P., 213
Féret, H.M., 236, 274

Feuillet, A., 7, 12, 13, 24, 50, 128, 133, 139, 145, 146, 167, 168, 170, 171, 221, 222, 243, 282, 290, 295
Filson, F.V., 62
Fiorenza, E.S., 1, 12, 28, 50, 79, 82, 89, 139, 140, 156, 158, 173, 183, 194, 253, 260, 261, 263, 288, 292
Firebrace, A., 202
Fischel, H.A., 283
Fischer, K.M., 235
Flack, E.E., 254
Flokstra, G.J., 191
Flynn, D.J., 322
Foerster, W., 119
Ford, A.R., 259
Ford, D.W.C., 319
Ford, J.M., 141, 150, 183, 211, 219, 227, 286
Fransen, I., 16
Franzmann, M.H., 196
Fredericks, R.L., 331
Frey, H., 205
Friedrich, E.J., 314
Fritsch, C.T., 307
Fritz, J.H.C., 316
Frontain, R.-J., 331
Fuller, J.W., 217
Furfey, P.H., 124
Gaechter, P., 94, 123, 160
Gahan, S., 296
Gangemi, A., 140, 167, 168, 260, 278
Garoffalo, S., 11
Garrett, J.L., Jr., 288
Gehardsson, B., 239
Geiger, A., 184, 304
Gelston, A., 212
Gentry, K.L., 68
George, A., 85, 214
Gerhardsson, B., 242

Gettys, J. M., 330
Geyser, A., 134
Giblet, J., 16, 147, 244
Giblin, C.H., 157
Giesen, H., 166, 238, 292
Giet, S., 84, 85, 273
Gillet, L., 123
Gilmour, S.M., 180, 306
Glasson, T.F., 90, 111, 187, 260
Glover, F.C., 316
Gnatkowshi, M.W., 174
Gollinger, H., 91, 185, 223
Good, E.M., 317
Goppelt, L., 293
Gordon, R.P., 134
Goulder, M.D., 153
Gourgues, M., 152
Graebner, T., 266
Graham, B., 193
Grant, F.C., 254
Grassi, J.A., 144, 278
Gray, J.R., 324, 325
Green, E.M.B., 218
Greenwalt, C.H., Jr., 64
Grillmeier, A., 283
Grimsrud, T., 329
Gruenthaner, M.J., 266
Grünzweig,, 180
Gryglewicz, F., 21
Gundry, R.H., 164
Günther, H.W., 251
Gunther, J.J., 69
Guthrie, D., 50, 239, 277, 304
Güttgemanns, E., 164
Gutzwiller, R., 244
Guyot, G.H., 148, 330
Gwynn, J., 52
Haag, H.J., 301
Hadorn, D.W., 189
Hahn, F., 91
Hailey, H., 195
Hall, G.F., 25

Hall, R.G., 125
Halver, R., 92
Hamilton, N.Q., 253
Hammenstede, A., 280
Hammer, J., 147
Hammerton, H.J., 268
Hanfmann, G.M.A., 64, 65, 66, 67
Hanhart, K., 135
Hanrahan, D.U., 321
Hansen, D.P., 66
Hanson, A.T., 186, 225
Hanson, P. D., 105
Harder, G., 92
Häring, P., 17
Harkness, G., 307
Harrington, W.J., 200
Harris J.R., 58
Harrison, N.B., 207
Harrison, W.K., 38, 258
Hartenstein, K., 208
Hartner, H.G., 326
Hatfield, D.E., 150
Hauret, C., 137
Heidt, W.G., 203
Heikel, I.A., 58
Heitmüller, F., 26, 214, 250, 294
Hellholm, D., 102
Hellriegel, M.B., 328
Helmbold, A., 72
Hemer, C.J., 6, 74, 80, 82, 217
Hendrick, W.K., 141
Hendricksen, W., 207
Héring, J., 289
Hill, D., 78, 107
Hillers, D.R., 225
Hillyer, N., 241
Hobbs, H.H., 21, 199
Hodder, A.D., 331
Hodges, Z.C., 54, 55, 171
Hofbauer, J., 264

Hohenstein, H.E., 317
Hohnjec, N., 277
Holtz, T., 240
Hooker, M.D., 285
Hopfgartner, L., 296
Hopkins, M., 272, 273
Horine, S., 101
Horton, S.M., 191
Hoskier, H.C., 59
Howard, G., 109
Hre Kio, S., 162, 300
Hubert, M., 159
Hughes, J.A., 30, 227
Hughes, P.E., 191, 255
Hultgren, A.J., 237
Hurtado, L.W., 131
Isbell, A.C., 70
Jacobsthal, P., 62
James, E., 9
James, P.P., 297
Janzon, P., 216
Jart, U., 169
Jarvis, D.E., 316
Jarvis, P., 311
Jenkins, F., 90, 139
Jeske, R.L., 2, 193, 245
Jochen, V.B., 309
Johnson, A.E., 181
Johnson, A.F., 181
Johnson, S.E., 61, 63, 81
Johnston, G., 312
Johnston, R.M., 280
Jones, B.W., 108
Jörns, K.-P., 157
Kallas, J., 108, 237
Karner, K., 271
Karrer, M., 103
Käsemann, E., 72
Kassing, A., 147, 297
Kealey, S.P., 192
Kealy, S.P., 49, 233
Keegan, T.J., 247
Keller, C., 295

Keller, J.E., 172
Kelly, B.H., 318
Kelly, J.F.T., 308
Kempson, W.R., 301, 332
Kent, J.L., 323
Ketter, P., 86, 188
Kiddle, M., 186, 189
Kienberger, V.F., 314
Kik, J.M., 228
Kilpatrick, G.D., 55
King, S.E., 51
King, W.L., 42
Kirban, S., 199
Kirby, J.T., 172
Kitter, P., 86
Klassen, W., 270
Kline, M.G., 255
Knoch, O.B., 101
Knowles, J.H., 213
Knox, W.L., 86
Koester, C.R., 174
Kolb, E.J., 313
König, A., 250
Kopecky, D.W., 42
Koser, R.E., 19, 46
Kraft, H., 6, 184
Kraybill, J. N., 96
Kreitzer, L., 74, 127
Kretschmar, G., 20
Kretzmann, P.E., 73
Krodel, G.A., 178
Kromminga, D.H., 264
Kuhn, C.L., 303
Kümmel, W.G., 56
Kusche, R.W., 301
Kuykendall, R.M., 103
Kuyper, A., 209
Ladd, G.E., 38, 104, 110, 198,
    228, 236
Lagrange, M.-J., 59
Lahaye,T., 198
Lähnemann, J., 78
Lambrecht, J., 4, 51

Lancellotti, A., 117, 120
Langenberg, H., 291
Langgärtner, G., 7
Läpple, A., 201, 275, 277
LaRondelle, H.K., 113, 266
Lauchli, S., 159
Lawton, A., 19
Leahy, D.J., 34
Leardi, J.C., 239
Leconte, R., 213
Lee, G.M., 72
LeFrois, B.J., 25, 223, 297
Légasse, S., 78
Lehmann, P., 293
Leiser, B.M., 145
Léon-Dufour, X., 49
Leveque, J., 167
Lew, T.T., 328
Lewis, G.R., 36
Lilje, H., 204
Lillie, W., 327
Lindsey, H., 198
Ling, T., 265
Lipinski, E., 70
Little, C.H., 17
Lo Bue, F., 57
Loasby, R.E., 226
Loenertz, R.J., 161, 206
Lohmeyer, E., 10
Lohse, E., 55, 101, 182, 240,
    241
Loisey, A., 209
Louttit, W., 315
Lowery, R., 6
Luce, S.B., 62
Lund, N.W., 124
Lurvey, J.M., 174
MacDonald, H.R., 324
Mackay, W.M., 215, 271
MacL. Gilmour, S., 24
MacQueen, H.Q., 326
Maier, G., 304
Maigaret, J., 216

Manns, F., 135, 162
Manz, J.G., 318
Marconcini, B., 22, 140
Marcus, R., 123
Martin, F., 162
Martin, G.M., 303
Marty, W.H., 300
Marx, M.J., 231, 293, 295
Mason, C.E., Jr., 39, 256
Mathers, J., 25
Matthews, H.F., 314, 326
Mauck, M.B., 332
May, E., 223
Maycock, A.L., 206
Mayer, F.E., 32
Mazzaferri, F.D., 96, 281
Mazzucco, C., 27
McCall, J.G., 301
McCall, T.S., 35
McCaughey, J.D., 83
McClain, A.J., 40, 41
McCorry, V.P., 320
McDermott, T., 262, 265
McDowell, E.A., 112, 205
McGinnis, J., 301
McLean, J.A., 173
McNamara, M., 143
McNeil, B., 136
McNicol, A., 154
Megivern, J.J., 4, 21
Meinardus, O.F.A., 60
Mellink, M.J., 60, 61, 63, 65, 68
Melton, L.D., 301
Mennicke, V., 33, 321
Menzies, R., 310
Métraux, G.P.R., 64
Metzger, B.M., 53
Michael, J.H., 161, 220, 229
Michaels, J.R., 255
Michaud, J.-P., 3
Michl, J., 25, 94
Mickelsen, A.B., 234

Miguens, M., 169
Milner, G., 266
Minear, P.S., 104, 118, 119, 171, 200, 248, 285
Mitchell, J.L., 41
Mitten, D.C., 65
Mitten, D.G., 66
Moberly, C.A.E., 161
Moellering, R.L., 325
Moffatt, J., 187
Molnar, A., 8
Monloubou, L., 153
Montagnini, F., 9, 160, 170, 222, 248
Montague, G.T., 223
Montgomery, J.W., 27
Moore, H., 10, 300
Moore, M.S., 166
Morant, P., 200
Morgen, M., 136
Morrice, W.G., 99
Morrill, M.F., 332
Morris, H.M., 36, 295
Morris, L., 178, 185
Morton, R., 125
Morton, R.S., 96
Mottu, H., 106
Moule, C.F.D., 257
Mounce, R., 183, 195, 251
Mowry, L., 219, 328
Mowry, M.L., 175
Mueller, E.E., 315
Mueller, J.T., 33
Mueller, T., 116
Muirhead, I.A., 250
Mulholland, J.H., 47
Mulholland, M.R., Jr., 177, 191
Müller, H.-P., 93, 144
Müller, U.B., 80, 90, 95, 179
Munck, J., 222
Murdock, W.R., 272
Murphy, R.E., 172, 298

Murphy, W.R., 322
Muse, R.L., 130
Mussies, G., 54, 119, 120
Mussner, F., 56
Nash, C.A., 214
Neall, B.S., 329, 332
Newbold, F., 306
Newbolt, M.R., 17
Newman, B., 24, 84, 201
Newport, J.P., 253
Newport, K.G.C., 114, 115, 116
Nikolainen, A.T., 235, 249
Niles, D.T., 203
North, R., 61, 67
O'Donoghue, N.-D., 297
O'Donovan, O., 287
O'Rourke, J.J., 274
Oberhuber, O., 305
Oberweis, M., 165
Oliver Roman, M., 156
Oliver, H.H., 56
Olivier, A., 100, 145, 206
Oman, J., 59
Ordonez, V., 291
Orna, M.V., 271
Orr, R.W., 198
Osburn, C.D., 117
Ozanne, C.G., 121, 134
Page, S.H.T., 136
Palmer, E.F., 11
Parker, H.M., 137
Parker, N.H., 113
Parnell, C.C., 197
Parsons, N.C., 314
Parvis, M.M., 62
Patrides, C.A., 305
Patterson, S.J., 75
Paul, A., 104
Paulien, J., 2, 127
Pax, E., 92
Payne, J.B., 258
Peake, A.S., 210

Peinador, M., 297
Pentecost, J.D., 38, 39
Pesch, R., 14, 211
Petersen, R.L., 331
Peterson, D.G., 299
Peterson, E.H., 120
Pétrement, S., 296
Pfeiffer, C.F., 93
Pierce, E.L., 72
Pietrella, E., 27
Pikaza, J., 222
Pilch, J.J., 5
Pilgrim, W.E., 291
Piper, O.A., 147, 328
Pippin, T., 287
Pitts, B.A., 332
Poellot, L., 327
Pohl, A., 186
Poirier, L., 301
Polatkan, K.Z., 67
Pollard, T.E., 283
Popkes, W., 134
Porter, S.E., 114, 217
Potin, J., 213
Poucouta, P., 128, 284
Poythress, V.S., 68
Prager, M., 330
Preston, R.H., 186
Prete, B., 22, 224
Price, A.W., 327
Prieur, J., 196
Prigent, P., 79, 81, 82, 94, 106, 140, 144, 154, 178, 181, 194, 235, 269, 274, 279
Quiery, W.H., 96, 300
Quispel, G., 195
Quitslund, S.A., 306
Raber, R.W., 324
Rakato, M.E., 173
Ramage, A., 64
Ramlot, L., 212
Ramsay, W.M., 87

Rao, K.P., 53
Reader, W.W., 88, 175
Reddish, M.G., 281, 301
Reicke, B., 83, 282
Repp, A.C., 213
Rewak, W.J., 268
Regopoulous, G.Ch., 83
Rhys, T.T., 326
Riach, J.L., 312
Richards, H.J., 23
Richardson, D.W., 17, 208
Rife, J.M., 148
Rigg, W.H., 311
Riley, W., 275
Rinaldi, G., 218
Rissi, M., 142, 144, 201, 251, 257, 272, 273, 276
Rist, M., 18, 188
Ritt, H., 179
Robb, J.D., 121
Robbins, R.F., 21
Robert, L., 67
Roberts, J.W., 8, 23, 252
Robinson, B.P., 221
Robinson, E.S.G., 62
Robinson, J.A.T., 70
Robinson, W., 259
Roffey, J.W., 289
Rogers, C., 308
Rollins, W.G., 108
Roloff, J., 180
Rösch, K., 298
Rosin, W.L., 325
Ross, J.E., 321
Ross, J.R., 35
Ross, M.K., 189
Rosscup, J.E., 294
Rossetti, C.G., 307
Rouner, A.A., Jr., 314
Rousseau, F., 95
Routley, E., 322
Rowland, C., 132, 137, 233, 303

Rowley, H.H., 109, 111, 112
Royse, J.R., 52
Rudnick, M.L., 313
Rudwick, M.J.S., 218
Ruiz, J.-P., 126
Rumble, L., 320
Russell, D., 311
Russell, D.S., 109
Russell, E., 147, 219
Rusten, E.M., 46
Ryrie, C.C., 39, 248
Sabugal, S., 240
Saffrey, H.D., 82
Sand, A., 101, 107
Sanders, H.A., 59
Sanders, J.N., 71
Satake, A., 84, 154, 156
Satre, L.J., 20
Saunders, F.B., 232
Scharlemann, M.H., 225
Scharrer, J.F., 320
Schellenberg, D., 206
Scherrer, S.J., 76
Schilling, F.A., 122
Schinzer, R., 167
Schlep, A.W., 312
Schlier, H., 242, 273
Schmid, J., 53, 55, 56, 57, 58, 59
Schmidt, J.M., 142
Schmitt, E., 243
Schrage, W., 216
Schwank, B., 272
Schwarz, O.J.R.A., 283
Schweizer, E., 246
Scofield, C.I., 42, 43
Scott, E.F., 19, 112, 208
Scott, N.A., Jr., 306
Scott, R.B.Y., 124, 212, 244
Segert, S., 149
Selwyn, E.G., 323
Senior, G.R., 319
Sharkey, S.A., 230

Shea, W.H., 88, 151, 153, 266
Sheerin, J.B., 315
Shepherd, M.H., 146, 216
Shepherd, N., 256
Shepherd, W.H., 1
Shute, A.L., 19
Sickenberger, J., 207, 250
Siegman, E.F., 291
Silberman, L.H., 121
Simpson, E.K., 124
Skehan, P.W., 245
Skiadaresis, J., 128
Small, R.L., 311, 321
Smalley, S., 128, 257
Smith, C.R., 125
Smith, D.C., 228
Smith, E.J., 223
Smith, P.K., 214
Smith, R.F., 259
Smith, S.O., 331
Smith, T.C., 263
Smith, U., 291
Smukal, G.H., 327, 328
Snyder, G.F., 108
Snyder, J., 305
Sokolowski, F., 215
Soule, C.D., 97
Sparks, H.F.D., 57
Spinks, L.C., 155
Sproxton, V., 12
Stagg, F., 23
Stamm, R.T., 18
Stancliffe, M., 316
Stanley, D.M., 9, 244
Stanley, J.E., 174
Staples, P., 90, 226
Stauffer, E., 85, 172
Stefaniak, L., 297
Stegner, W.R., 330
Steinmann, A.E., 173
Stevens, M., 331
Stewart, D., 317

Stewart, J.S., 324
Stewart, R.W., 317
Stierlin, H., 95
Stormon, E.J., 159
Stott, W., 121
Strand, K.A., 7, 21, 22, 88, 133, 135, 149, 150, 153, 155, 156, 165, 211, 221, 251, 281
Strobel, A., 71
Stuhlmacher, P., 142, 230
Summers, R., 30, 175, 205, 262
Surridge, R., 149
Sweet, J.P.M., 177, 182
Swete, H.B., 210
Tabbernee, W., 2
Tasker, R.V.G., 57
Tatford, F.A., 83, 206
Taylor, R.D., 332
Tengbom, L.C., 97
Tenney, M.C., 40, 216, 229, 309
Theissen, A., 10
Thomas, R.L., 23, 101, 159, 212, 242, 289
Thomas, R.S., 64
Thompson, L., 73, 75, 158
Thomson, R.W., 327
Thüsing, W., 261, 275
Tickle, J., 21
Tillich, P., 312
Todd, J., 218
Tolzien, G., 207
Topham, M., 114, 230
Torrance, T.F., 204, 254, 279
Torrey, C.C., 121, 124
Townsend, J.L., 34, 255
Trabucco, A., 25, 249
Tresmontant, G., 192
Trevès, M., 152
Trevett, C., 126
Trevijano Etcheverria, R., 247
Tribble, H.W., 245
Trites, A.A., 283

Trudinger, L.P., 54, 118
Trudinger, P., 68, 130, 141, 143
Tyciak, J., 280
Ulfgard, H., 126, 269
Ulrichsen, J.H., 69
Unger, D.J., 224, 298
Valentin, A., 72
Van Bergen, P., 276
Van Daalen, D.H., 329
Van den Eynde, P., 219
Van der Waal, C., 138
Van Dixhorn, L.J., 332
Van Unnik, W.C., 91, 93
Vangorder, J.J., 311
Vanhoye, A., 145
Vanni, H., 117
Vanni, U., 4, 5, 22, 117, 158, 167, 168, 278, 280, 294
Vassiliadis, P., 282
Vaucher, A.-F., 28, 221
Vawter, B., 110, 279
Veloso, M., 22
Venable, C.L., 207
Villiers, P.G.R. de., 163
Virgulin, S., 243
Vivian, A., 139
Vogelgesang, J.M., 132
Vogt, E., 172
Vögtle, A., 91, 194, 236
Von Balthasar, H.U., 260
Von der Osten-Sacken, P., 92, 241
Von der Ropp, Fr., 208
Vorster, W.S., 102
Vos, L.A., 143
Waldbaum, J.C., 64
Walden, J.W., 45
Walker, N., 146, 219
Wallace, H., 61
Wallis, W.B., 11
Walther, F.E., 252

Walvoord, J.F., 29, 34, 36, 37, 39, 40, 41, 43, 44, 123, 169, 202, 229, 246, 256
Warne, N., 55
Warren, W.L., 300
Wasson, M., 218
Weborg, C., 267
Wellman, S.E., 332
Wernecke, H., 204
Wessel, H., 26
Whale, P., 115
Whealon, J.F., 154
White, R.F., 149
Whiting, A.B., 259
Wikenhauser, A., 10, 160, 187, 189
Wilcock, M., 235
Wilder, A.N., 108
Wilkinson, R.H., 212
Williams, H., 319
Williams, R.B., 278
Willoughby, H.R., 58
Wilmot, J., 231
Wilson , J.B., 327
Winfrey, D.G., 117
Winkle, R.E., 220
Wishart, C.F., 310
Witherup, R.D., 99
Wittreich, J., 305
Wojciechowski, M., 163, 237
Wolber, V.E., 175
Wolff, C., 247
Wood, A.S., 252
Wood, P., 84, 214
Wright, J.W., 317
Wuest, K.S., 212, 258
Wulf, F., 325
Wulf, H., 276
Younce, D.R., 120
Zahn, T., 209
Zegwaart, H., 27

Index of Scripture and Ancient Texts

OLD TESTAMENT

Genesis
1-3   128
3   136
3:15   137, 167, 295, 299
13   44
15   44
37:9   146

Exodus 90, 141, 162
7   36
19:6   212, 263

Leviticus
16   133

Numbers
24:15-19   148
24:17   83

1 Kings
22:20-22   145

2 Kings
11:1-3   296

1 Chronicles
16   132
16:8-36   129

2 Chronicles
12:6   226

Psalms
2   80, 156
18   143
89   13
137:4   317

Ecclesiastes
1   312

Song of Songs
(Canticles)
5:2   137, 145
6:10   133, 145, 146

Isaiah 90, 162
6:3   145, 146, 219
6:8   145
7:14   133
24:1-6   325
40:2   165
43   230, 312
43:16-21   142
44:6   242
49   319
52:7-8   144
53   241
54:11-12   125
60   146
61:6   263
61:7   165
61:10   125
63:1-6   117
65:16   122
66:7   139

Jeremiah
4:30   131
12:1   226
15   144
16:18   165
17:18   165
30:7   42
31   42
50-51   164

Ezekiel 28, 90, 96, 126, 132,
    145, 153, 266
1:18 55
2:10 55
8:2 137
14 144
27:27-30 227
28:11-19 265
37 144
37:1 246
37-38 229
37-48 27, 228
38-39 228
39 144
40-48 133
48:31-34 220

Daniel 36, 79, 90, 101, 104,
    129, 131, 132, 234, 238,
    290, 291
2 37, 136, 174
3:25 114
4 130
4:37 238
7 37, 95, 147, 174, 221
7:1-14 293
7:2-3 13, 238
7:6 135
7:8-13 125
7:13 13, 132, 240, 244
9 35, 136
9:14 226
9:27 173
10:5-6 132, 137
10:5-7 125
10:13 146
11-12 136
12 147
12:1 42, 146, 287
12:3 249

Amos 111
1 91
1-2 148
2 91
6:11 165

Zechariah
1 144
2:1-5 133
4 135
4:1-21 269
9:12 165
12:11 113

Malachi
2:7 249

APOCRYPHA

Baruch
44:2 142, 230

2 Esdras 51

4 Ezra 27, 95, 96, 104, 132,
    133, 154, 260, 290
11-12 174
13 238

3 Maccabees
2:3 226

Tobit
3:2 226

PSEUDEPIGRAPHICA AND EARLY PATRISTIC BOOKS

Apoc. of Abraham 132

As. Moses 79, 260

Ascen. of Isaiah 83
4:16 133

2 Baruch 27, 51, 95, 132, 133,
    154, 260, 290

1 Enoch 95, 96, 104, 128,
    132, 133, 238, 260, 290

45:4   142, 230

Jos. Asen. 132

Jubilees 128, 260

Pss. Solomon 260

Ps-Philo 88

Sib. Oracles 127, 260
2:177-183   133
4-5 83
5 127
8 74

T. Joseph 132

Adv. Haer. (Epiphanius) 134

Didache
10:6   140, 241, 257

Epis. Apostles 43, 134

Epis. Barnabas 83

DEAD SEA SCROLLS
107

1QH
3:19-23   142, 230

1QM 127

1QpIsa 127

1QS
8:1-16   127
9:3-7   127
11:7-9   127

**TARGUMIC,
RABBINIC, AND**

**NAG HAMMADI
WRITINGS**

Tg. Exodus
19:6   143

Tg. Ps-Jonathan 139

Tg. Nahum
3:17   134

Gen. Rabbah 139

Lev. Rabbah 139

Ap. John 72

NEW TESTAMENT

Matthew
9 312
23:31-35   282
24 35, 36, 258
24:21   42

Mark
8:23 131
13 133, 146, 273

Luke
1:26-38   133
2:21 147
12:35-40   138

John 4, 148, 260
1 83
1:29 128
3:29 128
3:31 142
5:24-29   256
9:6 131
10:7 313
11:24-25   256
11:27 142
17 12, 13
17:15 117

19:25-27 138
20:8 114
21:11 114, 165

Acts 243, 273
19 62, 215

Romans
8 104
8:26 235
11:27 42
13 289
13:1-7 288

1 Corinthians 82
2:2 142
5:7-8 135
10:3 40
12-14 291
15 256, 259
15:23 256
16:20-24 140
16:22 241, 257

2 Corinthians
6:6-18 140

Ephesians 111

1 Thessalonians
4 251, 259
5:1-11 258

2 Thessalonians 36, 258
1 139
2 35, 251, 266

Hebrews 243
2:1-4:13 104
8 42
11:4 282
12:1-13:25 104
12:24 282

James 134

1 Peter 83, 104, 127, 134, 243
2:4-5 129
2:4-9 291

2 Peter 4
2:15 148

3 John 12

Revelation
Chap.1 118, 141, 157, 168,
  172, 211-212, 311-313
1:1 243
1:1-3 14, 103, 152, 211
1:1-8 177
1:1-3:22 165
1:2 282
1:3 292, 311
1:4 121, 130, 211, 246
1:4-3:22 152
1:4-5 132
1:4-8 118
1:5 92, 123, 152
1:5-6 53, 88, 241, 260, 290,
  292, 312
1:5-8 211
1:6 212, 263, 276, 291, 300
1:7 11, 178, 183, 184, 244
1:8 87, 121, 242, 312
1:9 59, 192
1:9-20 165, 250
1:9-3:22 103
1:9-4:11 151
1:10 70, 121, 211, 245, 246
1:10b-3:22 150
1:12 129, 143, 244
1:12-16 267
1:13 137, 240
1:13-16 132, 242
1:13-18 125
1:16 163, 171, 312
1:17-18 311, 313
1:18 87
1:19 15, 72, 93, 159
1:20 162, 163
1-3 60, 68, 128, 130, 161, 173
1-6 193

1-11   159, 273
Chap. 2   215, 313
2:1   163
2:1-7   215, 309
2:2   53, 123
2:7   80, 113, 140
2:8-11   216, 313
2:9-10   270
2:10   79, 313
2:11   130, 259
2:12-17   271
2:13   54, 84, 115
2:14   148
2:15   79
2:16   87
2:17   272
2:18   114
2:18-29   80
2:20   123
2:28   83
Chaps. 2-3   5, 6, 13, 20, 24, 36,
    40, 60, 61, 74, 79, 80, 82,
    83, 84-88, 90, 91, 97, 100,
    118, 119, 130, 134, 148,
    157, 159, 162, 212-218, 236,
    239, 249, 261, 262, 267,
    279,282, 294, 307
Chap. 3   313-316
3:1   84, 163
3:1-6   80, 315
3:2   315
3:2-3   82, 217
3:3   138, 313
3:4   123
3:5   217
3:7-8   314
3:7-13   81, 315, 316
3:8   123
3:10   42, 116, 117, 255, 286
3:12   123, 129, 213, 272, 315
3:14   118, 121, 122, 141
3:14-22   81, 314
3:15   314, 315
3:15-17   314
3:15-18   217
3:16   218
3:18   131

3:20   128, 138, 145, 218, 314
3:21   315
Chap. 4   100, 131, 171, 218-
    219
4:1   218
4:1-2   166, 270
4:1-11   147
4:1-8:1   104
4:1-11:9   50
4:1-16:21   7
4:1-19:9   273
4:1-21:4   150
4:1-22:21   103
4:2   316
4:3   316
4:4   139, 168
4:6   122, 125, 238
4:6-8   167
4:8   55, 121, 141, 146, 219
4:9   300
Chaps. 4-5   12, 106, 135, 158,
    162, 219, 278, 279, 293, 328
Chaps. 4-8   103
Chaps. 4-11   161, 273
Chaps. 4-22   13
Chap. 5   92, 147, 149, 171,
    219, 277, 316-318
5:1   55, 141, 219
5:1-5   145, 166
5:1-7   317
5:1-14   317
5:1-8:1   151, 251
5:2   317
5:5   134, 152, 318
5:5-6   127
5:6-7   238
5:6-14   277
5:7   317
5:8-14   318
5:9   272, 317, 328
5:9-10   244, 290, 292
5:10   212, 263
5:11   317
5:12   317
Chap. 6   124, 144, 219-220,
    294
6:1-8   115, 220

6:1-17   93
6:1-8:5   137
6:1-16:21   167
6:2   139, 168, 170, 171, 257
6:4   123
6:8   220
6:8-9   52
6:9   220, 262, 282
6:9-11   79
6:9-17   299
6:10   286
6:10-11   282
6:11   255
6:16-17   263
Chaps. 6-7   162
Chap. 7   38, 170, 171, 172,
   220, 221, 236, 247, 249,
   251, 269, 318-320
7:1-17   149, 162
7:2-12   172
7:2-4   220
7:2-14   127
7:4   319, 321
7:4-8   139, 168, 221
7:5-8   125
7:9   317, 319, 320, 321
7:9-14   220
7:9-17   126, 128, 178, 269,
   277
7:10   116
7:10-12   158
7:13-17   140, 321
7:14   130
7:16-17   319
7:17-8:3   57
8:1   322
8:1-14:5   156
8:2-14:5   151
8:5-11:18   309
8:8-9:21   93
Chap. 9   120, 143, 266
9:2   58
9:8   95
9:9   134
9:10-17:2   59
9:12   120
9:13-14   129

9:15   58
9:16   120
Chap. 10   277
10:1-11:13   149, 251
10:1-15:4   156
10:8-11   141, 219
10:10   57
Chap. 11   28, 35, 69, 70, 154,
   155, 221, 222, 285, 322
11:1   133
11:1-13   128
11:2   70
11:3   69
11:3-12   221
11:3-13   172, 222, 283, 331
11:4   135
11:7   69, 266
11:8   138, 163
11:10   69
11:11   144
11:12   52
11:15   152, 322
11:15-19   93
11:19   138
11:19-14:5   104
Chaps. 11-12   248
Chap. 12   8, 16, 25, 43, 61, 75,
   79, 82, 89, 91, 93, 94, 106,
   136, 141, 143, 146, 147,
   155, 163, 167, 170, 222-224,
   243, 249, 250, 265, 273,
   279, 295-299, 322
12:1   133, 145, 296-298, 322
12:1-6   136
12:1-17   88, 137, 151, 166
12:1-20:10   30
12:2   139
12:3-4   167
12:7-9   156
12:9   224
12:10   116, 152
12:10-12   156
12:11   322
12:14   221
12:17   143
Chaps. 12-13   287
Chaps. 12-22   74, 159

Chap. 13 37, 74, 132, 172,
  174, 197, 225, 251, 266,
  288, 289, 322-323
13:1 69
13:1-18 166, 322
13:2 135
13:3 171
13:6 54, 224
13:9 113
13:9-10 224
13:10 57, 79
13:13-15 76
13:16 266
13:16-17 289
13:16-18 3
13:17-18 169
13:18 136, 165, 169
Chap. 14 38, 155, 225-226,
  249, 323
14:1 114
14:1-3 251
14:1-5 127
14:1-13 149
14:3 272
14:4 294
14:6 144
14:6-7 129, 132
14:6-19:8 151
14:9-11 266
14:12 115
14:13 255, 283, 292, 323
14:14 240
14:14-20 116
14:20 225
Chap. 15 155
15:3 144
Chaps. 15-16 150, 158, 258
Chap. 16 226, 227
16:1-21 93
16:4-6 90, 91
16:4-7 89
16:15 138
16:16 113, 114, 226, 227,
  266-267
16:17-19:10 126
16:18 138
Chaps. 16-22 157

Chap. 17 69, 70, 74, 77, 89,
  164, 169, 197, 251, 296
17:1-6 166
17:5 77
17:9 69, 136, 169, 276
17:9-11 70
17:9-12 71
17:9-16 84
17:10 68, 169
17:10-11 83
17:12 69, 129
17:14 130
17:18 266
Chaps. 17-18 164, 249, 287
Chap. 18 70, 89, 96, 124, 153,
  164, 227, 287
18:1-3 153
18:2 57
18:5 138
18:6 165
18:17 58, 59, 227
18:20 165
Chap. 19 158, 227, 245, 250,
  251, 286, 323-324
19:1 116
19:1-7 323
19:4 104, 323, 324
19:5 261
19:6 323
19:7 128, 277, 279
19:7-8 125
19:9-22:5 151
19:10 227, 246, 282
19:11-16 257
19:11-21 116, 149
19:11-20:10 29
19:13 117, 147
19:15 38
Chaps. 19-22 252
Chap. 20 11, 19, 20, 27, 29,
  32, 34, 35, 38, 106, 178,
  227-229, 251, 255, 256, 259,
  260, 264, 276
20:1-3 229, 262
20:1-4 228
20:1-7 258
20:1-8 229

20:1-10   9, 34, 149, 151, 228
20:4   29, 136, 262, 283
20:4-6   28, 30, 35, 140, 228,
   229, 263
20:5   255, 256, 264
20:6   263, 291
20:7-10   229
20:11   138
20:11-12   324
20:11-15   229
Chaps. 20-21   253
Chaps. 20-22   37, 160
Chap. 21   2, 106, 230-231,
   237, 250, 255, 256, 276,
   312, 324, 327
21:1   272, 295
21:1-2   230
21:1-5   325
21:1-8   324, 326, 327
21:1-22:5   163, 164, 230, 268,
   275, 276
21:1-22:21   277
21:2   125, 325
21:4   231, 324
21:5   326, 327
21:5-7   325
21:5-8   142, 230, 325
21:5-22:5   150
21:6   87
21:7   326
21:8   140
21:9-22   275
21:9-22:2   174
21:9-22:5   163, 252
21:9-22:9   104
21:10   2
21:11   228
21:14   127
21:15-17   230
21:17   114
21:18-21   125, 169
21:19-20   88, 90
21:21   231, 326
21:24   299
Chaps. 21-22   34, 100, 131,
   249, 261
Chap. 22   106, 231, 327, 328

22:1   295
22:2   115, 240
22:3-5   263
22:4   327
22:6-7   88
22:6-21   152, 225
22:7   87
22:8-21   161
22:12-21   327
22:13   87, 242, 250, 327
22:14   88
22:15   166
22:16   83, 134, 166, 231
22:16-20   88, 140
22:16b   83
22:17   166, 295
22:18   101
22:20   241, 257, 328
22:21   327